The Rise and Fall
of an
American Army

The Rise and Fall of an American Army

U.S. Ground Forces in Vietnam, 1965–1973

Shelby L. Stanton

★
PRESIDIO

Published by Presidio Press
31 Pamaron Way, Novato CA 94947

Library of Congress Cataloging in Publication Data

Stanton, Shelby L., 1948–
    The rise and fall of an American army.

    Bibliography: p.
    Includes index.
    1. Vietnamese Conflict, 1961–1975—United States.
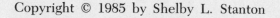
    2. United States. Army—History—Vietnamese Conflict,
    1961–1975. I. Title.
    DS558.S73   1985   959.704'342   84-26616
    ISBN 0-89141-232-8

Printed in the United States of America

Dedicated to the United States Soldiers and Marines
who served in Vietnam, Thailand, Cambodia,
and Laos from 1961–1975.

"The Call To Arms", by Auguste Rodin

Contents

MAPS

Annual Campaign maps (following Part openers):
  Part 1 South Vietnam, 1965
  Part 2 South Vietnam, 1966
  Part 3 South Vietnam, 1967
  Part 4 South Vietnam, 1968
  Part 5 South Vietnam, 1969
  Part 6 South Vietnam, 1970–1973
Battle Maps (following page 368):
  U.S. Military Presence in Vietnam
  The DMZ Front
  Hue and the A Shau Valley
  Phuoc Ha-Que Son-An Hoa Valleys
  Ia Drang Valley
  Junction City and Cedar Falls
  The Dak To Battlefield, 1967
  The Saigon-Bien Hoa-Long Binh Area
  Khe Sanh Area and Lam Son 719 Offensive

FOREWORD

On the wall of the War Plans Directorate in the Army General Staff used to hang a poster of a World War II infantryman with fixed bayonet advancing against the enemy. Underneath was the caption, "At the end of the most grandiose plans and strategies is a soldier walking point." It was a warning that if the soldier leading the attack could not carry the day, or if the mission was beyond his capabilities, then the plans and strategies were worthless. One of the terrible tragedies of the Vietnam war was that the reverse of that saying also proved to be true. No matter how bravely or how well the soldier on the point did his job, if the plans and strategies were faulty, all the courage and bloodshed were for naught.

Since the end of the war, several works have been published examining the grievous faults of America's Vietnam war plans and strategies. Some of these accounts—written, it is important to note, by self-proclaimed "experts" who never set foot in Vietnam itself, much less on the battlefield—have unconscionably extended these faults to the soldiers who fought the war. Tarred with the brush of America's defeat, their bravery, their dedication, and their sacrifices have been denied, ignored, and forgotten. Now for the first time Captain Shelby L. Stanton, a Vietnam combat veteran decorated for valor and now retired as a result of wounds suffered on the battlefield, gives us the full story of those soldiers on the point.

In so doing, Captain Stanton exposes some of the more pernicious myths that have distorted our understanding of the Vietnam-war battlefield. Born at the highest levels, these myths began to develop even before Army combat forces were committed to Vietnam. By the early 1960's, guerrilla war had become romanticized and quite fashionable among intellectual circles. Perceived as "a whole new kind of warfare," it was to be met with an equally romanticized response—counterinsurgency. Subsequently ordered into execution in 1962 by President Kennedy himself, then Army Chief of Staff General George H. Decker tried to explain to the President that "any good soldier can handle guerrillas." The President responded that "guerrilla fighting was a special art," and soon thereafter General Decker was removed from office. But from a lifetime as an infantry officer, General Decker knew something that President Kennedy's sophisticated civilian advisors could never know: that for the rifleman, there is only one kind of war—total war—where the stakes are kill or be killed. In Washington and in higher military headquarters, the fine academic distinctions between general war, limited war, revolutionary war, or guerrilla war may make some sense, but at the foxhole level such distinctions are meaningless.

But because these realities of war were dismissed as old-fashioned and out-of-date, the mythology of guerrilla war colored America's perception of the war. It created the impression that the war in Vietnam was a relatively minor struggle against simple, black pajama-clad peasants armed with bamboo stakes. However, with his series of vignettes on actual battlefield operations, Captain Stanton vividly illustrates that front-line combat in Vietnam was remarkably similar to the battles fought by those soldiers on the point who charged the Bloody Angle at Spotsylvania, who stormed the Nazi fortifications along the Siegfried Line, who broke through the Japanese defenses before Manila, and who assaulted the Chinese and North Korean entrenchments on Pork Chop Hill. The casualty figures tell the story. The 1st Cavalry Division, for example, suffered some 30,253 troopers killed or wounded in action during the Vietnam war, half again as many as the combined casualties it suffered during World War II and the Korean War. The 1st Infantry Division, which had led the assault in North Africa, Sicily, and the D-Day Invasion in Normandy during World War II, suffered more casualties in Vietnam than it did in that war. The 101st Airborne

Division, which had won fame for its jump into Normandy and who held the line at Bastogne during the Battle of the Bulge, suffered twice as many casualties in Vietnam as it did in World War II.

Another reality of war dismissed as old-fashioned and out-of-date was the histories and the traditions of the units involved. But just as Caesar's legions fought and died for their Imperial Eagles, so soldiers and Marines in Vietnam fought and died for the honor of their regiments. As Captain Stanton puts it, "These divisions and combat brigades had distinctive personalities which somehow reflected their essence. . . . Soldiers could sense it, and often these collective divisional and brigaded entities seemed tied to destinies which predetermined their combat performance." Bringing this critical and too often overlooked moral force to life, Captain Stanton draws on his earlier masterpiece, *Vietnam Order of Battle*, to describe not only the battles these units fought but the heritage of the units themselves.

One of the important but unstated conclusions of *The Rise and Fall of an American Army* is that General Decker was right, a fact too long obscured by the mythology of guerrilla war. Captain Stanton's compelling narrative of battle actions in Vietnam makes clear that "any good soldier" could, *and did*, "handle guerrillas," and American Army and Marine infantrymen handled this enemy the same way they had always handled the enemy—not by any new and esoteric techniques of guerrilla war but by the age-old infantry method of closing with the enemy and destroying him by fire and maneuver. Much has been made of the "horrendous" use of American firepower against poor, defenseless peasant revolutionaries. But, as Captain Stanton points out, the truth of the matter was that at the fighting level the war in Vietnam usually involved infantry assaults against well-armed Viet Cong or North Vietnamese Army forces entrenched in fortified positions. The terrain in Vietnam, as in the hedgerows of Normandy in World War II, gave the defender an enormous advantage. Fields-of-fire, invisible to advancing infantrymen, could be cut in the dense jungle undergrowth only a few feet off the ground. Caught in such "killing zones," entire companies could be wiped out in a matter of seconds. As in World War II, tactics changed from the traditional method of using firepower to fix the enemy and hold him in position so that he could be destroyed by maneuver—i.e., by infantry squads attacking on his flanks—to a tactic of using maneuver to find the enemy fortifications and then using massive firepower to destroy them.

The results of such tactics were revealed by the North Vietnamese Army's battlefield commander General Vo Nguyen Giap himself in a 1969 interview with the Italian journalist, Oriana Fallaci. Giap admitted that from 1964 to 1968 the North Vietnamese had lost over 500,000 soldiers killed in action on the battlefield. As a percentage of their population, University of Rochester Professor John Mueller has pointed out, this was a casualty rate "probably twice as high as those suffered by the fanatical, often suicidal Japanese in World War II."

For those on either side involved in fighting it, Vietnam was *not* a minor war. With his gripping descriptions of the Vietnam battlefields, Captain Stanton has not only shed new light on the ferocious intensity of the war, he has also reminded us of the timeless nature of the infantry. Too often fascinated by bright and shiny technologies of war, it is well to be reminded that it was the infantry—what has been called "the old-fashioned soldier on foot, the ancient and unglamorous 'Cinderella'" of war—who, for the United States and the North Vietnamese and Viet Cong as well, proved to be the decisive force on the battlefield.

The yet-to-be-built monument to the Korean war, no matter how artistic or well constructed, can never hope to equal the memorial provided by T. R. Fehrenbach's *This Kind of War*. Written ten years after the war by a former tank platoon leader and company commander in combat there, this memorial honors the men who fought and died in Korea much more than any stone monument ever could. While the stone monuments to the war in Vietnam—including the monument in our Nation's capital now complete with its "Three Fighting Men" statue—are important remembrances of our fellow countrymen who served with honor and distinction in that unpopular war, the enduring memorial to that war is only now coming into existence. But with the publication of *The Rise and Fall of an American Army*, the foundation has been laid. Writing, like Fehrenbach, ten years after the end of the war, former Special Forces advisor and combat infantry platoon leader Shelby Stanton has provided a lasting tribute to the men who fought and died in Vietnam. Those who served there—and those who would understand those who served there—owe him an enormous debt of gratitude.

HARRY G. SUMMERS, JR.
Colonel of Infantry
Army War College
Carlisle Barracks, Pennsylvania
7 December 1984

INTRODUCTION

The Rise and Fall of an American Army is a battlefield history of the United States ground forces in the Vietnam war from 1965 through 1973. This book covers both the U.S. Marine Corps *and* the Army, since the term American Army is being used in a larger sense to signify the combined military land forces of a nation.

This battlefield history concentrates on how the United States Army and Marine Corps raised combat units and deployed them to Vietnam, and then how these units were employed and fought during the war. The book highlights significant military factors which affected unit performance in Vietnam. To provide continuity within the framework of overall United States military history, the historical backgrounds of most line regiments fielded in Vietnam have been briefly summarized in the footnotes. Thus, matters of smaller unit heritage do not infringe upon the narrative, but are still readily available for the interested reader. Although the fall of Saigon and the fall of an American Army are two separate themes, the allied efforts in Vietnam were so intertwined that they directly impacted on American combat performance. The South Vietnamese actions and operations described in this work are believed necessary to tell the complete story.

The book is arranged chronologically, so that each of its six parts covers a specific span of time. The first chapter within a part gives the overall strategic campaign background for that period. The remaining chapters are divided so that each covers military activity during that time in a certain region of the country. Although this arrangement is somewhat imperfect, since January events in the northern sector of Vietnam are discussed after December battles elsewhere are concluded in a previous chapter, the geographical pattern of area warfare in Vietnam was most appropriately described using this organization.

Casualty statistics for specific actions and operations have been deliberately avoided in this narrative because of their general unreliability. Accurate assessments of North Vietnamese Army and Viet Cong losses were largely impossible due to lack of disclosure by the Vietnamese government, terrain, destruction of remains by firepower used, and the fact that allied ground units were often unable to confirm artillery and aerial "kills." The entire process of accumulating valid casualty data was also shrouded by the shameful gamesmanship practised by certain reporting elements under pressure to "produce results." American losses were subject to statistical manipulation as well. For instance, dying soldiers put aboard medical evacuation helicopters were often counted as only wounded in unit after-action tables. The author has relied instead on describing the intensity of a given battle, and quoting valid munitions expenditures to give the reader a fair gauge of the severity of actions included in the text.

The information in this book was derived primarily from the original unit records of the United States Army and Marine Corps. I owe a great debt of gratitude to the able personnel of the military history detachments who served in the Vietnam War. All sources utilized are arranged by chapter and section in a special section at the back of the book, where original Vietnam materials are further identified with their individual document accession codes. In this manner background data is fully described for each section without resort to extensive footnoting within the main narrative.

I also wish to acknowledge the assistance and suggestions given by the staffs of the Army Chief of Military History and Marine Corps History Division; the Directorate of Freedom of Information and Security Review of the Assistant Secretary of Defense; Dr. John Henry Hatcher; Mr. T. M. Colkitt; Ms. Wanda Radcliffe; Brigadier General E. H. Simmons, U.S. Marine Corps;

Dr. Jack Shulimson; Colonel Harry G. Summers, Jr., U.S. Army; Lieutenant Colonel John F. Sloan, U.S. Army, Retired; Colonel Robert V. Kane, U.S. Army, Retired; and Mr. Richard W. Marsh, Jr. Finally, this book would not have been possible without expertise of my editor, Adele Horwitz; the encouragement of my father, Samuel Shelton Stanton; and the loving cooperation of my wife, Kathryn.

PART 1

1965

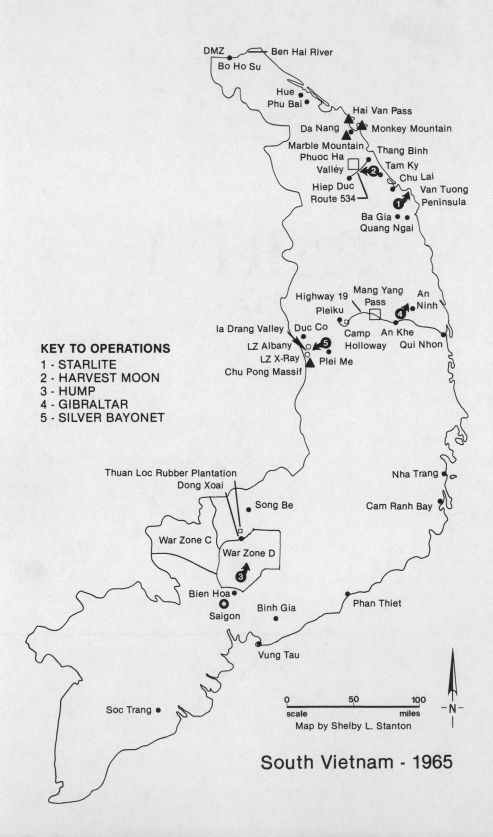

KEY TO OPERATIONS
1 - STARLITE
2 - HARVEST MOON
3 - HUMP
4 - GIBRALTAR
5 - SILVER BAYONET

South Vietnam - 1965

Map by Shelby L. Stanton

CHAPTER 1.

ADVISORS AND SPECIAL FORCES

1. Advisors at War

To many Vietnamese, their narrow S-shaped strip of land stretching along the seaward rim of Southeast Asia resembled a dragon facing the equator. The head and mane formed the southern region, with front legs thrust out into the Gulf of Siam, and the slender body curved around the Gulf of Tonkin to coil its massive tail against China in the north. Since the Geneva Conference on July 21, 1954, this dragon had been chopped in half, divided at a line of demarcation along the 17th parallel. This was the Demilitarized Zone (DMZ) separating North and South Vietnam. Vietnamese geomagicians were quick to point out that, in the position described, the Vietnamese dragon was a portent of national reunification.

Vietnam's southern half was officially the Republic of Vietnam, a thin 1,500-mile crescent-shaped country more commonly known as South Vietnam. Its long outer coasts are washed by the Pacific Ocean, and its interior mosaic of mountains, jungles, plains, and swamps are hedged in by the spine of the Chaine Annamitique, a western mountain range, which fades south into a vast alluvial plain created by the delta of the Mekong River.

Palm-lined white sand beaches fringe coves and bays where coral reefs can be clearly seen through the glassy sea. A vibrant

3

green mantle of rice paddies extends inland. These stretch almost endlessly across the flat delta, crisscrossed by ribbons of canals. At the time of the war, many areas of South Vietnam remained a wild and exotic wilderness. Mountain slopes dropped deep into luxurious growths of tropical flora, bracken, tuft-twisted bamboos, and majestic jungle trees. Silver rivers and waterfalls laced the deep rain forests. These were steeped in a wonderful variety of folklore and legend. Large rubber and coconut plantations stretched across rolling plains, and tigers stalked pine-forested plateaus.

Tropical monsoons allowed only two seasons; hot and dry and hot and rainy, and the alternation of the monsoons and dry seasons determined the pattern of life. The majority of the eighteen million inhabitants lived in the open lowland plains and rice-bearing deltas. Their hamlets and villages were generally self-governing. An old proverb states that the Emperor's law stops at the village gate. The people had existed through the centuries by cultivating rice on lands irrigated by primal pumps and sluices. The rugged uplands region was left to the ethnically alien and primitive mountain tribes.

South Vietnam was at war with a North Vietnamese-sponsored Viet Cong insurgency that was aimed at toppling the Saigon regime. The death of South Vietnamese President Ngo Dinh Diem and the collapse of his regime in the military-led coup of November 1963 ushered in a series of coalition governments replete with successive plots and counterplots. These political upheavals crippled central authority, while the division of military leaders between opposing cliques caused fatal turmoil in the armed forces. In the meantime, the Viet Cong were scoring major victories on the battlefront. The South Vietnamese Army's morale was wrecked, and its combat effectiveness was practically nil. In the majority of rural areas where governmental authority had collapsed altogether, the Viet Cong enjoyed firm control.

As 1965 was being ushered in, a newly formed and well-equipped VC division overran Binh Gia near Saigon and then stood its ground to challenge and destroy counterattacking South Vietnamese units during a four-day period.[1] In previous en-

1. The *9th VC Division* attacked and captured Binh Gia on December 27,

counters the VC had withdrawn shortly after attacking, and such a bold success was deeply troubling to South Vietnam's principal ally, the United States.

America's field advisory element of its Military Assistance Command, Vietnam (MACV), contained over 4,700 officers and sergeants during 1964, and their professionalism and dedication was the glue holding the South Vietnamese Army together as the year closed. They could be seen accompanying ARVN soldiers on routine patrols and in combat assaults, their tall lanky figures crowned with maroon berets or faded green, sweat-soaked baseball caps; while strapping shoulder holsters and World War II carbines. Wearing utility shirts adorned with brightly colored Vietnamese and American rank insignia crowding their gold-lettered U.S. ARMY tapes and white name tags, they represented an era that was rapidly slipping into oblivion on the eve of the "big war." These were the pioneers of a rising United States involvement in Vietnam, the pathfinders in a war destined to consume an entire American Army.

The military advisor's job was incredibly difficult and hazardous. The very nature of his work exposed him to constant political pressures and extremely dangerous situations. His responsibilities often extended beyond pure instruction to include combat planning, linking up needed communications, assuring the availability of medical assistance, and arranging for logistical support. He was given no command authority yet often had to provide direct leadership on the battlefield. In the midst of combat he was depended on to provide cool-headed advice and a steadying presence, as well as to ensure critical liaison with decisive American airpower. In many cases it fell upon his shoulders personally to rally units on the brink of panic.

One of these advisors was Capt. Donald R. Robinson, who was attached to the 51st ARVN Regiment's 1st Battalion, part of an undeclared war that was looming larger and more dangerous every month. A company of the battalion, dwarfed by oversized American helmets and clutching cumbersome Amer-

---

1964. Despite intense American helicopter gunship attacks, the Viet Cong demolished the 33d ARVN Ranger Battalion, which managed to reach the edge of the village, and the 4th VNMC Battalion sent in to assist.

ican M1 rifles, nonchalantly patrolled a road near the small hamlet of Ba Gia west of Quang Ngai on May 26, 1965. Captain Robinson's Son Tinh district was one of those backwater areas that had not seen battle, and he had been told the Viet Cong in the region were a bunch of ragtag guerrillas incapable of sophisticated military action. He had been gravely misinformed.

The Viet Cong of the *1st Regiment, Region V Liberation Army* had carefully prepared their attack positions. They had established a series of strategically placed ambush zones designed to annihilate this battalion as well as expected relief columns. When the lead company walked into the killing zone, the peaceful drone of tropical insects was shattered by a deafening fusillade of combined rifle and machine-gun fire which cut through the frail company ranks like a scythe.

Even at this point the trouble seemed to be little more than a hit-and-run ambush, which by 1965 could be expected anywhere in the Vietnamese countryside. The battalion commander immediately dispatched a second company to the scene of combat, but midway there it was bushwhacked from another direction. Leaving a small reserve behind, the rest of the five hundred-man battalion now went to the relief of its two engaged companies. The VC closed in from all sides, and the battalion disintegrated under a hailstorm of grenades and automatic weapons fire. In less than twenty minutes it had been wiped out. Only sixty-five soldiers and three advisors managed to escape.

It wasn't until four days later that a three-battalion ARVN relief force finally sauntered out of Quang Ngai, escorted by a mechanized troop of armored personnel carriers. The battalions advanced in three widely separated drives, intending to converge on the original ambush site. The Viet Cong were well prepared for any countermoves and had covered each approach route.

The 39th ARVN Ranger Battalion moved into its selected objective area without incident on May 30, but at two o'clock in the afternoon it was subjected to a furious barrage of recoilless rifle and machine-gun fire. The 2d Battalion of the 51st ARVN Regiment was ordered to reinforce the rangers, but before it could move it was also attacked. When the 3d South Vietnamese Marine Corps (VNMC) Battalion came under simultaneous attack all three battalions were effectively locked in isolated battles for survival.

Throughout the rest of the day each separate battalion perimeter was hit by numerous ground assaults. Viet Cong 75mm pack artillery howitzers sent shells crashing into the broken debris of foliage and toppled trees. Fallen soldiers from the 51st ARVN Regiment's second battalion were strewn all over the roadway. The tracked carriers hammered the tree line with heavy machine-gun fire as they coughed out clouds of engine exhaust and clanked into reverse. The infantrymen stumbled backwards, some exchanging desultory rifle fire but others tossing away weapons in dazed discouragement. Using the armored personnel carriers as cover, the decimated battalion managed to break away and retreat toward the town.

The other battalions were unable to pull back. Their circular defensive positions, hastily set up in fallen timber and clumps of vegetation, were caving in as the Viet Cong pressed their relentless attacks. With the onset of darkness, mortars began pounding the provincial capital of Quang Ngai and its airfield. The 39th ARVN Ranger Battalion had suffered particularly high losses. Swarms of Viet Cong, some clutching German burp guns, charged forward through the shattered thickets and into the shrunken ranger lines. They stormed past the dead and wounded defenders of the center company and overran the battalion headquarters.

Since that afternoon fighter aircraft had been roaring down to hurl bombs in the burning jungle below. Next came strafing runs over the forested battlefield. These aerial attacks continued throughout the night. Finally, just before daylight and after enduring 446 aircraft sorties, the VC broke off further combat. Airpower alone was credited with saving the South Vietnamese force from complete annihilation. This battle convinced Captain Robinson of the military proficiency of the Viet Cong and of the swiftly changing nature of the Vietnam War.

Viet Cong formations were attacking targets throughout the country, and the deteriorating South Vietnamese armed forces were being beaten in a series of sharp reverses. The United States decided to remedy the alarming situation by introducing large American combat formations in early 1965. This decision would stave off the total defeat of the Republic of Vietnam for ten years.

2. Special Forces at War

The United States Army first sent its Special Forces commando-advisors to Vietnam in 1957 as the vanguard of American front-line military assistance efforts. For nearly a decade they had been waging a localized guerrilla war through the battle-scarred tropical forests and delta marshlands of South Vietnam. There they had forged a lengendary reputation as one of the finest, yet most unorthodox, formations of the United States military. The new year of 1965 brought the realization that their antiguerrilla tactics were hopelessly outclassed by the increased tempo of conflict. The former, limited "Special Forces war" was ending, and they were now caught up in the full hurricane of conventional warfare.

The Army Special Forces was popularly known simply as the "Green Berets," in tribute to its trademark—the green beret awarded in 1961 by President John F. Kennedy. President Kennedy's enthusiasm had been the guiding force behind its creation as the elite nucleus of his counterinsurgency strategy. However, the Special Forces was not the ranger strike force that its heritage implied.[2] Instead it was a flexible grouping of highly trained sergeants and officers, designed to carry out a novel military doctrine being labeled "unconventional warfare." This complex program of guerrilla wars and countersubversion quickly translated into a very ancient military policy; the art of training, advising, and supporting foreign regular and irregular armed forces. The Army's Special Forces proved to be just the right combination for implementation of these training missions on a global basis, and so it came early to the tropical rice-and-jungle countryside of South Vietnam.

In the shadowy years of 1961 through 1964, before massive American military intervention in Vietnam, the Army Special

2. In its zeal to give the new Special Forces a solid heritage of special unit lineages upon its creation in 1952, the Department of the Army bestowed upon it the honors and lineage of the joint U.S.-Canadian mountain commando 1st Special Service Force ("Devil's Brigade") and the ranger battalions of World War II.

Forces had evolved into a unique and invaluable extension of American combat power. Traditional Special Forces orientation was the training of resistance forces in enemy territory. In Vietnam, the Special Forces mission was to teach government-sponsored forces in "friendly" territory. Instead of practicing guerrilla warfare, it found itself defending conventional fortified camps against Viet Cong insurgents. Slowly its influence permeated the remotest areas of South Vietnam, and the Special Forces became a mainstay of American presence. It was able to affect the battlefield in an all-encompassing manner unknown to conventional strategy.

The fundamental Special Forces responsibility throughout the Vietnam War was actually the Civilian Irregular Defense Group (CIDG) program, which had been started on November 1, 1961, under the operational control of the U.S. Central Intelligence Agency.[3] Begun as an experimental effort with the Rhade tribe of Darlac Province, the aim of the program was continued to gain the loyalty and cooperation of the isolated ethnic minority groups of South Vietnam, over which the Saigon regime had little or no control, and to create paramilitary (i.e., nonregular army) forces from their ranks. Hardworking teams of stalwart Special Forces members living under the most primitive conditions, disdainfully suspected as having "gone native" by senior military authorities, transformed hamlet militia and tribal bowmen into their beloved CIDG "strikers." By sharing common bonds of danger and hardship, a rare and lasting personal relationship was cemented between the gruff, burly Special Forces Americans and the small, wiry tribesmen.

The trend toward establishing Special Forces camps closer to Vietnam's rugged frontiers had been initiated by a U.S. Cen-

---

3. The CIDG (pronounced sid-gee) was the South Vietnamese country-wide Civilian Irregular Defense Group, civilian irregulars recruited from the local areas around the camps on a paramilitary basis by Special Forces. They were capable of conducting local security and limited reconnaissance operations, and were organized into 150-man light infantry companies. Their performance varied greatly depending on the amount of training and equipment they had received. While the 5th Special Forces Group in Vietnam boasted of 19,900 CIDG under arms at the beginning of 1965 (and 28,200 by year's end), these forces lacked the fire support, motivation, and inherent leadership to qualify them as conventional units.

tral Intelligence Agency border surveillance program cranked up in June of 1962 and dumped in the laps of the Special Forces a year later. The Montagnard tribal "trailwatchers" and "mountain scouts" inherited with this new mission were assimilated into a kaleidoscopic array of Special Forces-led native contingents. The four CIDG border surveillance camps of November 1963 had mushroomed to eighteen by mid-1964.

By the fall of 1964 the Vietnam War had heated up to the point where the Army decided to transfer the 5th Special Forces Group (Airborne) from the pines of Fort Bragg, North Carolina, to Nha Trang, Vietnam. The personnel of the group wore a solid black cloth "flash," or recognition patch, on their coveted green berets. The colors of the South Vietnamese flag were now sewn diagonally across the black background of the flash. The 5th Special Forces Group (Airborne) became synonymous with Special Forces duty in Vietnam.[4] There all training was put to the actual test of war. Already by the beginning of 1965, three out of every four Special Forces soldiers assigned to the group had a previous tour of combat in Vietnam behind them. They had received the best antiguerrilla experience possible—by fighting the Viet Cong guerrillas themselves.

In its formative years the CIDG program had been defensive in nature, the small camps being susceptible to overruns by swift Viet Cong attack. In 1965, in tune with the Army's buildup and offensive posture, the Special Forces role and the CIDG effort assumed an increasingly aggressive stance. "Eagle Flight" reserves designed to reinforce camp defenses were soon expanded to larger mobile reaction forces called "Mike Forces." Special missions, such as the long-range reconnaissance patrolling under Project LEAPING LENA, were formalized as part of the expanding hand of trump cards Special Forces could play. LEAPING LENA became Project DELTA, and a headquarters,

4. The 5th Special Forces Group (Airborne) was a Regular Army unit which was activated at Fort Bragg, North Carolina, on September 21, 1961. By that time Special Forces personnel were heavily engaged in action in South Vietnam. In September 1962 there was enough need for a group-sized Special Forces presence that the U.S. Army Special Forces, Vietnam (Provisional), was established. The 5th Special Forces Group (Airborne) arrived in Vietnam on October 1, 1964, and took over the missions and assets of the old provisional group, which was discontinued.

Detachment B-52, was organized in June to control it. Project DELTA operations would range throughout South Vietnam during the course of the war locating NVA/VC units and installations, gathering information, directing air strikes, conducting special raids, reinforcing camps, and performing a host of top secret assignments.

In theory the U.S. Army Special Forces was supposed to advise a South Vietnamese clone called the LLDB (Lac Luong Dac Biet), which would actually run the CIDG program. In reality the ineptitude of the South Vietnamese Special Forces permitted the Americans no choice but to continue full leadership themselves. Although it improved during the war and there were numerous individual exceptions, the LLDB in general suffered from a number of deficiencies, among them lack of training and capability. However, the American Green Beret soldiers most resented the unwillingness of LLDB personnel to lead CIDG soldiers in battle, and the racial animosity and distrust the Vietnamese expressed toward the Montagnards and other tribal minorities. These factors prevented the planned successful turnover of the CIDG program to the Saigon regime. The envisioned ability of the U.S. Army Special Forces to "work itself out of a job" never really materialized. When, in 1970, the 5th Special Forces Group (Airborne) was finally forced to turn over its camps and formally return to the United States, it left much unfinished and unresolved.

The Special Forces also worked a serious drain on the Army's leadership resources, which the Army could not afford after the big Vietnam buildup. The retention of thousands of excellent sergeants in such an elite organization, especially after the Army's expansion (which had created a grave shortage of noncommissioned officers), deprived the Army's regular units of valuable combat leadership at a most critical time. The hardship was so acute that the lack of available line sergeants, with their potential discipline and experience, ended up being a major factor in the Army's decline.

3. Special Forces Under Siege

By the summer of 1965, the blazing perimeters of Special Forces garrisons glowed throughout the length of South Vietnam like brushfires under the darkening storm of total war. On the overcast night of May 10 a heavy barrage of mortar and recoilless rifle fire crashed into the compound of Special Forces Control Detachment B-34 at Song Be. Behind this wall of exploding dirt and steel four battalions of Viet Cong regulars surged through the town and overwhelmed the scattered positions of the 36th ARVN Ranger Battalion.

The Special Forces defenders put up a resolute defense of the American compound, sandwiched between the ARVN ranger barracks and the province chief's home, but one sapper squad was able to fight its way across the barbed wire and storm the mess hall. The mess hall had been converted into a medical aid station and was now filled with aidmen frantically working on the wounded. Suddenly the Viet Cong squad burst inside where the fighting continued with grenades and pocket knives.

The low cloud cover had negated initial air support, but helicopters had flown through the swirling mists and were now overhead. However, they were initially unable to direct their rockets and aerial machine guns due to the smoke and confusion of the raging battle below. Around the compound hand-to-hand combat was deciding the outcome, and as dawn filtered through the cloud-banked sky the Special Forces was able to evict the Viet Cong who had broken through. A sudden spasm of action erupted around the mess hall as the VC squad survivors were killed making a break for open ground.

The Viet Cong force retired inside the center of Song Be where it entrenched itself in the town market and temple area. A hasty charge conducted by the reconsolidated 36th ARVN Ranger Battalion failed to dislodge the defenders. A reinforced two-battalion South Vietnamese reaction force cautiously approached the town the next day. En route a ranger battalion detected and avoided an elaborate ambush trap two miles in length. While the main infantry force was not ambushed, it did have to fight a running engagement with another VC force. After further combat, punctuated by repeated air strikes, the Viet Cong finally withdrew from Song Be.

On June 9, 1965, another successful Viet Cong attack was made, this time on the Dong Xoai Special Forces camp in the same province. The camp was defended by Operations Detachment A-342, backed up by local Vietnamese and tribal contingents with several artillery howitzers and six armored cars, and a U.S. Navy Seabee construction team. Just before midnight an intensive mortar barrage blanketed the post, followed by a ground assault a half hour later.

The mixed Special Forces and Vietnamese troops, native soldiers, and American sailors manned their gun pits and foxholes, firing furiously as detonations rocked the blazing skyline. Already groups of Viet Cong sappers were cutting through the mesh of barbed wire entanglements wrapped around the compound. Machine-gun fire riddled the Viet Cong assault pioneers, but others leaped forward to take the places of the fallen. Black-garbed bodies draped the broken wire, and crew-served weapons on both sides barked across the perimeter. Then bangalore torpedoes were shoved into the protective barrier and exploded.

The VC stormed through the smashed wire at 2:30 that morning. A hail of gunfire and exploding grenades blasted the air as the tumult spilled into the camp itself. Half of the armored cars were damaged and inoperable, but the Viet Cong scrambled into the other three. They spun crazily through the camp, raking it with machine-gun and cannon fire. Later on aircraft were used to destroy them. The surviving defenders fought backwards into a small cluster of positions. By daybreak this final defensive perimeter within the camp was closely surrounded.

At 9:40 that morning helicopters set soldiers from the 1st Battalion, 7th ARVN Regiment, into a landing zone north of Dong Xoai. These infantrymen were quickly overrun in a savage fifteen-minute skirmish. The remainder of the battalion then began airlifting into the Thuan Loi rubber plantation farther north. There the helicopter crews had to abort the landings after putting only eighty men on the ground, due to the terrific volume of mortar and automatic weapons fire directed against them. Within just twenty minutes all contact with the landed force was lost.

The 52d ARVN Ranger Battalion was landed on the road south of the compound following an intensive aerial bombardment late that afternoon. As they approached the camp the rangers came under heavy fire. A series of air strikes were called in on the camp's ruins, and then the rangers charged forward to take it, after a final sharp skirmish. On the morning of June 11, the 7th ARVN Airborne Battalion was helicoptered in near the recaptured compound and moved, against scattered resistance, to the ill-fated landing zones of the previous day. By this time the Viet Cong, subjected to continuous aircraft bombing and strafing, had started to withdraw. The district town of Dong Xoai was once again in South Vietnamese government hands.

Both battles had been extremely significant as they not only underlined the deepening crises in South Vietnam, but also highlighted the upgraded Viet Cong tactics of using large forces to overrun and hold district and province towns and setting up well-prepared ambushes to destroy relieving units. In such an atmosphere the Special Forces, tactically limited as training advisors, had to expand and conventionalize its combat resources in order to survive.

The Battle of Plei Me, fought in the fall of 1965, marked the first transition of the Vietnam battlefield from guerrilla clashes to a war between national armies. Instead of Viet Cong, the *32d, 33d,* and *66th NVA Regiments* would be used to assault this Special Forces campsite thirty miles south of Pleiku. In response the newly arrived American 1st Cavalry Division would be pitted against North Vietnamese regulars in the Ia Drang Valley, fully engaging the American military in another major war.

The Special Forces camp at Plei Me was garrisoned by the twelve-man Operations Detachment A-217, fourteen LLDB troops, and 415 Jarai, Rhade, and Bahnar tribal CIDG soldiers. On October 19, 1965, the camp had a large combat patrol of eighty-five CIDG strikers led by two Americans sweeping the area to the northwest. Local warning security was provided by five eight-man ambush teams and two regularly posted twenty-man outposts.

After nightfall had cloaked the surrounding tree line in darkness and introduced a new cycle of jungle noises, a muffled clatter of rifle fire suddenly erupted and then died away. An advancing NVA infantry column had brushed past one of the ambush positions. Later another distant crash of gunfire exploded the tropical night, this time accompanied by a barrage of mortar shells and recoilless rifle rounds sending up geysers of dirt throughout the compound. The NVA overran the southern outpost in barely twenty minutes. Shortly after midnight the North Vietnamese charged the camp itself.

The North Vietnamese shock troops ran forward, shouting and firing rapid bursts from their assault rifles. The bunkered machine guns rattled out concentrated bursts of grazing fire aimed at the first wave of sappers busily piercing the perimeter's barriers. Pith helmets and kit bags rolled across the open prewire zone as the bullets picked up running figures and flung them to the ground in writhing agony. Bodies were piling up like driftwood around the bent posts and bails of twisted barbed wire. Swiftly the NVA rammed explosive-filled pipe sections through the obstacles, and a series of detonations shook the fringes of the camp.

The NVA came pouring through the smoking gaps pitching grenades and blazing away with their submachine guns. Red tracer lines of machine-gun fire murderously converged to hammer against these packed clusters of onrushing attackers. Scores of men were skimmed from their ranks, collapsing and staggering as they fell behind to topple onto the battered earth. Flares and rockets flashed brilliant mixes of shifting colors and crossed shadows as they lighted the blackened landscape. At 3:45 A.M. the afterburners of jet engines could be seen darting through the darkened, overcast skies. Exploding yellow-white globular balls of jellied gasoline spewed over the jungled outskirts of the camp.

The northwest corner bunker was under direct assault. Its defenders desperately fought off each charge from behind shrapnel-riddled sandbags and blood-washed logpiles. A red dawn smeared with smoke and haze flooded the battlefield with the half-light of morning. At six o'clock a recoilless rifle round burst through the bunker aperture. Splintered wood and limbs were thrown into the air, and a final NVA lunge for the key position was made. The exhausted Special Forces, their jungle fatigues ripped and their webbing stripped of grenades, ordered tired and bloodstained tribesmen into the breach. The bunker managed to hold.

At daybreak a flight of unmarked medical evacuation helicopters arrived, escorted by several gunships. They descended into the smoldering camp to drop off a surgeon and pick up some of the wounded. Suddenly one of the hovering helicopters was hit and spiraled into the jungle below. The weary Special Forces team scratched together a rescue party, and sent it out in a vain attempt to reach the downed aircraft. After a harrowing encounter with an NVA machine-gun nest, during which one of the Special Forces sergeants was mortally wounded, the shaken survivors fell back into camp. By contrast the larger combat sweep patrol was notified to rejoin the camp and walked back through the gates without incident.

Maj. Charlie A. Beckwith's Special Forces unit known as Project DELTA, reinforced by two companies of the special 91st ARVN Airborne Ranger Battalion, received word to reinforce on the afternoon of October 20. They closed into Pleiku airfield at five o'clock that evening, just thirty minutes after a 1,200-man ARVN mechanized relief force headed south on Highway 14.[5] The mechanized group would run into a major ambush halfway to Plei Me, would suffer considerable personnel and vehicular losses, and would not reach the camp until October 25. Lack of helicopter lift forced Major Beckwith to spend the night planning. On the morning of October 21, Project DELTA was airlifted by a series of three flights into the thick tropical forest four and a half miles outside Plei Me.

Major Beckwith wisely decided to move his men due east a few miles before turning south toward the camp. The force slowly cut its way through the dense, vine-tangled jungle. The torturous trek was extremely difficult, and soon broken arms and heat exhaustion were reducing the strength of Beckwith's command. In mid-afternoon they ran into a three-man NVA recoilless rifle crew. As a result they turned deeper into the jungle. By five o'clock they were only thirty-five minutes from Plei Me, but the rangers couldn't decide what to do. Major Beckwith personally went forward with his machete and started cutting trail to con-

---

5. The relief force consisted of the 3d ARVN Armored Cavalry Squadron with M41 tanks and M8 armored cars, the 1st Battalion of the 42d ARVN Regiment, and the 21st and 22d ARVN Ranger Battalions.

tinue the advance. As night fell they formed a perimeter and prepared to enter camp the next morning.

At 1:40 A.M. on October 22, an Air Force A-1E Skyraider was shot down over the camp. The pilot was seen parachuting out but was never found. A second plane was lost, but its pilot was eventually rescued. Early that morning Project DELTA pushed through a brief firefight to move into the camp, where Major Beckwith took over command. At one o'clock in the afternoon a three-company force from the camp passed their wire and got into a skirmish line to clear a nearby hill. A bypassed heavy machine gun suddenly ripped into them, throwing the force into confusion, killing Special Forces Captain Thomas Pusser and twelve indigenous soldiers, and wounding scores more. The rest of the composite clearing force retreated.

The 91st ARVN Airborne Ranger Battalion's shortcomings continued to plague their performance the next day. During an assault on two other machine-gun positions, one NVA soldier suddenly charged the force. Before he was killed, the rangers fled back in disorder. On October 24, a recovery party managed to pull in the bodies from this botched attack. On the morning of October 25, a commando squad, led by two Special Forces flamethrower sergeants, charged light machine guns surrounding the camp. Although the flamethrowers malfunctioned, the commandos destroyed one of the bunkers. That evening the armored-infantry task force from Pleiku arrived in the camp.

Although clearing operations would continue for several days, the battle was over. The morning after the ARVN mechanized force showed up, a helicopter touched down at the camp carrying several United States Army combat officers. Col. Elvy B. Roberts, commander of the 1st Brigade (Airborne), 1st Cavalry Division (Airmobile), stepped onto the sun-scorched clay of the Plei Me Special Forces camp at nine o'clock on the morning of October 26, 1965, for a full briefing. He had moved an entire American infantry brigade to Camp Holloway outside Pleiku, and the rest of the division was now located at An Khe. The conflict in Vietnam was no longer a Special Forces affair. The 1st Cavalry Division's full-fledged efforts to punish the North Vietnamese attackers at Plei Me would transform it into a "big unit war," and the future conduct of miltary operations in Vietnam would leave the Special Forces in the background.

CHAPTER 2.

AN ARMY GIRDS FOR BATTLE

1. An Army Enters Vietnam

The beautiful South Vietnamese landscape, agrarian nature, and tropical climate posed a tremendous headache to American military planners faced with increasing support requirements as the expanding war erupted into full-scale conflagration. They bemoaned the lack of ports, terminals, warehouses, communications facilities, industrial complexes, or transportation networks. The United States had been fielding military advisors to South Vietnam since the French had pulled out ten years earlier. This military advisory effort was at the forefront of a massive American investment of money and material in an attempt to create a viable South Vietnamese state. However, the modern United States armed forces were tied to complex logistical considerations and a level of sophistication that required the overseas import of all supplies, equipment, and trained manpower. As more advisors, signal units, aircraft, aviators, and Special Forces were sent into the countryside, their support became increasingly difficult.

A logistical command, for U.S. Army Military Assistance Command Vietnam (MACV), had been recommended for Vietnam when the military had created the top headquarters there on February 8, 1962, but nothing had been approved. By the end of that year over twelve thousand American military technicians, advisors, and pilots were assigned to Vietnam duty.[1] At the beginning of 1965, Gen. William C. Westmoreland's MACV command had grown to over 14,700 Army and 700 Marine personnel,[2] and the need for immediate and responsive combat service support became more urgent.

American units were still principally located in the cities. They occupied the bustling capital of Saigon and adjacent Bien Hoa, the northern anchorage of Da Nang tucked underneath Hai Van (Clouds) Pass, the southern delta rice-farming town of Soc Trang, the beautiful beach town of Nha Trang, and the misty Central Highland crossroads of Pleiku.[3] These forces were mainly helicopter units, which were used to ferry ARVN troops and to provide aerial rocket and machine-gun fire in their support. It was just a matter of time before the Viet Cong would strike back at the bases housing these aviation resources.

In the early Sunday morning darkness of February 7, 1965, a cascade of mortar rounds blasted the American compound of Camp Holloway and the airfield of Pleiku. Viet Cong sappers charged through the flare-lighted night to hurl demolitions charges into barracks and planes. Nine servicemen were killed and 128 wounded, and scores of aircraft destroyed or damaged. Three days later the Viet Cong exploded the hotel billets in Qui Nhon, killing twenty-three American soldiers and wounding twenty-two others.

For years MACV headquarters had been urging that American combat units be sent to Vietnam to protect U.S. bases there. These two Viet Cong attacks had graphically demonstrated this

1. In December 1962 the major U.S. forces in Vietnam were U.S. Army Special Forces, Vietnam (Provisional), 45th Transportation Battalion, Utility Tactical Transport Aviation Company, and Marine Task Force Shufly (the marine medium-helicopter squadron HMM-163). The last three were helicopter outfits.

2. Gen. William C. Westmoreland had replaced Gen. Paul D. Harkins as MACV commander in June 1964.

3. Major U.S. forces in January 1965 were the Marine Unit, Vietnam (the Shufly force consisting of medium-helicopter squadron HMM-365), and the Army 5th Special Forces Group (Airborne) and 13th, 14th, 52d, and 145th Aviation Battalions.

need. The United States government also believed that strong American forces in South Vietnam would defeat the Viet Cong and discourage North Vietnam from continuing the war. On February 11, 1965, the Joint Chiefs of Staff decided that the 173d Airborne Brigade on Okinawa would be alerted for emergency Vietnam duty, and that a brigade of the 25th Infantry Division in Hawaii would be sent to Thailand.

General Westmoreland wanted a number of port and airfield centers along the coastline defended with American fighting troops. Ammunition and supplies could be dumped into these areas, artillery cannon and antiaircraft missiles installed, and fortifications carved out. Such enclaves would insure that a United States presence could be maintained in Vietnam, even if the South Vietnamese Army crumbled to the point of total ineffectiveness. American units could then take over offensive activity from such bastions while the South Vietnamese armed forces were rebuilt. This strategy was tagged the "enclave concept" (the troops called it "ink blot") and it was adopted despite Pentagon misgivings that it might lead the South Vietnamese forces to relax and lose interest. Da Nang would be garrisoned by Marines first, but plans were under way for other enclaves at Saigon, Bien Hoa, Vung Tau, Qui Nhon, Nha Trang, Tuy Hoa, Phan Thiet, and Chu Lai. To guard vital central Highway 19, which stretched through the jagged ridgelines from Pleiku to Qui Nhon, the 11th Air Assault Division (Test) at Fort Benning, Georgia, was targeted for insertion at An Khe.

The first Army troop arrival in response to the buildup decision was the 716th Military Police Battalion, which was flown into Saigon March 19–21, 1965, several days after two Marine combat battalions had landed at Da Nang. A platoon was immediately dispatched to each of Vietnam's four corps tactical zones. It heralded the arrival of a rapidly escalating number of regular Army combat formations in South Vietnam.

The increased American involvement had created a logistical nightmare, which was being resolved on a temporary emergency basis since planning envisaged an early reduction of this military commitment. Supply lines from Hawaii and Okinawa, six thousand and two thousand miles away, were already stretched to the limit. Suddenly an about-face was ordered. As the military situation deteriorated during 1965, logistics planners were directed to prepare for expanding troop levels instead of the expected withdrawals. They were also served notice that America expected to keep up the material comforts of its soldiers. The necessary facilities and bases would have to be built.

Practically overnight a major logistical foundation would have to be created in an undeveloped country, where all areas were subject to Viet Cong observation and attack. United States contingency plans for global situations requiring large-scale military response, which the conflict in Vietnam now threatened to become, assumed the National Guard and Army Reserves would be placed on active service. These were counted on to provide most of the special support units the Army would need in wartime. Even in the United States, combat units relied on a post's civilian supply and maintenance facilities. The Army's few mobile logistics units were oriented for a European battlefield, not tropical terrain.

President Lyndon B. Johnson announced on July 28, 1965, that United States forces in Vietnam would be expanded immediately to 125,000 men. The administration made it clear that it intended to meet these growing overseas requirements without mobilization. New soldiers would be gained through more drafting and increased enlistments. This political decision engaged the military in a major war without any of its anticipated National Guard or Reserve component assistance. The peacetime standing Army had a very thin crust of engineers, signalmen, logistics supervisors, and service units. Soon a crisis developed in supply and support of the combat formations going to Vietnam. The adverse consequences were legion, but this basic governmental policy never really changed.[4]

The ammunition situation was so chaotic that the 173d Airborne Brigade arrived in Vietnam with only fifteen days' worth of bullets. Daily cargo flights from Okinawa were instituted just to keep rifle magazines full. Ammunition for other deploying units was being sent on ahead and off-loaded, a good practice

4. Even the "mini-mobilization" that transpired after the Pueblo Incident in April 1968 only affected a small fraction of National Guard and Reserve components, hardly alleviating a chronic shortage of skilled manpower in critical service support jobs.

which was undone whenever the units were diverted from their original destinations. As a result ammunition crates and stacks of shells were piled up all over the beaches at Cam Ranh Bay and aboard leased sampans and barges floating on the Saigon River. The lack of transportation truck companies, another type of basic logistical unit, prevented ready transfer of such stockpiles to where they were needed.

A number of mad scrambles typified early logistical experiences in Vietnam. One of the worst happened during the summer deployment of the 2d Brigade, 1st Infantry Division, from Fort Riley, Kansas, to Vietnam. The unit was directed to secure the coastal town of Qui Nhon, where a natural harbor promised an ideal enclave site. Supplies were loaded by truck and aircraft at Saigon and hauled 250 miles north. Two days before arrival in Vietnam, the ships were diverted so that the brigade could secure the Saigon area.[5] A battalion was off-loaded to defend Cam Ranh Bay until the programmed American garrison (the 1st Brigade of the 101st Airborne Division) could get there, and the rest of the brigade then proceeded to Bien Hoa. A frantic last-minute relocation of supplies was made in an effort to get the tons of materials back south. The 1st Infantry Division's 2d Brigade arrived at Bien Hoa, located on the banks of the Dong Nai River outside Saigon, on July 16, 1965, minus large quantities of its supplies.

The only port worth its name in Vietnam was the bustling commercial dock fifty miles inland at Saigon. Its deep draft piers were in such demand that freighters were soon anchored the length of the channel for weeks on end. Warehouses and storage areas were scarce, and sabotage and pilferage abounded. Overworked logistical personnel often spent days searching through mountains of general cargo dumped at dockside for specific urgently needed items. Viet Cong sappers were having a field day destroying massive quantities of supplies, but no one could measure the losses. Without inventory control no one knew what was there. At Saigon the entire logistical command and control

5. Qui Nhon was secured briefly by the Seventh Fleet Special Landing Force, the 3d Battalion, 7th Marines, from July 1–7, 1965. It was then relieved by the 2d Battalion of the 7th Marines, which stayed until relieved in turn by Korean troops on November 4, 1965.

structure consisted of a U.S. Army major allotted one jeep and a briefcase, and he was seeking authorization to hire a driver.

The Vietnamese were uncooperative. When the first ship arrived at Cam Ranh Bay with desperately needed provisions, the South Vietnamese stevedore union balked at sending people to unload it. The entire ship was emptied by one transportation lieutenant and a handful of engineer soldiers dragooned from the local American garrison.

As the American buildup continued through the year, the ratio of service support units to combat forces kept slipping. At the Honolulu Conference of September 27, 1965, MACV decided to accept maneuver formations as they became available, even though their initial logistical support would be marginal. By December this calculated risk could no longer be accepted. All further tactical unit deployments were delayed as support components were rushed to Vietnam.

The 1st Logistical Command had unfurled its flag in South Vietnam on the last day of March 1965. It eventually grew in size to become one of the largest Army organizations in the world. Its superb support efforts soon dumped stacks of paper plates, hot meals, ice cream, and mountains of beer and soft drinks in the forward battle areas. The American Army quickly lost its appreciation of the harsh demands of a combat environment. The insistence upon large, luxurious base camps with snack shops and swimming pools erased the spartan lifestyle of the early advisors and Special Forces troops. In the end it greatly eroded the soldier's willingness to forego such comforts in extended field operations.

Even in the hard-driving line units, where the foot-slogging infantryman was not privy to such conveniences, too much of everything eroded combat prowess. In direct contrast to early ammunition shortages, a wealth of ordnance began to choke forward supply points. The American Army was making unbridled use of firepower. One could always find the officer who bragged that he would use any amount of supporting fire to save one American soldier. Since it sounded great, no one was ever faulted for saying so. However, casualties were taken while loading, unloading, transporting, and protecting the massive amounts of munitions required for such prodigious firepower. It led to catastrophic accidents in ammunition storage sites throughout the war. So many munitions were fired that alarming accident rates developed. Ammunition often killed or maimed the soldiers it was designed to protect. Commanders developed the habit of calling for artillery, gunships, and fighter-bombers to silence even the lightest opposition. More often than not, by the time this support was coordinated and arrived, the NVA or VC were gone.

The expanding American Army in Vietnam built a frightfully expensive but magnificent support system, capable of providing the wealth of resources needed to avoid any material sacrifice. In fact, its logistical achievement was unparalleled in the history of warfare. In so doing, the Army helped bring about its own decline.

2. A Battle for Troops

The United States Army had 970,000 soldiers worldwide on January 1, 1965. Just over half of them were stationed in the continental United States and the rest in various overseas locations scattered from Korea to Germany, including South Vietnam.[6] The Army was technically in a state of national emergency, still in effect since Korea, and depended mainly on draft calls for its soldiers. At this point the Army was in very good shape, having been put into fighting trim by three recent crises of the first magnitude: the Berlin crisis of 1961, the Cuban missile crisis of October–December 1962, and the assassination of President John F. Kennedy in November 1963. Each of these had placed the Army on a virtual wartime footing.

Generous budgetary allocations had produced high quality training programs, an expensive test division being personally

6. In January 1965 the U.S. Army had its major forces disposed as follows: Continental United States—1st and 2d Armored Divisions, 1st, 2d, and 4th Infantry Divisions, 5th Infantry Division (Mechanized), 11th Air Assault Division (Test), 82d and 101st Airborne Divisions, 194th Armored Brigade, 197th Infantry Brigade, 11th Armored Cavalry (Regiment), and 3d, 6th, and 7th Special Forces Groups; Panama Canal Zone—193d Infantry Brigade and 8th Special Forces Group; Alaska—171st and 172d Infantry Brigades; Hawaii— 25th Infantry Division; Okinawa—173d Airborne Brigade and 1st Special Forces Group; Korea—1st Cavalry Division and 7th Infantry Division; Vietnam—5th Special Forces Group; Germany—3d and 4th Armored Divisions, 3d, 8th, and 24th Infantry Divisions (Mechanized), 2d, 3d, and 14th Armored Cavalry (Regiments), and the 10th Special Forces Group.

pushed by Defense Secretary Robert S. McNamara, quantities of helicopters and other aircraft, and very modern technical equipment. The Army also had a considerable number of combat-experienced leaders and pilots, the result of years of advisory efforts in Vietnam. Senior officers and sergeants had World War II and Korean experience under their belts. While the Army still considered its most likely threat to be the European arena, its new airmobile doctrine being field-tested by the 11th Air Assault Division (Test) was unmistakably Asia-bound.

Basic and advanced individual training of soldiers was the responsibility of the Continental Army Command. The Army of 1965 had been on the brink of possible global war for the last four years. Recent experiences had led to emphasis being placed on realistic battle training. As a result instruction was serious, strenuous, and thorough. Although units were still expected to fight on a conventional European battlefield, their training was applicable to any combat situation. The best-trained units would be the first ones into Vietnam. However, the combat-experienced personnel of these initial units were lost after their first year in country. From then on units were filled over and over again by new replacements fresh from the States.

The military's training programs were geared in case of war to rely on mobilized Reserves and the federalized National Guard to provide sufficient cadre. This support never materialized, and as the war lengthened, the entire system of training soldiers in the Continental Army Command had to be altered. A major effect was the tremendous expansion of training facilities, their *raison d'être* now being the production of battlefield proficiency in the jungles and tunnels of Southeast Asia. Even as barracks doors stood ajar in posts across the United States, the former garrisons having departed for overseas service, "smokey bear"-hatted drill sergeants marched rows of fresh trainees down asphalt camp streets. U.S. Army infantry training center brigades dominated ten installations by the height of the Vietnam War.[7]

7. In February 1969 Army infantry training center brigades were located at Fort Benning, Georgia; Fort Bragg, North Carolina; Fort Campbell, Kentucky; Fort Gordon, Georgia; Fort Dix, New Jersey; Fort Jackson, South Carolina; Fort Lewis, Washington; Fort McClellan, Alabama; Fort Ord, California; and Fort Polk, Louisiana.

Training courses were chopped several weeks in order to assign trained soldiers rapidly to alerted units. While wartime conditions in Vietnam put more emphasis on training, they also produced a number of problems. Training still enjoyed very high priority, but now the number one priority for the Army was unquestionably the ongoing war in Vietnam. Sergeants and officers needed for training purposes were in even more demand for leading soldiers through the rice paddies and jungles of Southeast Asia. Training standards slipped due to rapid turnover. Many career soldiers even avoided training duty as not the choicest of assignments. Compressed and accelerated training programs became the order of the day, a situation further aggravated by the declining quality of incoming recruits as the war progressed.[8]

As the seemingly interminable Vietnam War dragged on, personnel turbulence grew more prevalent throughout the Army. Individual morale and discipline suffered. Stateside units, already skeletonized by the war's incessant replacement demands, were undermined by further demands from Continental Army Command's training establishments. Units in Europe, Alaska, Hawaii, and Panama were ruthlessly stripped. The battle-ready Army of 1965, its spit-shined shoes gleaming and full-color insignia neatly stitched on starched fatigues, had been replaced by a war-weary Army by 1969, with dull boots and peace beads draped under rumpled tunics.

Specialized training suffered most. One of the major hindrances to successful advisory performance was the absence of any requirement to communicate in Vietnamese or French. Vietnamese proved very hard for the few United States advisors who endeavored to learn it. While syntactically simple, it was a tonal language that proved to be phonetically difficult for Americans. Even those who diligently took lessons for months could only produce toneless, hence unintelligible, utterances. General Cao Van Vien stated, "Even later, over the war years,

8. The Marine Corps also reduced recruit training time from twelve to eight weeks beginning September 1, 1965, in an effort to process 30,000 additional men newly authorized without an increase in instructors or existing facilities. The Marines began drafting in January 1966.

I know of no single instance in which a U.S. advisor effectively discussed professional matters with his counterpart in Vietnamese."[9]

Equitable management of many critical skills was impossible. Some expertise required in Vietnam could not be filled by short-term training, and comparable civilian occupations were nonexistent. As a result individuals were ordered on involuntary second and even third tours of duty in Vietnam. Units fought over the limited skilled people available. Helicopter units urgently needed in Vietnam competed for the same quality personnel sought by equally needed aviation maintenance units. The lack of mobilization was soon taking its toll on the continued efficiency of the regular armed forces.

The one universal troop factor throughout the Vietnam War was the fixed "hostile fire area" tour, the combat zone service requirement of one year. The Army found it increasingly difficult to sustain this fixed tour length as the war dragged on. Unit readiness in the rest of the world was eroded, and personnel retention and combat effectiveness in Vietnam suffered. Many argued that just as a soldier was becoming a skilled tropical warrior he was yanked out, to be replaced by a green soldier who had to learn it all from the beginning. A popular military adage summed it up: the United States never fought in Vietnam ten years, it fought in Vietnam one year ten times over.

The American soldier tried to adapt to the climate and terrain of Vietnam and to fight courageously against a tough and battle-wise adversary. For the most part, he continued to exhibit good morale despite an inequitable draft system, training problems, high personnel turnover rates, occasional inadequate leadership, racial and drug problems, and a growing lack of public support at home. These took a larger toll of the American Army as the years exacerbated the effects, dulling the Army's fighting edge and ultimately reducing the combat potential of entire divisions and brigades.

For the individual American soldier, the overriding concern was how much time he had remaining in Vietnam. Daily "short"

9. General Cao Van Vien et al., *The U.S. Advisor*, U.S. Army Center of Military History, Washington, D.C., 1980, p. 31.

calendars were meticulously ticked off on everything from helmet covers to pin-up posters. Barring death or serious injury, every soldier knew his exact departure date as soon as he stepped on Vietnamese soil. His primary purpose became simply to reach his personal DEROS (date expected to return from overseas) intact. The fixed length of the hostile fire tour, for all its drawbacks, had undeniably overwhelming morale value.

The eager soldier of 1965, anxious to earn his Combat Infantryman's Badge, was replaced by the hardened but decorated Vietnam "survivor" of later years. By that time the privates and junior officers of the pre-Vietnam Army were the platoon sergeants and battalion commanders.

CHAPTER 3.

MARINES AT WAR

1. "Send in The Marines!"

The United States Marine Corps, the nation's amphibious strike force, is the *corps d'elite* of the American military. As a premier fighting organization, the Marines also have the role of protecting American interests on a global basis.

This dual responsibility has produced a rich and varied legacy extending from the first Marine landing in the Bahamas in 1776 to the Cuban missile crisis of 1962. In between, the Marines had captured a pirate fortress at Tripoli, taken the Mexican national palace, participated in the Civil War, defended Shanghai and Peking, cleared entrenched German troops from French forests, fought through a maze of Caribbean conflicts, stormed Japanese island bastions, landed on Korean shores, and defended Lebanon. This heritage had produced a common governmental response to military emergencies throughout the country's history: "Send in the Marines!"

As the situation in Vietnam began to unravel, the Marines were in a very high response posture. This was largely due to the triple crises of Cuba, Thailand in 1962, and the assassination of President John F. Kennedy the following year. During 1964, Marine capability was further tested and sharpened by a series of rigorous exercises extending from Norwegian Tremso, three hundred miles inside the Arctic Circle, to mock battles with French Marine commandos in the Mediterranean. That year training was conducted in Corsica, Sardinia, Spain, Norway,

Puerto Rico, Cuba, Panama, North Carolina, New York, California, Hawaii, Taiwan, and the Philippines.

Gen. Wallace M. Greene, Jr., who became commandant of the Marine Corps on January 1, 1964, stated on March 26 that the Marine Corps had "reached its best state of readiness in many years." On New Year's Day 1965, actual Marine strength stood at 188,505. They were poised for action anywhere in the world.[1]

In late 1964, the Pentagon considered strengthening the northern portion of South Vietnam by moving the Seventh Fleet's Marine Special Landing Force and a Marine antiaircraft missile battalion to guard Da Nang. Once the colorful French colonial city of Tourane, constant war had reduced it to a squalid, refugee-packed town. The crucial military significance of Da Nang was obvious. Its bay, hemmed in by the Chaine Annamitique spur of the Hai Van Mountains and Mon Ky (Monkey) Mountain, was one of the few good deep-water harbors in the country, and its single ten thousand-foot concrete runway was considered a major air base. By mid-February of 1965, MACV determined that the South Vietnamese military was no longer able to defend the area's installations against determined attack. It was imperative that the 9th Marine Expeditionary Brigade, on board naval ships in the South China Sea, be moved to Da Nang. The 1st Marine Brigade at Kaneohe Bay, Hawaii, preparing to outload for Exercise SILVER EAGLE in California, would be sent to Okinawa as backup.

The U.S. Marines became responsible for the five northern provinces known as I Corps Tactical Zone. At the upper boundary was the demarcation line separating North and South Vietnam. This was marked by the Song Ben Hai River until it reached Bo Ho Su, from which point the line ran straight to the border.

---

1. In January 1965 U.S. Marine Corps infantry was disposed as follows: Continental United States—1st Marine Division (1st, 5th, 7th Marines) and 2d Marine Division (2d, 6th, 8th Marines); Okinawa—3d Marine Division (3d, 9th Marines); Hawaii—1st Marine Brigade (4th Marines); Mediterranean Sea—1st Battalion Landing Team, 2d Marines; Caribbean Sea—3d Battalion Landing Team, 2d Marines; South China Sea—9th Marine Expeditionary Brigade (1st and 3d Battalion Landing Teams, 9th Marines); Vietnam—Company D, 1st Battalion, 3d Marines.

New flags are unfurled during the official activation ceremonies for the 199th Infantry Brigade (Light) at Fort Benning, Georgia, on June 24, 1966, as the United States Army goes to war. (Fort Benning Signal Photograph Laboratory)

Helicopters arrive over Camp Shelby, Mississippi, to ferry soldiers of the 199th Infantry Brigade (Light) into their final training exercise on October 1, 1966, prior to departure for Vietnam. (Fort Benning Signal Photograph Laboratory)

Marine Ontos vehicle, mounting six recoilless rifles, rolls ashore at Da Nang during the landing of the 3d Battalion, 9th Marines, on March 8, 1965. (U.S. Marine Corps)

U.S. Army soldiers disembark from a medium landing craft at Cat Lai in 1966. (U.S. Army)

Marines of the 2d Battalion, 9th Marines, come under fire while making an assault during Operation HARVEST MOON on December 12, 1965. (U.S. Marine Corps)

A recoilless rifle mounted on top of an amtrac of the 1st Amphibious Battalion, with the 3d Marine Division, fires at opposition west of Da Nang on August 19, 1965. (U.S. Marine Corps)

Paratroopers of the 173d Airborne Brigade combat assault near Bien Hoa in 1965. (Bell Helicopters)

Infantrymen of the 1st Infantry Division take automatic weapons fire from a treeline during an early search and destroy mission on October 4, 1965. (U.S. Army)

Precipitous border mountain ranges, with peaks eight to ten thousand feet high, formed the region's western frontier. This natural barrier reversed the monsoon seasons from what the rest of Vietnam experienced. Summers were mainly hot and dry, but the winters were warm and rainy.

I Corps Tactical Zone was also physically and culturally separated from the rest of South Vietnam. A series of ridges extended to the sea, dividing the inhabited coast into small mountain-ringed valleys wherever rivers washed out to sea. The old Mandarin Road, now called Route 1, connecting Da Nang to Saigon, had most of its bridges down. The trans-Vietnam Railway had large sections of track removed throughout its length. I Corps Tactical Zone was also traditionally part of old Annam, aloof from lower areas once known as Cochin China. The largest city of the region, Hue, was once the splendid Annamese imperial capital when Saigon was just a backward fishing hamlet.

The South Vietnamese commander and military governor of I Corps Tactical Zone was the former parachutist brigade leader, two-starred Gen. Nguyen Chanh Thi, the "Warlord of the North." Headquartered in the handsome yellow- and brown-trimmed French colonial compound near the Da Nang airfield, he had placed his 1st ARVN Division in the upper two provinces near the DMZ and the 2d ARVN Division in the lower two. The separate 51st ARVN Regiment was posted to central Quang Nam Province.

The 9th Marine Expeditionary Brigade landed at Da Nang on March 8, 1965. On April 10, a second landing force of Marines went ashore and began building a base farther north at Phu Bai. Nearly a month later, on May 6, still more Marines landed and began their southernmost installation in I Corps Tactical Zone at Chu Lai. By the end of the year they had established three operational enclaves, and the largest Marine force to be in combat since World War II was fully engaged in South Vietnam.

2. The Marines Land

The landing craft carrying the drenched Marines of Brig. Gen. Frederick J. Karch's 9th Expeditionary Brigade bobbed in the rough waters of Da Nang Bay. Overhead a cold, cloudy sky sent a stiff wind with drizzling rain across the harbor. An armada of warships clustered around the flagship USS *Mount McKinley* (AGC-7) disgorging tank-laden boats and amphibious tractors into ten-foot swells. Battle-equipped Marines grimly clambered down violently swaying nets. Mooring lines were snapping between the pitching landing craft and their mother ships.

The 3d Battalion of the 9th Marines had been embarked in naval ships off the Vietnamese coast for two months. On March 8, 1965, twenty years after the "Striking Ninth" had hit the beaches of Iwo Jima, four assault waves of the battalion landed through high surf in Vietnam.[2] They were greeted on the beach by General Thi, surrounded by a bevy of pretty college girls who draped the Marine vanguard, including Brigadier General Karch, with garlands of flowers. As the Marines were landing across the beach another battalion, the 1st Battalion of the 3d Marines, was en route from Okinawa in Marine KC-130 cargo planes. Since the territory just to the south of the airstrip was controlled by the Viet Cong, any aircraft approaching Da Nang had to run a gauntlet of VC ground fire. The planes flew past sniper rounds to begin landing the battalion at one o'clock that afternoon.

The Da Nang airfield, located in the middle of a densely populated area, was overcrowded with quantities of airplanes of all descriptions. These included Marine helicopters, stationed there since September 1962, and their company of Marine security. A Marine antiaircraft battalion had arrived that February.[3] Now it was becoming even more glutted with Marine in-

2. The 9th Marines had been part of the great expansion of the Marine Corps during World War I. It was activated November 20, 1917, at Quantico, Virginia, and posted to Cuba and then to Galveston, Texas. During World War II it fought in Bougainville, the northern Solomons, and Guam, before landing on Iwo Jima February 24, 1945. There it had captured Motoyama Airfield #2, broken the main line of Japanese resistance on the Motoyama Plateau, and made the final breakthrough to the island's northeastern shore. In 1948 it occupied Tsingtao and Shanghai, China, and had been posted between Japan and Okinawa since 1953, training in Korea, Formosa, and Borneo. In May–July 1962 elements had been sent to Udorn, Thailand, to counter the worsening situation in Laos.

3. The 1st Light Antiaircraft Battalion was activated at Twenty Nine Palms, California, as the Marine Corps's first HAWK missile battalion on May 2, 1960. It had been shipped from the United States for Vietnam duty in December 1964 but was held up in Okinawa due to facility construction costs.

fantry and artillery. Two companies secured hilltops enabling several HAWK missile batteries to leave the congested airbase and move beside them.

The five-thousand-man 9th Marine Expeditionary Brigade sent to Da Nang was assigned a single task: defend the airfield. The air base fence line was generally the boundary between friendly control and a strong pro–Viet Cong population. For several weeks the entire brigade had to subsist on fifteen days of rations one battalion had brought ashore and one emergency airlift from Saigon. The Marines felt besieged. A nearby undisciplined ARVN firing range, which routinely sent shots in their direction, and the scorching heat made them uncomfortable. Despite repeated pleas to extend aggressive patrolling, General Thi denied permission for the Marines to go outside a narrowly confined defensive perimeter. The only visible accomplishment seemed to be the revived sales of marble ashtrays, made from nearby Marble Mountain seven miles to the south and sold as souvenirs.

On April 10, the Marines in Da Nang were reinforced by the 2d Battalion of the 3d Marines, fresh from training in southern Thailand, followed by the regimental headquarters of the 3d Marines out of Okinawa. The reinforced 3d Battalion of the 4th Marines arrived from Hawaii via Okinawa on April 14. They were helicoptered to garrison Phu Bai, seven miles south of Hue, where a critical MACV electronic spy station and communications facility was located.

Another important enclave was established at Chu Lai, about sixty miles south of Da Nang, where the Marines were ordered to build an airstrip.[4] The headquarters of the 4th Marines along with its 1st and 2d battalions and the 3d Reconnaissance Battalion landed on the beaches May 7, 1965. A large sign had

It was on a firing exercise when President Lyndon B. Johnson announced over national television he had ordered it to Vietnam. After a hectic drive through the morning rush hour, it was shoved aboard planes at Naha Air Base and landed in Da Nang February 8, 1965.

4. The site had been selected by Marine Lt. Gen. Victor H. Krulak, the commanding general of Fleet Marine Force, Pacific, on a 1964 inspection tour. The naval officer with him agreed the place looked good, but it wasn't marked on the map. Krulak gave him the Mandarin Chinese characters for his own name, saying it was called Chu Lai. The name stuck.

been put up by the Ly Tin district Army advisors which read, "Ahoy Marines! Welcome Aboard, Area Secured." The area looked deceptively like Marine Camp Lejeune in North Carolina, but the terrible heat and bottomless, sugary sands ended the similarities as equipment was struggled ashore. Five days later they were joined by the 3d Battalion of the 3d Marines.

General Westmoreland had told the Marines to rename their headquarters, as the word *expeditionary* was unpalatable to the Vietnamese because of its French colonial association. The 9th Marine Expeditionary Brigade was folded down. The III Marine Amphibious Force (MAF) assumed control of Marine activities in Vietnam on May 7, 1965. The previous day the command group of the famed 3d Marine Division had arrived in Vietnam from Okinawa. Maj. Gen. Lewis W. Walt arrived in Vietnam at the end of the month to assume command of both III MAF and the division.

The 3d Marine Division was the westernmost United States Pacific response division. Originally formed in 1942 for World War II service, the division was highly regarded for its fierce 1945 battle at Iwo Jima, where it had earned the Presidential Unit Citation. Deactivated that December, it was reraised in California in 1952 and went to Camp Gifu, Japan, the next August. Since February 1956 it had been stationed at Camp Courtney, Okinawa. Known as a hard-training division, its proximity to Korea, Taiwan, South Vietnam, and Thailand had always kept troops and material at a high level of readiness. It was naturally the first American division into combat during the Vietnam War.

At 1:30 A.M. on July 1, a Marine sentry near the Da Nang air base fence line heard a suspicious noise. He tossed an illumination grenade into the darkness. It exploded, triggering a furious VC mortar barrage that swept across the Air Force side of the field. A squad of Viet Cong sappers, with an officer from the *3d Battalion, 18th NVA Regiment*, dashed through the perimeter fence and heaved satchel charges into a number of parked aircraft. As the demolition team scurried away, several groups of Marines scrambled over the concrete ramps toward the fence line. A short gunfight broke out between the Marines and Viet Cong. Two Marines were hit and went down. A recoilless rifle round crashed into a bunker. Then suddenly it was over. Flares and burning aircraft lit up the broken wire and bloodied grass in the blazing aftermath of the spectacular attack.

That month unrestrained authority for Marine offensive operations was granted. The headquarters of the 9th Marines landed in Da Nang on July 6, and the headquarters of the 7th Marines and the two remaining battalions on Okinawa were landed at Chu Lai on August 14. The III MAF now had four infantry regiments, and planned to swing immediately into action against the Viet Cong. Operation STARLITE was about to begin.[5]

3. The First Battle

For five months after the Marine landings at Da Nang, the Viet Cong had carefully avoided combat. However, by midsummer a major clash between the Marines and Viet Cong main force units was inevitable. The III MAF had steadily expanded its tactical enclaves at Da Nang, Chu Lai, and Phu Bai. The area actively patrolled by the Marines had grown from eight square miles in March to over six hundred square miles by August.

The Marine battalion, built to be part of a self-sustaining landing team designed to assault and hold a beach, was ideally suited for the fluid area warfare of Vietnam. A carefully structured and powerful force, it could be projected at considerable distance by the Marines's own helicopters and covered by the Marines's own jet aircraft. However, the Marines had been unable to employ their battalions this way in Vietnam. Then they were given an extremely crucial bit of intelligence information. The *1st VC Regiment* was pinpointed by a Viet Cong deserter on August 15, 1965. It was occupying hamlets in the vicinity of Van Tuong Peninsula, just fifteen miles south of Chu Lai.

The headquarters of Col. Oscar F. Peatross's 7th Marines with its 1st Battalion had just arrived to reinforce Chu Lai. The battalion was posted to base defense, but the command group

5. The infantry dispositions of III MAF would remain basically unchanged from mid-August until the end of 1965. These were Phu Bai—3d Battalion, 4th Marines; Da Nang—1st and 2d Battalions, 3d Marines; 1st, 2d, and 3d Battalions, 9th Marines; Chu Lai—3d Battalion, 3d Marines; 1st and 2d Battalions, 4th Marines; 1st Battalion, 7th Marines; Qui Nhon—2d Battalion, 7th Marines (under Army control); Special Landing Force—3d Battalion, 7th Marines.

of the 7th Marines was put in charge of the operation to hit the peninsula. The ground troops would be the seasoned Marines already in Chu Lai. Plans were drawn up to make a regimental assault. One Marine company would move overland from the north and dig in along the Tra Bong River as a blocking force. Shortly after dawn the next day a battalion would be landed by helicopter, simultaneously with a battalion hitting the beach in tracked amphibian vehicles. The Viet Cong would be driven between the seaborne and heliborne forces either into the blocking force or up against the coastline, where they would be trapped and eliminated.

A floating reserve battalion landing team could be provided by the Seventh Fleet Special Landing Force, but it was at Subic Bay in the Philippine Islands. Major General Walt insisted the reserve be present. The operation was scheduled to kick off based on its anticipated arrival off the coast of Vietnam. That would be daybreak, August 18. Fortuitous naval shipping for the seaborne attack battalion was readily available; a host of vessels were unloading reinforcements at both Chu Lai and Da Nang. They were quickly mustered for the operation. Plans were frantically put together, and in the rush the operational code name SATELLITE got mistakenly altered to STARLITE by a clerking error, the result of typing by candlelight after the electrical generators went down.

D-day for the seaborne assault battalion of the 3d Marines was August 18, 1965.[6] Marine A-4 Skyhawks repeatedly strafed the landing beaches as gargantuan forty-ton amtrac landing vehicles wallowed toward shore. The morning light reflected off the combing waves as the square-hulled titans thrashed across the beach, churning sand and grass as they moved inland. The machines jerked to a stop, their eleven-foot-high silhouettes towering stark against the rising sun like massive stone blocks

6. The 3d Marines was activated December 20, 1916, at Santo Domingo, Dominican Republic, where it served six years until deactivation. Raised again for World War II service, it was rapidly deployed to the Pacific, assigned to the 3d Marine Division, and invaded Bougainville and the northern Solomons. The 3d Marines went on to recapture Guam and take Iwo Jima in extremely hard fighting. It later occupied North China until 1949, and had been in Okinawa since March 1957.

left by some giant at water's edge. Dozens of green-clad warriors ran out of the gaping frontal ramp jaws. The men of the 3d Battalion, 3d Marines, formed up in long lines and advanced in open formation toward the seaside clusters of thatched huts, but there were no Viet Cong.

Out to sea, Marine-crammed landing utility craft backed out the well deck of the USS *Cabildo* (LSD-16), their dirty exhaust fumes mixing with salt spray to cloud the stern of the landing ship. Two other landing craft had sailed under their own power to the beaches and swung down their ramps. Big fifty-ton M48 main battle tanks and M67 flametanks rumbled onto shore, their turrets grinding around to swing long gun barrels from side to side. Nimble nine-ton beetlelike Ontos vehicles scurried down the beaches, their slender-barreled recoilless rifles balanced in triple mountings on each side. Vietnamese fishermen were putting their wooden boats into the water. Marine supplies were stacking up on the dunes, and already it was becoming a sweltering tropical day. Except for occasional pesky sniper fire, the operation was proceeding smoothly on the seaward side.

Company K was steadily advancing up the coast when it came under intense fire. VC machine guns and mortars were nestled into a fortified hill just ahead of it, and company attempts to maneuver forward were brought to a standstill. Company L was sent in to help, along with naval gunfire. The six-inch guns of the light cruiser USS *Galveston* (CLG-3) carefully measured out direct shots, each blast lighting the ship's tall array of antennas and lattice masts. The shells crashed against the hillside in devastating upheavals of dirt and timber.

The heat was unbearable. The noon sun beat down mercilessly on the sweltering Marines as they prepared to charge again. They refixed bayonets snugly into rifle sockets, and pulled spare bullet-filled magazines out of shirt pockets drenched in sweat. Then they surged forward through a smoking rubbish of vegetation, running past smashed trees riddled with shards of steel shrapnel. Suddenly a hail of deafening automatic weapons fire exploded from the Viet Cong trenchworks. Men sagged and dropped as bullets tore into them. The Marines leaped into the first VC trenchline where individual rifle shots and knifepoint dispatched the defenders. Dead Viet Cong gunners and Marine riflemen clogged the bottoms of weapons pits. The wounded from both sides, moaning for water, littered the collapsed trenches. The Marines continued to fight their way up the hill, and by mid-afternoon it was secured.

Action was intense on the landward side also. Early that morning the 2d Battalion of the 4th Marines had clambered aboard squat, green UH-34 helicopters for the flight to its western landing zones. The craft skimmed over flat rice paddies and dry fields dotted with hamlets, streams, and little wooded hills. The helicopters set down on three scattered sites, shortly after the first assault waves had crossed the beaches two and three miles distant. Company E immediately ran into a Viet Cong ridgeline off the landing zone. The Marines fixed bayonets on their M14 rifles and went into the attack. After a brief firefight the hill was taken.

First Lt. Homer K. Jenkins's Company H choppered in beside a small knoll, unaware that it had practically landed on top of a VC battalion occupying the adjacent hilltop. The first helicopters landed safely, but a furious fusillade of mixed rocket-propelled grenades and machine-gun fire met the next group. Jenkins pulled his men back into a small perimeter while Army helicopter gunships rocketed and strafed the wooded rise. He sent a platoon against the hill, but it was quickly pinned down by entrenched automatic weapons and couldn't get up the slope.

Three tanks and three Ontos vehicles were brought up, and jet aircraft roared down to send bombs plummeting into the dense shrubbery. Then Company H attacked again, working its way up the steep hillside against direct machine-gun fire. Grenades and bursts of rifle fire marked the advancing Marines as they closed the summit. Hill 43 had been taken, and Jenkins now advanced east with his tracked armor between two other small hamlets.

The hamlets, Nam Yen #3 and An Cuong #2, were strongly fortified with tunnels and trenchlines weaving through hedgerows laced with bamboo thickets. The latter had already been cleared, but Jenkins thought both were in Marine hands.[7] Mid-

---

7. Company I of the sea-landed 3d Battalion, 3d Marines, had secured An Cuong #2, the other hamlet in Jenkins's area. Capt. Bruce D. Webb's men

way across the rice paddy fierce machine-gun fire suddenly cut down the rear squads. A withering mortar barrage then rolled across the unit. The armored tanks and self-propelled recoilless rifles were bogging down. Jenkins desperately formed a mobile defensive circle with the vehicles and retreated back to the landing zone. Casualties had been heavy, and one platoon was cut off trying to reach medical evacuation helicopters. However, the separated group happened across another detachment of Marines sent after a downed helicopter. They combined into one defensive perimeter.

Meanwhile an amtrac resupply force with three flame tanks was moving inland from the beach to resupply Company I of 3d Battalion, 3d Marines, which was now pulling back from An Cuong #2. The column became disoriented in the maze of trails and ambled into a Viet Cong ambush. A series of jarring explosions swept the column, followed by an intense barrage of self-propelled grenades, recoilless rifles, and mortars. A hurriedly gathered task force of Marine infantry from Company I, several Ontos vehicles, and one M48 battle tank sallied out to rescue the beleaguered column. This relief group was also hit by concentrated fire as it neared the ambush area. The M48 tank was knocked out, and dead and wounded piled up as Marines attacked the fortified villages and tree lines. By the end of the action, Company I had taken so many losses it had to be pulled out of the battle. The supply column managed to hold its positions through the night, killing scores of Viet Cong soldiers who tried to overrun the amtracs and tanks.

The reserve Special Landing Force, the 3d Battalion of the 7th Marines, had arrived offshore on the helicopter carrier USS *Iwo Jima* (LPH-2) that morning. Companies from this unit were flown off the decks and helicoptered beside the other Marine units pushing steadily forward toward the coast. During the night the Marines halted on line. Naval warships fired star shells to keep the darkness flooded by artificial candles until morning.

---

moved into the innocuous-appearing village, but as they searched the huts a VC grenade was tossed into the midst of the command group, killing him instantly. An intense spasm of grenades and gunfire erupted, but the Marines were already inside the hamlet and took it after a sharp firefight.

The next day saw pockets of last-ditch resistance mopped up as the Marines pushed to the ocean.

Operation STARLITE had been a resounding Marine success. The *1st VC Regiment* had been taken by surprise and pushed against the sea, where it was systematically destroyed by Marine infantry, air power, and naval gunfire. The inherent flexibility of Marine doctrine was underscored by the timely insertion of the Special Landing Force, a move which completed the entrapment. The operation was also significant because it was the first battle between the United States and Viet Cong main forces. It was followed by Operation PIRANHA, another regimental amphibious-heliborne assault mounted on September 7, 1965, by the same Marine force, which was highlighted by the destruction of a large Viet Cong cave.[8]

Following Operations STARLITE and PIRANHA, Viet Cong main force units successfully avoided large scale engagements with the Marines for two months. That December the Marines would again clash with a revitalized *1st VC Regiment* on the battlefield, this time in the Phuoc Ha Valley in an operation called HARVEST MOON.

4. Battle in the Monsoon

By November the monsoons, which had arrived in I Corps Tactical Zone the previous month, had washed out roads and flooded facilities. Gray, misting clouds rolled down lush mountainsides to disgorge torrential sheets of rain that blotted out the horizon and socked in entire valleys for weeks. In this season of overcasts and downpours, the Viet Cong began a renewed offensive. On October 27, a night sapper raid hit the Da Nang airfield, causing heavy damage.

The district capital of Hiep Duc was overrun on November 17 as cloudbursts soaked the battlefield. Two battalions of the 5th ARVN Regiment were airlifted into landing zones that happened to be right under the heavy machine guns of an NVA flak battalion, sited on a commanding ridgeline. Twenty of thirty

---

8. Marine engineers exploded the cavern on Batangan Peninsula after the Viet Cong inside refused to surrender. While 66 Viet Cong were killed in the blast, six Marines searching it afterwards were overcome by oxygen starvation.

Marine helicopters involved were shot up by the *195th NVA Antiaircraft Battalion* attached to the *1st VC Regiment*. After a raging two-day battle, the 5th ARVN Regiment was ordered back to Quang Ngai, abandoning hard-won Hiep Duc in the process. The VC moved on into their base area in the Phuoc Ha Valley, and the Marines planned to trap them there.

Operation HARVEST MOON was to be a combined Marine-South Vietnamese search and destroy mission, the largest Marine operation since their arrival in Vietnam. Briefly, the plan called for three ARVN battalions to move overland from Thang Binh southwest into the Phuoc Ha Valley on December 9. At the same time two Marine battalions would be helicoptered to the rear and flanks of the Viet Cong, completing their entrapment. Another battalion of Marines, serving as the fleet Special Landing Force, would be a ready reserve on naval warships just off the coast of Vietnam.

The South Vietnamese forces were unable to make the road march into the area without getting ambushed. On the afternoon of December 8, the column was moving down both sides of Route 534, the 11th ARVN Ranger Battalion on the right and the 1st Battalion, 5th ARVN Regiment, on the left. Suddenly the right-hand battalion was hit by a withering concentration of machine-gun fire and grenade blasts. Waves of VC then charged them from all sides, firing assault rifles into the midst of the startled rangers. Ranger dead and wounded fell in twisted clumps, rifles and helmets clattered to the ground, and in fifteen minutes the battalion had disintegrated. The ranger commander was wounded, hit again, and carried out on the back of an American advisor. In another fifteen minutes the broken rangers were streaming to the rear, and the battalion was no longer in the war.

The 1st Battalion of the 5th ARVN Regiment couldn't get across the road. The roadway was exploding under a wall of up-turned clay and chunks of pavement hurled through the air by an intense VC mortar barrage. Screams, shouted orders, and small arms fire mixed in a din of crashing shells and roaring jets. Marine fighter-bombers thundered down to pound the other side of the road with cannon fire and an onslaught of exploding bombs. The 1st Battalion of the 6th ARVN Regiment was helicoptered into the positions held by the remnants of the ranger battalion, and the Viet Cong broke off the action during the night. The next morning both of the other South Vietnamese battalions were assaulted. The 5th ARVN Regimental headquarters and its 1st Battalion were overrun. The regimental colonel was killed in the desperate fighting.

At 10:00 A.M. the Marines stepped in. The flak-vested 2d Battalion, 7th Marines, was air-assaulted five miles from the battle to occupy a key hilltop and get behind the Viet Cong. Finding few VC there, they consolidated. That afternoon the 3d Battalion, 3d Marines, was helicoptered into a landing zone slightly south of the fragmented South Vietnamese positions, and pushed overland in an attempt to reach the 5th ARVN Regiment's lines. Company L immediately ran into a running engagement, which lasted until evening when firing ceased. The next morning the Marines linked up with the remnants of the South Vietnamese regiment.

The Marine counterattack continued early on the morning of December 10, as the two Marine battalions continued to compress the Viet Cong from two directions. Resistance was heavy, and the advance over hedgerows, jungle-covered hills, and rice paddies was slow and difficult. It was decided to commit the Special Landing Force. The men of the 2d Battalion of the 1st Marines donned full battle dress, drew rifles, and grabbed extra magazines of ammunition. They scrambled onto the flight deck of the old World War II aircraft carrier USS *Valley Forge* (LPH-8), which had since been converted into a helicopter carrier. This fresh battalion of reserves was to be inserted halfway between the two Marine battalions already on the battlefield. Loaded with the accoutrements of war, their rifles held firmly in their hands, they marched across the open deck in the stiff sea breeze to climb into fifteen UH-34 helicopters.

Captain James F. Page's Company F went in first. The helicopters whirled over flooded rice fields outlined by long dikes, neatly dividing them into an assortment of liquid boxes. The landing zone had been bombed and rocketed in advance, but as the troop-laden helicopters hovered close to earth they were met by a hail of Viet Cong machine-gun fire. The Marines dived out into a spray of bullets, and lunged into the shallow paddy water behind earthen berms. Mortar rounds started dropping among them. Crumpled bodies were strewn over the muddy fields, among them Captain Page. (He was left for dead but the next day medical corpsmen, checking through the bodies, picked up a very faint murmur of a possible heartbeat and flew him out. He later recovered.) The Marines desperately called for reinforcements, but the rest of their battalion had landed to the west.

Company E of the 2d Battalion, 7th Marines, fought its way forward to the pinned company. It took heavy losses, but finally managed to get a position to support the depleted Marines with covering fire. The trapped Marines wriggled back toward the relief force in bounds from dike to dike. Machine guns and rifles were waterlogged but still firing. Boots, open flak jackets, and shirts were drenched a muddy brown. Their painful withdrawal was marked by a trail of doubled-over comrades half sunk in the paddy ooze, and groups of naval corpsmen clustered over wounded propped up half out of the water beside dikes. Finally the two battered companies joined up and formed a defensive perimeter. Another reinforcing company arrived as darkness fell.

Throughout the next two days all three Marine battalions continued their steady advance against the southern rim of the valley. The Viet Cong pulled out of the entrapment, conducting effective harassing fire tactics. Four B-52 strategic bomber strikes were made December 12–14. Marines inserted to check out the effects of these bombings met only slight resistance. However, they uncovered extensive VC tunnel complexes containing large amounts of supplies and manufacturing equipment. Repeated sweeps of the entire operating area continued to draw only light Viet Cong fire. The battle was over except for one last parting shot.

On December 18, 1965, the 2d Battalion of the 7th Marines was ambushed by a large Viet Cong force west of Tam Ky, but a violent Marine counterattack and liberal use of artillery and air support routed the VC. Operation HARVEST MOON marked the Marines's last battle of the year, as well as their last major engagement during the rainy season. The 3d Marine Division was already drawing on elements of the 1st Marine Division, which had the 7th Marines and two battalions of the 1st Marines committed to Vietnam. The next year MACV planned to bring in the rest of the division as part of a continuing Marine buildup in an expanding war.

CHAPTER 4.

AN ARMY GOES TO WAR

1. The Rock Regiment

Brigadier General Ellis W. Williamson's 173d Airborne Brigade on Okinawa was the Army's own compact, two-fisted response force for the western Pacific, designed to drop in under canopies of silk and seize immediate objectives until something bigger could reinforce the situation. Its two fists were the 1st and 2d Battalions of the 503d Infantry (Airborne), which was the first parachute infantry regiment into the Pacific during World War II. There it had pulled off a dramatic parachute assault on top of fortified Corregidor Island, known as The Rock. This service gave the 503d Infantry a Pacific legacy and the appellation "The Rock Regiment."[1] The 173d Airborne Brigade enjoyed a close camaraderie, and in Vietnam would always be known to the troops as "The Herd," while its high percentage of blacks and racial cooperation would add another shibboleth, Two Shades of Soul.

General Westmoreland wanted the elite 173d Airborne Brigade in Vietnam as part of his enclave concept at once and got the green light on April 14, 1965. There was one proviso. The

1. The 503d Parachute Infantry was activated at Fort Benning, Georgia, on February 24, 1942, and arrived in Australia that November. It fought in New Guinea, Leyte, Luzon, and the southern Philippines. Its dashing airborne assault onto the small but well defended Japanese fortress island of Corregidor on February 16, 1945, was one of the most daring paratrooper assaults of history. The battalions were assigned to the separate 173d Airborne Brigade when it was formed on March 26, 1963. In Vietnam the brigade was later expanded to contain all four battalions of the 503d Infantry (Airborne).

brigade was understood to be in Vietnam merely on temporary duty and would later be replaced by another airborne brigade from the States. The paratroopers arrived in Vietnam on May 5, heavy duffel bags swung over their shoulders and full-color "flying butterknife" (a winged bayonet) shoulder patches on their sleeves. The first order of the day was rolled-up sleeves; the tropical heat blasted them like an open oven.

The brigade was the first Army ground combat unit to arrive in South Vietnam. It was headquartered at Bien Hoa, outside Saigon, where it expected to be used as a countrywide fire brigade. Instead, one battalion was detained to pull guard duty at Vung Tau, the landing point for Army units arriving by sea, and its other battalion dug in around the Bien Hoa air base as security. Then in early June the brigade was put back together, given a third maneuver battalion, the crack 1st Battalion of the Royal Australian Regiment, and ordered to start training for offensive combat.

The paratroopers had to be turned into a new kind of sky soldier: the airmobile infantry. They rehearsed day and night. They learned how to jump off helicopters and dash toward the tree lines in the right direction, firing from the hip. They learned to trust the helicopter gunship pilots zooming in just over their heads. They stopped mistaking the rain of falling cartridge links for bullets tearing into their own positions.

On June 27, 1965, the brigade's three battalions divided into hundreds of small clusters on the runway at Bien Hoa. Dozens of helicopters warmed their engines on the airstrip as the first lifts began soaring into the dense, humid skies. It was the largest airmobile operation to date in the Vietnam War, involving 144 helicopters, the 173d Airborne Brigade reinforced by two ARVN airborne battalions, and the 48th ARVN Regiment. They were helicoptered into the jungles of War Zone D, a large swath of Viet Cong–controlled territory just to the north of Bien Hoa, which no allied unit had entered in over a year.

The 173d Airborne Brigade stayed in the area until June 30. It simultaneously pulled out of three different landing zones within close distance of each other. It was a hectic experience for the green brigade. Artillery rounds sailed through the air to crash into the thick forests, troop helicopters flew underneath to pick up shrinking bands of infantry deliberately collapsing their perimeters, and gunships orbited in tight circles firing machine guns and rockets. As the young paratroopers clambered into the wildly vibrating open cargo bays of the Huey helicopters, their helmets sprouting rather exotic combinations of tropical leafage, they grinned at the door gunners. There hadn't been much action, but they were now veterans. That August the new sky troopers were taken off temporary duty orders. The brigade was in Vietnam on a permanent change of station.

The 173d Airborne Brigade had made another excursion into War Zone D on July 6 in conjunction with the 48th ARVN Regiment. The brigade was moved to Pleiku on its first mobile response mission on August 10, after the attack on the western border Special Forces camp of Duc Co. There it held Thanh Binh Pass on Highway 19 as South Vietnamese units retreated through it on August 17. After other sweeps around Kontum it moved back to Bien Hoa on September 6. A month later on October 8, back in War Zone D, the brigade pushed through heavy jungle and the shattered remnants of rain forest, where B-52 bombing strikes had reduced massive timber to broken deadfall littering gigantic craters torn out of the earth. Constant sniper fire and occasional ambushes plagued the sweltering paratroopers.

By the time the 173d Airborne Brigade went into War Zone D on its fifth incursion November 5, 1965, the exhilarating edge of war had long worn off. The pugnacious soldiers even gave the operation a petulant title, HUMP. The soldier's term for marching under the heavy weight of rucksacks crammed with extra rations, water, and ammunition, their straps biting into shoulders already burdened by equipment harnesses loaded with pouches, canteens, and grenades, was "humping." The search and destroy missions to find, fix, and destroy Viet Cong personnel, supplies, and installations were becoming instead long and exhausting "walks in the sun."

The operation began with two airmobile assaults by the 1st Battalion of the 503d Infantry (Airborne) and the Australian battalion. The two units established separate fire bases without any major contact. For several days they toiled through the dense forests, finding tunnel systems, fortifications, and abandoned huts, but no Viet Cong. At eight o'clock on the morning of November 8, the 503d Infantry's 1st Battalion ran into the VC in force in thick jungle composed of trees 250 feet high. The soldiers fought in a hail of fire raking their lines from the wall of jungle. Platoons were cut to pieces by close range machine guns and charging swarms of VC soldiers. Snipers aloft fired down with automatic weapons and pitched grenades. Rockets exploded, showering dirt and steel through the ruins of vine and torn bark.

The battle rapidly escalated in brutal intensity. The paratroopers desperately called in for air support. All that could be granted were blocking fires; the fighting was too close. They radioed for immediate employment of 2d Battalion, the brigade reserve. Reinforcements were impossible; there were too few helicopters to fly them in. Soldiers grappled in hand-to-hand combat, swinging axes and entrenching tools as ammunition ran out. The perimeter became a jagged ring of paratrooper squads flat against the roots of jungle trees. Assault after assault was made by the Viet Cong against the battalion's lines.

In the late afternoon the Viet Cong attacks began subsiding. Although the battalion sustained heavy fire for the rest of the day and through the night, they were able to hack out a landing zone on November 9 for evacuation of the wounded. By seven o'clock that night the entire battalion had been extracted, and the 173d Airborne Brigade's first battle in Vietnam was over. Over 117 Air Force tactical air strikes and 1,747 helicopter sorties had been used. By this time, however, the 173d Airborne Brigade wasn't the only American paratrooper force seeing heavy combat in South Vietnam. They had been joined in the meantime by the 1st Brigade, 101st Airborne Division, which had originally gone to Vietnam so that the 173d could return to Okinawa.

2. The Eagle Brigade

When the 173d Airborne Brigade was expedited to South Vietnam in May of 1965 the Pentagon planned to pull it back to reconstitute the Pacific response force, as soon as another brigade from the United States could get into country. The 1st Brigade of the 101st Airborne Division was selected by General Westmoreland as its permanent replacement, and it arrived at coastal Cam Ranh Bay on July 29, 1965. Like the 173d, this brigade was fully paratrooper-qualified, but it was somewhat stronger, having three intrinsic airborne infantry battalions.

The 1st Brigade was part of one of the most famous divisions in the United States Army; the 101st Airborne Division, which had held the key town of Bastogne during the German Ardennes counteroffensive of World War II. The paratroopers wore a Screaming Eagle shoulder patch, an insignia so lionized that the division never adopted a subdued version when the Army mandated that all formations adopt camouflaged insignia in combat. Eventually the entire division would be committed to Vietnam, but initially only one brigade was called for. The division sent three of its finest battalions, among them the 2d Battalion of the 502d Infantry (Airborne).[2]

Col. James S. Timothy moved his brigade north in August. His orders were to open up the stretch of Highway 19 between Qui Nhon on the coast and the inland town of An Khe. This clearing operation was designed to permit the 1st Cavalry Division (Airmobile) to deploy peacefully to An Khe one month later. The paratroopers moved to An Khe and began Operation HIGHLAND. The sweep proceeded smoothly and the operation concluded without incident. However, a Viet Cong main force battalion of the *2d NVA Regiment* had been reported in the Song Con River valley to the north of An Khe Pass, and Colonel Timothy wanted to get a crack at it. On September 18, 1965, he set Operation GIBRALTAR into motion.

The ground arm of the operation was to be a mechanized column, which would move north beside the Song Con River. The airmobile force consisted of the 2d Battalion, 502d Infantry (Airborne), under Lt. Col. Wilfrid K. G. Smith. It was to air-assault the jungled hinterlands near An Ninh, consolidate its landing zone, and then push the Viet Cong into the advancing armor of the other task force. As it turned out, the air-assault battalion became heavily engaged and needed rescue, but the

2. The 502d Parachute Infantry had been formed from a battalion activated at Fort Benning, Georgia, on July 1, 1941, and was one of the 101st Airborne Division's original components of World War II. It had gained fame making a spectacular bayonet charge at Carentan, France, shortly after parachuting in on D-Day in 1944.

composite armored-infantry force couldn't get to them. It encountered great difficulty moving its armored personnel carriers and heavy tanks forward in the soggy terrain.

The paratroopers of the 2d Battalion, 502d Infantry (Airborne), boarded a medley of Army and Marine helicopters for the air assault. The airmobile force made a swift morning flight and set down on the marshy rice paddy landing field which had been selected near An Ninh. Lieutenant Colonel Smith and Company C unloaded the craft shortly after seven o'clock and established a perimeter to await the second lift. Occasional rifle shots rang through the air.

The second flight of helicopters swung low into the approach and started to set down. Their blades twirled impatiently through the dank air as door gunners crouching behind pedestal-mounted machine guns nervously scanned the tall trees. The paratroopers began to scramble out. Suddenly intense automatic weapons fire swept the landing zone. Splashing water and dirt exploded among the wobbling helicopters as their brownish frames were hammered by shells. Doors and windows were shattering, and pilots slumped in blood-splattered seats. Paratroopers were being killed and wounded as they tumbled out of the helicopters and fell into the thrashing water. Dead and dying mounds of equipment-laden men were peppered by the storm of ground fire. Other men slithered desperately across the flat killing zone.

Helicopters struggled into the air as door gunners fired feverishly back into the surrounding jungles, their smoking guns cranking through long belts of linked ammunition. Other door guns were silent, swinging jerkily to the motion of the helicopters gaining altitude, the gloved arms of their crewmen dangling out the cabins.

The additional helicopters carrying the rest of the battalion had to be waved off, aborting what remained of the rest of the planned airmobile assault. The commander of Company B had been hit before he could get off his craft, and the single surviving officer was a second lieutenant who took over the decimated company. Capt. Robert E. Rawls of Company C directed him to use his men to plug gaps in the perimeter. Without air reinforcement they would have to hold on to the landing zone until the ground column reached them. Then the combined force could clear the area sufficiently to permit safe evacuation.

Lieutenant Colonel Smith looked about the field. Smoking helicopters sat dizzily in the water, broken skids and shattered blades tilting them like capsized boats. He had exactly 224 men, many of them wounded, in a tattered circle of paddy dikes and tree line. Their positions were pounded by concentrated mortar barrages. A platoon that had clawed out some room on a nearby ridge was forced to pull back to an earthen berm on the side of the rice field. Then another platoon was brought back in to the shrunken perimeter. As it was being maneuvered, Captain Rawls was killed. Armed helicopters overhead maintained a shield of rocket detonations and machine-gun fire all around them. Artillery was called in to form a barrier of exploding shells. At nine o'clock Air Force fighter-bombers arrived to begin their incendiary bombing runs.

Twenty minutes later another air assault to the south was tried by Company A and the aborted portion of Company B. They were only able to get thirty-six live soldiers on the ground, and in the process the battalion lost another company commander. They were forced to form a separate perimeter, which was held until morning when rescued by paratroopers advancing overland. Three more helicopters were added to the ground wreckage. The others were nursed back to the takeoff point at Khu Pho, often by crewmen or severely wounded pilots. Short of power and riddled with bullets, many helicopters were struggling just to make the fifteen-minute return flight. Some crashed on landing. Every one of the twenty-six helicopters of the failed reinforcement attempt had to be scrapped or grounded due to battle damage.

The hill was now becoming the center of a prolonged series of charges and counterattacks as the VC fought to get in closer to the Americans. Medical evacuation helicopters continued to try to dash in during slack periods, pick up wounded, and race out before concentrated fire was directed at them. During one such attempt the crew chief of a Marine Sea Knight helicopter was killed and the copilot wounded. Late that afternoon another battalion and the ARVN rangers were air-landed over a mile away without incident, and began moving overland to link up.

Throughout the night, flares kept up illumination. Although the perimeter was probed, it was never attacked en masse. As morning arrived, the Viet Cong withdrew, and at 6:15 A.M. the ground force reached Smith's lines. During the battle over a hundred tactical fighter sorties had been flown and some eleven thousand artillery rounds fired. Two shattered companies of the 1st Brigade of the 101st Airborne Division had managed to hold on to their perimeter against heavy odds. While the United States government was labeling its Vietnam involvement a "police action," early Army operations like GIBRALTAR quickly demonstrated that the American Army was actually caught up in a full-scale war.

3. The 1st Cavalry Division Goes to Vietnam

At Secretary of Defense Robert S. McNamara's insistence a new test formation, tentatively titled the 11th Air Assault Division, was formed in February of 1963 at the infantry school post of Fort Benning, Georgia. McNamara was convinced that a new type of division could move rapidly about using large numbers of helicopters. He wanted the test unit (actually a brigade in size) built so he could "fill in the facts and figures" as justification for it. Many senior Army generals were adamantly against the idea. They weren't sure helicopters were thick-skinned enough to survive on the battlefield, but they were sure such a conglomeration of expensive gadgets would eat up the Army's budget. There was also a nagging fear that the Air Force was somehow scheming to get in the picture.

The Defense Department never gave the Army a chance. The Howze Board was set up under a couple of high-ranking believers, and McNamara handed out deadlines so short the Army couldn't do anything but say yes. One of the staunch supporters was Maj. Gen. Harry W. O. Kinnard, handpicked by the Secretary of Defense to head up the project. He would later take the first air assault division into the maelstrom of war and make airmobility a household Army word.

The Army staff was both right and wrong. The 11th Air Assault Division turned out to be frightfully expensive, but on the other hand, the new production models of Bell helicopters, being called Hueys, were proving fairly dependable. The division members worked day and night with their three carefully nurtured battalions and crusading nucleus of officers and sergeants. This was their baby. They took it up to the pines of North Carolina in the cold fall of 1964, and then moved back to Fort Benning to prepare for spring and summer exercises in the northern swamps of Florida. The plans for this third-phase test, called Operation GOLDFIRE, were never used. The division would receive its final test instead in the western Highlands of Vietnam.

Fort Benning was filled with soldiers in June of 1965. The 2d Infantry Division, the school's 197th Infantry Brigade, the 11th Air Assault Division (Test) with its associated 10th Air Transport Brigade, and the parachute school swelled the post's green-fatigued legions. Then came the first call for Vietnam troops. It barely shook the Army tree and never touched the reserves, but it whirled through Fort Benning like a hurricane, leaving it a naked oak stripped of every leaf. Later Vietnam would send its gales through other posts, then through cities, and finally through every hometown in America.

On June 29, 1965, the flag of the 1st Cavalry Division at Tonggu, South Korea, was put on a plane and presented to the small band of test soldiers of the 11th Air Assault Division at Fort Benning on July 1. The test unit finally had a Regular Army name; it was redesignated the 1st Cavalry Division (Airmobile). The ex-cavalrymen in Korea were handed the Indian head patches of the 2d Infantry Division; they now became the new 2d Infantry Division. The 2d Infantry Division at Fort Benning disappeared in one gulp as the embryo 1st Cavalry Division (Airmobile) filled to wartime strength. The parachute school was also denuded; the new airmobile division needed pathfinders and enough parachutists to make its first brigade "airborne."[3] The only unit left intact at the post was the school's own brigade, the 197th Infantry Brigade. It was turned upside down for every deployable soldier, "recycled" with the nondeployable ones the 1st Cavalry Division couldn't use, and became known as the

3. The airborne brigade of the 1st Cavalry Division ended soon enough in Vietnam. With the inroads the 5th Special Forces Group was making on paratroopers, the Army was hard pressed to keep its two airborne brigades already there (173d Airborne Brigade and 1st Brigade of the 101st Airborne Division) filled. Things were made worse by the fact that paratroopers liked to fight, which meant that they usually got killed and wounded faster, and that more replacement paratroopers were needed to replace the higher losses in their units.

"Dollar Ninety-Worst" 197th Infantry Brigade. It never went overseas.

Soldiers hurriedly tacked on their new, oversized 1st Cavalry Division insignia. The big patch shields featured a horse head over a diagonal black bar slashing through the bright cavalry-yellow cloth. Functionally designed by an officer's wife to be large enough to be spotted through the Fort Bliss, Texas, dust which the horses used to kick up, it was a reminder of the days when the 1st Cavalry Division was truly cavalry. As a result the division was sometimes known as the Blanket Division. Officers and sergeants frantically in-processed soldiers into companies, out-processed them for overseas duty, inventoried equipment, organized units, and drew up training schedules. The Army had given them only thirty days to get the entire division formed and ready to go overseas.

Every shortcut possible was used or invented as the division rushed to meet its deployment date. Soldiers arrived at all hours on buses and planes. They were dispatched to the divisional replacement center, given a hot meal and forms to fill out, and were then trucked off to their assigned companies almost as fast as they turned in their trays. Some arrived with orders in hand and their families at their sides. They inquired about housing, looking forward to a comfortable change of station at Fort Benning. The dependents were advised to go back home; the soldiers would be overseas in a month.

The men of the 1st Cavalry Division heard about their ultimate destination on television two weeks before the Army told them officially. Less than twenty days before the division shipped out, some were still on emergency riot duty in the Dominican Republic. They were quickly rushed back to Georgia. Three hundred critically needed new aviators arrived July 15. Their manifest of origin represented almost every Army post, arsenal, and depot in the world, even some the sergeant majors hadn't heard of. They shook their heads in bewilderment; the Army must have scoured the entire globe for them. In fact the Army had done just that. There was already an aviator shortage and the war was just starting.

Actual training was largely out of the question for the time being. Weapons firing and even squad tactics would be rehearsed on the decks of ships carrying them across the Pacific Ocean. Things got worse during out-loading. The accommodation assignments led to hopeless overcrowding on the naval transport ships MSTS *Kula Gulf* (T-AKV-40) and *Card* (T-AKV-8), old World War II merchant hulls converted to escort aircraft carriers and now finishing their days unceremoniously as cargo ferries. Last-minute transfers had to be made in the mass confusion at dockside. To alleviate crowding, the Army decided to utilize unused portions of the crew billeting area. The civilian crews balked and refused to sail. The Army relented. The division literally sailed into the sunset, heading west on the high seas toward the Republic of Vietnam.

Brig. Gen. John M. Wright, the divisional assistant commander, was already in Vietnam with a small advance party. He was told the division was going to safeguard the rugged central heartland of the country, the western badlands of Pleiku and Kontum provinces. He decided to locate it outside a small town along key Highway 19 near the Mang Yang Pass where excellent flying weather usually prevailed. The town was called An Khe, presently occupied by a Special Forces camp that had seen hard fighting that February.

The division advance group decided its base camp would have to be heavily fortified, accommodate a heliport for the division's four hundred fifty aircraft, and yet be as small as possible. Within three days they had laid it out. On August 25, one thousand advance troops of the 1st Cavalry Division arrived and were put to work with shovels and picks building the camp. Everyone from full colonels to privates toiled clearing brush. The composition of the advance party was rank-heavy with senior sergeants and officers who had at least one thought in common. They all wished they had sent over the engineers first.

On September 21 the bulk of the division arrived at the new campsite. Soon a full division and a borrowed engineer battalion were constructing everything from showers to mess halls. Five wire barriers and two cattle fences were strung around the new base. When Maj. Don G. Radcliff became the first person from the division to lose his life in Vietnam, it became Camp Radcliff. On October 1, 1965, the 1st Cavalry Division assumed responsibility for its new An Khe base and most of Highway 19.

The men continued to build. On October 19 they received word that a Special Forces camp at Plei Me had been hit hard by the NVA. At last the relabeled 11th Air Assault Division was about to undergo a combat test of the airmobile concept.

4. The Ia Drang Valley Campaign

Maj. Gen. Harry W. O. Kinnard's 1st Cavalry Division (Airmobile) was providing traffic security along Highway 19 with both heliborne and dismounted sweeps, when it was called into action as a result of the North Vietnamese Army attacks against Plei Me, south of Pleiku. The division would call it Operation SILVER BAYONET, but its airmobile actions over the fifteen hundred-square mile battlefield of western South Vietnam would be registered in military history as the Ia Drang Valley campaign.

The Chu Pong massif marked the southwestern corner of the division's area of responsibility. Dense tropical forests, extensive grasslands, and red clay typified the geography. Clear blue, cloudless skies and starry nights offered optimum weather for massive helicopter flights which typified the air cavalry's most successful engagements. On October 23, the division committed a battalion, which was quickly reinforced to a brigade. Four days later, this force was told to search and destroy everything between Plei Me and the Cambodian border. The 1st Cavalry Division (Airmobile) was at war.

The 1st Squadron of the 9th Cavalry, the division's air reconnaissance arm, was unleashed across the landscape. The scout helicopters swarmed over the woods and streams of the rolling country, spotting and firing at isolated bands of soldiers below who sometimes fired back. The NVA were moving back to their base camps in the Chu Pong Mountain area, and were taking considerable harassment from the ranging aerial cavalrymen. However, they were unsure of what to do about it. This airmobile screening was as new to them as it was to the Americans.

On November 9, 1965, Col. Thomas W. Brown's fresh 3d Brigade with its three cavalry battalions arrived in the area of operations to relieve the 1st Brigade. By now the North Vietnamese regiments had returned to their mountainous base area.

The new brigade would have to go in after them to execute the destruction phase of its assignment. The first few days were spent flying battalions around to get them into position for further offensive movement. Just before midnight on November 12, the brigade command post and aviation refueling point were subjected to a heavy mortar barrage. The next day was uneventful, and on November 14 Lt. Col. Harold G. Moore, Jr.'s 1st Battalion of the 7th Cavalry landed at Landing Zone X-Ray, adjacent to the Chu Pong range.

The 7th Cavalry was perhaps the most well-known Army unit in American history. It was the one that went down at Little Big Horn River, in Montana, in what is known to the public as Custer's Last Stand, when it dared attack the Sioux Indian bands of Chiefs Crazy Horse and Sitting Bull during the Indian Wars.[4] Now in Vietnam, deep in NVA territory, it was about to undergo another jarring experience.

Just before eleven o'clock in the morning, Company B touched down at LZ X-Ray, and an hour later most of the battalion had joined it. With Company C securing the landing zone, Capt. John D. Herrin's Company B moved north and west up a heavily jungled ridge extending from the Chu Pong hill mass. Shortly after noon one of the platoons was pinned by heavy ground fire, and another platoon was sent in to assist. This second platoon, led by Lt. Henry T. Herrick, spotted some other NVA soldiers along a well-traveled jungle trail and decided to pursue.

His soldiers crossed a dry creek bed and were moving forward toward a large anthill when a volley of automatic weapons fire ripped into them. Several soldiers were spun around by the bullets and thrown to the ground. The other cavalrymen managed to dive into the red dirt as the hail of bullets tore through shrubbery and grass only inches above them. Many were hit in several places and painfully wounded. The officers and senior

---

4. The 7th Cavalry had been formed on September 21, 1866, at Fort Riley, Kansas, for the express purpose of fighting Indians. Actually, only Troops C, E, F, I, and L under the command of Lt. Col. G. A. Custer were destroyed on June 25, 1876. Troops A, B, D, G, H, K, and M under Maj. M. A. Reno took heavy losses but survived. The regiment later participated in the Mexican Expedition of 1916–17 and fought as foot infantry in the Pacific in World War II and in Korea.

sergeants were either dead or so badly wounded they were unable to move. The men laid their rifles flat against the ground and sprayed the grass in front of them whenever they heard movement. All attempts by Captain Herrin's company to force its way across the creek bed and link up with the pinned platoon were repulsed with heavy losses. This westerly platoon would remain an isolated island of resistance until it was retrieved the next day. Although several night attempts to overrun them were made, intensive artillery protective fires formed a ring of blazing steel that broke up the North Vietnamese attacks.

As Company B became heavily committed to securing its separated platoon, mortars started shelling the landing zone and rocket-propelled grenades slammed into the cavalry lines. Company A was moved into position alongside Company B and became tied down in a firefight countering an NVA infantry assault across the tall grass. The firing was so furious that the rest of the battalion helicopters had to be waved off.

Company C moved off the landing zone to the east. Machine guns opened up and two companies of North Vietnamese regulars charged them. Company D was thrown into the fray. Air strikes and massed artillery were frantically called in, almost up to their positions. This horrendous series of closely packed, earth-filled explosions from rockets and shells shattered the NVA assault. By three o'clock the rest of the battalion landed and was fed into the eastern fringes of the landing zone. They began digging in. Company B from the 7th Cavalry's 2d Battalion was helicoptered into the fire-swept landing zone after dark and held as the battalion reserve. Ringed by the NVA, the cavalrymen formed a tight circular defense around LZ X-Ray. Parachute flares floated gently through the night sky, casting moving shadows on the ground, underneath the shifting variety of colored lights.

At first light, the battalion ventured small scout teams out immediately in front of its positions. Shortly before seven o'clock that morning Company C's lines were swept by heavy automatic rifle fire and then stormed by the North Vietnamese. The charging groups of NVA infantry bounded forward through the explosions of rocket artillery and into the American positions. There the combat was hand to hand.

The other portions of the perimeter were also under attack

and the landing zone itself was in a crisscross of grazing fire. The reserve was thrown into the breach of Company C's crumbling ramparts. Thick colored smoke was set off to mark the battle line's forward edge. Helicopters strafed and rocketed as artillery was used to form a curtain of explosions just yards from the billowing clouds of pinkish smoke. The fresh cavalrymen moved in firing short bursts from their rifles and then resorted to knives and shovels in close-quarters combat. American dead and wounded lay sprawled across the dirty, bloodstained khaki of North Vietnamese bodies. Every one of Company C's officers had been killed or wounded.

By nine o'clock that morning the threat against Company C's portion of the perimeter had subsided. The shambles of smoking grass and scalloped dirt in front of its positions was strewn with broken corpses and equipment. About one o'clock that afternoon the 2d Battalion of the 5th Cavalry, which had trekked overland to reach the beleaguered 7th, walked in from the east. The *66th NVA Regiment* had left, and the battle of LZ X-Ray was over.

Strategic B-52 bombings were made on November 17. That day the 2d Battalion of the 7th Cavalry, less elements lost at LZ X-Ray, was sent out through dense jungle to skirt the B-52 strike area and then turn north to a grassy clearing coded LZ Albany. It was temporarily loaned Company A from the 1st Battalion of the 5th Cavalry as substitution for its missing components. The new company was put to the rear of the file. It hacked and cut its way through the tropical foliage, picked up two NVA prisoners too startled to offer resistance, and reached the predetermined landing zone site.

The lead elements passed through the clearing without incident. Then a sudden fusillade of machine-guns mixed with rifle and grenade fire cut into the 7th Cavalry's column. Soldiers toppled lifelessly to the ground. Others quickly dropped to fire back with automatic rifles, light antitank weapons, and their own machine-guns. The North Vietnamese regulars came charging across the brush, shouting and firing their assault rifles from the hip. They ran straight into Companies C and D and fought their way through the battalion's ranks. Company A and the reconnaissance platoon made a stand on the landing zone itself. The rear of the column was cut off.

Soldiers desperately fought individual battles at point-blank range. Helicopters circled helplessly, unable to call in tactical air support or artillery because of the general melee going on below them. Slowly the Americans started falling back into clustered perimeters, and the spotting aircraft could distinguish enough semblance of the flow of the battle to call in air strikes. The first runs were made by low-flying, rocket-spitting helicopter gunships which raked the NVA soldiers still pressing the attack. Then fighter-bombers swooped down to discharge loads of napalm, which tumbled through the tree lines and engulfed at least one entire North Vietnamese company in rolling balls of jellied fire.

Lt. Col. Robert A. McDade, Jr.'s battalion remnants had formed a tight circular perimeter on LZ Albany. Company B was helicoptered in after dark, when the firing against the smoldering clearing had slackened. The perimeter experienced gunfire and periodic assaults, but illumination by Air Force flare ships and a continuous ring of artillery fire held the NVA at bay. Groups of soldiers made a number of forays outside their perimeter during the night. They carried back scores of American wounded. From midnight to dawn there was sporadic sniper fire, but the major threat was over.

It had been a sanguinary initiation for the 1st Cavalry Division. A smaller attack was mounted November 18 against an artillery fire base, which proved to be the last contact of the Ia Drang Valley campaign. It had lasted thirty-five grueling days, during which time the division had used its airmobile flexibility to the utmost advantage. The NVA regiments had been forced from the area and defeated in open combat. Despite damage to fifty-nine helicopters, the 1st Cavalry Division (Airmobile) had demonstrated that its sturdy aircraft could survive on a modern battlefield. The division's bold tactics and hard-fighting resolution displayed during the first big Army battles gained it a nickname it would carry throughout the Vietnam War: the First Team.

On November 26, 1965, the air-assault troopers moved back to An Khe. They left behind fields littered with empty C-ration tins, expended ammunition boxes, and water cans. Even as the last helicopters droned drowsily into the distance, North Vietnamese Army soldiers cautiously moved back to reclaim the territory. However, the American Army was not attempting to physically occupy Vietnam's trackless wilderness. Instead, formations like the 1st Cavalry Division were seeking battlefield destruction of NVA and VC units wherever they could be found. The Ia Drang Valley campaign proved that punishing blows could be swiftly administered in retaliation for assaults made on allied installations, even in remote areas such as the Plei Me Special Forces camp. MACV hoped that enough military victories of this nature would cause North Vietnam to desist in its war against the South.

PART 2
1966

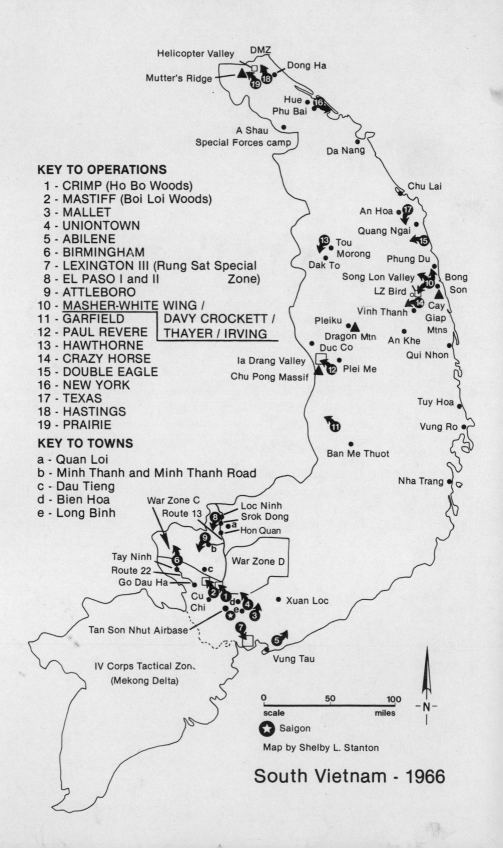

South Vietnam - 1966

KEY TO OPERATIONS

1 - CRIMP (Ho Bo Woods)
2 - MASTIFF (Boi Loi Woods)
3 - MALLET
4 - UNIONTOWN
5 - ABILENE
6 - BIRMINGHAM
7 - LEXINGTON III (Rung Sat Special Zone)
8 - EL PASO I and II
9 - ATTLEBORO
10 - MASHER-WHITE WING / DAVY CROCKETT / THAYER / IRVING
11 - GARFIELD
12 - PAUL REVERE
13 - HAWTHORNE
14 - CRAZY HORSE
15 - DOUBLE EAGLE
16 - NEW YORK
17 - TEXAS
18 - HASTINGS
19 - PRAIRIE

KEY TO TOWNS

a - Quan Loi
b - Minh Thanh and Minh Thanh Road
c - Dau Tieng
d - Bien Hoa
e - Long Binh

Helicopter Valley
DMZ
Dong Ha
Mutter's Ridge
Hue
Phu Bai
A Shau
Special Forces camp
Da Nang
Chu Lai
An Hoa
Quang Ngai
Tou Morong
Dak To
Phung Du
Song Lon Valley
Bong Son
LZ Bird
Vinh Thanh
Cay Giap Mtns
Pleiku
Dragon Mtn
An Khe
Duc Co
Qui Nhon
Ia Drang Valley
Chu Pong Massif
Plei Me
Tuy Hoa
Vung Ro
Ban Me Thuot
Nha Trang
War Zone C
Route 13
Loc Ninh
Srok Dong
Hon Quan
Tay Ninh
War Zone D
Route 22
Go Dau Ha
Cu Chi
Xuan Loc
Tan Son Nhut Airbase
Vung Tau
IV Corps Tactical Zone
(Mekong Delta)

scale
0   50   100
miles
-N-

★ Saigon

Map by Shelby L. Stanton

CHAPTER 5.

THE BUILD-UP

1. Higher Headquarters and More Battalions

After the Ia Drang Valley campaign, the North Vietnamese Army avoided further major confrontation during the 1965–66 dry season, and concentrated instead on expanding and rehabilitating its forces. Since the American military was engaged in the same process, and both sides were trying to formulate acceptable strategic doctrine to cope with the military capabilities of the other, 1966 was spent largely in mutual buildup.

The United States Military Assistance Command, Vietnam, already had 116,700 Army soldiers and 41,000 Marines in Vietnam as 1966 began, and more battalions and troops would continue to pour in throughout the year. To the 3d Marine, 1st Cavalry, and 1st Infantry Divisions would be added, in the course of the year, the 1st Marine, 4th Infantry, 9th Infantry, and 25th Infantry Divisions. To the separate Army 1st Brigade of the 101st Airborne Division and 173d Airborne Brigade would be added the 11th Armored Cavalry Regiment, and the 196th and 199th Infantry Brigades. As a result, MACV spent much of 1966 realigning the assets represented by this flood of American combat forces and getting new units settled in. The huge buildup of 1966 set the stage for large-scale field operations and escalating combat levels on the eve of 1967.

Vietnam had been blocked off into four military areas, the U.S. Marines responsible for the north and the South Vietnamese for the far south. This left the Army with one field force headquarters handling the two middle regions. II Field Force, Vietnam, became operational March 15, 1966, at Long Binh to work the III Military Corps Zone, which included Saigon. These larger headquarters were being designated "field forces," instead of corps to avoid confusion with the Vietnamese corps zone concept, as well as being flexible command-and-control formations not tied to particular size limitations.[1] Personnel for this new field force were pulled out of the III Corps headquarters at Fort Hood, Texas. The Army gave this new structure the lineage of the old XXII Corps of World War II Europe fame, and the main shipment of men arrived in Vietnam on March 28. The commander of the 1st Infantry Division, Maj. Gen. Jonathan O. Seaman, was promoted to head the new headquarters, which was given initial control over his old division, the 25th Infantry Division, the 173d Airborne Brigade, and an artillery and an aviation group (the 23d and 12th). At the same time the previous field force, already in Vietnam since the preceding November under Maj. Gen. Stanley R. Larsen, was redesignated as I Field Force, Vietnam, at Nha Trang.

The fighting edge of this enormous American buildup leaped from the twenty-two Army and thirteen Marine infantry and tank battalions of January 1966 to fifty-nine and twenty-four, respectively, by the end of the year. President Johnson and Defense Secretary McNamara had decided by mid year to reject any call-up of the reserves due to political ramifications, but still planned to have 390,000 troops in Vietnam by the end of 1966. The commandant of the Marine Corps, Gen. Wallace M. Greene, Jr., mirrored the sentiments of many high-echelon military leaders when he later stated that the decision not to use the reserves was a "fatal mistake."[2]

The Marines and the Army shared a common dilemma: there wasn't enough manpower. In addition to new units being raised or brought up to strength and shoved into the combat zone,

1. The Army was also probably copying the title of the successful III Marine Amphibious Force, which seemed to have harmonized easily with its increased command, advisory, and Vietnamese counterpart responsibilities in I Corps Tactical Zone.

2. Jack Shulimson, *U.S. Marines in Vietnam, 1966, An Expanding War*, Headquarters, U.S. Marine Corps, Washington, D.C., 1982, p. 283.

individual replacements still had to be provided for those already there. Due to shortages of critical skilled personnel, certain scheduled aviation and logistical units could not be formed or deployed on time. Combat units were forced to operate in the field with far fewer riflemen than they were authorized to have. For example, 1966 saw many Marine infantry companies, with a normal strength of six officers and two hundred ten enlisted men, down to one officer and only one hundred ten men. Already the ability of the United States to respond on a global basis was being largely negated, and in Vietnam combat response was being hampered. Furthermore, the continued dizzy deployment of divisions and brigades into Vietnam was absorbing the cadre needed to sustain the training base in America. This vicious cycle threatened future military posture—as well as any Vietnam replacements or reinforcements.

In the meantime, 1966 witnessed a steady flow of new units into the Vietnam battlefield. These divisions and combat brigades had distinctive personalities that somehow reflected their essence. This would vary from war to war, and from commander to commander. It could even be manipulated by replacement policies and compositional changes. However, their larger being was a product of so many years and so much tradition that it became almost fused into a soul-like quality. Soldiers could sense it, and often these collective divisional and brigaded entities seemed tied to destinies which predetermined their combat performance.

2. The 1st Marine Division Arrives

Maj. Gen. Lewis J. Fields's 1st Marine Division headquarters had transferred from Camp Pendleton, California, to Camp Courtney, Okinawa, in August 1965. At the beginning of 1966 the division already had its 7th Marines, with artillery support, and two battalions of the 1st Marines in Vietnam.[3] Late in 1965 the Secretary of Defense had recommended doubling Marine forces in Vietnam during 1966, and the 1st Marine Division was tagged for Chu Lai.

3. The 1st and 2d battalions of the 1st Marines were actually in Vietnam as part of the Fleet Marine Force, Pacific, intratheater rotation system, allowing two other Marine battalions to be rested and refitted.

The 1st Marine Division, called The Old Breed in the Corps, was not only a premier Marine division, but also one of the finest formations of the United States military. It was the direct descendant of the Marine Advanced Base Brigade activated at Philadelphia in 1913 to serve in the troubled Caribbean area. There it had engaged in the Banana Wars from Vera Cruz, Mexico, to Haiti and the Dominican Republic. It was given its present title on February 1, 1941, at Guantanamo Bay, Cuba, as the first division in Marine Corps history. The 1st Marine Division initiated the ground offensive against territories held by the Imperial Japanese forces of World War II. It gained immortality on Guadalcanal and went on to victory through eastern New Guinea, New Britain, Peleliu, and Okinawa. Afterward it participated in the occupation of North China and the Korean War, and had sent elements to assist in the Cuban missile crisis of 1962. The 1st Marine Division's six years in Vietnam would confirm its reputation as a first-class fighting formation.

The division embarkation officer was alerted to the scheduled deployment at a Fleet Marine Force, Pacific, conference held in Honolulu during December 1965. He briefed General Fields five hours after arriving back on Okinawa on December 27. Some thirty ships would be needed over a $2^{1}/_{2}$ month period. There were doubts whether the Navy could in fact provide such support. These matters were resolved at a later meeting between division representatives and the Seventh Fleet Amphibious Force at Subic Bay, Philippines. The Navy indicated the job could be done "with judicious scheduling." The 1st Marine Division met every shipping date and deadline and arrived in Vietnam exactly as planned.

The incremental deployment of the 1st Marine Division into Vietnam heightened the buildup of forces in southern I Corps Tactical Zone. The insertion of this division freed the 4th Marines from the Chu Lai sector to counter a new NVA threat in the Phu Bai area. That sector was also reinforced by two battalions of the division's 1st Marines and the Korean 2d "Blue Dragon" Marine Brigade, enabling Marine reinforcements to continue flowing undiverted into Da Nang and Chu Lai. On January 17, 1966, the headquarters of the 1st Marines arrived at Chu Lai to reinforce the 7th Marines which had been there since August 1965. Throughout the first three months of the year more elements of the division continued to arrive. Plans to establish a division rear headquarters on Okinawa were dropped in order to avoid administrative and fiscal complications. Major General Fields moved his command post to Chu Lai at the end of March, and the 5th Marines arrived in April.

By June, the 1st Marine Division was firmly planted in the Chu Lai vicinity and busily engaged in numerous small-unit actions that typified activities there during late spring. Less a battalion serving as the Seventh Fleet's Special Landing Force and a regiment dispatched to the Da Nang area, by June 1966 the division had over seventeen thousand men to include all its artillery, engineer, tank, amphibious tractor, antitank, and reconnaissance elements. III MAF finally had the two-division ground force with which it would fight during the major part of the Vietnam War.

3. The 4th Infantry Division Goes to War

The 4th Infantry Division was a good, solid Regular Army outfit popular with its men. For ten years, since 1956, it had been stationed at Fort Lewis, at the southern end of Washington's Puget Sound region. There, in the tranquil wooded fringes of the snow-topped Olympic Mountains near Tacoma, it had trained for atomic and mechanized warfare. Its shoulder patch was of World War I vintage and featured four green ivy leaves. This design gained it the simple title Ivy Division, which the troops fondly modified to the Poison Ivy Division. Its other nickname, The Famous Fourth, had likewise been modernized by the soldiers to The Funky Fourth. The 4th was a dignified veteran of two world wars, and at first it appeared that Vietnam, like Korea, would leave it undisturbed.

The 3d Brigade of the 25th Infantry Division had been rushed into its future area of operations, the Central Highlands around Pleiku, in December 1965. The Hawaii-based 25th was the Pacific response force, and one infantry brigade had been deemed large enough to tame that portion of Vietnam wilderness. The war in Vietnam heated up fast, however, and Westmoreland's incessant demand for more battalions soon tagged the western highlands as requiring the presence of a full American division.

In April 1966, the 4th Infantry Division commander, Maj. Gen. Arthur S. Collins, received word his division was going over. By July 11, the division's advance planning party was set up in Vietnam, and the three brigades were dispatched as soon as they could be shipped.

The division move unfortunately put them into their new base camp at Dragon Mountain outside Pleiku in the midst of torrential rains and fog brought by the southwest monsoons. The 2d Brigade was airlifted into Pleiku in August, and the rest of the division arrived by early October. Its 3d Brigade was diverted south, its last units arriving at Dau Tieng on October 18, 1966. It was being exchanged for the 25th's 3d Brigade, which had already been posted to the highlands where it was now well established. By August 1967, after some Army infighting over lineage considerations, the swap became permanent. Maj. Gen. William R. Peers was officially slated to take command of the 4th Infantry Division on January 3, 1967. His command later included three full brigades—a complete division—and he was anxious to gain mastery over Pleiku and Kontum provinces.

4. The Raising of the 199th Infantry Brigade

In the hectic summer of 1966, a new Army separate brigade was formed at the infantry school post of Fort Benning, Georgia. The 199th Infantry Brigade (Light) was activated that June expressly for Vietnam duty. The Army's timetable scheduled the unit to be overseas that November. Things became too rushed as a result. To save time, the Army raised the unit without the usual cadre development period. The brigade was created in a confused spasm of simultaneously activating, equipping, and training.

The newborn brigade command post was planted in the pines on the post's remote Kelley Field. In the red clay, dust, and sweltering heat, the serious business of training for real war began. The grueling program kept its soldiers in the field every week, with one third of their time spent on night exercises. At the beginning of September everyone was piled into commercial buses and sent off to the rejuvenated World War II post of Camp Shelby, Mississippi. There the brigade crashed through advanced unit training, although handicapped by lack of assigned soldiers. One of its battalions, the 3d of the 7th Infantry, had less than half of its authorized personnel.

However, the brigade was now rapidly starting to take shape. It was given its own shoulder patch, a flaming spear, and was dubbed the Redcatchers, a macho nickname so ludicrously self-exalting that it stuck. Under intense pressure to deploy as close as possible to schedule, its men moved by sea and by air in five groups. It arrived through the port of Vung Tau and closed its Long Binh staging area on Christmas Day. Since a permanent base-camp site was lacking, the brigade would remain at Long Binh indefinitely.

Despite the fact that the brigade's heavy equipment was still in transit and would not arrive until January, its battalions were farmed out immediately in Operation UNIONTOWN. There in Vietnam the brigade continued its wartime preparation on the field of battle. For example, its very first airmobile mission was an actual combat air assault conducted December 17 by the 4th Battalion of the 12th Infantry in Vietnam itself.

5. The 25th Infantry Division Deploys

The Army's Pacific reserve was the 25th Infantry Division, stationed at time-honored Schofield Barracks on the diamond-shaped Hawaiian island of Oahu. The post was pleasantly sandwiched on the central plateau between two volcanic mountain ranges. It was built to protect the Pearl Harbor naval base, ten miles distant, from possible enemy landing on the northwest coast. The 25th Infantry Division was a lineal descendant of the old Hawaiian Division established in 1921, and it had been thrust into World War II twenty years later by Japanese aircraft descending to strafe its neat palm-lined barracks parade fields. The division had earned a rugged reputation for hard jungle fighting in that war, from Guadalcanal through Luzon in the Philippines which was summed up by its proud nickname, Tropic Lightning. Its destiny irrevocably tied to United States interests in the Pacific area, it was rushed into the Korean conflict from occupation duty in Japan. It had returned to spend two decades again in Hawaii, where it had been modernized for trouble-shooting throughout the Orient.

It was no secret that the 25th Infantry Division was slated

for some sort of Southeast Asian duty; the only question was where. While it had been providing helicopter door gunners to Vietnam since January of 1963, the division as a whole was preparing for deployment to Thailand where it had briefly posted a battle group in 1962. MACV proposed the division be moved to Vietnam at once, but there was concern over stripping the Pacific reserve, which couldn't be replaced for two years. However, when a stateside airborne division was slated to assume this role, the green light was given for accelerated deployment of the 25th.

Fifty-five tons of maps that had been issued for other contingency areas were burned as the division's 3d Brigade boarded planes for direct airlift into Pleiku Province, central Vietnam, on December 23, 1965. There it would shore up the highlands region, which had seen heavy fighting against the 1st Cavalry Division that fall. As the planes taxied off the runways, the division's Hawaiian Jungle and Guerrilla Warfare Center was putting the 2d Brigade through twelve Vietnamese village training sites on a crash basis. The 2d Brigade boarded ship just after the New Year, landed at Vung Tau during the last week in January 1966, was airlifted to Bien Hoa, and was then trucked on to Cu Chi. The 2d Brigade was immediately committed to combat to secure the base area, which would be used by the division to guard the western approaches to Saigon for the next five years.

Back in Hawaii the Dependents' Assistance Center was working on a twenty-four-hour basis, and soldiers were turning in their private cars around the clock at a special "vehicle boneyard" with or without "post decals." Almost one hundred pilots and fifty-seven aircraft were requested at once to make up for shortfalls. Meanwhile various other division elements continued traveling all over the Pacific in the hectic but upbeat rhythm of a major force optimistically heading toward a new war. The 1st Battalion of the 69th Armor arrived in Ryukyuan Okinawa on February 6 where it was outfitted with new M48 Patton tanks and armored personnel carriers. Two new battalions arrived in Hawaii from midwinter Alaska to join the 1st Brigade on January 30. Both were at full strength with high morale, and the moderate Hawaiian climate provided an ideal intermediate adjustment en route to Vietnam.[4] The remaining original divisional infantry battalion in Hawaii, the 2d Battalion of the 14th Infantry, had been stripped to fill vacancies in the 2d and 3d Brigades. Now it was refilled with new replacements.

On January 23, General Westmoreland requested that the rest of the 25th Infantry Division be speeded up to Vietnam, with special emphasis on the cavalry squadron and the engineers. Two of the cavalry troops had already been sea-lifted to Okinawa and were being given brand-new tracked M113 vehicles. When the hastily refreshed 1st Brigade arrived in Vietnam on April 29, it completed the move of Maj. Gen. Fred C. Weyand's division into country some five months ahead of the original schedule.

The only real confusion was occasioned by MACV's indecision regarding the employment of the armor. Initially the 69th Armor's 1st Battalion had been programmed for Pleiku, but in mid-February it was decided to move it, less a company, to Cu Chi. This was due as much to the VC threat there as to trafficability and divisional integrity considerations. Late in April, alarmed at NVA strength in the highlands region, MACV ordered the battalion to proceed from Cu Chi to Pleiku at once in order to beat the upcoming southwest monsoon season.

Major General Weyand vehemently protested. He had insisted on deploying his armor battalion to Vietnam in the first place over the loud howls of Army staff planners in both Vietnam and the Pentagon. Through his foresight a valuable asset had been brought over, and it was being yanked away from him. He was told simply that the decision had already been made. The tanks reached Pleiku on May 22. As the monsoon season approached, however, General Westmoreland decided to give Weyand the needed tank battalion at Cu Chi after all. To do so, Westmoreland now asked that the armor battalion from the deploying 4th Infantry Division be diverted to replace the one that had gone to the highlands.

---

4. These were the 4th Battalion, 9th Infantry from the 171st Infantry Brigade and the 4th Battalion, 23d Infantry, from the 172d Infantry Brigade. At the time these were the two combat brigades stationed in Alaska, and each was reduced to provide a full battalion for Vietnam service.

6. The 11th Armored Cavalry Adds Armored Punch

General Westmoreland's concept for the use of army tanks in Vietnam dated from 1965, when the 11th Armored Cavalry stationed at Fort George G. Meade, Maryland, had been requested for highway security along Route 1 operating out of Xuan Loc as part of the 1966 buildup. Since he now desired to use this regiment on missions beyond road security, he became concerned over its organization, maintaining it was too heavy for Vietnam's heavy rains, difficult terrain, and shaky bridges. Late in 1965 he suggested that the Department of the Army replace its medium tanks with M41 light tanks (or armored personnel carriers in its cavalry platoons), substitute armored cars for certain other armored personnel carriers, and delete the armored vehicle-launched bridges. The Pentagon replied that since its scheduled deployment was already fixed as mid-1966, such a radical equipment change was out of the question. They also agreed with Pacific command that such modifications were probably unnecessary anyway.

General Westmoreland replied that in that case he preferred a mechanized infantry brigade in Vietnam instead of the armored cavalry. He stated flatly he had no need for two more tank battalions, which the 132 tanks of the regiment in fact represented. Continental Army Command noted that the 199th Infantry Brigade, then training at Fort Benning, could be mechanized, but in turn the 11th Armored Cavalry would have to be inactivated. As this would cost additional training time and cause greater complications to the programmed assembly of units for Vietnam duty, the Pentagon compromised. The 11th Armored Cavalry would go, but with certain changes that had the effect of cutting its strength down to fifty-one tanks. The warning order that it was going to Vietnam was sent to the 11th Armored Cavalry on March 11, 1966.

The 11th Armored Cavalry was known as The Blackhorse Regiment, and a rearing stallion dominated the red and white shield of its patch. It had been organized at Fort Myer, Virginia, in March of 1901, saw service in the Philippines and rendered notable service along the Mexican border in 1916. During World War II, this cavalry regiment was used as a basis for the

11th Armored Regiment of the 10th Armored Division, and a new cavalry group by the same number was raised thereafter. Both saw extensive combat service across France, Belgium, and Germany. After the war they were consolidated as the 11th Armored Cavalry, since the the Army combat arms regimental system had dropped the use of the word *regiment* as part of titles. This official Army directive on terminology was usually ignored, and the unit in fact always continued to refer to itself as the 11th Armored Cavalry Regiment—often shortened to the popular abbreviation, 11th ACR.

The Blackhorse Regiment was, at one-third strength, busy training 988 newly assigned soldiers and trying to get its recently reactivated 2d Squadron in shape. It was headquartered at Fort George G. Meade, Maryland, twenty miles equidistant from Baltimore, Annapolis, and Washington, D.C. Its orders to Vietnam came simultaneously with a reorganization directive—the second since the previous October. The substitution of up-gunned armored personnel carriers for tanks was not well received by most armor officers, and in fact the alteration was later regretted as an unfortunate diminishing of needed armored shock power in the Vietnam War. Still short over eighteen hundred men, its updated April orders to achieve personnel readiness by May 7 were simply scoffed at. It continued intense but scattered training at Camps Pickett and A. P. Hill, Virginia, since any stateside maneuver room was now at a premium. One of the many last-minute equipment switches did prove most beneficial: everyone was issued a brand new black, lightweight rifle called the M16.

By June a regimental planning team was in Vietnam. Hosted by the 1st Infantry Division, the 919th Engineer Company arrived by air August 16 to prepare a base site. The main portion of the regiment went to Friendship Airport outside Baltimore and got on planes bound for Oakland, California. There they boarded three transport ships and, after several weeks at sea debarked at the port of Vung Tau on September 7–19, 1966. Surmounting serious problems due to lack of consistent guidance, constant changes in personnel deployment criteria, and a drop in morale due to the loss of over four hundred individual finance pay records, the 11th Armored Cavalry was firmly in

Vietnam by the end of the month. It was a highly potent combat force of tremendous value. Now forty-two hundred strong with attachments, the regiment was moved to Long Binh under Col. William W. Cobb, a World War II veteran of the 503d Parachute Infantry in the Pacific.

The 11th Armored Cavalry would become one of the Army's finest units in Vietnam. It rapidly moved beyond conventional expectations regarding armor's ability to cross difficult tropical terrain. Often parceled out in squadron increments to avail larger commands of its precious armored firepower, the regiment would see action in many areas, with many different units. A series of excellent commanders and aggressive flak-vested cavalrymen would ensure that the 11th ACR gained an enviable combat reputation far out of proportion to their actual numbers. Combined with the exploits of the 1st Cavalry Division, the handful of air cavalry squadrons, and divisional and brigade components, the prestige of modern cavalry, whether in a ground or air mode, would reach a new zenith as a result.

7. The 196th Infantry Brigade Is Diverted

The 196th Infantry Brigade was activated as the Army's first light brigade on September 15, 1965. The unit was designed to be an infantry stability force for peacekeeping duty in the Dominican Republic. The 196th was organized at the wooded, lake-dotted Massachusetts post, Fort Devens, forty miles inland from Boston. It was given two thousand recruits from Fort Knox, Kentucky, and Fort Dix, New Jersey, along with a depleted tank battalion turned into infantry and artillerymen from the remnants of the 2d Brigade, 5th Infantry Division.[5]

While awaiting the arrival of the first recruits in mid-October, the brigade tried to prepare for its anticipated training difficulties. The billets and training areas were prepared for the influx of new soldiers. To eliminate unnecessary administrative processing, prior arrangements were made with the two reception stations on post. The brigade's small cadre was hopelessly insufficient for the task at hand. The shortage of basic unit lead-

5. The other two infantry battalions of the 2d Brigade, 5th Infantry Division, at Fort Devens were being shipped out for Vietnam service with the 1st Infantry Division.

ers was so acute that selected recruits had to be immediately promoted to privates and privates first class, to take the place of missing noncommissioned officers. The colorful patch being issued to the raw trainees of the new brigade featured a yellow twisted match on a blue shield enflamed at each end, symbolizing the old matchlock musket days when the match was lighted at both ends to ensure readiness.

Personnel problems were further aggravated when three high priority levies stripped the brigade of 120 critical sergeants and officers who were doing most of the training. Since the ranges and training areas at Fort Devens were too cramped for brigade preparation, Camp Edwards on Cape Cod had to be used to provide the expanded terrain necessary for advanced training requirements. In late December, 1965, the 196th Infantry Brigade was secretly alerted to begin planning for possible overseas movement, contingent on the results of upcoming June elections in the Dominican Republic. There it would replace elements of the 82d Airborne Division, which the Army wanted off the island. While the brigade was told to be combat ready by May 15, the expected pace of Caribbean duty lessened any operational anxiety. The Secretary of Defense intended to make the move on July 15, 1966.

The entire unit reported to Camp Drum, New York, on March 30. There it rehearsed brigade maneuvers on the vast training site, assisted by a U.S. Army Special Forces Operational Detachment A for added realism in counterguerrilla warfare. The 196th returned to Fort Devens on May 17. After many months of training, it assembled as a full brigade for the first time to march in the Armed Forces Day parade. By now its movement to the Dominican Republic was well known, and all ship-loading plans and movement schedules were finalized on June 23. However, a week earlier the Defense Department decided that the 196th was no longer required in the Caribbean area and offered it to MACV either in substitution for the 199th Infantry Brigade or in addition to it. Such an unexpected boost to Army strength in Vietnam was considered a godsend by General Westmoreland. He immediately replied that the unit could be accepted as soon as it was available, and that it should be in addition to the 199th. True to form, he also asked that its closure date be expedited.

On June 24 the brigade was told it was going to Vietnam. Three weeks of frantic activity followed. Soldiers were offered preembarkation leaves; nondeployable personnel were reassigned; radios were exchanged for more modern types, and M14 rifles were traded in for M16s once qualification on the new weapons was completed. The brigade had to be practically rebuilt in a matter of days. The main body left Boston on the USNS *Patch* and the USNS *Darby* July 15, 1966, and arrived at Vung Tau a month later.

Meanwhile MACV was happily deciding where to place this unexpected reinforcement. It had been initially slated for the security of Tuy Hoa. However, it was decided better use of the brigade could be made in the Tay Ninh area where it could open and secure Route 22 from Go Dau Ha to Tay Ninh city, and prepare for large-scale operations in War Zone C. Its presence in that vicinity could add further pressure against the Viet Cong northwest of Saigon, allowing the 25th Infantry Division to concentrate on what was proving to be a very troublesome Hau Nghia province. By August 16 the brigade had been airlifted to its Vietnam camp at Tay Ninh, and the 25th Infantry Division's 1st Brigade provided initial security and joint training as the 196th prepared its base site.

8. The 9th Infantry Division Goes Over

The 9th Infantry Division was the first Army division activated, organized, equipped, and trained for deployment into a combat theater in two decades. Formed for operations in the Mekong Delta, it had originally been scheduled under the coded designation Z Division. Approval for activation of the division was issued by the Department of the Army on January 26, 1966, and Maj. Gen. George S. Eckhardt was placed in command. The division began organizing at Fort Riley, Kansas, on the first day of February as a standard infantry division with eight infantry battalions and one mechanized battalion. That September, as a last-minute predeployment change, the 2d Battalion of the 47th Infantry was reorganized to a mechanized mode, giving the division two mechanized battalions.

The 9th Infantry Division was known as The Old Reliables, a fitting salute to its Regular Army background. The florid octofoil shoulder patch represented the heraldic symbol of the ninth son. The Vietnam generation of soldiers referred to the strange-looking design as Flower Power, or the Psychedelic Cookie. The 9th was in training for World War I but an outbreak of Asian flu prevented its deployment overseas. It was reconstituted at Fort Bragg, North Carolina, in 1940, and became one of the Army's finest divisions in World War II. The 9th Infantry Division participated in the campaigns for Algeria, Tunisia, and Sicily, and landed in France during June, 1944, to fight into Germany. After postwar service at Fort Dix in New Jersey, Germany, and Fort Carson in Colorado, it was inactivated in 1962. Four years later it was being raised again, this time on the historic post of Fort Riley, Kansas. Its final selection as the planned Z Division was largely a result of General Westmoreland's extensive service with the division in World War II. He had commanded the 60th Infantry Regiment and had served as divisional chief of staff.

Due to a shortage of men and equipment, the division was formed in increments. The division headquarters, support command, and brigade headquarters were activated first. Battalions of each brigade were phased for activation according to a schedule commencing in April for 1st Brigade, May for 2d Brigade, and June for 3d Brigade. The division began training on April 4, but the post staff of Fort Riley had to double as divisional staff until late June. The division was very short on signal equipment and ammunition during training.

The authorized cadre strength of 3,301 was insufficient and serious training problems resulted. By late March only nine hundred had been provided, and many were inexperienced, low in rank, and of low physical quality. Fortunately, during February two thousand soldiers being trained at Fort Riley for assignment to Fort Carson, Colorado, were transferred into the division. Most of these were placed immediately in schools and used to fill vacancies not provided by cadre allocations. Another two thousand unprogrammed soldiers arrived in March and April and alleviated a crisis in forming the 15th Engineer Battalion.

Initially the 9th Infantry Division was formed as an ordinary stateside division. However, some officers assigned directly from Department of the Army staff knew that it was being built to serve in the southern wetlands and canal-crossed marshes of Vietnam. As a matter of fact, its training schedule was compressed by shaving off twelve weeks in order to move the division to Vietnam in December 1966, so that arrival in the Delta area would be at the beginning of the dry season. In early May the division was formally alerted for movement to Southeast Asia at the end of 1966. Its 15th Engineer Battalion had to be in Vietnam by September to help prepare the base camp.

Meanwhile, in Vietnam, increasing NVA pressure in I Corps Tactical Zone was causing MACV to have second thoughts on its delta deployment. It considered diverting the division in its entirety to the northern portion of the country, and by the middle of October some sort of decision on location was becoming urgent. Finally, it was decided to move it in as originally planned. The majority of the division arrived aboard eight troop transports. On December 19, 1966, as divisional support personnel debarked from the USNS *Barrett* at Vung Tau, the 9th was officially declared completely in Vietnam.

The 9th Infantry Division marked the last major unit arrival for the year. For MACV, 1966 had been a year of great expansion and critical choices. While many of these concerned troop deployment, decisions had also been reached regarding area warfare strategy and the use of military airmobility. These are discussed in the next chapter.

CHAPTER 6.

THE AREA WAR

1. 1966 Campaign Strategy

The battlefield of Vietnam was far different from the continuous fronts of both world wars and the Korea War. Traditional military doctrine, based on seizing and holding a series of successive terrain objectives, was largely inapplicable. The multidirectional, nonlinear nature of military operations in Vietnam was being given a new label, "area warfare." Since Army dogma and training were still oriented toward conventional warfare, Army strategy had to be redefined. Exactly how area warfare would be fought was still evolving, and additional tactics and techniques were being assiduously developed. Goals were redefined and inevitable setbacks experienced. Such directional changes were questioned by civilian government policy interpreters, who frequently cited operational failures. In actual fact Army strategists were simply trying to adjust to the conflicting demands and novel principles of area warfare.

Army combat commands arrived in Vietnam eager for open confrontation with the VC and the NVA. They wanted to bring superior American firepower and new airmobile flexibility to bear on the open battlefield, winning a decision in the classic sense where they could "find, fix, and finish" the enemy. The frustration of warfare in Vietnam stemmed from the inherent difficulties posed by antipartisan warfare. While Americans looked to French and British experiences in subduing native revolt, the war of liberation in Vietnam was no longer a squabble between midnight partisans and colonial police. Both North Vietnamese and United States armed forces represented excellently equipped, professional modern armies. By 1966 the war in Vietnam had moved well beyond the guerrilla warfare skirmishes that typified the pre-1965 battlefield, although there was just enough local Viet Cong activity to compound problems. It was now a regular war being fought between two main-force armies with divisional establishments, although the basic "frontless" nature of it confounded traditional linear-bound solutions.

MACV strategy from 1965 through 1966 was dictated by the initial necessity of supporting and protecting its buildup. This consisted of unit deployment matters, protecting the multitude of military installations being constructed, organizing logistical support, and securing main lines of communication. Until late in the year this essentially static posture was broken only by limited "spoiling attacks." Available forces had to ensure stability in selected areas first.[1] Only with the advent of additional large combat formations would MACV have enough battalions to mount any truly punishing offensive. Despite the desire to break away and openly confront the NVA and VC main force elements, the United States military was tied to base and lines-of-communication considerations.

As 1966 began the South Vietnamese armed forces were largely combat-ineffective. The string of 1965 military defeats, lopsided combat losses, skyrocketing desertion rates, and widespread draft evasion had deteriorated ARVN manpower further. Military inefficiency and corruption were rife. Food and clothing allowances were being embezzled. Much time would have to be spent in rehabilitation to bring units up to levels of basic combat proficiency. The Vietnamese had a saying, "Using a man is like using wood." All wood, whether rare, common, hard, or soft, is beneficial if used properly. However, from 1965 through 1968 a lot of wood was disappearing, and good wood was being wasted.

1. At the beginning of January 1966 major U.S. forces in Vietnam consisted of 3d Marine Division (reinforced), 1st Cavalry Division (Airmobile), 1st Infantry Division, 173d Airborne Brigade, 1st Brigade of the 101st Airborne Division, 3d Brigade of the 25th Infantry Division, and 5th Special Forces Group. The 1st Battalion of the Royal Australian Regiment and Korean Capital Division and 2d Marine Brigade were also in Vietnam.

A Joint General Staff Honor Battalion and the regimental-sized crack Palace Guard, all under the Capital Security Group, were guarding the Independence Palace, various guest quarters in plush vacation camps, and the president's house.

The ten regular ARVN divisions were little more than static security formations. The latest, titled the 10th Division in a society where the number ten had come to signify the very worst imaginable, and under a commander who relied on an inept astrologist for military advice, was sent to a critical area near Cambodia outside Cu Chi. Its performance was so miserable that it later had to be withdrawn to Xuan Loc, redesignated the 18th Division, and completely overhauled. The marginal 5th and 25th ARVN divisions were also ineptly led, and both suffered from a steady stream of deserters to the capital, a situation so common it was being termed "the Saigon syndrome."[2] Even the reliable 1st ARVN Division was to be seriously undermined by the political furor in Hue and Da Nang that spring.[3]

Taking all these factors into consideration, the annual combined United States/South Vietnamese Campaign Plan coded AB-141 went into effect on the last day of 1965, with the optimistic hope that serious inroads could be made into NVA and VC combat capacity by the end of 1966. Four "national priority areas" were established in heavily populated regions inclusive of Saigon and adjacent areas, the middle of the Mekong Delta, and two selected coastal plains areas around Qui Nhon and Da Nang. The American military would establish and defend major bases, serving as a shield while South Vietnamese units were tasked with defending governmental centers and resource security. Of

2. The South Vietnamese commanding general of the 25th ARVN Division was so upset at adverse reports about his unit that he published an order of the day castigating his senior advisor, which ended quoting a poem referring to the Vietnamese expulsion of the Mongols, interpreted as a reference to the Americans.

3. In July 1966 the regular South Vietnamese military consisted of the Airborne, 1st, 2d, 5th, 7th, 9th, 10th, 21st, 22d, 23d, and 25th Divisions, Palace Guard (Regiment), 51st Regiment (Separate), 1st–7th and 10th Armored Cavalry Squadrons, 111th and 301st LLDB Groups, 1st–5th Marine Battalions, twenty ranger battalions (11th, 21st–23d, 30th–39th, 41st–44th, 51st, and 52d), six separate artillery battalions (28th, 34th-38th), and five separate infantry battalions (JGS-Honor, 10th, 12th, 14th, and 16th).

that army, only the airborne, ranger, and marine battalions were to be consistently employed in offensive operations. Except for special circumstances, other ARVN battalions would serve on garrison duty and support rural development. The exception was IV Corps Tactical Zone—the Mekong Delta area—where the South Vietnamese would continue full offensive operations. However, during 1966 the low, flat, and poorly drained Mekong Delta experienced major flooding which curtailed military operations there.

During the Honolulu Conference of July 1, 1966, the Secretary of Defense outlined six major goals in Vietnam by year's end for Adm. U.S. Grant "Oley" Sharp, the Commander in Chief Pacific, who replied that the first three were hopelessly farfetched under current conditions. By the end of 1966, the NVA and VC forces were to be *attritioned* at a rate as high as their capacity to place men in the field. Forty to fifty percent of all North Vietnamese and Viet Cong base areas were to be eliminated and fully half of all critical roads and railways were to be opened. Sixty percent of the South Vietnamese population was to be secured, the four national priority areas were to be pacified, and finally, defense was to be insured over all military bases, political and population centers, and food-producing areas under governmental control as of February 8, 1967.

Guidance concerning restrictions on border operations in the DMZ and Cambodian and Laotian frontiers was fragmentary and tardy. After July, the Joint Chiefs of Staff authorized aerial, naval, and artillery bombardment of, and troop incursions into, the southern half of the DMZ if it was in actual or imminent danger of enemy contact—provided no public disclosure was made and the Pentagon was immediately notified of each case. Additionally, in December permission was granted for artillery counterbattery fire across the DMZ.

At the beginning of 1966, no rules of engagement had been established for combat operations near the Laotian border. Therefore, unit commanders operating in the area were told that with prior approval they could act in "self-defense" against any attack launched from Laos. In emergency situations, as determined by the field commanders, no prior approval was required. Washington was to be kept closely informed of all instances in which American troops returned fire, attacked Laotian towns, or maneuvered troops into Laos under this guidance, and this information, or knowledge of it, was to be highly safe-guarded. Guidance covering Cambodia issued by MACV in the last month of 1965 was similar, except that restrictions on at- tacking populated areas were tighter.

In the fall of 1966 the United States first field-tested its new search and destroy pattern of area warfare. Coded Operation ATTLEBORO, it was designed to penetrate War Zone C in northwestern Tay Ninh Province along the Cambodian border and root out NVA and VC forces located to the west of the Michelin plantation. Initiated by a single infantry brigade, the 196th, on September 14, 1966, it rapidly expanded to include the 1st Infantry Division, the 3d Brigade of the 4th Infantry Division, the 173d Airborne Brigade, and the 11th Armored Cavalry Regiment. Terminated toward the end of November, its results led to the foundation of a new strategic cornerstone. Search and destroy operations on a multidivisional corps level might provide a key to solving the riddle of area warfare, thereby en-suring military success in South Vietnam. The test would come in 1967.

2. Army Tactics in 1966

Wider area warfare strategy faded on the actual battlefields themselves, as American soldiers approaching, or inside, tree lines found themselves face-to-face with Viet Cong or North Vietnamese Army Regulars. In these instances, ten-man squads and thirty-man platoons (often at half strength) decided the out-come of skirmishes by fire and maneuver. Their faces soiled by the heat and toil of combat, infantrymen huddled around twisted brush and fallen trees, blazing away with rifles and grenade launchers. This was the "base of fire." Standing fast and often reinforced by comrades, they waited for any stoppage or slack-ening in enemy return fire. They crawled or dashed forward by bounds; advances often measured six yards at a time. With enough firepower, teamwork, and luck the advance would either drive the enemy from their defensive positions or close with them. Even a small drive could result in a toll of dead and wounded. Actions were finished by point-blank rifle fire, grenade, and knifepoint. The Army called the means to accomplish this hellish job, "tactics," and tactical proficiency could only be gained by battle rehearsal, time, and actual combat exposure.

In 1966 the United States Army was still striving for tactical proficiency. Statistically, Army operational reports revealed 88 percent of all fights were being initiated by the NVA or the VC, and half of these (46 percent) began as ambushes. These reports also showed that some 63 percent of all encounters were against bunkers and fortified trenches. Units collided into combat against North Vietnamese and Viet Cong entrenched in streams laced with foxholes, rice field dikes lined with spider holes, and even nests in giant anthills. The NVA and VC forces were able to seek or break off combat with relative freedom, using rocket and mortar attacks if their front-line losses became unacceptable in a given area. Their aggressiveness resulted in bushwhacked landing zones and halted units unable to move forward, yet they also possessed an uncanny ability to fade into nearby woods and avoid a fight. The American military found the situation maddening; the battlefield initiative was still in the hands of the enemy.

Actually, the real problem was that the American soldiers being fielded were simply green, and faring poorly as a result. Lessons had to be learned the hard way. Command groups, readily identifiable by collections of radio antennae protruding out of tall grass and dense undergrowth, took critical losses until they dispersed. Treetops had to be liberally sprayed with automatic weapons and grenade fire to shake out sniper teams. Close jungles compressed companies into single files with exposed flanks. Soldiers were frozen and pinned by the unexpectedly heavy fire initially received in engagements, and their equally inexperienced officers and sergeants were not taking charge. Unpredictably high ammunition expenditures forced soldiers to rely on their machetes and cutting tools instead of bullets midway through fierce firefights. Even medical evacuation of wounded sometimes led to panic on the line if nearby soldiers thought they had missed getting word to withdraw.

Slowly the military adjusted its tactics to cope with this new battlefield. Soldiers learned to accept the fact that the Viet Cong would usually have the advantage during the first five or ten minutes of any clash, since they were initiating the combat from prepared positions at a time and place of their choosing. Officers and sergeants became firm as they called in air strikes and heavy artillery, and the combat odds began to shift rapidly in their own favor. The profusion of American technological firepower became a casualty-preventing mainstay, and burning napalm, phosphorous, and exploding steel were used in mass quantities to shatter resistance.

Some lessons were harder. Viet Cong snipers capitalized on the American habit of immediately going to the aid of injured comrades by deliberately wounding a soldier and then killing several would-be rescuers. In the midst of combat it was found that little more could be done for casualties beyond foxhole help. In order to keep the perimeter intact and every available man shooting, wounded were evacuated later. Since the Viet Cong were well versed in delay tactics, which allowed time for further preparation of ambush and defensive positions or escape, the Americans learned to press the attack. Sergeants had to use all their forceful professionalism to drive wearied troops on. Situation miscalls and underestimations of enemy strength were inevitable and produced unfortunate results. Ability to guess enemy capability or intentions intelligently could only be gleaned from fighting experience.

Battalion and company commanders learned to expect water obstacles and other hazards, not shown by maps or observable from the air, underneath jungle canopies. Night positions had to be constantly patrolled. Large captured rice caches impossible to remove were found to be destructable if gasoline, diesel oil, or artillery powder was mixed in. Work priorities in defense became digging positions and cutting fields of fire.

The 1st Infantry Division was having difficulties reminiscent of its first experiences in North Africa in World War II, when it was trounced by German desert warriors at Kasserine Pass in 1943. The division was also painfully assimilating jungle warfare experience through trial and error. Lack of divisional battle prowess caused several unfavorable situations where on-hand reserves were either unprepared for immediate commitment, not under control, or lacking altogether. Personnel turnover, illness, and battlefield losses threatened to undo the lessons mastered.

In March 1966 General Westmoreland put his MACV chief of operations, Maj. Gen. William E. DePuy, in command. General DePuy immediately began relieving so many subordinate officers that the Army Chief of Staff expressed open concern. Despite a temporary loss of morale, the 1st Infantry Division slowly mastered its tactical problems. Under Maj. Gen. DePuy, the "Big Red One" was soon living up to the combat performance expectations it had earned in two World Wars, and became one of MACV's hardest-fighting outfits.

3. Air Assault

Perhaps the most novel tactical innovation of the Vietnam War was the air assault. In these attacks the smoldering green-gray wash of earth and sky would tilt dizzily as helicopters banked into their final approaches toward the blazing, smoking landing zone ahead. Huddled four to a side on the edge of doorless cargo compartments, legs dangling into space, young American infantrymen sucked in deep gasps of the charred jungle air as they flipped their rifles off Safe onto Full Auto. Eruptions of artillery could be clearly seen exploding down one side of an assault corridor while last minute air strikes ripped up the other side with fragmentation bombs and intense 20mm-cannon strafing. Armed helicopters lazily suspended in the sky poured concentrated rocket and machine-gun fire into the far and rear approaches. Sergeants had explained this landing zone preparation and how it had to be of critical intensity to maximize shock effect. At a time like this, though, all their teaching slipped past senses too dazed to think. The blurred tropical landscape flashed by eyes singed by burning gunpowder. Ears were pounded by the roar of whirling rotor blades and detonations. For the veterans of previous "hot LZs," battle instinct surfaced, but, for the newer soldiers, whatever rudimentary drill they had received in stateside training mills had to suffice. Such superficial training became overwhelmed by the impact of actual war.

Flak-vested door gunners hammered the blazing tree lines with a steady stream of tracer-laced machine-gun fire. The aircrews secretly prayed that nervous grunts wouldn't accidentally fire their weapons or drop loose grenades. Many helicopters had been lost due to careless rifle discharges through cabin roofs or unsecured grenades rolling across metal floors. As the helicopters slowed and descended, some soldiers lowered themselves to stand on the outboard skids while still clinging to the aircraft sides. Then the soldiers leaped out and the transport helicopters swiftly left the corridors by executing roundabout turns and taking off downwind in the same direction they had entered.

The sudden availability of rugged, dependable helicopters in mass quantity allowed these craft to dominate the battlefield. They became the basis of a new doctrine—airmobility—a potentially devastating means of battlefield technology. Slightly over fifty aviation companies and air cavalry troops had been sent to Vietnam by the end of 1965, and they would be joined by twenty-two more in 1966. Most of these were helicopter units, and for the first time ground commanders were being offered massive vertical assault capabilities, extra aerial firepower, and a degree of mobility never before experienced in warfare. Airmobility meant attacking from any direction, striking targets in otherwise impossible terrain, overflying barriers, bypassing enemy positions, and achieving tactical surprise. It was counted on to resolve the problems of area warfare since the rapid tempo of fighting operations, unhampered by normal ground restrictions—even in marginal weather—gave the U.S. commanders great flexibility in employing their soldiers very quickly from a variety of distant locations.

Bold and aggressive use of massive combat power, linked with a choice of unexpected times and places for attack, had been instrumental in securing success for the 1st Cavalry Division in the Ia Drang Valley campaign of 1965. As a result, airmobile tactics were perfected quickly, and all Army maneuver battalions became skilled in their use. Soon throngs of green-clad warriors, garbed in rip-stop cotton and loaded with bandoliers of ammunition, were departing their base areas on waves of helicopters. Shepherded by armed helicopter escorts, they assaulted predetermined landing zones which were already under artillery and aerial fire bombardment. Like everything in Vietnam, this airmobile thrust entailed considerable risk, since it could lead to an unwanted general engagement under unfavorable conditions if it mistakenly tripped a hornets' nest.

Airmobility was most effective when it was used as the cavalry it had replaced had been used. It reigned supreme in exploitation and pursuit, after an enemy force had been broken or enveloped. Its purpose then became to destroy the opponent's ability to reconstitute and conduct an organized defense. While small-scale exploitations seemed insignificant, especially if local setbacks were experienced, their cumulative effects could be decisive. Introduced whenever the enemy was perceived as having difficulty maintaining its position, ruthless execution could block withdrawal and complete the destruction. The NVA and VC became adept at avoiding entrapment this way by abandoning ground at opportune times. Flexibility, speed, and a hunch for enemy intentions were required to maintain pressure on such a proficient adversary.

One of the finest scout formations that excelled in this type of work was the 1st Squadron of the 9th Cavalry, the air reconnaissance arm of the 1st Cavalry Division. Descended from the famed "Buffalo" cavalrymen of the Indian Wars and previously an all-Black unit, it was the first air cavalry into Vietnam.[4] On August 19, 1966, two light observation helicopters from Troop B spotted ten NVA soldiers hiding in tall grass beside a trail. Two helicopter gunships joined them four minutes later, and the troop's rifle platoon was sent aloft. The troop commander raced into his helicopter and was overhead in fifteen minutes. He marked a landing zone 150 feet away by dropping smoke, and the riflemen who arrived ten minutes later were set down. Meanwhile the two scout helicopters kept the NVA corralled. One made a low orbit, keeping them in constant sight, while the second flew a wider circle. The scout observer in the first craft discouraged two attempts at escape by firing short bursts from his M16 rifle.

The rifle platoon formed a diamond with its four squads and moved up to within fifty meters of the NVA, guided by the scout helicopter crew, who could see both groups. The platoon then swiftly fanned out into a line with one squad dropping back

4. The 9th Cavalry had been first organized in October 1866 at Greenville, Louisiana, and fought Comanches and Utes out West. It garrisoned Texas, New Mexico, and Colorado until 1881, when it moved to secure Kansas and Indian Territory. It had also seen action in the Spanish-American War, the Philippine Insurrection, and in Korea.

for rear security, and charged the pinned NVA soldiers. Thirty modern cavalrymen lunged forward with guns firing from the hip, and the cornered North Vietnamese infantrymen blasted back. One trooper fell dead in the charge but the others pressed forward. Through the din of battle, the helicopters whisked overhead and radioed instructions. Two hours and twenty minutes from the first sighting the skirmish was ended. Sixteen NVA lay dead and nine wounded gave themselves up.

Scouting and screening were natural helicopter missions, and entire air cavalry squadrons exclusively dedicated to this function were raised and dispatched to Vietnam in 1967. To the 1st Cavalry Division's 1st Squadron of the 9th Cavalry, would be added another divisional aerial reconnaissance cavalry squadron, the 2d Squadron of the 17th Cavalry, for the 101st Airborne Division (Airmobile). Three separate air cavalry squadrons also served: the 7th Squadron of the 1st Cavalry, and the 3d and 7th squadrons of the 17th Cavalry.

4. Helicopters At War

For the Army, the widening war in Vietnam promised to be like no other in its potential airmobile success over nearly all terrain restrictions. With enough helicopters and their intrinsic lift capacity, there seemed no end to the possibilities. Every Army concept seemed to mesh with their remarkable versatility, from troop and cargo hauling to firepower assistance and surveillance. Commanders were quick to cram their cargo compartments with radios and use them as airborne command posts. Soon the squat, olive drab Army aerial workhorse, the ever present Bell Corporation Huey helicopter, became an integral part of nearly all Vietnam missions. The incessant, pulsating whoosh of their rotor blades labored continually through the humid Southeast Asian skies.

Armed helicopters were especially reassuring to the "crunchies," the ground infantrymen who depended on them to deliver accurate supporting fire whether conducting raids or in "deep serious" trouble trying to disengage. In their own peculiar jargon, the soldiers called the UH-series Huey gunships Hogs, and the later, sleeker AH-1G Cobra attack helicopters Snakes. Both delivered high concentrations of destruction whether using running fire delivered in forward flight, hovering fire, or stationary fire while grounded. Their armament came in various combinations of dual or singular machine guns, 2.75-inch rocket launchers, 40mm grenade-launching systems, 20mm automatic guns, miniguns, and mine dispensers. These weapons were fitted onto the helicopters using side mounts to nose turrets.

In fact the armed helicopters were so powerful, fast, and effective that they created control problems that became extremely critical, especially in poor weather. In an effort to guide the lethal and rapid fire into enemy targets and safely around friendly forces, soldiers used smoke grenades, visual panels, flare devices, all types of star clusters, tracer ammunition, and radio communications.

To command and control the tremendous Army aviation forces in Vietnam, the 1st Aviation Brigade was created in May 1966. It eventually became one of the largest military commands there, with over 24,000 men and 4,230 aircraft of all descriptions organized into a multitude of aviation groups and battalions as well as air cavalry squadrons. During the course of the conflict some 142 separate Army aviation companies and air cavalry troops participated in the most lavish airmobile effort in history, but its toll of helicopter personnel was staggering. Nearly six thousand helicopter pilots and crewmen were killed in aircraft losses over Vietnam.

While the advent of airmobility allowed the Army unparalleled ability to surmount many of Vietnam's jungled obstacles, flying conditions often remained severely restricted. Weather and geography were foremost in determining range and power. South Vietnam's landscape varied from the flat, open rice fields of the Mekong Delta, where lack of dense vegetation gave antiaircraft gunners excellent opportunities, to the rugged mountains of the Central Highlands where suitable landing zones were difficult to select and high trees presented numerous flying hazards. The coastal plains resembled delta areas except for their fewer and poorer roads and the east-west mountain ridges extending inland from the shore. Added to these terrain difficulties were the northeast monsoons between September and April, and the southwest monsoons between April and September. The former brought heavy clouds along the coastal mountains and hot, dusty conditions to the Delta and mountain areas, while low cloud ceilings and poor visiblity prevailed over the Central Highlands and the Delta during the southwest monsoon period.

The maximum distance airmobile units could travel was based on the helicopter's ability to deliver its assault forces and then return to the nearest refueling or rearming point. In Vietnam such operations were conducted anywhere from less than a mile up to roughly forty miles from pickup to landing zone. Seldom was there enough aviation available to meet demand, and control between ground and air units was often difficult. Aircraft fuel was consumed in tremendous quantities; for example, a utility aircraft on an average day consumed over four thousand pounds of fuel. Ammunition was expended rapidly. Maintenance was a major effort that received the highest command emphasis in Vietnam. As a result the 34th General Support Group was formed at Tan Son Nhut air base in January 1966, specifically to handle aviation supply and support. Due to the lack of qualified military personnel, the group had to be heavily augmented with civilian mechanics hired on a contractual basis.

All those associated with airmobility faced grave personal hazards apart from enemy action and mechanical failure. In order to achieve surprise and escape ground fire, helicopter pilots were forced to skim over Vietnam at treetop level. The Army termed this "nap of the earth," or terrain/contour, flying, and all agreed it left little margin for error. Other general hazards became associated with helicopter employment. Hovering helicopters wallowed in their own toxic engine exhaust gases, magnified by downward rotor wash. Crew members had their breathing stifled by the visible haze and cordite odor of side machine-gun fire, despite ventilation through open cargo doors. Pilots suffered from spatial disorientation episodes, magnified by a helicopter's peculiar ability to produce total viewing changes instantly. Shuddering helicopter motions produced vibrations that played havoc with eyesight. Main rotor noise swamped low frequency ranges and combined with higher frequency antitorque system noise to devastate eardrums, which were further aggravated by sounds from open doors and windows. Loss of auditory response threatened the safety of soldiers in battle, as leaders might not be heard or orders understood.

Early on, the helicopter was employed to evacuate the mounting toll of combat wounded. By locating three litters on each side of the transmission support structure, six seriously injured soldiers could be carried and the center forward-facing troop seat used for the medical attendant. Two blood-bottle hangers were placed on the inside of the cabin roof and electrical receptacles furnished direct current for heated blankets. Additionally, rescue hoists with electrically operated winches and "forest penetrator" litter devices were installed to allow extraction of wounded from jungles where landing was impossible. Resuscitators, telescoping splints, and surgical instrument sets were shoved into the aircraft in an effort to save soldiers suffering from shock, severe bleeding, multiple burns, and wounds to the head, chest, or abdomen. In such circumstances survival was directly linked to the skills of aidmen and crew chiefs, working feverishly to open air passageways or tie tourniquets, and to the flying ability of pilots who shaved minutes off the time separating their wounded from medical facilities. The feats of these "Dust-Off" crews, so called in tribute to the call-sign of the first medical evacuation helicopter lost in Vietnam, were legendary and resulted in a number of awards of the Medal of Honor, the highest United States decoration for valor.

Special medical air ambulance companies and detachments were introduced as fast as crews and helicopters became available. Each company consisted of four air ambulance platoons totaling twenty-four helicopters, while detachments contained six aircraft. These units operated in conjunction with ordinary helicopters on call, and soon Americans hit on the battlefield had a good chance of receiving quicker first-class medical aid than highway accident victims back home. However, problems constantly hampered this airmobile answer to prompt medical evacuation. Not only did surrounding terrain and climatic conditions limit lift capacity, but pressured ground troops often called in urgent requests before the wounded were collected, or in areas too small for the helicopters, or not yet clear of enemy fire. This sometimes resulted in downed medical helicopters and more casualties.

Whatever advantages airmobility had, the fighting soldier valued the promise of speedy medical evacuation the highest.

He realized that a wounded man's condition could worsen in seconds, that shock was quick to set in, and that only aerial evacuation could prevent potentially overwhelming death rates. Line units were suffering grievous casualties in close combat, and these were occurring in some of the most rugged terrain on earth. The soldier viewed helicopter evacuation as an absolute necessity and its ready availability became an accepted, overriding morale consideration.

5. A Crisis of Pilots

If aviation was the key component of airmobility, then certainly the number of available pilots was a key determinant of the possible extent of airmobile presence. MACV was already aware that its airmobile potential wasn't keeping pace with growing troop strength because of a widespread shortage of aviators. Now this lack of personnel was so acute that the entire promise of airmobility was in danger of foundering. Already field operations were being premised on the amount of helicopters on hand, rather than on whatever objectives or enemy threat existed.

In January 1966, the Department of the Army had informed General Westmoreland that all aviation sources had been exhausted, and that nearly five hundred aviation-qualified Vietnam veterans were being recycled back overseas. The rapid deployment of Marine aviation units had likewise precipitated a critical shortfall. By October the Marine Corps was deferring both releases and retirements and shortening its helicopter courses.

The Army squeeze was underlined by the 9,700 pilots on hand compared to its June requirement for 14,300. A rash of letters went out begging previous aviation personnel to come back as part of a voluntary recall, but the response wasn't promising. Of nearly two thousand individual letters mailed in the first half of 1966 inviting nonactive aviators back in, only sixty were answered. In Vietnam itself urgent steps were taken which trimmed any aviator requirements in nonflight jobs, and posted everybody up to and including the rank of major in actual flying assignments.

Still more drastic measures were required beyond stepped-up pilot training and abbreviated flying courses. In order to beef up the Southeast Asian war zone, the Defense Department reduced global manning levels in other areas to only a fourth of that authorized. Even this dangerously low profile was sliced by a further emergency withdrawal from Europe and Korea in May. By the end of spring, for instance, there were only thirty-four Army pilots on the entire Korean peninsula. Any aviator below the rank of lieutenant colonel was informed that his time between Vietnam tours was being cut to a year.

At this point the Army's aviation school at Fort Rucker, Alabama, was geared solely to cranking out as many pilots as possible for Vietnam duty. The Army was now desperately seeking officer pilot material from all sources. Graduates in the upper portion of advanced individual training courses were being called into the offices of their training commanders. There they were reviewed as potential volunteers for flight training. Some recalled the questions being hardly more than whether they could read, see without glasses, and ever thought about racing cars or flying. If response was positive, they were packed off to Fort Rucker as new warrant officer candidates.

To the Army's surprise, these young soldiers—who often possessed no college background or career aspirations, but only the desire to fly—proved to be just the answer. Full of zeal, and bold to the point of recklessness, young and unmarried, they became the best helicopter pilots in the business. As young as eighteen, their chests soon adorned with dozens of distinguished flying crosses and air medals, they were heroes to the military, district, and province chiefs of South Vietnam, to the front-line combatants and support personnel, to unit commanders and planners, and to anyone else connected with the allied cause. Their efforts and dedication enabled airmobility to flourish, and by mid-1968 increased school output and force leveling combined to alleviate the pilot crisis.

CHAPTER 7.

THE CENTRAL FRONT

1. Battles for Base Camps, Plantations, and Roads

The American military focused its 1966 campaign efforts in the critical regions north and west of Saigon, on securing base areas for its incoming units, and opening lines of communication through threatened areas. Regular Army forces were summoned into battle wherever outlying South Vietnamese and U.S. Army Special Forces garrisons were threatened, and maintained as much pressure against known VC sanctuaries as assets permitted. As the year progressed and more units became available, larger operations were initiated in suspected Viet Cong fortified zones. In the Central Highlands and coastal areas the swift and powerful 1st Cavalry Division conducted all-out efforts to locate and destroy NVA and VC concentrations.

The "Tropic Lightning" 25th Infantry Division was emplaced west of Saigon at the start of the year, and its 2d Brigade assumed operational responsibility for the future divisional base camp near Cu Chi. The division's placement directly challenged the prime Viet Cong lifeline to Cambodian supply points, which was guarded by a maze of VC fortifications and tunnel networks. Hau Nghia and Tay Ninh provinces represented a dangerous slice of terrain covered by swamp and jungle, which was never effectively subdued throughout the length of the Vietnam War.

The security of the Cu Chi vicinity had top priority. The 2d Brigade contained the famed 27th Infantry "Wolfhounds," whose 1st Battalion was tasked with clearing the southwest portion of the perimeter to a distance sufficient to prevent any mortaring of the compound.[1] Thus a large abandoned village a mile west of the base camp became a battalion objective. The village contained rows of bamboo thickets around each hut, as well as an elaborate tunnel system. For four days the battalion's companies took turns assaulting the village, and each was repulsed and took heavy losses in turn. Although air and artillery bombardment would precede the infantry, each charge would inevitably be met by withering machine-gun and automatic rifle fire and stopped cold. Then the Viet Cong would break off the action by splitting into small groups and fading in the jungle. Returning later from another direction, they would suddenly shoot up soldiers trying to search through the empty houses.

Company B was determined to clear the place once and for all. Air Force fighters, helicopter gunships, howitzers, and battalion mortars were called in. The infantrymen advanced toward the village behind a moving curtain of exploding artillery rounds. The Viet Cong rapidly lobbed their own mortar shells to burst among the Americans, and the line started to waver because men suspected their own artillery was falling short. The coolness of a platoon sergeant prevented a rout, and slowly the village was closed. As suspected hot spots around it were hit by continued artillery fire, the soldiers began pitching thermite grenades into the structures. Aerial rocket fire was directed at bamboo thickets containing snipers. The company then withdrew behind a smokescreen which was mixed with high explosive shelling to prevent VC use of its concealment. A stay-behind ambush team was left in place to discourage Viet Cong return.

The clearing process was slow and tedious. In late July the

1. The 27th Infantry was one of the most renowned Regular Army regiments. Its traditional designation, "The Wolfhounds," commemorated its service in Siberia after World War I, and the insignia of the American Siberian Expeditionary Force—a giant wolf head—and the motto *Nec Aspera Terrant* (Frightened by No Difficulties) were embossed on the regimental shield. Organized in February 1901 at Plattsburg Barracks in New York it had rendered outstanding service during the Philippine Insurrection, especially in the Lake Lanao Expedition. Assigned to the Hawaiian Division in 1921, it had been part of the 25th Infantry Division in the Pacific during World War II and the Korean War.

division's base camp was struck by an intense recoilless rifle and mortar attack. In the meantime, other "Wolfhound" elements were probing deeper into Viet Cong territory. On July 19, 1966, Company A of the 1st Battalion, 27th Infantry, was airlifted to the edge of the Ho Bo Woods. They immediately ran into entrenched elements of the *1st Battalion, 165A VC Regiment*, complete with camouflaged uniforms and steel helmets, and a furious five-hour battle resulted. The length and intensity of these early encounters convinced Army planners that the Viet Cong would fight tenaciously if forced to defend their base areas. This experience later shaped operational directives, which massed allied formations against certain areas in the hope of inducing decisive engagements.

MACV directed the 1st Infantry Division and the 173d Airborne Brigade into several other western areas of III Corps Tactical Zone. The paratroopers of the 2d Battalion, 503d Infantry (Airborne), from the airborne brigade, air-assaulted into sharp action along the Oriental River during the first week of the year (Operation MARAUDER), and on January 8 they stabbed into the Ho Bo Woods (Operation CRIMP). The 1st Infantry Division swept the Boi Loi Woods (Operation MASTIFF) and the Long Than district (Operation MALLET) in February. "The Herd" 173d Airborne Brigade ventured into the Be River area northwest of Saigon on March 7, which triggered a fierce four-hour counterattack. In these early 1966 encounters the price of entry was costly, but then the pace of action fizzled out. The slow and deliberate clearance of bunkers and tunnels, always a hazardous and painstaking procedure, began. The large amounts of material captured and earthen fortifications razed seemed to indicate that Viet Cong capabilities were being seriously eroded. The violence of sudden firefights in the sunless, vine-choked tropical forests cheered MACV into believing they were offering the VC no respite.

Company C of the 1st Infantry Division's 2d Battalion, 16th Infantry, was decimated by the *D800 VC Battalion* in deep jungle on April 11 while engaged in Operation ABILENE sweeping coastal Phuoc Tuy Province.[2] They had been hacking their way

2. One of the traditional regiments of the 1st Infantry Division, the 16th

through the jungle against sporadic rifle fire when a "friendly" artillery round fell short and burst in the tree-masked canopy overhead, spraying their ranks with shrapnel. The company halted to evacuate the two dead and twelve wounded Americans, unaware that they had selected a spot only yards from the VC battalion's base camp. Automatic rifle and grenade fire suddenly swept their perimeter. During the night the soldiers desperately fought off three main charges as 1,086 rounds of artillery plummeted down through the trees in support. Reinforcements were pushed toward the beleaguered company but were forced to wait for first light before attempting a linkup. Early the next morning engineers and medical personnel reached the unit, descending through the jungle canopy on "Jacob's ladders" dropped from the rear of hovering CH-47 Chinook helicopters. Only then were the engineers able to carve out a landing zone so the wounded could be lifted out by evacuation helicopters.

The 1st Infantry Division, the "Big Red One," went north of Tay Ninh in Operation BIRMINGHAM commencing April 24, but only squad- and platoon-sized encounters were made. MACV considered minor actions only irritants and directed the division to make more substantial contact with the Viet Cong. The climax of the drive was to be a four-battalion surprise infantry air assault on the suspected South Vietnamese communist headquarters May 7–9, secretly coded HOLLINGSWORTH. The hot, parched weather suddenly evaporated into a violent series of thunderstorms which dumped so much rain that helicopter operations had to be suspended. With that cut in mobility, MACV was forced to cancel out.

The division sent units into some of the most inaccessible regions of Vietnam as it strived to produce significant combat results. The infantrymen of the 1st Battalion, 18th Infantry, sloshed through mud up to their hips during Operation LEX-

---

Infantry had a long history of desperate fighting. At the Wheatfield and Devil's Den in Gettysburg during the Civil War, it had lost approximately 50 percent of its effective strength. It had been initially formed in Massachusetts in February 1862, and was consolidated as the 16th Infantry from the 11th, 16th, and 34th Infantry Regiments in 1869. It had also seen intense combat during the storming of Fleville, France, on October 4, 1918, during the Meuse-Argonne Offensive of World War I.

INGTON III, fought April 17–June 9, 1966, in the mangrove-choked swamps of the Rung Sat Special Zone. While sampan kills proved easy in the murky nightly marsh gloom, results were limited since the companies had to be rotated every other day to avoid immersion foot. Finally, with the approach of the summer monsoons, the 1st Infantry Division was urged to deal a punishing blow somewhere, in order to forestall a suspected VC offensive with the onset of the rains.

In early May a Viet Cong lieutenant was killed southeast of Loc Ninh, and a search through his possessions turned up a plan to attack both the town and its Special Forces camp. As a result the 1st Infantry Division spent the month fruitlessly sweeping the area in Operation EL PASO I. Maj. Gen. William E. DePuy was looking for battle, so he decided to strike deeper into Viet Cong-dominated territory. With the commencement of June he pushed his 1st Infantry Division into War Zone C. This operation, EL PASO II, was designed to block the *9th VC Division* from taking the offensive northwest of Saigon during the upcoming monsoon season. The area heated up fast, and in less than a week the *9th VC Division* had sprung into action, determined to repel this major United States intrusion.

On the afternoon of June 8, Troop A of the 1st Squadron, 4th Cavalry, was churning down Route 13 with its tanks and armored personnel carriers. As the cavalry passed through Tau-O toward Hon Quan, the *272d VC Regiment* conducted a massive ambush. Troop A's lead tank was hit by recoilless rifle fire, and the rear of the column was also disabled. The Viet Cong then charged the vehicles trapped in between. Fierce combat raged for four hours before the assault was finally broken off.

Three days later action erupted at the rubber plantation northwest of Loc Ninh. Company A of the 2d Battalion, 28th Infantry, was ordered to clear plantation village #10 by a combined ground-air assault. The day promised to be fair and hot, but heavy morning fog delayed the helicopters two hours. After it dissipated, helicopter gunships made a five-minute "gun run" across the landing zone, followed by two platoons which were airlifted in. The remainder of Company A moved into the area by foot to establish blocking positions. Rifle fire from a small hill wounded three of these advancing soldiers and the battle was on. Before it ended the entire 2d Battalion of the 28th Infantry became involved.[3]

Company A immediately fired off a barrage with its light mortars, while the heliborne troops shifted their village approach to move against the hill. By now bunkered machine guns were causing trouble, and the company hurled an attached South Vietnamese CIDG platoon, led by one Special Forces advisor, into the attack. This impromptu charge was repulsed. Company C was alerted to join the fight, but it ran into more entrenched defensive positions on another hill. At noon the battalion's reconnaissance platoon was ordered in to assist. The 28th Infantry was up against a dug-in battalion of the *273d VC Regiment*.

After intensive artillery bombardment and considerable anti-sniper work, Company C got into line formation and assaulted the Viet Cong trenchlines on the second hill. The recon platoon was attached as ordinary infantry to bolster the left side of the advance. The platoon started receiving intense automatic weapons fire. As grenades showered down from the rubber trees they began to fall back in disorder. The VC quickly moved around them, and sited a machine gun by the trenchline occupied by reconnaissance members providing covering fire for their retreating comrades. The gun suddenly fired down the trench and killed all its occupants. A serious reverse was avoided as Company C threw its reserve platoon into the fray. By late afternoon the Viet Cong had been pushed off the hill.

Meanwhile, repeated attacks by Company A had failed to dislodge the Viet Cong on the first hill. Another CIDG unit, a company that happened to be wandering nearby on patrol, was grabbed to help encircle the Viet Cong position. During mid-afternoon Lt. Col. Kyle W. Bowie committed his final reserves, Company B. At this juncture the interpreter of Company A's attached CIDG platoon was killed by VC gunfire, and the platoon bolted from the battlefield. The Special Forces sergeant

3. The 28th Infantry was officially known as "the Lions of Cantigny," having been the attacking regiment at Cantigny in the ancient province of Picardy, France, during World War I. The regiment had been formed in Vancouver Barracks, Washington, during March–June 1901 and sent to the Philippines. It fought in World War I with the 1st Expeditionary Division (later 1st Division), but served with the 8th Infantry Division in World War II.

stayed to fight with Company A, but a gap had been created around the hill.

Following a sixteen-volley artillery barrage, accompanied by an equal number of sorties from Air Force and Navy aircraft dropping incendiary and fragmentation bombs, the fresh troops of Company B charged the hill. Bunkers were stormed in furious hand-to-hand combat. The Viet Cong scattered, many making their escape through the hole that the missing CIDG platoon had created. The battalion consolidated, evacuated casualties, resupplied its ammunition, and policed the charred shambles of the plantation.

The next encounter, on June 30, was destined to be one of the classic engagements of the Vietnam War, the Battle of Srok Dong. For the previous two weeks the 2d Battalion, 18th Infantry, combined with the 1st Squadron, 4th Cavalry, to sweep the Quan Loi vicinity. A destroyed bridge on Route 13 limited this ability, and the banks of the stream had to be prepared to support an armored vehicle-launched bridge near the demolished structure. A threefold operation was planned in order to get the bridge site repaired. Lt. Col. Leonard L. Lewane, the cavalry squadron commander, was given the mission.[4]

Both sides of the road were heavily forested, the only openings formed by rice paddies and streams, where chest-high grass grew up to the edges of the road. The tropical weather was clear and hot as the armored scissors bridge arrived at the stream. Troop B was returning down Route 13 to Loc Ninh when recoilless rifle and machine-gun fire ripped through the column as it crossed a rice paddy. Wearing a variety of khaki, green, and black uniforms, the *271st VC Regiment* had lined the western side of the road and was firing from log piles and the thick tangle of jungle hardwood. The troop's four tanks were quickly

---

4. The 4th Cavalry was one of the Army's finest. Formed in March 1855, at Jefferson Barracks in Missouri to fight Indians in Kansas, it was involved throughout the Civil War where it gained honors storming the entrenchments at Selma, capturing Hood's artillery, and routing Confederate cavalry at Murfreesborough. The Bud Dajo campaign against the Philippine Moros was still represented by a triumphant sabre across the volcano on the 4th Cavalry's regimental crest. As a mechanized cavalry group it had seen action across northern Europe in World War II.

neutralized by repeated hits which blasted the turret-top cupolas, decapitating commanders and killing or wounding their crews.

The armored personnel carriers of Troop B replied with heavy machine-gun fire. Artillery was called in and armed Huey and Chinook helicopters made strafing and rocket passes up and down the fringes of the road. The armored personnel carriers of Troop C raced toward the action, with infantrymen piled on top. A sudden rain of mortar shells started blowing soldiers off the vehicles. A checkpoint with some armored mortar carriers and infantrymen had been established earlier at a crossroad. This road junction was under mortar fire and jammed with vehicles from Troop B, bringing in wounded and replenishing ammunition, as well as Troop C vehicles trying to maneuver through.

As Troop C's vehicles pulled around the clogged checkpoint to reach the ambush area, the turret of the lead tank took a direct hit. The seriously wounded commander and loader were taken out, and the tank-led line of carriers continued on. The brush was so thick on both sides of the road that the vehicle crews just lobbed grenades over the sides. The tank was hit a second time, and the gunner was wounded badly. He was removed and the tank driver kept going. Troop C's column finally arrived at the tail of Troop B's stranded position. All power to the tank turret was gone, but three more men joined the sergeant inside. With a replenished crew, the tank stormed through the burning wrecks in the ambush site. The sweltering substitutes manually swiveled the cannon around to point northwest and fired off all sixty rounds of ammunition. Meanwhile the rest of the reinforcing armored personnel carriers rumbled along both narrow shoulders of the road to form a shield around the battered remnants of Troop B.

Troop B's operable vehicles retreated to the checkpoint. There a lieutenant of Troop C had been left behind with several armored personnel carriers to guard the crossroad and assist in the evacuation of dead and wounded. He now moved his mechanized platoon forward to clear a landing zone for troop-laden helicopters arriving to reinforce the battle area. As he stood in the hatch, a VC bullet hit him in the chest. Several more men were wounded and the armored personnel carriers were unable to break contact. A mechanized flamethrower rammed through the snarl of underbrush and high grass and lashed the VC strongpoint with a fiery tongue of spray in an effort to extract the lieutenant's vehicles.

For a week prior to the battle, the 2d Battalion of the 18th Infantry had kept Company B on thirty-minute alert to reinforce any armored cavalry trouble spots. After a mix-up getting helicopters, they hopped in twelve small 3/4-ton trucks and drove to Quan Loi. Helicopters had already lifted Company A, which was there previously, into the battle. Company B turned its trucks north on Route 13 and headed to an alternate pickup zone. However, it was full of medics frantically collecting dead and wounded, and medical evacuation helicopters buzzing in to retrieve them. The company was diverted to another spot and finally lifted into action. One of the helicopters landing in the last lift struck a dud cluster bomblet and burst into flames. Its crew and passengers managed to scramble out. The company went into action, but by this time the Viet Cong were already leaving the battlefield.

Lieutenant Colonel Lewane pushed Companies A and B across the smoking road. They soon ran into sharp resistance at a nearby creek. Two more infantry battalions, the 1st Battalion, 2d Infantry, and the 2d Battalion, 28th Infantry, arrived in the battle area the next morning. July 1–2 would be marked by continued sporadic fighting, accented by nocturnal attacks on American overnight positions. As contact faded, the Battle of Srok Dong was declared ended. Major General DePuy would brief General Westmoreland in July:

> This was a complete surprise . . . . U.S. forces nearly lost this battle. However, air superiority proved to be the deciding factor and inflicted severe losses on the enemy.

On July 9 the cavalry went out again, this time as bait. A feint was made to the northeast with a B-52 bombing strike, and information was leaked through the local Vietnamese that one cavalry troop would be coming down the road. However, two cavalry troops with infantry were sent, and the result was the Battle of Minh Thanh Road. The mixed column of tanks and troop-filled armored personnel carriers waited until fog and overcast dissipated, moved out, and was hit one hour before noon right where expected. Due to the tremendous volume of fire from the vehicles and the denseness of the jungle, the overhead command helicopters were initially confused as to the main direction of the *272d VC Regiment*'s attack. As the column compressed under the fury of the onslaught, the helicopters darted out of the way so that a wall of artillery fire could blanket the north side. One CH-47 Chinook helicopter was brought down but managed to force-land on the roadway to the southwest. It was later retrieved by a CH-54 Flying Crane.

The second troop moved back, closing the column by doubling it. While 22,200 rounds of artillery saturated its targeted area, 99 air strikes blasted the south. At one time five flights of Air Force fighter-bombers were stacked up waiting for their turn to go in. The Viet Cong dug deep into foxholes with overhead cover and used the roadside drainage ditches as fire lanes. The 1st Infantry Division prepared to move three reaction battalions into the battle—the 2d of the 2d Infantry by road, the 1st of the 28th Infantry by air, and the 1st of the 18th Infantry overland. The latter immediately set out on a difficult cross-jungle trek that pitched them right into a web of Viet Cong fortifications. The soldiers of the 18th Infantry, just back from nearly two months of swamp combat, started doggedly fighting their way forward.[5] Meanwhile action in the ambush site continued unabated, and the VC swarmed out to charge the stranded vehicles. One tank and four armored personnel carriers were completely destroyed, and many others were crippled by this time. The other tanks replied with devastating canister fire.

The 1st Battalion of the 28th Infantry had been moving parallel to the road to reinforce but had also run into strong defensive works. The 1st Battalion of the 16th Infantry was now brought forward to try to close a ring around the battle area.

5. The 18th Infantry was organized for Civil War duty in July 1861, at Camp Thomas, Ohio. After campaigning in that war with Sherman through Atlanta and the southern heartland, it went to Wyoming. It was posted back south for a ten-year span of occupation duty and returned west to Montana in 1879. It later fought in the Spanish-American War, in the Visayas during the Philippine Insurrection, and in the Soissons Offensive in World War I. It was one of the traditional regiments of the 1st Infantry Division.

In a sharp engagement in the forested tangle of undergrowth, its commander, Lt. Col. Rufus G. Lazzell, was wounded. The 2d Battalion, 2d Infantry, finally closed the area by road march. They then discovered the dust had completely clogged their new M16s, and cursed the absence of their old trusted M14 rifles. The Viet Cong, however, had failed to overwhelm the column and were now rapidly retreating from the battlefield. The heavy jungle enabled their escape from a tightening ring of advancing American infantry struggling in from different directions. By the next day the battle had faded into a series of inconsequential running skirmishes.

The *9th VC Division* moved into well-concealed base areas and was rebuilt with North Vietnamese Army replacements. In early November it moved back around Michelin plantation, west of Tay Ninh, where it planned to attack the Special Forces camp at Suoi Da and other targets in the province. Instead it collided into the 196th Infantry Brigade (Light), which happened to be in the area searching for Viet Cong rice and sundry supplies under a new concept being called search and destroy. The ensuing battle, fought through the snarled thickets of War Zone C, highlighted both Operation ATTLEBORO and the Army's 1966 campaign in III Corps Tactical Zone.

Operation ATTLEBORO had been initiated by Brig. Gen. Edward H. DeSaussure's light infantry brigade with a single battalion air assault by the 2d Battalion, 1st Infantry, on September 14, 1966. Only light contact resulted, and the brigade shifted its attention to operations around Dau Tieng. A month later, on October 19, the brigade reentered the area to look for more supply caches. The next day considerable quantities of rice were discovered and continued probing uncovered even larger amounts. Acting on documents found in a sweep of the Ten Cui plantation on the last day of the month, the 196th moved into deeper woods. The attached 1st Battalion, 27th Infantry, had its Company C cut off in high elephant grass after it had landed uneventfully but then stumbled into the *9th Reconnaissance Company* of the *9th VC Division* on November 3.

Moving down a trail through gnarled jungle forest to aid Company C, Company A itself ran into a well-concealed bunker line. It was suddenly engulfed in a furious hail of machine-gun and rocket fire that took down scores of Americans, wiped out radio contact, and prevented anyone from reaching them. After several hours of hard fighting, the company continued its push forward. These clashes of November 3 rapidly absorbed the available reinforcements (both battalions of the attached 27th Infantry "Wolfhounds" from the 25th Infantry Division), and by the next day all American companies on the operation were engaged in heavy fighting.

November 4 brought increasing action. The 1st Battalion of the 27th Infantry was engaged in a grisly, sustained battle for survival. By afternoon its commander, Maj. Guy S. Meloy III, had been wounded, and Company A fought for its positions against three major frontal assaults. Lt. Col. William C. Barott, who had just taken over the sister 2d Battalion of the 27th Infantry that August 22, was killed leading a squad in an attempt to link up the battalions. A full company of his battalion had been isolated and surrounded by Viet Cong regulars. When medical evacuation helicopters descended into the shattered lines after dark, they flicked on landing lights. An immediate mortar attack resulted. Major Meloy angrily told them to come in blind and land by flashlight or wait until morning. The response from the helicopter pilots was typical of their dedication: the landings were made blind.

Shortly after midnight the Suoi Cau Regional Force camp was attacked by the *272d VC Regiment*. Bangalore torpedoes and satchel charges were carried in a pitched charge, but the assault was repulsed. The 196th Infantry Brigade command post was also plastered by mortar fire. The Wolfhounds held on as combat renewed on November 5. Six massed Viet Cong frontal assaults surged out of fortified bunker lines to crash against the 1st Battalion, 27th Infantry. Infantrymen of the brigade's 2d Battalion, 1st Infantry, and 4th Battalion, 31st Infantry, navigated toward the 27th Infantry by the sound and smoke of battle. By now the *70th, 271st* and *272d VC Regiments* and the *101st NVA Regiment* were in action. Losses were mounting, and help was needed at once.

The 1st Infantry Division dispatched a battalion, then a reinforced brigade, and by moving all night managed to assemble near Dau Tieng. It took over direction of the battle and sent two of its own brigades into action on November 6, keeping

The elite 1st Squadron of the 9th Cavalry, the aerial reconnaissance arm of the 1st Cavalry Division, picks up troopers in Quang Ngai Province during summer operations north of the Bong Son Plains on June 9, 1967. Helicopter is a Bell Huey. (U.S. Army)

The hazards of aeromedical evacuation clearly demonstrated by the loss of this Bell Huey helicopter during 25th Infantry Division operations in Long An Province on September 26, 1966. (U.S. Army)

A heavy lift CH54 Skycrane helicopter prepares to pick up a 5-ton truck loaded with equipment for movement with the 101st Airborne Division (Airmobile). (U.S. Army)

Powerful gunship support to ground troops was offered by rocket-firing AH-1G Cobra helicopters such as this one from the 1st Squadron of the 10th Cavalry (4th Infantry Division) west of Ban Me Thuot. (Army News Features)

The Battle of Minh Thanh Road, fought July 9, 1966, by the 1st Infantry Division, was one of the year's roughest encounters. The downed CH47 helicopter mentioned in the text is clearly seen after force-landing on the roadway. (Author's Collection)

Armored Personnel Carriers of the 2d Battalion, 2d Infantry, move up to reinforce the Battle of Minh Thanh Road on July 9, 1966. (Author's Collection)

Marines of the 3d Battalion, 4th Marines, struggle up "Mutter's Ridge" (Nui Cay Tre) during Operation PRAIRIE in September, 1966. One Marine carries forward a rocket round while his comrades work their radio and compass in the heat of action. (U.S. Marine Corps)

Casualties are lifted out on the double by the 2d Battalion, 7th Marines, after combat near Duc Pho on December 30, 1966. (U.S. Marine Corps)

another in reserve. The 3d Brigade of the 4th Infantry Division and the 173d Airborne Brigade (reinforced by two ARVN battalions) also arrived, and the 25th Infantry Division moved up to screen. With such overwhelming concentration of force now mustered on the scene, the *9th VC Division* refused further combat and retreated west. By November 15, contacts were sputtering out, and late that month Operation ATTLEBORO, the harbinger of things to come, was over.

For the hastily deployed 196th Infantry Brigade, diverted at the last minute from its expected Caribbean duty, Operation ATTLEBORO had been a particularly rough initiation to full-scale Vietnam combat. By the closing days of the battle, MACV reluctantly came to the conclusion that the brigade had "cracked," posted Brigadier General DeSaussure to field force artillery, and appointed Brig. Gen. Richard T. Knowles to command of the 196th on November 14, 1966. The American Army, forced to rush more and more units into Vietnam without the benefit of orderly mobilization planning or reserve component assistance, was already beginning to show signs of strain under fire.

2. Battles for Jungles, Valleys, and Plains

The twelve provinces of II Corps Tactical Zone remained untamed, and a host of operations were unleashed on the region during the year. These were designed to safeguard installations and to secure the national priority area of Binh Dinh Province. Some, conducted in the thick bamboo and forested slopes of rugged mountain valleys, would result in bloody battles of great violence.

Maj. Gen. Harry W. O. Kinnard's 1st Cavalry Division (Airmobile), stationed at Camp Radcliff outside An Khe, was ordered to clear four important valleys located along the coastal plains of northeastern Binh Dinh Province. Reinforced by the ARVN Airborne Brigade, 22d ARVN Division, and the 1st Regiment of the Korean Capital Division, Col. Harold G. Moore Jr.'s 3d Brigade entered combat there on January 25. It was followed by the 2d and, later, 1st brigades. On February 4, Operation MASHER was redubbed WHITE WING to mollify President Johnson's concern over public opinion. Militarily it would become known as the Bong Son campaign.

For forty-two days the First Team division hopped across

the mountain ridges crowding the South China Sea, the waves of helicopters depositing battalions of cavalrymen into sandy fortified villages and lush, verdant jungle strongholds. In marginal weather typified by driving rain, skirmishes abounded, and the *2d VC* and *18th* and *22d NVA Regiments* fought with determination against the aerial onslaught. Company C of the 2d Battalion, 7th Cavalry, air-assaulted January 28 into a hamlet-studded landing zone at Phung Du. It was quickly pinned by a vicious cross fire from a battalion of entrenched Viet Cong, and its sister company, Company A—already decimated by the loss of forty-two members killed in a C-123 aircraft crash on the operation's first day at Deo Mang Pass—had a hard time getting across an intervening rice paddy. The next morning both companies had to be bailed out by the 2d Battalion of the 12th Cavalry. Massive heavy artillery barrages using delayed fuses and tear gas were employed to root out such entrenched village defenders.

On the morning of February 15, Company B of the 2d Battalion, 7th Cavalry, encountered opposition along a jungle-banked stream off the Soui Run River in the Son Long Valley. Two platoons were rapidly locked in an escalating firefight against entrenched and well-camouflaged positions. As artillery and aerial bombing runs were directed on the defensive works, the company's 3d Platoon fixed bayonets and prepared to attack. Just before noon, as the shuddering echoes of the last bomb explosions reverberated through the battered landscape, the signal was given and the men stood up and bounded forward. At a point only forty yards from the VC line they surged together at a dead run, yelling at the top of their lungs, their bayonets gleaming starkly in the sunlight. The unnerved Viet Cong broke and ran into a lethal cross fire laid down by the supporting platoons. Their position was quickly rolled up.

The operation was terminated on March 6, 1966, as the division completed its full circle of airmobile sweeps around Bong Son to arrive back in the Cay Giap Mountains. As a grand finale cavalrymen rappelled on ropes and clambered down Chinook helicopter-launched Jacob's ladders, dropped through holes bombed out of the jungle canopy of this suspected mountain fortress. The NVA had already left the vicinity, but the division was destined to return several times throughout the year in Operations DAVY CROCKETT, CRAZY HORSE, IRVING, and THAYER.

The other American formations in the zone, the 3d Brigade of the 25th Infantry Division at Pleiku and the 1st Brigade of the 101st Airborne Division near Tuy Hoa, were also active. The former dallied northwest of Ban Me Thuot in the Darlac Plains during Operation GARFIELD, instituted shortly after its arrival in Vietnam, and then struck west toward the Chu Pong Mountains on the Cambodian border. Already General Westmoreland had requested permission to maneuver troops around this range and into Cambodia to block escape avenues, but was refused. Now I Field Force, Vietnam, requested permission again to employ this option for Operation PAUL REVERE. In view of State Department sentiments on widening the war, MACV decided against making a further request to Washington. There would be no major Cambodian incursions until 1970.

Operation PAUL REVERE was initiated by the brigade on May 10, 1966, to counter possible NVA offensive activities during the southwest monsoon season against Special Forces border camps at Duc Co and Plei Me. It was the first time large American units had entered the Chu Pong-Ia Drang River area since the campaign of 1965. The *1st "Yellow Star" NVA Division* was all around the U.S. forces, but resorted to long-range observation and light contact. On June 24, the 1st Battalion of the 35th Infantry got into a heavy firefight, but disengaged due to the proximity of the international border. A platoon of Company B, of the same battalion, which had been further divided into patrols, was surrounded and cut up in early July. A mechanized assault with armored personnel carriers enabled the rest of the company to combine into one defensive perimeter. Survivors from both patrols were extracted with help of liberal artillery and air power. On August 1, the 1st Cavalry Division was called in to assist and Operation PAUL REVERE II began, later followed by III and IV.

The elite 1st Brigade of the 101st Airborne Division combined with the tough Korean 2d "Blue Dragon" Marine Brigade to protect the Tuy Hoa rice plains as the Korean Capital Division closed its last elements into Qui Nhon. In May, Brig. Gen. Willard Pearson's paratroopers scoured the vicinity around

Phan Thiet, but contacts were negligible. Minus a battalion (the 2d of the 327th Infantry operating around Tuy Hoa), the airborne brigade was moved west into Kontum Province to begin Operation HAWTHORNE on June 2. The brigade mission was to withdraw the Tou Morong Regional Force outpost back to Dak To.

The separate 24th NVA Regiment had the locality completely surrounded; a normal pullout was impossible. The 1st Battalion of the 327th Infantry (Airborne) was helicoptered northeast of Tou Morong, and the 1st Battalion of the 42d ARVN Regiment and the 21st ARVN Ranger Battalion fought past moderate resistance by June 6 to rescue the garrison and truck them out. This left the battalion of the 327th Infantry (Airborne) alone at the abandoned camp that evening, with a detached company and artillery battery farther out 2 1/2 miles away in the adjacent jungle.[6]

The detached company was commanded by Capt. William S. Carpenter, Jr., who in West Point had been an All-American football player nicknamed the Lonesome End. Beginning on the evening of June 6, his company was attacked with mortar and grenade fire, and waves of NVA regulars incessantly stormed his positions. The situation rapidly worsened and Captain Carpenter called in air strikes on his positions. Fighter-bombers streaked down to blast the jungle battlefield with rolling, exploding balls of napalm. Americans and North Vietnamese alike were singed and burned in the blazing inferno, but the NVA assault was defeated. By 8:45 on the morning of June 7, the NVA had pulled back.[7]

The rest of the 1st Battalion of the 327th Infantry (Airborne)

6. The 327th Infantry (Airborne) was the "Bastogne Bulldogs," a title officially bestowed by the Army in recognition of its defense of the encircled town of Bastogne during the German Ardennes counteroffensive in December 1944. It was considered one of the finest units in the United States Army. The 327th Infantry had been originally formed for World War I duty in September 1917, at Camp Gordon, Georgia, and served in the St. Mihiel, Meuse-Argonne, and Lorraine campaigns. It was reorganized in August 1942 as a glider infantry regiment, and after World War II as a paratrooper unit.

7. Capt. William S. Carpenter later received the Distinguished Service Cross, America's second-highest award for valor, for his heroism.

formed two columns and plunged into the twisted jungle to cut through to the isolated company. Immediately they ran into well-entrenched NVA soldiers. The 2d Battalion of the 502d Infantry (Airborne), in reserve at Dak To, was air-assaulted to the north and closed into the battlefield. To ensure better odds against the North Vietnamese regiment, the 1st Battalion of the 5th Cavalry and a provisional brigade paratrooper company were inserted into the action, as well as a rifle company from the 2d Battalion, 327th Infantry (Airborne), flown in from Tuy Hoa. Unrelenting combat continued against the tropical earthworks as the combined forces hacked through tangled undergrowth to take out NVA strong-points one at a time. A total of 463 air strikes were delivered around the clock.

Trimming safety margins to a bare minimum, thirty-six strategic B-52 bombing sorties were used. On June 13, the brigade dumped nine hundred CS gas grenades in the center of one North Vietnamese Army position. Then, for twenty-seven minutes B-52 bombers pounded the target with high explosive bombs, which shook the entire jungle with their earth-shattering detonations. Within thirty minutes after the last bomb fell, the brigade was on top of the NVA lines and finished the killing task with rifles and axes. On June 20, 1966, as NVA resistance crumbled and the regiment withdrew, Operation HAWTHORNE was ended.

The 1st Brigade, 101st Airborne Brigade, then turned its attention to coastal Phu Yen Province, securing the Vung Ro Bay vicinity during August and guarding the rice harvest around Tuy Hoa that September. Labeled Operations JOHN PAUL JONES and SEWARD, respectively, the latter would be marked by another company mishap. Operation SEWARD was typified by saturation patrolling through the mountainous jungles, rolling hills, sandy beaches, and rice paddies, and a lot of stay-behind night ambushing. On the night of September 17, the command post of Company B, 2d Battalion, 327th Infantry (Airborne) was suddenly overwhelmed by a surprise attack from an estimated VC company and overrun. Among the dead were the company commander, executive officer, and artillery observation officer.

Maj. Gen. John Norton took over the 1st Cavalry Division on May 6, 1966, as Operation DAVY CROCKETT was underway. It recombed the same area near Bong Son fought over in earlier Operation MASHER/WHITE WING. Again the NVA and VC offered resolute resistance, often entrenched or firing out of large, hardened clay anthills. This operation terminated May 16. The day previous, a local CIDG patrol had ambushed a Viet Cong mortar team, discovering plans for an attack against their Vinh Thanh Special Forces camp. Under threatening storm clouds the next day, the 2d Battalion of the 8th Cavalry air-assaulted its Company B into a patch of elephant grass on the highest nearby mountain. As it walked the ridgeline, the forward platoon suddenly had a squad overrun, and the company was rapidly engulfed in combat. Operation CRAZY HORSE had begun.

Capt. John D. Coleman's command group of Company B was also under fire as he tried to deploy more men to assist 3d Platoon, which was now in full retreat. Dead and wounded were all over the place, and local counterattacks to retrieve them were defeated by concentrated automatic weapons fire. A heavy downpour washed out the horizon, but two helicopters of the division's 2d Battalion, 20th Artillery, edged up the side of the mountain and discharged volleys of rockets just yards from the trapped company's collapsed perimeter. That broke the attack long enough for sister Company A to reach them after nightfall. Early next morning the position was blasted with recoilless rifle and grenade fire, and for two hours ground assaults closed the weakening lines. Only the approach of a relief column from Company C saved the force from ultimate annihilation.

The 1st Cavalry Division had entered the most difficult terrain in the province. Steep forest-cloaked mountains peaked to razor-backed summits three thousand feet above sea level. Helicopter landing zones were often suitable for only one craft at a time, and descents through the triple-canopy jungle resembled sudden elevator drops to the cavalrymen. Many insertions were made using Chinook helicopter Jacob's ladders. The big problem was determining how long such operations were beneficial. Though it was obvious the Viet Cong were there, the division would shut down the operation on June 5. Moving on to Kontum and Phu Yen Provinces, it would leave Binh Dinh Province until fall.

On September 18, the 1st Cavalry Division returned to Binh

Dinh Province. It commenced activities there in Operations THAYER I and II, and IRVING. The latter was aimed at clearing out the Phu Cat Mountain area, and the THAYER series kept pressure on the *5th NVA Division*. These operations would continue to spark heavy combat in Binh Dinh Province throughout the rest of 1966. One of the fiercest battles occurred when the *22d NVA Regiment* nearly overran the lst Cavalry Division's Landing Zone Bird on December 27.

Landing Zone Bird was established as an artillery support site southwest of Bong Son. It contained two howitzer batteries and a depleted company of infantry recovering from intense pre-Christmas combat.[8] The uneasy Christmas Truce of December 24–26 was spent with the knowledge that the NVA was planning something for immediately after the truce, and both batteries had been warned of impending attack. As a result, December 26 had been spent firing blindly at the surrounding palm trees in an effort to break up possible troop concentrations.

The North Vietnamese soldiers crawled up to edge of the landing zone's perimeter by evading two outposts, slicing the thin wires leading to command-detonated claymore mines, and silently defusing trip flares. At one o'clock on the rainy morning of December 27, they surged forward with fixed bayonets as a concentrated mortar barrage smothered the American positions under the swift impact of multiple explosions. The NVA quickly overran the cavalry lines and charged into the gun positions, where combat was hand-to-hand. Several howitzer crews were overpowered making last stands around their weapons, and the defenders were forced back to final defensive positions around the three remaining howitzers. At that point a battery executive officer fired two Beehive rounds point-blank into a dense throng of NVA preparing to charge.[9] That stopped the assault, and the North Vietnamese retreated as helicopters arrived overhead and began dropping flares.

8. Units stationed at LZ Bird were Battery C, 6th Battalion, 16th Artillery (155mm); Battery B, 2d Battalion, 19th Artillery (105mm); and Company C, 1st Battalion, 12th Cavalry.

9. The Beehive was a 105mm shell composed of 8,500 steel flechettes. Designed after the Korean War to stop massed infantry assaults, its powerful burst maimed and killed in a most devastating manner.

The action had lasted one hour, but LZ Bird was in shambles and losses had been severe. While all three units were later presented the Presidential Unit Citation in light of the remarkable valor displayed against overwhelming odds, larger questions of adequate security and preparation remained unsettled. The American Army ended its 1966 campaign on a somber note, and similar incidents continued to plague its performance for the duration of the Vietnam War. Military laxity and combat inexperience, the latter a product of the one-year tour policy, continued to invite surprise attack. In many such cases, total disaster was only averted by superior artillery munitions and readily available air support.

CHAPTER 8.

THE NORTHERN FRONT

1. The Marine Offensive

The Marine 1966 campaign was centered around the defense of the three northern I Corps Tactical Zone base enclaves of Chu Lai; Phu Bai, outside Hue; and Da Nang. The Marines were also actively engaged in combat operations in Quang Ngai Province just south of Chu Lai and, as more reinforcements arrived during the year, guarding the Demilitarized Zone in upper Quang Tri Province against North Vietnamese Army units moving south across the border. During the year the security of the Marine zone would be jeopardized by a large South Vietnamese uprising in I Corps Tactical Zone against the Saigon regime, and the loss of key Special Forces camps on the western frontier.

The Marines initiated the campaign from its Chu Lai base enclave, which was garrisoned by two reinforced regiments, the 4th Marines and the 7th Marines. The area surrounding Chu Lai was a Viet Cong stronghold and contained at least two North Vietnamese Army divisions, the *2d*, to the west, and the *3d*, to the south. The Marines assembled a three-battalion amphibious strike force to move into Quang Ngai Province just below Chu Lai in conjunction with the 2d ARVN Division. The operation was coded DOUBLE EAGLE. It was to be launched as part of MACV's converging efforts to entrap large NVA and VC forces in a vise between the Marines and the ongoing Army 1st Cavalry Division/22d ARVN Division operations in the next province to the south, Binh Dinh.

The battle started on the Marine front on January 10. The 1st Force Reconnaissance Company, searching the extremely rugged western portion of the upcoming operational area, fought a savage jungle action on Hill 829. As a result DOUBLE EAGLE was launched on the sullen, rainy, overcast day of January 28. Landing craft buffeted by heavy seas unloaded two Marine battalions on the rocky sand coast at Thach Tru, twenty miles south of Quang Ngai. Huge bow-doored LST landing ships nosed onto the beach in worsening weather as amtracs and dozers, half-buried by mounds of sand, struggled to discharge their cargo. Two days later the Marine Special Landing Force battalion was helicoptered off the rolling decks of the USS *Valley Forge* (LPH-8) into an old French fort five miles west of the beaches.[1]

The Marines moved inland through punji-filled gullies and steep forested slopes, their rain ponchos draped over flak vests. The operation was hampered by foul weather, which prohibited the widespread use of helicopters until it cleared toward the end of February. The ponchos disappeared. Sleeves were rolled up and extra canteens were strapped onto web belts. The Marines then split into helicopter search teams, which bounded from hilltop to hilltop, striking deep into suspected Viet Cong regions of southeastern Quang Ngai Province. Sniper fire was intermittent as the Marines toiled up grassy knolls, bent under the weight of mortar baseplates and tubes, recoilless rifles, and ammunition shells strapped to their packboards. At the beginning of March, after weeks of frustrating searches and few solid contacts, DOUBLE EAGLE was terminated.

The Marine enclave at Da Nang had been heavily mortared at the end of January. The Marines stationed at Phu Bai saw hard fighting barely a month later. A composite Marine battalion known as Task Unit Hotel (built around the 2d Battalion, 1st Marines) had been formed there as a special reserve for the

1. In the early years of Marine involvement in Vietnam, battalions from different regiments were often put together in composite task forces. The sea-landed battalions were the 3d Battalion, 1st Marines, and the 2d Battalion, 4th Marines. The 2d Battalion, 3d Marines, was serving as the Special Landing Force. Part of a fourth Marine battalion, the 2d Battalion of the 9th Marines, was moved in to search B-52 bomber strike areas after the weather cleared several days later.

1st ARVN Division in nearby Hue. On the evening of its activation, the division had scrambled the unit into an emergency night heliborne air assault on an objective that proved deserted. In less than twenty-four hours, on the night of February 27, the South Vietnamese were calling again for its immediate employment. A battalion of the 3d ARVN Regiment was in the thick of battle with the *810th VC Battalion* on "pacified" Phu Thu Peninsula, just outside Phu Bai, and needed help. The Marines, tired and hungry, had just returned to their base when they were alerted for a second night air assault. They wearily shuffled back to their helicopters, silhouetted in the glare of airfield floodlights. The mechanical birds lifted vertically into the darkness and then set down just two miles away under the illumination of multicolored flares. Operation NEW YORK was on.

It was two o'clock in the morning of February 28 as the Marines arrived on the battlefield. The South Vietnamese troops stepped aside; they were assigned blocking positions. The three Marine companies formed up in one frontal skirmish line and began moving across the peninsula's powdery sand, sparse grass, and pine barrens. The Marines on the right began taking sniper fire, which was mixed with a rising crescendo of mortars, machine guns, and rocket grenades. The Viet Cong, who were dug into strong defensive positions, held their fire until Marine squads had advanced nearly on top of them. Then they cut loose with a heavy dosage of bullets and grenades that sent the exhausted Marines into the dirt. The depleted groups of Marines returned fire, called in artillery and fighter-bombers, and slowly crawled forward to clean out the opposing weapons nests.

Bunker after bunker was methodically assaulted. The expertly camouflaged, earth-level logworks were arranged in a maze of mutually supporting positions, which often caught advancing Marines in lethal cross fires. The Marines discovered the bunkers extended to a depth equal to the length of two football fields. As the artificially lighted night faded into a murky, smoking dawn, the VC battalion withdrew. The operation dwindled to sporadic contacts as the peninsula was searched for another week.

The Marines began encountering North Vietnamese Army infantrymen in early March south of the Chu Lai base. Several Marine battalions were air-assaulted into Operation UTAH, northwest of Quang Ngai city, after South Vietnamese para-troopers had helicopters into a hot landing zone brisk with ma-chine-gun fire on March 4. More Marine and ARVN reinforce-ments finally forced the *36th NVA Regiment* to retreat after a hard two-day battle.[2]

Another battle, Operation TEXAS, was triggered on March 19 in the same area when the *1st VC Regiment* attacked the South Vietnamese Regional Force outpost of An Hoa, just fif-teen miles south of Chu Lai. Marine helicopters became in-volved immediately, delivering ARVN reinforcements and evac-uating wounded. By evening it appeared doubtful that An Hoa could hold through the night. Nevertheless, plans were made to reinforce the garrison with Marines and paratroopers at first light. After dawn on March 20, the 3d Battalion, 7th Marines, and the 5th ARVN Airborne Battalion were landed and went into action. When the Viet Cong started withdrawing, the 2d Battalion of the 4th Marines was quickly helicopters south of the fort to intercept. The VC were sandwiched between the al-lied units and largely decimated in the ensuing battle.

2. Trouble in I Corps Tactical Zone

The mobile Marine success in rapidly eliminating NVA/VC threats against vital areas on the northern front was countered by two crises in early spring. The most serious was caused by the South Vietnamese and imperiled all American efforts in the northern five provinces.

In April 1966, political violence and civil disorders erupted in Hue and Da Nang due to Premier Ky's dismissal of Major General Thi, the result of severely strained relations between Saigon and I Corps Tactical Zone. Near the large Marine bases there were riots, demonstrations, and confrontations between Vietnamese that verged on combat. Not far distant, South Viet-namese regular military units refused orders and exchanged fire with other South Vietnamese Army units. The 1st ARVN Di-vision, long considered the second-best division in Saigon's in-

---

2. Marines engaged, in order of insertion, were the 2d Battalion, 7th Ma-rines; 3d Battalion, 1st Marines; 2d Battalion, 4th Marines; 1st Battalion, 7th Marines; and a company of 2d Battalion, 7th Marines.

ventory (the Americans judged the ARVN Airborne Division as first), declared itself in sympathy with the antigovernment "struggle forces." To their shock and dismay, all United States advisors were pulled out. The division was out of the war for the time being. Divided South Vietnamese forces made moves and countermoves in the Da Nang vicinity. There was deep concern over the worsening situation at the highest levels in Washington.

On April 9, South Vietnamese planes struck a dissident mechanized column moving toward Da Nang. This reckless act infuriated the Americans; the vital United States military facility was surrounded by anti-Saigon ARVN troops. The Marines insisted that the airfield not be used for such purposes, and the South Vietnamese Air Force resentfully consented. Meanwhile, the mechanized column was blocked from moving its 155mm howitzers within range of the Da Nang air base by a Marine truck deliberately blocking the bridge. The South Vietnamese gunners broke out ammunition and started fusing rounds. Their commander, Col. Dam Quang Yeu, was told that if he fired on the airfield, he would endanger American lives and Marine artillery would fire on his artillery. By that time Marine rounds had been chambered and Marine F-8 Crusader jets were flying overhead. Colonel Yeu, a Harvard-educated officer very conversant in English, threatened to fire. Marine Captain Reckewell replied, "I'll see those 155s and raise you two F-8s." After about an hour the Vietnamese leveled two howitzers at the truck blocking the bridge instead. The Marines then aimed the recoilless rifles of two Ontos vehicles at the howitzers. After a brief but tense period, the ARVN gunners elevated their tubes. The incident was over.

The political turmoil continued to affect adversely all Marine operations throughout the next three months. The Marines took an active part in defusing a number of potential flash points as the troubled weeks continued. Ammunition dumps and bridges became scenes of standoffs which were only settled by Marine intervention. During the March–June crisis, the Marines evacuated American civilians once from Da Nang and twice from Hue.

Heavy street fighting costing hundreds of lives erupted in

Da Nang on May 12. That same day the new III MAF command headquarters was hit by eight South Vietnamese mortar rounds, wounding eight Marines. On May 21, the building was "accidentally" strafed by South Vietnamese aircraft. Six days later the United States Consulate in Hue was sacked and burned. These events proved to be the high-water marks of outward anti-American activity, and by June 19, continued organized resistance to the Saigon regime had collapsed.

The North Vietnamese also forced the abandonment of several Army Special Forces camps along the western border, and wrested control of the A Shau Valley from the allies. Although the Marines initially considered this setback an "Army problem," the NVA developed the remote region into an important staging base for strong incursions into the populated cities of I Corps Tactical Zone. MACV never regained control over the valley and in later years had to resort to massive raids contingent on favorable weather. Some of these became milestone battles of the Vietnam War.

The isolated A Shau Army Special Forces border surveillance camp was located two miles from Laos, in the southwestern corner of Thua Thien Province. It sat astride three major NVA infiltration routes leading east into the A Shau and A Loui valleys. The only inhabitants in the region were highly secretive and hostile Katu tribesmen. The camp and its Operations Detachment A-102 had always been in imminent danger. The South Vietnamese LLDB had already abandoned two nearby camps at A Loui and Ta Bat on December 8, 1965.

The A Shau Special Forces camp was surrounded by old minefields, long since overgrown by the dense, eight- and twelve-foot high elephant grass that covered the entire valley floor. Steep jungle-covered mountains towered above to disappear into a vault of rain-swollen clouds, the parting storms of the monsoon season. The camp was shrouded by thick ground fog in the mornings. Patrols and overflights detected increasing NVA buildup around the site, and the camp commander, Capt. John D. Blair IV, requested reinforcements. 5th Special Forces Group (Airborne) headquarters at Nha Trang dispatched a mobile strike force company, which was flown into the compound on March 7.

With them Captain Blair had exactly 434 people.[3]

In the morning darkness of March 9, just before 4 A.M., the camp was blanketed by a heavy and accurate mortar barrage which lasted for two and a half hours. The Special Forces team house, supply area, and water supply were blown to pieces. Communication was temporarily lost. Casualties had been heavy; a quick count tallied ten dead, including two Special Forces sergeants, and forty-seven wounded. Two companies of North Vietnamese regulars stormed the south wall a half hour after the mortaring started, but they had been quickly repulsed by heavy machine-gun fire. Sniper and mortar fire continued through the gloomy daylight.

Since A Shau was beyond the range of friendly artillery, the camp defenders had to rely on air support. Heavy antiaircraft fire and marginal visibility made this extremely difficult. An Air Force AC-47 "Puff the Magic Dragon" fire support plane was shot down in flames that day. Two light observation planes managed to fly through the low cloud ceiling to attempt an emergency ammunition resupply and medical evacuation. They took intense ground fire and were only able to get one wounded master sergeant out. Two UH-34 Marine helicopters also got into the camp, but one was hit in the oil line and crashed. The other Marine helicopter picked up the downed crew and managed to whisk them away to safety. Three resupply drops were made by CV-2 Caribou aircraft, but the parachutes drifted both inside and outside the camp. Recovery parties, braving constant automatic weapons fire, were only able to retrieve part of the precious water and ammunition that had fallen beyond the wire. Just before dark an Air Force CH-3 helicopter lifted out twenty-six more wounded.

The overcast night sky of March 10 was lit by continuous flares. Then, at four o'clock in the morning the camp received another pasting from extremely accurate mortar and close-in

3. The camp defense strength was 17 Army Special Forces members, 51 civilians, 6 LLDB, 7 interpreters, 143 indigenous Mike Force, and 210 CIDG. Of this total, 172 would be known dead, 248 missing or presumed dead, and the rest wounded. As the Katu tribesmen were all Viet Cong, Captain Blair's CIDG company members were not natives of the area.

57mm recoilless rifle fire. Most structures were leveled, and over half the defenders' mortars and machine guns were knocked out. One hour later, a massive NVA ground assault swept across the runway and onto the east wall. The south wall was hit at the same time. Many CIDG company irregulars manning the southeast corner of the perimeter suddenly turned their weapons on their Special Forces sergeants and other camp defenders. The Americans and Mike Force soldiers made a fighting withdrawal to the north wall and communications bunker, a hard three-hour struggle in which they fought hand to hand against both North Vietnamese regulars and former Vietnamese comrades.

Armed with machine guns, M16 rifles, and two mortars, the camp survivors defeated another mass attack on the bunker that came at 8:30 A.M. Captain Blair was forced to request bombing and strafing of the entire camp, including the American bunkered strong-point. Although a heavy volume of ground and mortar fire continued to blast the remaining Special Forces portion of the compound, the ground attacks stopped. The Special Forces and Mike Force soldiers then made several local counterattacks to regain the southern wall but were defeated. By afternoon it was apparent the camp was lost. The cornered defenders not only lacked the ability to retake lost areas, but their very survival was questionable. They had been without sleep, food, or water for thirty-six hours, and their ammunition was about out.

At three o'clock that afternoon Captain Blair decided A Shau would have to be abandoned. Marine helicopters made a harrowing rescue approach underneath the cloud bank and immediately came under intense ground fire. Two helicopters were shot out of the sky, and twenty-one of the twenty-four others were so badly shot up they later had to be scrapped.

An ugly episode awaited them on the ground. The South Vietnamese panicked, dropped their weapons, and stormed the descending helicopters, trampling over the wounded. The hysterical pack of Vietnamese reached the craft and started clawing and shoving among themselves to get on. One wounded American was yanked out of a helicopter and thrown to the ground. The Special Forces began clubbing them with rifle butts in order to restore order. Finally both Army Special Forces and Marine crewmen began firing into the mob. Sixty men were evacuated that day, including seven downed Marine airmen and one Special Forces defender.

The next morning the Marine helicopters returned to lift out more of the camp personnel. Another panic-stricken South Vietnamese dash ensued. It ended when one of them pitched a grenade into a mass of struggling fellow soldiers, killing ten in the explosion. By March 12, the rescue mission was over, having taken out 186, mostly wounded, defenders. Marine helicopters scouring the camp and vicinity for another few days could not locate any further survivors.

3. Guarding the DMZ

The Marines were soon forced to focus attention on the critical military situation developing along the Demilitarized Zone. In July the *324B NVA Division* moved across the Ben Hai River into Quang Tri, the northernmost province of South Vietnam. The thrust of Marine combat activity now shifted from the southern tip of Quang Ngai Province north to the DMZ almost 250 miles away. Guarding this region would become a prime Marine mission, with large conventional formations confronting each other in reference to a fixed battle line. During 1966 the Marines resorted to mobile fire brigade tactics, sending units into action in response to specific intrusions.

Both Quang Tri and Thua Thien provinces had been watched closely by the Marines for over a year. Rumors of large North Vietnamese Army formations infiltrating across the Demilitarized Zone had always been rampant, but evidence was lacking. After weeks of combat scouting by the 3d Reconnaissance Battalion, intelligence and captured documents confirmed the actual presence of the NVA division. The Marines established a large forward base at Dong Ha on Route 9 and then helicoptered forces into Cam Lo, near the seven-hundred-foot pinnacle of the Rock Pile. Six Marine and five ARVN battalions were propelled by sea and air into Operation HASTINGS, the largest combined offensive of the Vietnam War up to that time.

Inside the twin-rotored Marine CH-46 helicopters approaching the Ngan River, rows of Marines adjusted helmet chin straps and equipment belts, and rechecked watches. They were from the 2d and 3d Battalions of the 4th Marines.[4] It was nearly eight o'clock in the morning on July 15. Preceding them, Marine F-4 Phantom and A-4 Skyhawk aircraft made their final napalm bombing and strafing runs over the landing zones.

The helicopters began descending into the Ngan Valley. As they set down, two collided, their blades spinning off to slice Marines in half as they scrambled out. Another helicopter smashed into a tree and yet another was suddenly flamed by ground fire. The place was christened Helicopter Valley. The 3d Battalion pushed slowly through dense jungle and elephant grass in the sweltering tropical humidity. Company K was repulsed assaulting across the Song Be River, surrounded during the night and hit hard by repeated NVA ground assaults. For two days the two battalions relied on close Marine air strikes as heavy combat continued.

On the afternoon of July 28, the Marines were leaving the valley. Foxholes had been filled in. Engineers, protected by Company K, were preparing to blow up the downed helicopters. Suddenly, after a brief but furious mortar barrage, a massed one thousand-man NVA human wave assault hit the Marines. Bugles rang through the air as hundreds of soldiers charged forward. Company K machine gunners and riflemen fired as fast as they could. The Marines could see banners falling above the tall grass as North Vietnamese flag bearers ran into the hail of bullets.

Suddenly the khaki-clothed NVA infantrymen were in the Marine lines. Groups of bypassed Marines fell back in fire-team clusters that blazed a bloody pathway through swarms of NVA

---

4. The 4th Marines were known as the China Marines, one of America's most colorful regiments. Formed in response to the 1914 Mexican Revolution, the 4th Marine Regiment had been hurled into the Dominican Republic Civil War and then used as a special western U.S. Mail Guard force during the robbery epidemic of 1926. It was sent to Shanghai, China, the next year where it served until November 1941, becoming forever linked with guard duty at the American settlement and along the international barricades. The regiment was lost soon afterward at Bataan as Japanese forces captured the Philippine Islands. Reraised from the crack 1st Raider Regiment in February 1944, the 4th Marines stormed Guam and fought on Okinawa. The regiment had been stationed at Kaneohe Bay, Hawaii, for ten years previous to its arrival in Vietnam in 1965.

regulars, cutting down North Vietnamese officers who were blowing whistles and shouting orders. Company K bayoneted, clubbed, and shot its way back while carrying its wounded. Marine dead had to be left where they fell. Company L doubled back to provide covering fire from high ground. The Marines called in artillery fire and directed napalm as close as fifty feet away to drive the NVA off. After a four-hour battle the rear guard Marines managed to retreat and join the two-battalion perimeter of the 4th Marines. Helicopter Valley was abandoned.

After the battle of July 28, the operation continued in a series of hill fights and smaller skirmishes. Three more Marine battalions had reinforced the battleground, while the Seventh Fleet Special Landing Force secured the eastern seaward flank.[5] All these battalions saw considerable action, and HASTINGS was ended on August 3 as further contacts with the *324B NVA Division* faded out. Three Marine battalions remained in the area to guard against reentry, and the North Vietnamese division attacked again. The battle went into a second round, which the Marines named Operation PRAIRIE.

As action intensified in early September, the Marines added a fourth battalion to the PRAIRIE forces, increased their reconnaissance efforts, and again requested that the east flank be secured by amphibious assault. On September 16, 1966, the Special Landing Force, the 1st Battalion of the 26th Marines, reinforced by the 3d Reconnaissance Battalion, made heavy contact after coming ashore. The battle raged for seven days in the Cua Viet River valley just south of the DMZ. North Vietnamese Army fortifications, consisting of covered trenches, bunkers, and tunnels, were reduced by ground assault; air, artillery, and naval gunfire; and direct fire from tanks. On one occasion three Marine companies launched a coordinated attack under a rolling barrage to envelop an NVA company. The Special Landing Force drove the NVA back across the Ben Hai River and the Marines reembarked on their warships on September 25.

For the other battalions involved in Operation PRAIRIE, the

5. The Special Landing Force, composed of the 3d Battalion, 5th Marines, landed at Pho Hai. The 1st Marines sent in its 2d Battalion on July 16 and 1st Battalion on July 20. The 1st Battalion, 3d Marines, was committed on July 22.

latter half of September would be marked by violent battles ranging far into central and western Quang Tri. Maneuvering by helicopter and by foot, the Marines systematically isolated North Vietnamese groups defending well-prepared strong-points. One of the fiercest battles was the attack on Nui Cay Tre, defended by elements of the *324B NVA Division*. The hill was nicknamed Mutter's Ridge by the Marines. On September 8, the 1st Battalion of the 4th Marines had just returned from Dong Ha to the Rockpile, where it relieved the 2d Battalion, 7th Marines, on line. On September 15, two of the 4th Marines companies moved out in column toward the ridgeline, with Company D at the front.

Suddenly an ambush caught Company D halfway through its file. Men went down in a burst of grenade and automatic weapons fire. Other Marine platoons were shoved desperately into the fight as Companies B and D formed a defensive circle, dug in, and tried to carve out a landing zone. Captain McMahon radioed back, "We have 'em just where we want them, they're all around us!" The 2d Battalion of the 7th Marines managed to link up with the two companies on September 18, two and a half days later.

Mutter's Ridge itself was assaulted on September 22. The 3d Battalion of the 4th Marines was helicoptered in to the east and struggled for days through dank, vine-tangled triple-canopy jungle as it approached the heights. Bamboo forests rose to mingle with trees eight feet in diameter, forming a solid ceiling of vegetation, which choked off sunlight. The Marines of point companies K and L had discarded all equipment except for their rifle, two canteens, one poncho, and socks stuffed with canned rations, which were crammed into their pockets. Working their way up the steep jungled slopes against dogged NVA rear-guard resistance, the Marines managed to secure part of the ridge by September 26.

Company K was counterattacked as it continued the advance on the morning of September 27. North Vietnamese infantrymen surged downhill into its lines. The Marines dropped behind bomb-blasted tree trunks, clinging onto branches to keep from slipping downhill themselves, and opened up at point-blank range. NVA riflemen tumbled down into the gulleys. Twisted clumps of scorched foliage broke their fall down the sheer slopes. Grenades careened down, bouncing madly into the air to spin into the Marine positions and explode. Machine guns tore splinters out of tattered logs and pitched them through bodies like wooden stakes. Marines draped with belts of ammunition fed chains of bullets into their machine guns, which were propped up at dizzy angles in order to fire uphill. After an hour of hard fighting the groups of NVA soldiers pulled back to their reinforced bunkers, which were built flush into the ground.

Heavy fighting continued for days as the Marines worked their way up the higher hills composing Mutter's Ridge, using a wall of advancing artillery to shield their methodical advance. On October 4, Company M of the 3d Battalion, 4th Marines, carried the crest of Mutter's Ridge in a sharp fight that ended at 1:30 that afternoon. The ridge was secured, but Operation PRAIRIE would continue into 1967.

Marine operations along the Demilitarized Zone in 1966 had been characterized by a number of small unit engagements, with occasional large encounters. Well-trained and determined North Vietnamese regulars were pitted against Marine assault troops in locked combat. In each case the Marines had sent their NVA opponents retreating north with heavy losses into areas safe from pursuit. There they regrouped with fresh manpower and equipment before recrossing into South Vietnam. This pattern set the tone of the DMZ campaign, which would engage the Marines in continual combat until their departure from Vietnam.

PART 3

1967

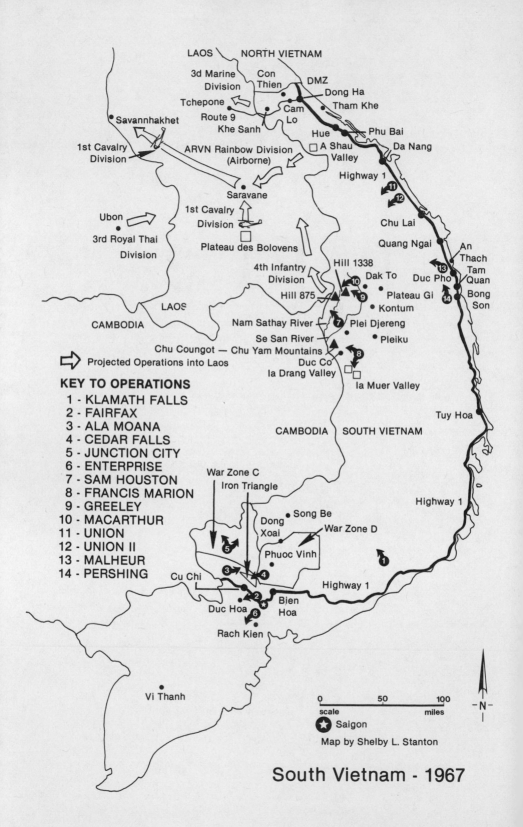

South Vietnam - 1967

LAOS   NORTH VIETNAM

3d Marine Division
Con Thien
DMZ
Dong Ha
Tham Khe
Tchepone
Route 9
Cam Lo
Khe Sanh
Hue
Phu Bai
Da Nang
Savannhakhet
1st Cavalry Division
ARVN Rainbow Division (Airborne)
A Shau Valley
Highway 1
Ubon
3rd Royal Thai Division
Saravane
1st Cavalry Division
Plateau des Bolovens
Chu Lai
Quang Ngai
An Thach
Tam Quan
4th Infantry Division
Hill 1338
Dak To
Duc Pho
Bong Son
Hill 875
Plateau Gi
Kontum
LAOS
Nam Sathay River
Plei Djereng
CAMBODIA
Se San River
Pleiku
Chu Coungot — Chu Yam Mountains
Duc Co
Ia Drang Valley
Ia Muer Valley
Tuy Hoa
CAMBODIA   SOUTH VIETNAM

Projected Operations into Laos

KEY TO OPERATIONS
1 - KLAMATH FALLS
2 - FAIRFAX
3 - ALA MOANA
4 - CEDAR FALLS
5 - JUNCTION CITY
6 - ENTERPRISE
7 - SAM HOUSTON
8 - FRANCIS MARION
9 - GREELEY
10 - MACARTHUR
11 - UNION
12 - UNION II
13 - MALHEUR
14 - PERSHING

War Zone C
Iron Triangle
Dong Xoai
Song Be
War Zone D
Phuoc Vinh
Highway 1
Cu Chi
Highway 1
Duc Hoa
Bien Hoa
Rach Kien
Vi Thanh

0   50   100
scale   miles

⭐ Saigon

Map by Shelby L. Stanton

— N

South Vietnam - 1967

CHAPTER 9.

THE YEAR OF THE BIG BATTLES

1. 1967 Command Performance

The new year arrived on a rising flood tide of American ground forces that had already tasted blood in the limited country-wide battles of 1966. These had culminated in the multibrigade November confrontation in Tay Ninh Province during Operation ATTLEBORO. MACV already visualized that engagement as providing the key to large-scale destruction of North Vietnamese Army and Viet Cong main force units, and forged jumbo operational plans as the dominant pattern of strategy for the upcoming year.

After a decade of military advisors to South Vietnam lamenting the absence of "just one good American battalion" during a multitude of preintervention battles between the ARVN and VC, General Westmoreland now had seven United States divisions, two paratrooper and two light infantry brigades, one armored cavalry regiment, and a reinforced Special Forces group.[1] Two and a half Korean divisions and one mixed Australian-New

1. The U.S. 1st and 3d Marine, 1st Cavalry, 1st, 4th, 9th, and 25th Infantry Divisions, the 1st Brigade of the 101st Airborne Division and the 173d Airborne Brigade, the 196th and 199th Infantry Brigades (Light), the 11th Armored Cavalry Regiment, and the 5th Special Forces Group (Airborne).

133

Zealand force added another excellent boost in combat power.[2] The burgeoning South Vietnamese forces included eleven divisions, a number of separate units, and a welter of territorial forces, police forces, and the like.[3] He hoped to fuse this polyglot military command into a blade honed to a fighting edge of American units. The very design of the MACV shoulder patch, which consisted of a white-bladed sword thrusting upwards through a red field to pierce a yellow wall, incorporated this symbolism.[4] General Westmoreland confidently looked forward to wielding this multitudinous force to open Highway 1, campaign along Vietnam's borders, neutralize War Zone C, disrupt War Zone D, eradicate the Iron Triangle, force NVA and main force VC contingents away from populated areas "into a vulnerable posture," and police the South Vietnamese population. 1967 would be the year of the big battles.

II Field Force Vietnam, the headquarters with geographical responsibility for that slice of country including the targeted war zones and triangle area, planned to begin with a major excursion into War Zone C. After some last-minute wrangling over objective areas, and against the advice of his 1st Infantry Division commander, Lieutenant General Jonathan O. Seaman substituted a preliminary thrust into the Iron Triangle January 8–26. Dubbed Operation CEDAR FALLS, it represented the first corps-sized American mission of the war as well as the first ma-

2. The Korean Capital and 9th Infantry divisions and 2d Marine Brigade, and the 1st Australian Task Force with a New Zealand artillery battery.

3. The South Vietnamese regular military in July 1967 consisted of the Airborne, 1st, 2d, 5th, 7th, 9th, 18th, 21st, 22d, 23d, and 25th Divisions, 42d Infantry Regiment (detached) and 51st Infantry Regiment (separate), Marine Brigade (six marine and one artillery battalions), Palace Guard (Brigade), 1st–10th Armored Cavalry Groups (redesignated from squadrons May 1 but still battalion-sized), twenty ranger battalions (11th, 21st–23d, 30th–39th, 41st–44th, 51st, 52d), six separate artillery battalions (34th–39th), and the LLDB Command.

4. The pattern and colors of the MACV command insignia had been carefully chosen. They also reflected early American military sentiments; the implications of "red" communist hordes and the "yellow" wall of China being blatantly represented.

jor combined U.S.-ARVN operation involving formal planning.[5] While defoliants, bombings, and land-clearing Rome Plow dozers carved an extensive network of pioneer approaches for future area access, this ephemeral foray was insufficient to jeopardize continued Viet Cong utilization.

Operation JUNCTION CITY, the move against War Zone C, was supposed to follow immediately on the heels of Operation CEDAR FALLS, but got off a month late. Finally begun on February 22, it was planned to remedy the deficiencies of its predecessor. To eliminate a repetition of the Viet Cong escape apparently managed through the cordon around the Iron Triangle, South Vietnamese presence was reduced (only four ARVN battalions being trusted to participate). To ensure more lasting and destructive results, it became a far larger and more ambitious search and destroy operation, lasting a quarter of the year.

The militarily successful results of JUNCTION CITY had disturbing long-range strategic consequences. Aware that the inviolability of their base areas in South Vietnam had evaporated, the main force Viet Cong began moving their supply depots and headquarters into adjacent Cambodian sanctuaries. Instead of pushing the NVA/VC into the "vulnerable posture," as MACV had envisioned, the *9th VC Division* had simply been pushed into Cambodia, where it was immune to any attack whatsoever. It joined the NVA division base areas already firmly entrenched along the Laotian and Cambodian sides of the Vietnamese border,. where refurbishment could be effected unimpeded.

Rules of engagement for Cambodia and Laos remained stringent. While the Pentagon gave MACV permission to fire artillery against valid military targets inside Laos beginning February 23, only in emergency situations requiring force preservation could U.S. troops maneuver into these nations, and no Cambodian village or populated area could be attacked regardless.

Both during and after the Vietnam War some senior officers felt that MACV should have been allowed the strategic ability

5. South Vietnamese participation in CEDAR FALLS consisted of the 1st Airborne Brigade, elements of the 5th Division's 7th and 8th Regiments, and one ranger battalion.

to pursue opposing conventional forces to their destruction, preventing their reappearance on South Vietnamese territory. Under the circumstances MACV remained hopelessly mired in a defensive campaign with the negative aim of wearing the NVA and main force VC units down through attrition. The larger parameters of the conflict had been fixed by American governmental policy, and the United States military was limited to a ground war within the geographical boundaries of South Vietnam until 1970.[6]

Plans for sealing South Vietnam off from northern attack altogether had been in the works for years, as well as various plans for far-reaching ground operations into adjoining countries. In 1966 General Westmoreland had considered planting the 1st Cavalry Division on the Bolovens Plateau of Laos for a drive north toward Saravane and then on to Savannhakhet, while the 3d Marine Division headed due west along Highway 9 into Tchepone (the later route of the ill-fated ARVN drive into Laos during Operation LAMSON 719 in 1971), and the 4th Infantry Division and an ARVN division pushed into Laos from Pleiku and the A Shau Valley. On October 27, he began forming the reinforced ARVN "Rainbow Division," based on a nucleus of the ARVN Airborne Division, for employment against Laos in case permission was granted for a South Vietnamese incursion with the change of presidential administrations foreseen in 1968. Another contingency plan was produced for a Laotian invasion involving a Thai division from the west and two ARVN divisions and one U.S. division from the east. All these plans came to naught, until the 1970s.

6. Larger strategic questions are considered from a military standpoint by Gen. Dave Richard Palmer, *Summons of the Trumpet,* Presidio Press, Novato, California, 1978; and Col. Harry G. Summers, Jr., *On Strategy: A Critical Analysis of the Vietnam War,* Presidio Press, Novato, California, 1982. An interesting theoretical military solution to the war proposed by Gen. Bruce Palmer, Jr., former deputy commander of U.S. Army, Vietnam, is presented on p. 76 of the latter work. It proposed a tactical offensive along the DMZ across Laos to tie into U.S. positions in Thailand, thus isolating South Vietnam from NVA intrusion. This was claimed as possible without mobilizing reserves or invading North Vietnam, thus avoiding the risk of Chinese intervention. The logistical reality of this plan and whether it would have entailed indefinite American defensive presence, as still exists on the Korean DMZ thirty years after that war, are not discussed.

Although the United States was unable to follow retreating or staging North Vietnamese forces into neighboring lands, neither could the NVA or VC divisions remain indefinitely in other countries if victory was to be pursued inside South Vietnam. In this manner MACV's powerful army—well endowed with the wings of airmobility—became committed to ranging throughout the country in an effort to defeat the NVA/VC wherever their forces could be found.

The general MACV doctrine of employment tied American divisions and brigades to specific geographical areas inside South Vietnam, which were called tactical areas of responsibility. Whenever a major operation such as JUNCTION CITY packed several of these formations into a given locality, especially for any duration, it drew them away from their normal assignments and exacerbated difficulties elsewhere.[7] An expanded war of big battalions seeking out NVA divisions inside South Vietnam required exploiting forces of tremendous flexibility, which could respond and "pile on" top of contacts. As 1967 began there was only one airmobile division capable of delivering such concentrated punch, the 1st Cavalry Division. Although envisioned as a country-wide exploiting force, the deteriorating situation around Khe Sanh had forced its deployment north beginning in October. The commander of MACV wanted a second airmobile division to back it up.

2. A Matter of Muscle

Defense Secretary Robert S. McNamara still favored forming a second airmobile division either by converting the remainder of the 101st Airborne Division at Fort Campbell, Kentucky (its 1st Brigade was already in Vietnam), converting an infantry division in Vietnam, or bringing together three infantry brigades there. On April 18, 1967, General Westmoreland decided against converting the 9th Infantry Division, preferring to make a triphibian division out of it (consisting of one brigade of three riverine battalions, one brigade of two mechanized battalions, and

7. The MACV formula for neutralization of war zones required massing 25–30 battalions in "sustained operations," but competing requirements for available units did not permit long-term operations of such magnitude.

one brigade of four airmobile-capable infantry battalions). The 101st was selected to be this second airmobile division but lack of aviation resources postponed the full transition until July of 1969, by which time the war in Vietnam had regressed to enclave security.

As 1967 began, the III Marine Amphibious Force had its 3d Marine Division around Phu Bai and the 1st Marine Division divided between Da Nang and Chu Lai. The Korean 2d Marine Brigade had been moved to III MAF control on September 1, 1966, and was presently reinforcing the Chu Lai sector. As more Army forces were moved into the southern portion of I Corps Tactical Zone the Marines concentrated their forces in the northernmost three provinces for the DMZ campaign.

The Pacific command reserve in the western Pacific consisted of the two Special Landing Forces of the 7th Fleet. Each was composed of a Marine Battalion Landing Team and a Marine helicopter squadron, and their versatile striking power had been used to conduct forty-four amphibious landings along the South Vietnamese coast by the end of September 1967. However, the Special Landing Forces were also charged with maintaining the ability to respond to contingencies anywhere in the western Pacific Ocean area. After a special landing force amphibiously assaulted Vietnam and completed its mission there, it would return to sea and resume its readiness posture.

The 26th Regimental Landing Team from Camp Pendleton and Twenty-Nine Palms, California, had reconstituted the two-battalion 9th Marine Amphibious Brigade at Okinawa in this status on August 21, 1966. This also enabled resumption of the intratheater battalion rotation system. In April of 1967 its battalions were directed to Vietnam. To provide a controlling regimental headquarters, the headquarters of the 26th Marines was airlifted to Da Nang on April 25 and attached to the 3d Marine Division the next day. On May 16, 1967, it was announced that the Marine intratheater battalion rotation system was again suspended.

To further facilitate Marine buildup along the DMZ, in April the Army formed Task Force Oregon to secure the southern portion of I Corps Tactical Zone. However, this stripped the Army of its II CTZ mobile fire brigade, the 1st Brigade of the

101st Airborne Division. General Westmoreland dispatched the 173d Airborne Brigade to Pleiku on May 24 to fill its place, with the understanding that it could not be committed to action without his permission. That came soon enough, and the 173d would be consumed in the frightful Battles of the Highlands and Dak To before the year was out.

In the meantime the Army was still experiencing great difficulty in prying soldiers out of rear echelons and replacing losses in line units. A MACV survey of its divisions found each comfortably above authorized strength but the number of foxhole infantry in combat companies at critically low levels. The 1st Cavalry Division's 920-man battalions were commonly fielding less than 550 men, and rifle companies were persistently short at least a third of their allowances.

The South Vietnamese Army was plagued with grave desertion and leadership problems, but the massive introduction of American troops and material was shoring up belief in ultimate victory. As a result its forces began to exhibit better battlefield performances, and by May of 1967 U.S. advisors were rating 148 out of 153 battalions as combat-effective. During that month the 2d ARVN Ranger Group conducted an airmobile operation deep into the rugged jungles of central Vietnam, a feat U.S. advisors considered an impossibility just six months earlier.

In the fall, the 1st ARVN Division's 2d Regiment was retrained to take over a portion of the DMZ defensive line. Farther south in Phuoc Long Province, the 3d Battalion of the 9th ARVN Regiment successfully staved off a midnight attack by the *88th NVA Regiment* at Song Be on October 27. Two days later half of Loc Ninh fell, but reinforcements from the previously lackluster 5th ARVN Division managed to pin the Viet Cong in close combat. The 1st Infantry Division was called in and battled through adjacent plantations and dense scrub brush, where the soldiers of "The Big Red One" defeated the VC several days later.

In Vietnam's delta region, the 21st ARVN Division launched an attack up the Kinh O Mon Canal near Vi Thanh in Chuong Thien Province on December 8. Supported by Air Force AC-47 Spooky gunships and plenty of artillery, the division and its attached 42d, 43d, and 44th ARVN Ranger Battalions distinguished themselves in a spectacular battle. As a result MACV decided to reward them with special recognition—they would receive priority on issuance of the M16 rifle.

3. The 101st Airborne Division Flies In

As 1967 came to a close, General Westmoreland, very optimistic about the war's progress, became concerned about the possibility of an extended holiday moratorium over the 1968 New Year which might result in an agreement between North Vietnam and the United States freezing force levels. Before he left in November for a public relations pitch in the United States, he wanted the 101st Airborne Division's deployment to Vietnam accelerated. On October 21, McNamara approved special aerial flights to get the rest of the division in country as fast as possible.

Maj. Gen. Olinto M. Barsanti's 101st Airborne Division had been originally scheduled for departure to Vietnam in June of 1968. Located on the rugged post of Fort Campbell, Kentucky, five miles north of Clarksville, Tennessee, on the state line, it had fielded a brigade in Vietnam since July 1965. The 101st Airborne Division enjoyed a glorious heritage of tough paratrooper action on the battlefields of France and Germany in World War II, as well as a close personal connection with General Westmoreland, who had commanded the division in 1958. The division insignia consisted of the famous Screaming Eagle shield, over which a black tab was arched with AIRBORNE lettered in gold.

When Barsanti received notification on August 2 that the entire division would go over, the 101st was hardly more than a cadre-level nucleus feeding replacements to Vietnam-based parachutist brigades. It was located on two separate areas of Fort Campbell. Just to fill its two remaining brigades to 75 percent strength would require more than forty-five hundred men. The bulk of enlisted filler personnel would have to come from regular Third Army assets; there was no way to get more paratroopers. A series of dispatches kept moving up the division's deployment date, compressing an already tight schedule.

The battalions were filling up quite unevenly. There was considerable noncooperation from other commands tasked to send personnel to help fill the division. More last-minute frustration resulted when the Army suddenly levied the division for 450 emergency paratrooper replacements for the 173d Airborne Brigade. These were urgently needed due to that unit's losses in the Battle of Dak To. The division was unable to meet its projected deployment strength, but it was going anyway.

MACV meanwhile had tasked the 1st Infantry Division as its sponsor. The lead brigade of the 101st Airborne Division into Vietnam was planned to go to Phuoc Vinh, and the second to arrive would go to Dong Xoai. However, the 1st Infantry Division couldn't open the road between the two towns. It was decided to switch the 2d Brigade to Bien Hoa, and truck it to Cu Chi for in-country training there instead. In view of the changes, Major General Barsanti now wanted his projected command post location changed to Bien Hoa. When the last troop-crammed planes arrived on December 19, 1967, the division was scattered from Bien Hoa to Phuoc Vinh to Cu Chi, while its 1st Brigade was off on Operation KLAMATH FALLS in Binh Thuan and Lam Dong provinces a hundred miles away.

CHAPTER 10.

BATTLE FOR THE SAIGON APPROACHES

1. Saigon Defense and "Iron Triangle" Attack

The 199th Infantry "Redcatchers" Brigade began patrolling the villages and hamlets around Saigon during January 1967. Small-scale airmobility and river transport gave the brigade ability to seal off villages and search them, sweep around the flat countryside, and check roads and waterways. However, the brigade activities were often typified by nothing bigger than extensive night ambushing. The emphasis was on magic words such as "revolutionary development" and "pacification," techniques more suited for the South Vietnamese government than for American combat units designed to combat the North Vietnamese Army and main force Viet Cong. The smattering of ARVN airborne, marine, and ranger battalions in the area were tasked to help out. This assistance was given another fancy catchword, "the double force," which meant that for every U.S. unit engaged in operations, a similiar-sized ARVN unit was also supposed to be shouldering the load.

The 5th ARVN Ranger Group was given new M16 rifles and American food, promised a lot of help from artillery and aircraft, and shoved outside the city gates. The whole thing was called Operation FAIRFAX, and it lasted throughout the year, phasing in the South Vietnamese as the primary participants that November. The first test came soon enough. On the night of May 14, a battalion command post of the 50th ARVN Regiment was overrun by the Viet Cong. The 3d Battalion of the 7th Infantry had to conduct an airmobile assault to retake the compound. The resulting "battle" lasted for the next two days, netting a total of twelve VC killed. Things were so shaky that a combined force had to be inserted into Tan Binh during a bold night airmobile operation on May 20 to protect the western approaches to the sprawling Tan Son Nhut Air Base. From May 24 to 28 these forces searched through the pineapple area of western Binh Chanh, destroying empty bunkers and killing less than a dozen Viet Cong. An antisampan offensive was conducted next.

The brigade found the duty routine, the results elusive, and any surprises invariably unpleasant. On the afternoon of August 7, Company E from the 4th Battalion of the 12th Infantry, and a 30th ARVN Ranger Battalion company, jointly air-assaulted into Nhi Binh in the Hoc Mon district. Upon landing, they were hit by rifle and automatic weapons fire from a Viet Cong company of the 2d Local Force Battalion concealed in bunkers and spider holes around the landing zone. The VC concentrated their fire on the hovering helicopters, damaging seventeen and destroying two. Each battalion sent in reinforcements, which reached the area that evening. Brigade companies ended up spending six days clearing out a forty-man VC contingent. In this slow and imperturbable manner the 199th Infantry Brigade continued its operations outside Saigon. The lethargic pace was one the attached ARVN forces could keep up with, and on September 24 the brigade parted ways with the 5th ARVN Ranger Group and each returned to independent sweeps. On December 14, the South Vietnamese took over responsibility completely.

The 199th Infantry Brigade's joint 1967 effort with the ARVN Rangers was one of the earliest experiments in what was to become known two years later as Vietnamization. The brigade's dual task, training South Vietnamese soldiers to defend Saigon and ferreting the Viet Cong out of densely populated areas without undue civilian damage, all under the immediate command scrutiny of MACV, was immensely difficult. The brigade must be given due credit for good performance under such trying circumstances. However, the main objective—enabling the South

Vietnamese to defend their own capital—was never attained.
General Westmoreland was in too much of a hurry to get the
199th out of the camera's eye so that he could claim the 5th
ARVN Ranger Group responsible for Saigon defense. Only one
month after the 199th left the South Vietnamese totally in charge,
Saigon was subjected to major Viet Cong infiltration and attack
during Tet-68. Unfortunately, MACV never learned from this
early failure at putting the ARVN forces in charge of their own
territory. Later the same inadequate combat familiarization cycles,
teaming up other American formations with counterpart ARVN
units, were repeated in rushed programs aimed at token satis-
faction of political pressure to "Vietnamize" the war.

The 25th Infantry Division was busy trying to keep the Viet
Cong away from the rice-producing areas adjacent to the "Ho
Bo" and Boi Loi Woods, an operation begun on the first of De-
cember, 1966, and coded ALA MOANA in fitting tribute to the
Tropic Lightning Division's Hawaiian home. By the first of the
year, the action had shifted to Duc Hoa in Hau Nghia Province.
On February 26, its 4th Battalion, 9th Infantry, and the divi-
sional reconnaissance squadron, the 3d Squadron of the 4th
Cavalry, ran into a tough fight in the Filhol Rubber Plantation.
However, larger events in the area would soon overshadow these
events.

General Westmoreland was going after bigger game. Two
Army divisions, one infantry and one paratrooper brigade, and
one armored cavalry regiment prepared to assault the fortified
Viet Cong sanctuary known as the Iron Triangle. Located fairly
close to Saigon itself, this sixty square-mile chunk of territory
was interspersed with dense forests and wet, open rice lands.
The area had been dominated by the Viet Cong since anyone
could remember, and previous efforts to uproot them had failed.
This time it was determined that systematic destruction of
everything in the Iron Triangle might do the trick. The entire
civilian population was to be evacuated, and twenty thousand
air-dropped leaflets advised them to leave.

The "Iron Triangle" was generally bounded by the winding
Saigon River, Thanh Dien Forest of Binh Duong Province, and
the Song Thi Thinh River. The plan was to move the 25th Infantry Division and 196th Infantry Brigade against the Saigon

River to form an anvil. The 1st Infantry Division, 173d Airborne Brigade, and the 11th Armored Cavalry Regiment would then crash right through the Iron Triangle from its eastern side, splitting it in two, and hammer the enemy against the anvil. The operation was dubbed CEDAR FALLS. The *9th Viet Cong Division* simply eluded the area during the mass American sweep, rather than get hammered against anything. However, several significant underground complexes they left behind were uncovered.

The weather was most favorable in January. For four days Air Force B-52 bombers devastated the region. On January 8, twenty battalions moved into the Iron Triangle. Operation CEDAR FALLS had begun. The elite paratroopers of the 173d Airborne Brigade and the famed 3d "Iron Brigade" of the 1st Infantry Division spearheaded the drive, looking for action. The key Viet Cong fortified village of Ben Suc was the first target.

In the darkness of early morning, January 8, a sergeant from the 1st Aviation Battalion stood on the Dau Tieng airstrip, armed with an oversized flashlight and two baton lights. He waved his beacons and directed the landing, loading, and lift-out of sixty troop-packed helicopters and their ten armed gunship escorts. In an airmobile move timed to the second, he safely got all of them into the air by 7:25 A.M. With twenty minutes allocated to form two giant V formations, each containing three flights of ten helicopters, pilots jockeyed their craft over, under, and between the other ships. The helicopters were less than fifty feet apart. Then the massed flight headed toward Ben Suc.

The helicopters, loaded with soldiers of Lt. Col. Alexander M. Haig's 1st Battalion, 26th Infantry, roared over the forests at treetop level. Skipping the usual preparatory bombardment to achieve surprise, they landed in the midst of the village and cordoned it off. The Viet Cong were too stunned to react, though the unit suffered losses from sniper fire and minefields. A thorough search of the hamlet uncovered a massive supply complex. Three levels of carefully concealed storage rooms were discovered under some houses. Chinook helicopters and South Vietnamese patrol boats dragged the six thousand villagers away, and the 1st Engineer Battalion bulldozed their dwellings into the ground. Viet Cong continued to pop out of the tunnel networks and were taken prisoner. The first objective of Operation CEDAR FALLS had been accomplished—Ben Suc had ceased to exist.

The rest of the 1st and 25th infantry divisions sealed off the other legs of the Iron Triangle. Then the armored personnel carriers and tanks of the 11th Armored Cavalry Regiment plunged west from Ben Cat; the hammer had swung into action. They were beefed up by advancing paratroopers of the 173d Airborne Brigade, one company of which was riding captured VC bicycles found in a cache. Both within the Iron Triangle and on its fringes, soldiers of most participating units were stumbling across increasing amounts of stored supplies, base complexes, and tunnels. Numerous small skirmishes ensued. The 25th Infantry Division swept along the Saigon River, pushing down its waters in open boats. They probed darkened shores with searchlights and raked riverbanks with machine-gun fire.

On January 19, along the banks of the Rach Son stream near a rubber plantation, soldiers of the 1st Battalion of the 5th Infantry, 25th Infantry Division, found elaborately camouflaged tunnel openings.[1] The battalion formed "tunnel rat" teams to investigate. These tunnel soldiers carried silencer-equipped .38-caliber pistols to clear out any remaining Viet Cong. Deep inside the tunnels, caverns opened up to reveal rooms for hospitals, mess halls, munitions factories, and living quarters. What they saw had taken twenty years to build. It was part of the Viet Cong military headquarters controlling activities throughout a large portion of South Vietnam, including Saigon. Stuffed among forty pounds of recovered documents and maps were detailed diagrams of the U.S. billets in the capital. For six days the 5th Infantry soldiers slowly probed the four-level labyrinth of passages and chambers carved beneath the jungle floor.

1. The 5th Infantry was one of the Army's oldest, dating back to 1808. It was also one of the Army's most distinguished Indian-fighting regiments. It had escorted the Westward movement from Tippecanoe to Montana, and the only Civil War action it saw was in New Mexico. Led by the legendary Col. Nelson A. Miles, and famous for riding captured Indian war horses, the 5th had racked up glory for its pathfinding ability to track Indians from Sioux to Comanches. In Panama from 1939 to 1943, it was trained as a jungle warfare regiment before being sent to Europe in World War II. It also served in Korea. On January 19, it had been in Vietnam exactly one year to the date.

On January 26, Operation CEDAR FALLS was terminated. The excursion into the Iron Triangle had turned up significant finds but few Viet Cong. The VC had successfully avoided combat, and would infiltrate back when the soldiers and helicopters left. The Army wasn't especially worried about that now. With the large units now at its disposal, a sojourn under the code-name JUNCTION CITY was planned less than a month away in another Viet Cong bastion, War Zone C. It was destined to be one of the largest U.S. operations of the war, and this time there would be a fight.

2. Into War Zone C

War Zone C occupied a flat and marshy corner of Vietnam which gradually faded into thin-forested rolling hills as the region closed the Cambodian border. Heavy jungle prevailed, and the solitary 3,235 foot-high Nui Ba Den Mountain dominated the landscape. Like the Iron Triangle, this war zone had been Viet Cong-controlled since South Vietnam had been formed. The military hoped a multidivisional pounding would crush War Zone C as a continued threat, and evolved a complex plan of attack. Basically, the 25th Infantry Division would block west along the Cambodian frontier, and the 1st Infantry Division would block the eastern side of the zone along Route 4. On the first day of the operation, the 173d Airborne Brigade and a brigade from the 1st Infantry Division would move to seal off the northern portion. When all blocking forces were in place, a giant inverted horseshoe would result. A brigade of the 25th Infantry Division and the 11th Armored Cavalry Regiment would then be "pitched" into the horseshoe from the south.

During February, the 1st and 25th infantry divisions positioned themselves along the east and west sides, and on February 22, Operation JUNCTION CITY began as the north side was enveloped. Led by Brig. Gen. John R. Deane, Jr., the 173d Airborne Brigade jumped its 2d Battalion, 503d Infantry (Airborne), out of aircraft over Katum, less than seven miles from Cambodia. Parachutes blossomed under the tropical blue skies as the troopers glided to earth without incident. It was to be the only major U.S. Army combat jump of the Vietnam War, but some saw it as a "glory" exercise in reminiscence of the last big jumps in Korea. Although mass parachute landing was still a viable military doctrine, as the postwar Grenada expedition of 1983 demonstrated, airmobility may have sufficed here.

February 22 witnessed one of the largest mass helicopter lifts in the history of Army aviation. Over 249 helicopters were used in the eight battalion-sized airmobile assaults required to complete the northern rim of the horseshoe. The rest of the 173d Airborne Brigade was helicoptered into its preselected landing zones. At the same time, the 1st Brigade of the 1st Infantry Division was airmobiled in. The troops had already coined a phrase for the upcoming battles. They called it "Playing horseshoes with Charlie."

The next day the 2d Brigade of the 25th Infantry Division and the 11th Armored Cavalry Regiment swept north. Things started happening on February 28. The 173d Airborne Brigade discovered the Viet Cong Central Information Office, complete with an underground photographic laboratory containing 120 reels of film, stacks of photographs, and busts of communist leaders. Farther south, toward the western tip of the horseshoe, the 1st Battalion of the 16th Infantry tripped into battle off Route 4 near Prek Klok. The outfit was led by Lt. Col. Rufus Lazzell.[2] Capt. Donald S. Ulm's Company B had been moving over thick deadfall from trees and jungle brush, and was approaching the Prek Klok stream, when it clashed with the *2d Battalion, 101st NVA Regiment*. The point platoon was temporarily cut off, and Company B was engulfed by combat.

As soon as the company started taking concentrated rocket and machine-gun fire, Captain Ulm called in artillery and air strikes. The company formed a circular defensive perimeter. The fighting was intense. Airdropped cluster bomb units (CBUs) exploded with terrible effect at treetop level. The blast waves tore through the woods and toppled men and trees. At around midnight, after fifty-four Air Force tactical bombing sorties, the Viet Cong broke off the action. Air power had decided the firefight, and the Army had employed this support to good effect.

At Prek Klok, the 168th Engineer Battalion was busy con-

2. Lt. Col. Lazzell had been wounded commanding the same battalion in the July 1966 Battle of Minh Thanh Road; see Chapter 7. After recovery in the United States, he had asked for his old command back.

structing a future U.S. Army Special Forces camp and an airfield. The mechanized 2d Battalion of the 2d Infantry protected the 168th by forming a giant "wagon train" circle out of its armored personnel carriers, with foxholes in between. On the night of March 10, after a thirty-minute mortar and recoilless rifle barrage, a battalion of the *272d VC Regiment* attacked the eastern half of the perimeter. It was mowed down by crushing return fire from the heavy vehicle-mounted machine guns, over five thousand rounds from the 2d Battalion of the 33d Artillery inside the circle, and a hundred Air Force air strikes. The night sky was made brilliant by continuous pyrotechnics and bomb bursts. Helicopters darted in to deliver ammunition and take out wounded, their landing light beams stabbing through dust and smoke. At five o'clock the next morning the lopsided battle was finally over. Once again the American Army had utilized its prodigious artillery and aerial resources to ensure absolute victory on the battlefield.

On March 18, Operation JUNCTION CITY entered a new phase. The action shifted east with the construction of a new Special Forces camp northeast of Tay Ninh. The 173d Airborne Brigade was pulled out, and a brigade of the 9th Infantry Division was brought in to substitute. All units involved were now given sectors and began search and destroy operations. The 11th Armored Cavalry Regiment was escorting about two hundred trucks a day during convoy runs up Route 13 to An Loc. Along Route 13 a fire base was posted by Troop A of the 3d Squadron, 5th Cavalry, with six tanks and twenty-three armored personnel carriers.

The 5th Cavalry was known as the "Black Knights," and its 3d Squadron was the 9th Infantry Division's reconnaissance arm. It had been in Vietnam barely a month, but circular "wagon wheel" fights were part of its heritage.[3] The *273d VC Regiment*

3. The 5th Cavalry was organized in 1855 at Louisville, Kentucky, and it had charged Longstreet's Confederate lines at Gaines Mill, Virginia, in 1862—a charge that saved the Union artillery. After the Civil War, the 5th Cavalry had a most distinguished career in the Indian campaigns, where it fought just about every tribe from Comanches and Apaches to Cheyennes. It served in the Philippine Insurrection, participated in the 1916–17 Mexican Expedition, helped to clear New Guinea and the Philippines in World War II, and had served in the Korean War.

initiated its attack on this unit during the night of March 19 in a bizarre fashion. A wheel-mounted machine gun was rolled down a stretch of abandoned railroad track near the destroyed village of Ap Bau Bang. At ten minutes past midnight it furiously opened fire on the armored cavalry troop.

Tank-mounted searchlights soon pinpointed it and the gun was blown to pieces. Then a VC ground assault surged forward and was met with crippling fire from heavy machine guns, mortars, tank cannons, and artillery. However, Viet Cong soldiers succeeded in swarming in on the 5th Cavalry lines. Armored personnel carrier crewmen frantically buttoned up their vehicles as VC infantry swarmed over them. Artillery cannister rounds were fired directly at the armored vehicles, and dozens of attacking soldiers were blown off the carriers. Foxholes were being overrun in hand-to-hand combat. Machine guns were being stripped off wrecked armored personnel carriers, some of which were now on fire.

Troop A urgently radioed to its sister troops that it needed help. They crashed past preset ambushes and blasted their way in to help sustain the shrunken American positions. Eighty-seven Air Force bombing runs under flareship illumination pounded the continuous Viet Cong attacks. The 5th Cavalry held their lines and repulsed the charge. Again, armored personnel carriers packed in a tight laager, liberally supported by artillery and aircraft, had proved their ability to survive in isolated outposts.

The foot infantry was having a more difficult time. Near the center of War Zone C, near Suoi Tre, Fire Support Base Gold had been established by the 3d Battalion of the 22d Infantry and the 2d Battalion of the 77th Artillery. On March 19, helicopters began to descend into the jungled clearing, which had been doused with Agent Orange. As they touched down, five explosive charges tore through the small open area, destroying three helicopters and badly damaging six others. Strewn through the smoldering wreckage littering the landing zone were fifteen dead and twenty-eight badly wounded Americans.

Throughout the rest of the day the *272d VC Regiment* continued to take helicopters under accurate fire. Claymore mines were set off against the infantrymen as they dug in positions.

Clearly there would be trouble ahead. On the morning of March 21, a small night patrol of the 22d Infantry was returning to the fire base, when it was overrun by a mass VC attack behind an advancing mortar barrage which suddenly blanketed the area. Heavy return fire, air strikes, and artillery failed to stop the waves of attackers. Company B on the western edge of the perimeter was overrun, and artillerymen began desperately ramming Beehive flechette canister rounds into their leveled howitzer tubes.

Fire Support Base Gold positions caved in under the melee of close combat. Fighting was conducted with entrenching tools, chain saws, and bowie knives. The battalion's crucial quad .50-caliber machine gun was captured. The Viet Cong scrambled to turn the four-barreled gun around on the surviving American positions. The artillery crewmen of a remaining howitzer frantically chambered a round to destroy the swiveling multi-barreled machine gun. The howitzer managed to fire first, and the threatening gun was destroyed. Other howitzers had created a wall of steel by continuous Beehive discharges, but now the precious ammunition was suddenly exhausted. The few rounds of high explosive were being shot off as a final gesture, when reinforcements suddenly appeared. Soldiers of the 2d Battalion of the 12th Infantry took up positions alongside them.

The Viet Cong reassembled and counterattacked the new American force. Disabled VC soldiers were being carried piggyback into the attack, both bearer and rider firing submachine guns. The situation was again worsening for the defenders when a second relief force appeared out of the jungle, this time tanks of the 2d Battalion of the 34th Armor escorted by an entire battalion of mechanized infantry in armored personnel carriers. At 10:45 that morning the battle was ended.

The final large engagement of Operation JUNCTION CITY was fought on March 31 between Lt. Col. Alexander M. Haig's 1st Battalion of the 26th Infantry, and the combined *271st VC Regiment* and *1st Battalion, 70th VC Guards Regiment*. On March 26, under threatening storm clouds, Haig's infantrymen had airlanded in the tall, meadowlike grass near the Cambodian border. Signs were found nailed to trees, with warnings in English not to venture out. Even though they were deep in War Zone

C, they had obviously been expected. The battalion would shortly see one of its most violent actions in Vietnam as a result of relentless pursuit of the enemy.[4]

On March 31, the soldiers set out from LZ George to sweep their assigned area. At noon the battalion's reconnaissance platoon was hit hard, resulting in the loss of the platoon lieutenant, and everything started becoming unglued. Americans had learned by now not to advance without a shield of artillery and aerial support all around them, but due to lack of control, Company B ran off to assist without proper preparatory fires. Lieutenant Colonel Haig wasn't aware of the extent of Company B's actions until he was aloft in a helicopter. Company B was pinned and unable to move, under intense fire and low on ammunition and its wounded commander was in shock. Haig was forced to land in its midst and take over the battle personally and managed to avert disaster.

Company A was directed in to extract its sister company from the rapidly worsening firefight. By five o'clock the two companies were able to break contact and retreat back to the perimeter. In the meantime the landing zone had been reinforced by another battalion, the 1st Battalion of the 16th Infantry. In the morning darkness of April 1, a mortar barrage heralded a mass Viet Cong assault on the American lines. Rushing through a hail of bullets and artillery explosions, the VC quickly engaged the infantrymen in close combat. Air Force strikes loosing antipersonnel bomblets and napalm, artillery and mortar supporting fires, and helicopter minigun fire enabled the perimeter to defeat the attackers soundly.

In mid-April the big-battalion phase of Operation JUNCTION CITY ended. A third phase was tacked on, in which a "floating brigade" composed of a mechanized battalion of the

4. The 26th Infantry was one of those Army units formed at the turn of the century, which had picked up most of its heritage from World War I. The insignia of the regiment was dominated by a giant Mohawk arrowhead, selected by its World War I commander, Col. Hamilton A. Smith, to indicate the regimental spirit of courage, resourcefulness, and relentless pursuit of the enemy. Colonel Smith was killed shortly afterwards, leading the regiment in the first great offensive in which it took part. It later served in World War II, and had been in Vietnam since October of 1965.

25th Infantry Division combined with an ARVN battalion would rove throughout War Zone C. For the next month constant sweeps revealed only empty countryside, and the operation was terminated on May 14. The 196th Infantry Brigade, which had originally been intended to garrison War Zone C, had been sent north to bolster military efforts in I Corps Tactical Zone.

Operation JUNCTION CITY remained a hallmark of the Vietnam War. The multidivisional attack was destined to be the apex of Army efforts in III Corps Tactical Zone in 1967. Although War Zone C was not neutralized, three regiments of the *9th VC Division* had been temporarily shattered. Corps-sized Army forces had demonstrated their ability to mass and use great mobility in tackling any area of Vietnam. However, due to later enclave and pacification strategies, the mobile shock power of such a colossal effort was rarely repeated.

The 25th Infantry Division kept pressure going to the northwest of Saigon throughout the rest of the year in a series of operations that were insignificant in contacts produced, but were marked by extensive jungle-clearing efforts. On December 8, the major strength of the division was committed through Operation YELLOWSTONE back into War Zone C. Through the end of 1967, this operation was marked by frequent Viet Cong mortar attacks but light ground action. However, it did prove that War Zone C was still being used as a major VC logistical base.

3. Enterprising in Long An Province

The 39th Infantry arrived in Vietnam in January 1967 as part of another massive dose of American power injected into South Vietnam: the 9th Infantry Division. The regiment took its motto and most of its history from service to France.[5] This French connection remained unbroken as it entered a country French interests had shaped, and it prepared to take up the fight against an old French enemy.

5. The 39th Infantry regimental motto was *D'une Vaillance Admirable* (With a Military Courage Worthy of Admiration). Five French Croix de Guerre decorations for heroic action had been bestowed on the 39th from the Marne front of World War I to Cherence le Roussel in World War II. It had been formed in June 1917 at Syracuse, New York.

When its 3d Battalion slipped into Long An Province to the south of Saigon during February as the first 9th Division force to dwell there, the area was undisputed Viet Cong territory. As soon as the Americans planted their flag at Rach Kien they came under harassing fire, and any platoon or company that moved 350 yards outside the camp could count on a good-sized fight. The 3d Brigade of the 9th Infantry Division was colocated there, while the division's mechanized 2d Battalion of the 60th Infantry was stationed at Binh Phuoc. A long-term operation labeled EN-TERPRISE was initiated by these elements on February 13, 1967, to clear Long An Province. During April 9–11, the 3d Battalion of the 39th Infantry was airlifted into battle just outside Rach Kien, coming under heavy fire from the *506th VC Battalion* upon touchdown at the landing zone. The 2d Squadron, 10th ARVN Cavalry, and two battalions of the 60th Infantry were tossed into this battle along the Rach Dia River. Rapid shifting of forces in lightning airmobile assaults kept the Viet Cong off balance. Company-sized sweeps were executed for three days, but the VC managed to escape despite considerable loss. Six months of hard combat in the adjacent countryside may have scattered the Viet Cong, but it hadn't made a dent in their popularity. They continued to travel at will, depending on local villagers for information on U.S. movements. Determined to take a swipe at these farmer-soldiers who melted into the population every twilight, Lieutenant Colonel Anderson of the 3d Battalion, 39th Infantry, banded together his most trusted sergeants and formed a "killer patrol" under Capt. Donald Price.

On August 16, 1967, the battalion's Company A made a large sweep of the rice paddies around Rach Kien. The patrol clambered into a helicopter and landed in the midst of hundreds of Company A soldiers at one o'clock that afternoon. Captain Price picked out positions near a suspect cluster of huts and old bunkers near the thickly vegetated Rach Doi Ma River. The men of the patrol sweated through the afternoon preparing hidden positions, stringing wires for their claymore mines through the bushes, and covering up their gear. Meanwhile, the other soldiers made a lot of noise and tramped all over the place like a herd of elephants. The plan was simple but the risk was great. When Company A left for the night it was hoped nobody would notice six men left behind and dug into a perfectly camouflaged ambush site.

At six o'clock that evening six men and women began working the rice paddies, a signal to the Viet Cong that everything was safe. An hour later eight VC ambled around them, and shortly afterward two more entered the area and one of them stayed. He was armed with an M79 grenade launcher. Crossing the log bridge, he squatted on the far bank and looked right at Captain Price and his patrol sergeant, who were standing in the corner of a hut. Already it was fairly dark. They nervously exchanged stares, but the Viet Cong couldn't figure out who was there. A minute later he rose and, keeping his weapon ready, walked into their hut and squatted down in the far corner. Although Captain Price had his M16 rifle beside him, he didn't reach for it for fear the Viet Cong would fire first. He was counting on his sergeant, who had his AR15 rifle in his hands, to shoot the intruder. However, the patrol sergeant was shaking so badly when the VC came in that he didn't know what to do.

Suddenly the Viet Cong realized who the strangers were and with lightning speed fired a grenade at them and bolted for the door. The 40mm round bounced off the sergeant's leg and cut through the wall of the hut without exploding, since it never had time to arm.[6] The sergeant leaped behind the running VC and shot him twice in the back. The enemy soldier fell, mortally wounded, and the two men dragged him back into another corner.

Another team member who heard the gunfire had the sickening feeling his comrades had been hit. He was in the middle of tall grass and very nervous. When they had set up in the daylight he had been confident. After dark the whole thing looked different, and he wasn't sure he could see everything necessary. After getting no response to several whispered calls he crawled over to talk to the patrol sergeant and then went back to his own position. Everybody was now set for more Viet Cong, and fifteen minutes later two came down the eastern dike. Captain

6. The American 40mm grenade round was deliberately set to arm at a certain distance from the launcher, a result of early Vietnam experiences with rounds that bounced off trees and flipped back into Army positions during close jungle fighting.

Price had claymore mines set in position to kill them, but never triggered the electrical devices because he was hoping the VC would enter the main hut. There he had planted a GI rucksack and several *Playboy* magazines as bait, and he was hoping they would call in more of their friends.

The two Viet Cong walked right past the hut and the patrol's lieutenant spotted them next, fifteen yards from his own position. He could see their faces clearly in the moonlight. He picked up his .45-caliber automatic pistol and followed them for five feet. Then he thought to himself, "Naw, I can't hit the broad side of a barn with a .45." So he turned around, picked up his M16 rifle, and followed them another five feet until he realized they were entering another claymore mine killing zone. He dropped back and in the dark had to guess when to fire his mines. He set off the device but they had stepped off the dike. The explosion dazed and wounded them, but both were able to run away.

The explosion apparently discouraged any more Viet Cong activity in the area that night. The patrol members quietly listened to the familiar night noises of the delta—frogs croaking, crickets, and rats moving about in the rice paddies. That morning the patrol laid out their one kill and rifled through his pockets. The wallet had pictures of his friends, a girl, and a certificate honoring him for killing nine American soldiers. When the patrol sergeant was later asked if he thought the killer patrol tactic was valid, he could only quip, "I hope so; it took a lot out of me."

The 3d Battalion of the 39th Infantry continued its participation in Operation ENTERPRISE, though contact with the Viet Cong was to remain at a low level throughout the year. As their French associates had already experienced, time ran out for the men of the 9th Infantry Division long before a war of attrition could ever pay dividends.

CHAPTER 11.

BATTLE FOR THE HIGHLANDS

1. Western Battles

Major General William R. Peers took command of the 4th Infantry Division two days after it had marked its first New Year's Day in Vietnam. He moved it into the western portion of the Central Highlands plateau, a dangerous area occupied by both *1st NVA* and recently formed *10th NVA Divisions*. Tagged as Operation SAM HOUSTON, two infantry brigades would be pushed into the steep-walled valleys and rugged jungles falling off the Chaine Annamitique mountain spine which marked the Cambodian border.

The 4th Infantry Division was one of those divisions that mirrored the distinctive slogan officially bestowed upon it. The motto, Steadfast and Loyal, reflected the division's image perfectly. It was dignified, traditional, and definitely Regular Army. Perhaps that was needed in the rough, mountainous western wilderness of South Vietnam. Anyway, in case more gunslingers were needed to help out, the paratroopers of the elite 173d Airborne Brigade could always be slammed in.

The first phase of the operation was a piece of cake. Conducted over the rolling tropical plains of Pleiku and Kontum provinces, the only resistance encountered was occasional mortaring and road mines. January was spent uncovering tunnel

157

complexes and fortifications and then demolishing them. Armored cavalry personnel carriers hauled in captured rice, and infantrymen spent their time pitching riot-gas grenades into the mouths of caves. February began with the division dispatching a tank platoon to Duc Co, a Special Forces camp located in the southern portion of the Kontum plateau astride Highway 19. There the U.S. Army Special Forces was engaged in a confrontation with their South Vietnamese LLDB counterparts inside the joint compound. Only intervention on February 3 by high-ranking officers on both sides restored order. However, General Peers was determined that his "steadfast and loyal" 4th wasn't going to be a glorified police division. He looked northwest toward the mist-shrouded ridges of the Cambodian border to determine the future axis of advance. In mid-February a brigade was moved into the heavy jungle west of the Nam Sathay River to fight the NVA. There the battles that would typify Operation SAM HOUSTON were decided.

This region contained some of the most difficult tropical terrain in the world, consisting of continuous rain forests with huge 250-foot hardwood trees seven feet in diameter, which crumpled chain saws and defied small clearing explosives. Where the sunlight filtered through the canopy of trees, the jungle floor was covered with dense undergrowth restricting visibility to a matter of yards and making any movement extremely difficult. Valleys intersected the area, caged in by jagged mountains rising as far as six thousand feet above them. Daylight temperatures soared above 105 degrees, and nighttime temperatures could plunge to 45 degrees. Since it was the end of the dry season there was very little available water except in the valleys, and the troops were forced to carry at least a two-day supply with them. Wading through the seasonally low waters of the Nam Sathay, men of the division's 12th and 22d Infantry entered NVA territory.

On February 15, soldiers from Company C, 1st Battalion of the 12th Infantry, began patrolling around their landing zone across the river.[1] As the men moved outside their new fire base,

1. The 12th Infantry was a good Army regiment, forged at the beginning of the Civil War where it secured fame during its first engagement at Gaine's Mill, Virginia. Twin moline crosses still decorated its insignia, representing the iron fastening of a millstone and recalling the crushing losses it had sus-

the jungle exploded with intense automatic rifle fire. One squad was trapped in a ravine and unable to move for an hour. Only the heroic actions of one wounded private, killed covering the others, enabled the rest of the squad to rejoin its company. Dozens of NVA soldiers now charged the surrounded landing zone. Concentrated rifle fire tore through their ranks. Artillery and air strikes were called in closer and closer to the belea- guered defenders, and the attacks were finally beaten back. The rest of the 12th Infantry's first battalion was now airlifted into the battle. Helicopters coming in were subjected to murderous ground fire, but eventually another company was landed. Com- pany B immediately sallied forward but was hit hard and soon had two of its own platoons cut off and pinned down.

By late afternoon Company A, accompanied by the battalion heavy mortars, had been successfully landed. It charged forward to form a corridor through which Company B could evacuate its dead and wounded. Fighting was especially fierce in the gath- ering twilight, and soldiers used knives and entrenching tools as ammunition supplies ran out. Earth and vegetation was thrown into the air by blocking fire from the battalion's mortars. By eight o'clock that night the battered companies had managed to pull themselves back to the landing zone. To keep the NVA at bay through the night, the jungle around them was saturated by artillery and bombing runs.

The next day, in another sector of the battlefield, a platoon of the 2d Battalion, 8th Infantry, came under enemy fire at noon. Underestimating the force being engaged, the soldiers returned fire and began moving forward. In minutes the platoon was being swept by a storm of bullets and grenade shrapnel. It gathered in a tight circle and desperately called for artillery, but the thick morass of twisted jungle made accurate placement impossible. Charging NVA soldiers were killed in close combat. Only the efforts of the platoon sergeant, who was slain in the action, saved the unit from total annihilation. A relieving company was soon

---

tained that day in June 1862—over 50 percent of its strength. It served in the Indian Wars, captured the blockhouse at El Caney, Cuba, during the War with Spain, participated in the Philippine Insurrection, and assaulted France during D-Day in World War II.

hard-pressed itself by well-equipped NVA concealed in the jungles. Air strikes were called in so close that deadly fragments rained down on both sides.

Elsewhere other soldiers, this time from the 22d Infantry, were moving west. The point squad ran into an NVA unit moving east. Taking advantage of the extremely dense undergrowth, the North Vietnamese opened up with a hail of submachine-gun fire and sent snipers aloft into the trees. Soon the entire company was taking casualties. The Army had issued the grenadiers the new dual purpose rifle with grenade launcher located underneath (the XM148), promising the advantages of both methods of fire. Now they were having great difficulty loading, cocking, and firing the launcher portion. Cursing the loss of the traditional M79 and its trusted firepower, they were reduced to ordinary riflemen. Napalm and cluster bomb units shattered the jungle in front of them, and a relief force was able to link up. The tempo that dominated the battle for the highlands had been set.

Every day more soldiers, their torn jungle fatigues frayed and drenched with salt and sweat, went forward. They were under constant physical strain and mental pressure, painfully aware that every step in the jungle could bring death if they didn't react quickly enough. Individuals were overloaded by rucksacks crammed with additional ammunition, extra gear, rations, and water; and survival equipment such as mosquito repellent, head nets, and ponchos. Minimized "essential loads" still required each soldier to "hump" from forty to sixty pounds. The constant exertion demanded of troops hacking and moving through dense jungle day after day exhausted their fighting ability. Search patterns had fancy military names, "cloverleaf," "starburst," and "zig-zag," but the infantrymen only cursed as they struggled to push on ahead and keep within sight of their comrades. To keep oriented in the deep forests, units were forced to periodically drop artillery rounds along their route of advance.

Thin olive drab ribbons of men moved like ants, slowly toiling through the natural maze of green jungle. They were carefully tracked by NVA reconnaissance teams and trailwatchers, often moving behind them or in parallel directions. Snipers would suddenly open fire, the sharp crack of their rifles reverberating through the foliage. Bursts of submachine-gun fire also sprayed advancing personnel, dropping key leaders and radiomen. The soldiers responded with a fusillade of automatic rifle fire and shotgun canister rounds that tore through the trees. Splintered branches, leaves, and other debris were hurled through the air. Such skirmishes could last for hours, caused serious delays, and often masked larger NVA troop movements.

At the end of each day, the weary, aching soldiers had to dig in and construct individual shelters consisting of at least one layer of overhead sandbags to ward off the inevitable nighttime mortar attacks. Only then could they settle down to a night too frequently punctuated by the terror-filled cries of "Incoming!" followed by the crash of dreaded explosions. Deprived of decent sleep and drained of energy, the soldiers had to move out every morning. Sergeants maintained brutal pressure to keep their men combat-ready. Accidents became more frequent, and the hazards of jungle warfare increased. Throughout February, firefights were sudden and unexpected, engulfing units in a whirlwind of death and confusion.

The 4th Infantry Division's 1st Brigade was helicoptered into Plei Djereng, and two full brigades were now committed in the area. The new brigade assumed responsibility for the lower Plei Trap and Nam Sathay valleys, while the 2d Brigade pushed farther west toward the Cambodian border. Throughout the rest of February and March, the American units experienced the most dreaded pattern of Vietnam jungle marching and fighting. The North Vietnamese Army regulars would attack moving rifle companies at times and locations of their own choosing. The assault would close too quickly for the defenders to call in effective supporting fire. Mortars and snipers would try to drive the surrounded unit into smaller fragments. Invariably, counterattacking the prepared NVA brought intense flanking fire from positions established in depth to the right and to the left. The entire 2d Battalion of the 35th Infantry was subjected to such an attack on March 12. Only after dark would the NVA break off the battle, using short ropes and hooks, if needed, to retrieve their dead and wounded comrades.

These actions only lasted from one to six hours, but the violent force of the enemy attack, combined with a feeling of claustrophobia resulting from the dense jungle, created an unbearably high degree of tension. This strain worsened with proximity to the Cambodian border. Americans found they could no longer count on massive dosages of firepower to break resistance. As usual, generous use of available artillery and air power was made, but its effectiveness was diminished by the rugged terrain. Smoke grenades and flares could not penetrate the triple-canopy jungle, and units could not be located by aircraft seeking to deliver supporting ordnance.

Although thirty-one B-52 ARC LIGHT bombing runs were brought against the NVA, even this formidable weapon failed to assure results when needed. The NVA knew that a troop safety distance of three thousand meters was required before the B-52 bombers could be used, and initiated close-quarters combat inside these bounds. They also took full advantage of the Cambodian border to rush a few companies into Vietnam, mount mortar barrages, and get back across. One of the fire bases was hit by twelve separate mortar attacks in a day and a half, taking three hundred rounds.

There were so few suitable areas for landing helicopters that North Vietnamese Army forces could pick them out and prepare them in advance. Pilots soon expected every landing site to be "hot and mined." NVA ingenuity was remarkably efficient. One device had several grenades tied to a ten-foot board with a charge placed underneath. As the helicopters descended for landing, the charge would be set off by an observer, tossing the grenades up to explode in the midst of the aircraft. Strong bunkers were dug in around the periphery of open areas, ringed by command-detonated mines. In fact, the jungle was so heavy that a road had to be constructed westward to establish a series of fire bases from which operations near the Cambodian border could be supported. Only the airlifting of D-4B dozers into remote areas made this effort possible.

From March 16 through the end of the month, both brigades moved back east from their areas west of the Se San River in the face of continued ambushes and firefights. When they moved, units habitually left their fire bases cluttered with accumulated litter ranging from empty ration boxes to shell cartridges. NVA forces then entered such areas to clean up the wealth of material left behind, much of which was put to good use. All efforts to educate Americans to this fact failed, and deserted bases remained piled high with "trash." The military finally decided to take advantage of it. For the first time, antipersonnel mines were sewn across selected areas by Air Force A-1E Skyraiders. Recondo patrols were inserted to report on the losses the NVA suffered as a consequence of entering the freshly abandoned fire support sites.

The next major action of the operation erupted when radio contact with a reconnaissance patrol was lost on March 21, and the 1st Battalion of the 8th Infantry was sent to search for it the next day. At 7:30 in the morning Company A, moving in two columns, suddenly came under intense machine-gun fire. While trying to maneuver their company, the captain and the artillery forward observation officer were both blown to pieces by a direct hit from a B-40 rocket. Without leadership, communications, or the ability to direct supporting artillery fire, the company broke in two. Men discarded equipment and rucksacks and fought from separate perimeters.

The company first sergeant raced over to the point of heaviest contact and adjusted the lines. He then directed artillery fire and aircraft by running over to a clearing where he could be spotted, climbing a tree, and tying an identification panel from its highest branches. A relief column, composed of Company B, moved toward them on line, keying on the sound of battle for direction. Then it too came under attack. It was also split, but managed to reconsolidate. The NVA eventually left the field, but losses had been heavy.

The 4th Infantry Division's extra tank battalion, the 1st Battalion of the 69th Armor, was useless in the jungled mountains. During Operation SAM HOUSTON it was engaged in road security to keep Highway 19 open. The tanks were also used to drive cattle from villages to new relocation sites.

The foot soldiers of the 4th Infantry Division were thoroughly fatigued. On April 5, Company C of the 3d Battalion, 8th Infantry, was firing mortars when a deflection error sent the rounds exploding in American positions. Twelve U.S. servicemen were wounded as a result. Operation SAM HOUSTON was terminated that midnight. The division's after-action report ruefully commented:

> The most difficult tactical problem found in fighting the NVA in large areas of difficult terrain is *finding the enemy*. That is, finding him without having tactical units shot up and pinned down by automatic weapons and snipers, also armed with automatic weapons, at close range.

2. Guarding the Border

With the advent of the summer monsoon season, Major General Peers nestled two brigades of his depleted 4th Infantry Division up against the Cambodian border in the flat rolling hills of western Pleiku Province south of the Se San River. The 1st Brigade covered the area from Duc Co north across forested plains into the rugged Chu Goungot–Chu Yam massif and Plei Djereng, while the 2d Brigade worked south of Duc Co through the Ia Drang Valley. There he hoped to stop the *1st* and *10th NVA Divisions* if they tried to push into South Vietnam's western heartland. This frontier guard duty turned out to be arduous and costly, but it did stifle NVA attempts to cross large forces through that particular area during most of 1967.

The 4th Infantry Division relocated in these areas on April 6, 1967, the day after Operation SAM HOUSTON ended. The new operation was labeled FRANCIS MARION, and before it ended in October the division would fight eight hard battles. It must be mentioned that in April many soldiers who had deployed with the division were scheduled to rotate home. Line companies were fielding less than one hundred men, and almost all the officers and sergeants were brand new. This would have considerable impact on combat in the coming months.

Border brushes with NVA recon parties became common in late April. The 2d Battalion of the 8th Infantry was being mechanized that month and was trying out its new armored personnel carriers. The 8th Infantry had never been spectacular, but it enjoyed a reputation for steady dependability.[2] On the last day of April, Company A got off its tracked vehicles and began moving slowly along the Ia Muer River on foot.

Early that morning one of its platoons scattered thirty NVA by hasty ambush, the stunned North Vietnamese soldiers picking up their wounded without firing a shot in return. The rest of the company moved up to destroy an apparently small enemy patrol on the run. The NVA tried to set up a defense line in order to treat those injured, but the pursuit was so hot that the casualties were abandoned. The chase continued toward a tree line which suddenly spattered the field with machine-gun fire, pinning two squads in the open. Half the company became engaged in the searing tropical heat, and over three hours were spent trying to pull back the dehydrated squad members.

After napalm and bombs blistered the tree line, a combined late afternoon attack was made behind two armored personnel carriers of the battalion scout platoon. They were almost to the trees when a volley of automatic weapons fire ripped across the company front. The soldiers scrambled back as the tracked carriers shifted into reverse. They were up against the *2d Battalion, 95B NVA Regiment*. All night long, artillery explosions lit up the forest. Captain William R. Harvey used the darkness to bring up all his armored personnel carriers, as well as two tanks from Troop B, 1st Squadron, of the 10th Cavalry.

After intensive air and artillery preparation, the company moved forward in the morning, passing through the initial ambush site of the previous day. Sniper fire erupted over the noise of diesel engines, and the tanks roared into line beside each other, their steel tracks tossing back clods of dirt. Two squarish armored personnel carriers, top-heavy with cupolas and gunshields, kept up on the left, and four churned alongside to the

2. The 8th Infantry was organized in Detroit, Michigan, in July 1838 and served in both Mexican and Civil wars, occupied the Carolinas, and moved to fight Indians in Arizona during 1872. It invaded Cuba during the war with Spain, and in June 1913 fought the four-day Battle of Bagsak Mountain on Jolo Island, Philippines, which ended the long struggle against the fierce Moro pirates. It assaulted Normandy, France, in World War II and deployed to Vietnam in August 1966.

right. One of the carriers threw a track and drunkenly ground to a stop. Its soldiers scrambled out, quickly dismantled its guns, locked hatches and doors, and clambered onto other advancing vehicles.

As the war machines relentlessly neared the tree line, NVA soldiers raced out to heave grenades under their tracks. The medium tanks blasted back with powerful 90mm cannister rounds, throwing out great clouds of smoke-filled death which chopped through men and shrubbery. Personnel carriers swung their armored cupolas around to hose clinging NVA soldiers off other vehicles with machine-gun fire. Resulting sparks flew wildly off the sides of blood-streaked tank turrets. Tanks looked like iron beasts emitting electrical discharges in the thick haze of the battlefield. Their crushing weight beat down the dense undergrowth, and the company drove through the tree line.

The mechanized onslaught carried them into a large bunker complex. NVA soldiers desperately tried to aim anti tank rockets, but the dense jungle and the flow of battle obstructed their efforts. Cannister discharges and machine guns swept the foliage like scythes, and slaughtered gunners were strewn like broken dolls over unused B-40 rockets. Topside bunkers were blown to pieces by point-blank cannon fire. The mechanized infantrymen periodically opened the back doors of their carriers and emerged to stalk the jungle and grenade remaining bunkers. Mechanized firepower had given the men of the 8th Infantry a mailed fist.

Its sister 1st Battalion of the 8th Infantry, was normal foot infantry. On May 18, Company B was trudging through the undergrowth of light tropical forest, composed of trees ranging from fifteen to seventy-five feet in height. A platoon was detached to check out a well-traveled trail, spotted a lone khaki-clad NVA soldier, and started pursuit. Lieutenant Allen, the company commander, radioed the platoon to rejoin him. A "lame duck" ambush was then triggered by the *K4 Battalion, 32d NVA Regiment* between them, and the platoon was trapped. The rest of Company B was unable to break through to the isolated men.

Seven platoon soldiers ran over to a small creek bed where all but one were immediately killed by a machine-gun. The NVA initially tried to overrun the rest of the platoon from the creek, but were repulsed. Continuous machine-gun fire raked the pinned men, and the platoon lieutenant, sergeant, and radioman died in rocket explosions. The NVA then moved across the shattered platoon in perfect line formation, firing as they advanced. They stopped at each body, kicked it several times in the back and ribs, and then searched through clothing and rucksacks. Hands were stripped of watches and rings. They spent forty minutes gathering weapons, ammunition, canteens, and other gear. The only survivors were seven soldiers who played dead or were unconscious from their wounds. Company B had a total of twenty-nine killed, one never found, and another thirty-one wounded.

The next two days passed with only light contact. On the night of May 20, however, the entire battalion was attacked in its hilltop defensive positions. After an intense mortar barrage, three waves of soldiers from the *K5 Battalion* of the *32d NVA Regiment* stormed up the slopes bathed in the ghostly, discordant flarelight. Planes illuminated the battlefield. The shifting glare of their airborne searchlights swept the hill. Blinding bursts of ignited powder silhouetted broken wire, heaving earth, and maimed men. The assault was defeated at heavy cost to the 1st Battalion of the 8th Infantry.

The neighboring 3d Battalion of the 12th Infantry was ordered to link up and reinforce the 8th Infantry. As the men left their defensive positions on the morning of May 22, they were showered by enemy mortars. Soldiers of the *66th NVA Regiment* then charged down from a high ridgeline. Under concentrated grenade and rocket fire, infantrymen were shifted from one side of their perimeter to the other to meet the onslaught. Soldiers dropped under the furious shelling as they dashed over, but enough made it to shore up the line and prevent a breach. They were dangerously low on ammunition and requested immediate resupply. As U.S. artillery fire was temporarily shifted, Air Force fighters arrived and made low-level bombing runs. Helicopter gunships followed, strafing and rocketing the jungle up to the very edge of the perimeter. After the gunship attack, artillery fire was brought back all around the perimeter, and helicopters delivered two loads of vital ammunition. Shortly afterwards, the North Vietnamese broke off their attack.

The NVA initiated a series of mortar and rocket attacks against strategic Pleiku city itself beginning on June 9, but the 4th Infantry Division refused to budge from the Cambodian border. Fierce actions there continued, and on July 12 in the rock-covered hills south of Duc Co two companies from the 1st Battalion of the 12th Infantry ran into a hard fight again with the *66th NVA Regiment*. Company B was attempting to reinforce a surrounded platoon. Instead, it was driven from the field toward its fire base position. The rest of the battalion combined to stop the NVA assault.

The last significant encounter of the operation took place on a torrid July 23, when a platoon out of the 3d Battalion, 8th Infantry, became separated from its company just south of Duc Co. Both the platoon leader and the radioman were killed by NVA riflemen aiming at radio antennae, and the platoon was practically wiped out. A battalion of the *32d NVA Regiment* charged forward, and the shattered company dodged behind bushes in the light forest. They hastily set up extra claymore mines, which were detonated in the face of the NVA attack. Twice the North Vietnamese charged their lines. Jet fighters darted through the clear skies to pulverize the massed NVA battalion in great explosions of spewing napalm and phosphorous. Both attacks were hurled back, and a second rifle company reinforced their position. Twelve Air Force fighter strikes were used during the course of the action, which not only demolished the attacking NVA battalion, but also annihilated the reserve battalion just a thousand yards away.

This border guard duty was destined to remain under the code name FRANCIS MARION only until October 12. By October it was apparent that the main North Vietnamese Army effort was being made in western Kontum Province, directly to the north. Consequently, FRANCIS MARION was consolidated with Operation GREELEY, taking place there. Both tasks then became Operation MAC ARTHUR, which encompassed the greater portions of Kontum, Pleiku, and Phu Ban provinces. History would subordinate the name MAC ARTHUR to its pivotal battle which decided the highlands campaign: the Battle of Dak To.

3. The Battle of Dak To

The opening rounds of the Battle of Dak To actually started in June 1967 when the U.S. Army Special Forces camp at Dak

To, situated in the towering mountains of central Kontum Province, was pounded by mortars. Then its local garrison sent out a patrol force which was bushwhacked. The monsoon season blanketed the region with low clouds and moving ground fog, but two paratrooper battalions of the crack 173d Airborne Brigade managed to airlift into Dak To on June 17. The operation would be initially tagged GREELEY. It would span a rugged wilderness covered by thick double- and triple-canopy jungle. The only clearings in the mountainous primeval rain forest were choked with bamboo fifteen to twenty feet high.

On June 22, a company of the 2d Battalion, 503d Infantry (Airborne), clashed with the *6th Battalion, 24th NVA Regiment* in one of the most violent battles of the Vietnam War. That morning, Company A left its night position in the triple-canopy jungle and began threading its way down a steep ridgeline. It planned to reach the brigade command post at Dak To that afternoon. The point squad collided with a North Vietnamese Army force, and the battle quickly engulfed the parachutists. Artillery fire crashed down and helicopter-delivered rockets pierced the dank green foliage. All failed to check the assault. Two platoons were fed into the tangled jungle cauldron. At eleven o'clock all contact was lost with the forward platoons. Then a band of disheveled, wounded troopers stumbled into the company lines. Their shredded tropical combat uniforms, the cloth jump wing insignia blackened and bloodied, and exhausted faces told the story. The rest of the company scrambled back up the smoking ridge, and began frantically cleaving a landing zone out of the thick vegetation.

Companies B and C were ordered forward at once. The former air-assaulted a distance away, but was shot up as soon as it tried to leave the clearing. Company C was able to reach the area by two o'clock that misty afternoon. However, when the fresh company tried to get down to the overrun area of the lost platoons, heavy fire repulsed it. The next day the weary paratroopers managed to sweep the area where the platoons had made their last stand. Littering the trampled underbrush, broken trees, and the clutter of war debris, were the crumpled bodies of seventy-six dead parachutists.

The rest of Brigadier General Deane's elite brigade moved to Kontum city a week later, along with Colonel McKenna's 3d

Brigade of the 1st Cavalry Division. The hard-fighting South Vietnamese paratroopers of the 5th and 8th ARVN Airborne Battalions and a battalion of the 42d ARVN Regiment were also moved in. A forward tactical command post of the 4th Infantry Division was set up to control activities. The gunslingers that General Westmoreland needed to subdue the Central Highlands had arrived.

The next few months were spent in grueling marches into the western depths of Kontum Province, where the NVA were firmly entrenched in bunker complexes. The paratroopers suffered mounting losses in attacks on these fortifications. The bunkers were always covered by mutually supporting machine-gun positions, undetectable until they suddenly blazed into life. The supporting 299th Engineer Battalion struggled through torrential rains to replace the blown bridges along Route 14, the single road linking Kontum and Dak To. Despite its best efforts, the monsoons turned land routes into impassable quagmires. At times Dak To had to subsist on aerial delivery of supplies for days on end. Aircraft crashed and burned with alarming regularity.

A particularly grisly aspect of this fighting involved the constant discovery of human skeletons from past battles. On June 20, 173d Airborne Brigade paratroopers found the osseous remains of two Special Forces, eight of their indigenous CIDG strikers, and one NVA soldier. Three days later the bones of a missing radioman from one of their own patrols was found. Still more skeletal corpses of Army Special Forces and their CIDG soldiers were discovered throughout the period. Ghosts seemed to haunt every tropical mist-shrouded sepulcher, and the unnerved parachutists freely admitted the whole area "spooked them out."

The 3d Brigade of the 1st Cavalry Division systematically searched north of Kontum throughout July. A combined Special Forces-CIDG force working out of its Plateau Gi camp ambushed a withdrawing NVA unit on July 12. 1st Cavalry Division artillery supported the action. Near Dak Seang, on August 3, the South Vietnamese airborne battalions helicoptered into combat. A battalion of the 42d ARVN Regiment was hung up on a bunkered hilltop it had assaulted. In a sanguinary night

engagement on August 6, the tough South Vietnamese paratroopers of the 8th ARVN Airborne Battalion threw back five
mass attacks of the *2d Battalion, 174th NVA Regiment*. Ten days
later the combat-fatigued ARVN airborne battalions left Kontum, followed by the bulk of the 173d Airborne Brigade which
departed for coastal Tuy Hoa. On October 11, Operation
GREELEY was folded into Operation MAC ARTHUR. At the
end of the month, the 1st Brigade of the 4th Infantry Division
was air-landed at Dak To. Attached to it was the 4th Battalion
of the 503d Infantry (Airborne) from the 173d Airborne Brigade.
The decisive Battle of Dak To was about to commence.

The town of Dak To lies on a valley floor next to a river,
ringed by mountains covered by tall, thick trees capped by triple-canopy jungle soaring a hundred feet off the ground. These
peaks and ridges sloped steeply up to elevations of over four
thousand feet. Throughout the first two weeks in November,
west and southwest of Dak To, a series of attacks would be
launched against the well-prepared, fortified NVA positions on
the ridgelines. At the beginning of the battle only five battalions, two of them ARVN, were stationed near Dak To. By mid-
November the numbers had tripled, and Dak To became a major logistical support site.

On November 4, at a spot only a thousand yards from the
173d Airborne Brigade's fierce June action, the 3d Battalion of
the 12th Infantry from the 4th Infantry Division ran into an NVA
position on a high ridge. Since the unit was unable to take it
frontally, forty air strikes were used to paste the area. The soldiers then advanced over the shattered defensive works. Meanwhile, on November 6, the 4th Battalion of the 503d Infantry
(Airborne) got into heavy combat on Hill 823. Losses were making major inroads into combat power; one 164-man company was
down to 44 men.

Brigadier General Leo H. Schweiter, who had taken over
the 173d Airborne Brigade on August 24, moved his paratroopers back into Dak To at once. Along with the brigade came
eleven teams of the 39th Scout Dog Platoon. The dogs were
used as part of point elements. These scout dogs went ahead of
the point man in open terrain, while in tropical forest they moved
just behind him. In this manner the canines' energy was saved

by having the trail broken for them. Their endurance was also stretched by having handlers carry them over more difficult jungle obstacles. The dogs kept up a lively interest in these varied regions, and alerted their masters to enemy presence, tunnels, food caches, and bunkers. Once a battle was joined, the dogs were moved to the rear as the din of mortar, artillery, and bombing nullified their keen hearing.

The 4th Battalion of the 503d Infantry (Airborne) had suffered so many losses south of the Ben Het Special Forces camp, that the decision was made to replace it. The paratroopers of its sister 1st Battalion had to fight through entrenched NVA bunkerworks just to get to them. On November 12, the 2d Battalion was also combat-assaulted into the spreading battle. That night the North Vietnamese began mortaring the lucrative target that supply-packed Dak To airfield now presented. On November 14 the confrontation was enlarged as the 42d ARVN Regiment crashed into NVA forces northeast of Dak To. It was promptly reinforced by South Vietnamese paratroopers of the elite 2d and 3d ARVN Airborne Battalions.

The 4th Infantry Division was pushing its 3d Battalion, 12th Infantry, from ridge to ridge. By the time the soldiers reached Hill 1338, they resorted to standard procedures: after striking bunkered positions, massive air and artillery fire were used to obliterate hilltops. The 173d Airborne Brigade was also moving down one ridge, crossing a valley, and then climbing up the next ridge. Riflemen strained under full rucksacks crammed with extra ammunition, smoke grenades, trip flares, and claymore mines.

On November 13, Company B of the 2d Battalion, 503d Infantry (Airborne), was checking out a potential mountainside for a suitable night defensive position. They were taking the usual intermittent sniper fire, when two bunkers were spotted. They had been carrying a large 90mm recoilless rifle and twenty-two rounds of ammunition for it, a real hardship in the mountain jungles. Now they saw their chance to put it into action and brought the gun forward. After one cannister round was fired into the NVA bunker, the gunners looked back toward one of their squad members. He was sitting on his rucksack to make sure no one was in the back-blast area of the gun. Suddenly he tipped sideways and fell over, shot through the head. A furious barrage of small-arms and rocket fire swept through the entire company. Radiomen and officers were quickly gunned down. The remaining men managed to set up a hasty perimeter as the *3d Battalion, 174th NVA Regiment* attacked.

The 90mm recoilless rifle crewmen quickly shot off their last rounds as hand grenades exploded around them. They crawled back to a pile of logs which was already being clipped by vicious cross fire. North Vietnamese soldiers tried to close in on the logs. One private got off a shot which missed, raised his head to fire again, and was shot between the eyes. Another paratrooper was hit in the chest and died as a medic administered first aid. Then the log pile was shaken by the blast of a B-40 rocket, and the NVA bounded forward. Again the paratroopers repulsed the charge.

Hand-to-hand combat, rocket and grenade blasts, and clattering automatic weapons filled the bamboo thickets and shrub brush. The right flank of Company B collapsed under the NVA assault. Shouted orders to withdraw were impossible to execute; breaking contact was no longer a viable option. American standbys such as artillery and air support were useless in such close combat. The bamboo was so thick many parachutists believed their M16 bullets weren't penetrating the jungle. Company A fought its way inside the perimeter to help hold it as darkness descended.

All night long the two companies were raked by heavy NVA weapons. Ammunition was air-dropped into a large bomb crater near the position's center by helicopters, which were guided in by flashlight. Both sides tried to recover their wounded comrades from the fringes of the battle line, and more dead were added in the thin space separating the two forces. No flares were fired for fear of silhouetting positions. At dawn the NVA withdrew. The fighting had been so intense that one log was found in the morning with six dead paratroopers on one side and four dead NVA soldiers sprawled out on the other side. At the end of the log were two more NVA, one of them an officer who still clutched a captured M16 rifle taken from one of the Americans.

On November 15 a major U.S. setback for the ongoing Battle of Dak To occurred when a mortar attack on the Dak To airfield touched off the ammunition dump there. Exploding ordnance threatened the entire base camp, and the accumulated ammunition supplies required to continue the battle were lost. Additionally, two C-130 cargo planes were destroyed. Disaster was averted by emergency airlift of massive quantities of replacement ammunition during the next few days. Heavy fighting on both sides of Dak To flared up again on November 17 and soon became centered on Hill 875. The fight for Hill 875 would ultimately climax the Battle for Dak To, as well as the 1967 campaign for the highlands. The weather was now excellent, but mountain temperatures still ranged from a daytime 91 degrees to lows of 55 degrees at night.

On November 18, the 26th Special Forces Mobile Reaction (Mike) Company ran into a large North Vietnamese Army force entrenched on the east slope of Hill 875, about twelve miles west of Dak To. Encountering a complex system of interconnecting bunkers and trenches manned by the *174th NVA Regiment,* the company quickly retreated. It was later determined that these defensive works even included tunnels between bunkers and had been constructed three to six months previously, allowing ample growth of concealing natural vegetation in the meantime. The next day Lt. Col. James R. Steverson's 2d Battalion of the 503d Infantry (Airborne), the combat-jump veterans of the parachute assault into War Zone C that February, drew the tough mission to "move onto and clear Hill 875."

Companies C and D of the battalion tackled the tree- and bamboo-covered northern slope of Hill 875 on the morning of November 19. After four hours of increasingly heavy return fire, they were abruptly assaulted by waves of North Vietnamese Army infantrymen of the *174th NVA Regiment,* the hill's defenders. The paratroopers dropped their rucksacks and retreated in the thick underbrush. Desperately they clawed into the ground with knives and helmets to carve out a defensive line. The NVA gave them no respite, rushing the troopers in groups of twenty to thirty men. The NVA attackers were well camouflaged, their faces painted black and their weapons wrapped in burlap. Machine guns, rifle grenades, mortars, and well-placed snipers riddled the paratroopers of the two lead companies.

Company A was in reserve at the bottom of the hill cutting a landing zone out of the jungle. Waves of screaming North Vietnamese Army regulars charged through its positions in such force that two platoons simply evaporated. Now split and under fierce assault, the battalion's reserve was in imminent danger of being overrun as well. Most of the paratroopers there were already dead when the six-man command group was completely wiped out in hand-to-hand combat.

The rain of steel was mowing down parachutists so fast all seemed lost. A sergeant was hit and the medical specialist dragged him over to a tree, where the latter was shot through the head himself. One private had his M60 machine gun blown out of his hands by a rifle grenade. Their lieutenant tried three times to get to the sergeant and was hit each time. The sergeant died crying, "For God's sake, Lieutenant, don't come out here; there's a machine gun behind this tree!" He had been shot seven times. With scores of paratroopers already killed, many missing, and hundreds wounded, the survivors of the shattered battalion tried to shore up their front with an emergency perimeter.

As fallen and severely wounded men were being dragged into the relative safety provided by the center of the perimeter, a bomb from an Air Force fighter plummeted into their midst. There it exploded in a horrendous blast which tossed limbs and pieces of clothing over the entire area. Twenty men literally disintegrated, and another thirty were horribly wounded. The battalion had lost most of its leaders; even the chaplain was mortally wounded.

As fast as the paratroopers fired, the NVA appeared in more numbers on all sides. The 335th Aviation Company had six of its helicopters shot out of the sky as they started to descend. Supporting artillery fire was now starting to hit the battalion, and a platoon sergeant went from shattered radio to radio until he found one that worked. Frantically he turned the frequency knob, trying to raise any friendly station. He happened to turn it to the artillery fire direction center network and was able to adjust the errant shells.

The night was filled with more terror. Soldiers hollered on both sides and tossed grenades across the burning boundaries of the perimeter. The NVA were yelling, "Now You *Chieu Hoi*, G.I.!"[3] The sister 4th Battalion, spent the night preparing to move up Hill 875 to break through to its fellow paratroopers. They stuffed their rucksacks and pockets full of ammunition. Everything else was left behind except for one meal, one canteen, and one poncho for carrying dead and wounded.

On the morning of November 20, Lt. Col. James H. Johnson's 4th Battalion started up the slope. They found it littered with empty C-ration tins that the NVA had captured. Bloodied Chinese first-aid dressings and expended ammunition cans dotted the hillside. By one tree a young paratrooper was found dead in a pile of empty shell casings, still clutching his jammed M60 machine gun. They began passing so many dead Americans that soon some of the advancing men wondered openly if there was anyone left alive to link up with. However, there was no resistance and seven thousand yards up the hill the 4th Battalion reached the worn perimeter at ten o'clock that night. The survivors of the 2d Battalion openly cried as the union was finally made.

The following day a new landing zone was cut out of the twisted jungle, and for the first time the brigade was able to lift out its wounded from the November 19th battle. For seven hours Hill 875 was plastered with every artillery and air asset available. Air strikes streaked in every fifteen minutes, scorching the crest with seven and a half tons of burning napalm. Then the paratroopers made an afternoon attack. They prepared to advance by forming ranks behind a wall of last-minute artillery fire which pounded the hillside. Suddenly an NVA mortar counterbarrage rained down. The men dove into their foxholes as the explosions tore through their positions. Crowded six or seven to a hole, direct hits decimated the attackers before they could even begin the climb.

At three o'clock the attack began, but return fire reduced the advance to a crawl. The paratroopers found themselves up against mutually supporting bunkers built flush to the ground, with up to fourteen feet of protective dirt and logs piled over-

3. *Chieu Hoi* was the "open arms" program promising clemency and financial aid to guerrillas who stopped fighting and returned to live under South Vietnamese government authority.

head. These defensive works were usually spotted only after they opened fire, and then had to be painfully reduced one by one. Ordinary grenades, flamethrowers, and recoilless rifles proved useless. One group of troopers fired twelve antitank rockets directly into a bunker aperture and then charged forward to clear it. They were met by a hail of grenades and submachine-gun fire from the bunker occupants, who had taken refuge in a connecting tunnel during the rocket attack. The battalion resorted to sending individuals forward to heave twenty-pound satchel charges through bunker openings or dump concentrated napalm mixture inside and then ignite the substance with grenades.

The tenacious NVA defenders responded by firing rockets, which skidded along the ground and slid into the paratroopers who were huddled behind logs and mounds of dirt. There they went off, killing and wounding dozens. Fortunately for the Americans, the Chinese grenades also sprinkling their pinned ranks were almost all duds. The NVA even managed to charge the flanks and rear of the battalion. After two trenchlines were captured in close combat, the advance finally ground to a halt within 250 feet of the top of the hill. After darkness the word to "hold in place" changed to "fall back." More intensive air and artillery bombardment was used the next day.

Throughout November 22, continuous air strikes pummeled Hill 875 and the surrounding area with bombs, napalm, and rockets. The top of Hill 875 had been blown bald by the terrific bombardment, which continued throughout the night. The 4th Battalion was reinforced by fresh soldiers airlifted into the valley near the southeast slope. These infantrymen were from two fresh companies helicoptered in from Darlac Province by the 4th Infantry Division's 1st Battalion of the 12th Infantry. They combined and spent the night under mortar fire preparing to assault the hilltop the next morning. They prepared for the renewed attack by checking weapons and distributing more ammunition and satchel charges.

The final attack was launched against Hill 875 on November 23. The paratroopers and infantrymen started back up the hill, but this time there was hardly any opposition. They scrambled past empty man-deep trenches and huge bunkers. The NVA had left, their covering mission completed. At 11:55 that morning the paratroopers reached the abandoned summit. They cheered with the chants they yelled when jumping out of aircraft, slogans inherited from the victories of World War II—"Airborne!" and "Geronimo!" However, their shouts were tempered by the realization that many gold-starred veterans of Vietnam's only parachute assault were now dead. Other soldiers reaching the hilltop simply sat down in the dust and charred wood splinters around them, opened their cans of C-ration turkey loaf, and had lunch.

The Battle for Hill 875 was over, and by November 28 it was obvious that the 1967 Battle for the Highlands was over also. The battered *1st NVA Division's 32d* and *66th Regiments* had retreated beyond the South Vietnamese borders, shielded by the division's Laotian War veteran *174th Regiment*. From October 25 through December 1, a tremendous military effort had been waged by some of the Army's best units. They had crossed some of the most hostile territory in South Vietnam and battled against some of the finest light infantry in the world. The expenditures matched the stakes involved; 151,000 rounds of artillery, 2,096 tactical air sorties, and 257 B-52 bombing strikes had been used. The losses had been high also. The 179th Aviation Company, which flew recovery Chinook helicopters, picked up over forty carcasses of downed helicopters.

The Battle of Dak To had driven the NVA off the field of battle into Laos and Cambodia. The Army had secured victory by surmounting great logistical difficulties to close with and defeat an entrenched first-class opponent. As 1967 closed, the ability of the NVA to stage major operations in the Central Highlands had been largely negated. However, as events in 1968 were to prove, the long-range effects were less satisfactory. The setback the NVA had sustained was temporary, and the 1967 Battle for the Highlands had caused extremely heavy losses to both the 4th Infantry Division and the 173d Airborne Brigade.

CHAPTER 12.

HOLDING THE LINE

1. The DMZ Spring Campaign

On February 26, 1967, Army heavy artillery planted on the scraped laterite of Hill 158, at the Con Thien Marine fire base two miles below the Demilitarized Zone, unleashed a deafening cannonade that stirred up miniature whirlwinds of red dust. The 174-pound projectiles were being fired over the DMZ, and the North Vietnamese counterbatteried the next day. Con Thien and Gio Linh were shelled, while Camp Carroll farther south was subjected to a fierce rocket attack. These opening salvos initiated a savage artillery exchange that would last throughout the year, thunderclaps in the storm gathering over the northern fringes of South Vietnam.

The entire Marine DMZ campaign was hinged on the combat bases hugging the length of Route 9, from western mist-shrouded Lang Vei, past Khe Sanh, the Rockpile, Camp Carroll, and Cam Lo, to the key Marine command post of Dong Ha. Four Marine battalions had been skirmishing in the territory beyond this line since the previous August as part of Operation PRAIRIE. Only two fortified outposts had been thrust closer to the DMZ, Con Thien and Gio Linh, both forward gun positions under the shadow of the zone itself. Desultory local actions were waged against the *324B NVA Division* through the drenching winter monsoons, but the tempo quickened as the artillery duels intensified and the dry season approached.

The North Vietnamese Army periodically infiltrated large

combat formations directly south into Quang Tri Province through the DMZ. The 3d Marine Division, lacking the strength physically to cover the length of South Vietnam's northern border, resorted to a mobile defense. It depended on a roving advance guard to detect crossing NVA forces, which were counterattacked by Marine elements stationed at the major bases along Route 9. In this manner a reconnaissance patrol from the 4th Marines tripped over the advancing *812th NVA Regiment* in the scrub brush outside Cam Lo on February 27. One of the tanks accompanying the relief company (Company L, 4th Marines) threw a track in the dense undergrowth, forcing the advancing Marines to laager overnight deep in hostile jungle.

Daybreak was accompanied by an intense mortar barrage which sent geysers of dirt tearing through the Marine positions. As clumps of earth and grass were still falling to the ground, waves of North Vietnamese soldiers stormed out of the jungle. Rocket-propelled grenades exploded against two tanks, setting one on fire. The Marine defenders defeated three determined NVA infantry charges with the help of massed close artillery support. The North Vietnamese pulled away as Lt. Col. Victor Ohanesian of the 2d Battalion, 3d Marines, reached the stranded company with reinforcements later that morning.

Another company of the 4th Marines had also been sent in from another direction. It was now ordered to take a hill blocking the suspected North Vietnamese withdrawal and unwittingly sallied up the slope directly into perfectly camouflaged fortifications. The NVA abruptly opened up at point-blank range, killing the company commander and forcing the Marines back under a vicious cross fire. Another line company was helicoptered north of the hill and began moving toward the stricken unit. That afternoon Ohanesian's group also set out toward the new scene of action. Since the disabled tanks were still stuck, Company L was left in place as security.

Lieutenant Colonel Ohanesian's column was beset by a thick snarl of jungle and began moving down a trail just beyond Company L's lines, confident that the NVA forces had departed. The North Vietnamese triggered a massive ambush along the trail, showering the Marines with a hail of grenades and machine-gun fire which tore the entire column in shreds and killed both

Lieutenant Colonel Ohanesian and his Sergeant Major. Tightly bunched in platoon clusters and under heavy fire from the dense walls of vegetation on each side, the Marines desperately crawled over abandoned equipment and dozens of dead comrades, dragging their wounded back to Company L. The North Vietnamese then kept the armor-supported perimeter under such devastating rifle and grenade fire that medical evacuation helicopters were unable to land.

Marine units throughout the area were redirected toward the remnants of Ohanesian's group. The North Vietnamese soldiers left the battlefield, and the Marines consolidated without incident. They swept the entire vicinity, but the tropical forest around Cam Lo was now deserted. Maj. Gen. Bruno A. Hochmuth took over the 3d Marine Division on March 20, as the Special Landing Force battalion came ashore south of the Gio Linh fire base. That battalion fought a week-long battle through a maze of interconnecting North Vietnamese tunnels between Gio Linh and Con Thien.

The next threat that Hochmuth's division faced was sparked along the western part of Route 9 near Khe Sanh. The Khe Sanh combat base consisted of an airstrip carved from a small plateau overshadowed by Dong Tri Mountain. The surrounding territory was composed of a tangle of piedmont hills with jungle-webbed slopes, which disappeared in groves of bamboo and saw-toothed elephant grass. Four peaks covered by sixty-foot-high tropical hardwood trees dominated the most advantageous northwest approaches, Hills 558, 861, and 881 North and South. Khe Sanh was being defended by solitary companies on a rotating basis, which pushed reconnaissance patrols into the rugged hills around it. On March 16, 1967, a platoon from Company E of the 9th Marines was ambushed returning from an overnight patrol position on nearby Hill 861. Another platoon was sent to help, and both were badly shot up trying to get casualties out of an emergency landing zone. The opening shots in the incipient struggle for Khe Sanh had been fired.

On April 24, a Marine forward observation party from Company B, 9th Marines, was bushwhacked in a bamboo thicket on the slope of Hill 861. The action engulfed several platoons in heavy combat on the hillside, and a company from the 3d Marines was sent in from the Rockpile. The new Marines were fed into the battle the next day, but the well-fortified NVA bunkers, supported by mortars on the reverse slopes, stopped all further advances. Instead of another brief patrol engagement it developed into the first of The Hill Fights, which lasted until mid-May.

After Khe Sanh was heavily shelled during the night of April 25, it became apparent that the *325C NVA Division* was also in command of other hills overlooking the base. The next morning another company from Camp Carroll joined in the attack up Hill 861, but it was also repulsed. In the meantime Company B had also attempted to link up, but was decimated and pinned in place. The battalion pulled back down the hillside at sundown and was able to extract the remnants of Company B under the cover of rain showers and night fog.

Colonel John P. Lanigan, commander of the 3d Marines, arrived at Khe Sanh to take charge. The regiment's 2d Battalion was made available from the Quang Tri area by closing out its role as Special Landing Force. Together with several companies of the 9th Marines, he had roughly three rifle battalions committed.[1] They were outfitted with an unfamiliar weapon, which was about to undergo its first Marine test in battle. The 3d Marines had exchanged their reliable wooden M14 rifles for lightweight black M16s.

More Marines slipped into muddy positions on the battle line in the nightly downpours. Incessant air strikes and heavy artillery pounded Hill 861 into a smoking, cratered heap of upturned earth and shrapnel-riddled, branchless tree stalks. The North Vietnamese soldiers abandoned their positions, and the Marines met no resistance as they marched to the hilltop on the afternoon of April 28. The 3d Battalion of the 3d Marines tackled the next NVA strong-point, Hill 881 South, on April 30. It had also been worked over by intensive bombardment. Two platoons had almost reached the summit when perfectly cam-

1. The exact Marine units and arrivals in The Hill Fights were Company M, 3d Marines (April 27); 2d Battalion, 3d Marines with Companies E, F, G, H (April 26); 3d Battalion, 3d Marines with Company K (April 25); Company B, 9th Marines (already at Khe Sanh); Company E, 9th Marines (May 1); Company K, 9th Marines (April 25); and Company M, 9th Marines (April 27).

ouflaged, earthen-timber casemated defensive works struck the
Marines on all sides with machine-gun and grenade fire. Men
were spun around and thrown into the broken ground before
they could return a shot. Mortars added to the carnage, and
snipers finished off the screaming wounded. Helicopter gunships and fighter-bombers carved out a channel of exploding
ordnance, through which the battalion managed to retreat down
the hill. Company M of the 3d Marines had been rendered
combat-ineffective.

Another day was devoted to massed aerial and artillery dev-
astation, which raked the hill and flattened scores of bunkers.
The battalion attacked again and took Hill 881 South on the
afternoon of May 2. That same morning, after extensive clearing
skirmishes, the 2d Battalion had worked its way into attack positions against the single remaining NVA hillsite, Hill 881 North.
The Marines toiled up the slippery clay in driving rain. NVA
machine guns and rockets suddenly blazed through their ranks
and the attack faltered, then stalled, and finally stopped for the
night.

In the early morning darkness of May 3, the battalion suffered a sharp reverse. A North Vietnamese Army counterattack
overwhelmed Company E and reoccupied several bunkers. More
waves of North Vietnamese attackers were disclosed under flarelight, and direct Marine 106mm recoilless rifle fire was used to
break up the charge. The battalion spent the next day painfully
reducing each recaptured bunker with close-in assaults and
demolition charges. Hill 881 North was plastered by air and artillery bombardment, and the Marines pressed to its summit in
the afternoon of May 5. Mopping up and final destruction of
the extensive fortified positions continued for another week, but
The Hill Fights were over. On May 13, 1967, the 1st Battalion
of the 26th Marines took over the defense of Khe Sanh, and
they were reinforced by the 2d Battalion the next month. Their
mission would become a harrowing ordeal when the regiment
was besieged there during 1968.

2. The DMZ Campaign Continues

Con Thien, the Marine forward artillery post perched on a
small knoll near the DMZ, soon developed secret strategic significance in addition to its crucial observation role. It was des-

tined to be the western terminus of an infiltration barrier extending to Gio Linh, which Defense Secretary Robert S. McNamara planned to stretch across Vietnam and eventually Laos. Initially coded Project PRACTICE NINE, but popularly known as the Electric Fence, this mine-sewn, sensor-saturated, obstacle-swamped swath of bulldozed land was to be backed by a fixed system of elaborate strong-points.[2] The Institute of Defense Analysis had sold the idea to the Defense Department, and General Westmoreland noted it could potentially substitute for additional troop requirements.

The Marines were bluntly opposed to the whole concept, which they considered impractical and immensely expensive, and which relegated them to building and manning futile static defenses. However, the McNamara Line had the highest national priority, and a trial segment was ordered emplaced by the end of the year. The 3d Marine Division began devoting most of its energy to the preparatory clearing and construction of this preliminary section. The enormous construction resources required placed a tremendous strain on Marine logistical support. That April, Army Task Force Oregon had been created at Chu Lai to free several Marine battalions for mobile area warfare. Instead, barrier security consumed all additional Marine manpower assets made available.

Con Thien, conceived as a key PRACTICE NINE Barrier strong-point, quickly developed into a magnet for NVA shellings and maneuvering. It dominated operations in the DMZ area, and an entire line battalion was stationed there to guard the engineers razing the surrounding countryside. On May 8, 1967, the base was hit by a predawn mortar barrage followed by a sapper-led ground assault. North Vietnamese soldiers pierced the perimeter wire with bangalore torpedoes and raced through a hail of automatic weapons fire to leap into the trenches of Company D, 4th Marines. NVA flamethrowers scorched bunkered machine guns as close-quarters combat raged through the Marine lines. Two armored amphibious tractors sent into the breach were knocked out by satchel charges and rocket-pro-

2. Project PRACTICE NINE was relabeled ILLINOIS CITY in June 1967, and DYE MARKER on July 14, 1967.

pelled grenades. The Con Thien defenders managed to eject the assailants after a bitter fight lasting most of the morning.

The Marines began large sweep and clearing operations for the PRACTICE NINE barrier in the second half of May. For the first time in the war, a multibattalion attack was launched into the southern half of the Demilitarized Zone. The drive began early on May 18 under an umbrella of helicopter gunships and fighter-bombers.[3] To the east a motorized South Vietnamese force dashed straight up Highway 1, reached the border and Ben Hai River at first light, and wheeled around to sweep back south. Shortly after the South Vietnamese jumped off, the Marine Special Landing Force Battalion hit the beaches near the mouth of the Ben Hai River and drove inland against entrenched resistance.

The western prong of the drive was launched by Marine battalions near Con Thien north into the zone, while another battalion air-assaulted just south of the Demarcation Line. Its major purpose was to evacuate the civilian population from this region so that the barrier could proceed. Hard fighting developed immediately. Bunker complexes and fortified hills, well built and camouflaged to blend into the ground, presented formidable obstacles to the Marine advance, but the NVA pulled back under pressure. After two raging battles on Hills 117 and 174 during the last week of May, the operation was successfully concluded.

The Marines continued to scour the southern DMZ afterwards, pulverizing massive bunker and tunnel emplacements through early June. Afterwards, company-sized ambuscades prevailed in the lower zone area. Lt. Gen. Robert E. Cushman, Jr., took over III Marine Amphibious Force on June 1, and throughout the summer and fall the main arena of conflict remained Con Thien. Increasing artillery and rocket barrages against

---

3. The South Vietnamese portion, consisting of five battalions, was called Operation LAM SON 54. The Special Landing Force Alpha (1st Battalion, 3d Marines) portion was Operation BEAU CHARGER. The western prong was Operation HICKORY, executed by the 2d and 3d Battalions, 9th Marines, and 2d Battalion, 26th Marines, from the Con Thien, with an aerial insertion of the 3d Battalion, 4th Marines, north near the Ben Hai River. Later the 2d Battalion, 3d Marines, was also committed. The NVA *31st*, *32d*, and *812th Regiments* were engaged.

Marine fire bases were coupled with violent infantry clashes. Operation BUFFALO was among the fiercest.

Capt. Sterling K. Coates's Company B of 1st Battalion, 9th Marines, was ambushed along hedgerow-lined Route 561 within earshot of Con Thien on July 2. North Vietnamese soldiers of the *90th NVA Regiment*, backed by flamethrowers and massed artillery, shattered the Marine attempts to disengage. Pinned platoons were rapidly cut up and in minutes the company was destroyed. The rest of Lt. Col. Richard J. Schenning's tank-supported 1st Battalion, 9th Marines, counterattacked. Tanks exploded in minefields, ferocious mortar barrages blistered helicopter insertions, and artillery on both sides blasted infantry movements. After considerable fighting, the Marines reached the remnants of Company B. Staff Sergeant Leon R. Burns reported to the relief column, "Sir, this is the company, or what's left of it." Out of three hundred men, only twenty-seven shaken survivors were able to walk out. With the company suffering nearly two hundred severely wounded and another hundred dead, it had been one of the worst Marine battle disasters of the Vietnam War.

Colonel Schenning's battalion was still locked in heavy combat, and two more battalions were shoved into the battle (3d Battalion, 9th Marines, and 1st Battalion, 3d Marines). Heavy artillery exchanges continued as the Marines swept north. One 152mm shell impacted directly on top of a 9th Marine battalion command post on July 5. The violent ground fighting culminated in a massed NVA regimental attack on July 6. Aircraft swooped down to strafe and bomb lines of fully combat-equipped North Vietnamese regulars. Artillery shellfire blanketed the battlefield with smoke and burning powder. Many North Vietnamese soldiers reached Marine positions despite horrendous losses, hurling blocks of TNT before they were gunned down or stabbed. Two days later the battle was over, leaving hundreds of torn North Vietnamese corpses and acres of demolished equipment crushed into the smoking earth.

Dong Ha was subjected to a fierce rocket and artillery attack in August which exploded both the ammunition and fuel dumps, and left them burning for days. Marine medium helicopter squadron HMM-361 had so many of its aircraft destroyed and severely damaged that it was temporarily put out of business. As a result, III MAF was forced to relocate Marine Aircraft Group 16 (Forward) to Quang Tri, which was outside NVA artillery range.

By the end of August, the Marines had completed much of the test barrier section, but work on this massive undertaking continued. In September events moved to a climax at Con Thien. During the month the Marine fire base was pounded by one of the most intense shellings of the Vietnam War. In one week, that of September 19–27, Con Thien was lashed by 3,077 rounds. Occasional NVA ground attacks struck the base but were stopped at the wire. Outside the perimeter several Marine battalions tried to keep the NVA forces at a safe distance from the base. These efforts produced frequent, sharp firefights.

In the fading twilight of September 10, 1967, the *812th NVA Regiment,* garbed in Marine helmets and flak jackets, struck the perimeter of the 3d Battalion, 26th Marines, near Con Thien. Circling aircraft flashed across the darkening sky, tumbling bombs that crashed across the attacking formations in gushing explosions of jellied napalm. As the NVA infantry ran forward a medium battle tank and a flame tank unleashed a torrent of cannister projectiles and scorching fire. Both armored vehicles were rocked with salvos of rocket-propelled grenades. The flame tank disintegrated in a tremendous blast which left its hulk blazing through the night. The other tank rolled into a ditch. The Marines hammered the onrushing North Vietnamese soldiers with claymore mines, machine guns, and automatic weapons. The Marines fell back to a final defensive position and called in a solid curtain of protective shellfire, which broke the NVA attack.

At the end of the month the bombardments of Con Thien began tapering off, and on October 4, 1967, MACV declared that the siege of Con Thien was over. One segment of the McNamara Line section was largely implanted before the mid-October torrential monsoon rains drenched the northern provinces with flooding waters. Roads were turned into red ooze, and mud caked equipment and weapons. While fighting became light and intermittent the next month, the 3d Marine Division lost its commander. Major General Hochmuth's helicopter exploded and crashed en route to Dong Ha on November 14, 1967, and two weeks later Maj. Gen. Rathvon McC. Tompkins arrived to take his place.

The last action of the 1967 DMZ campaign occurred in late December when the 3d Battalion, 1st Marines, ran into a heavily fortified beach village in trouble-plagued Operation BADGER TOOTH. Naval landing craft had brought the Marines ashore the previous day to search several seaside hamlets in southern Quang Tri Province. Captain Thomas S. Hubbell's Company L spent the night at Tham Khe and then moved out to search other villages. At noon it was ambushed trying to reenter Tham Khe. Two companies of the *716th NVA Regiment* had infiltrated behind them.

Although the village was literally in the middle of the Marine battalion, there was an inordinate amount of confusion trying to coordinate an attack. The fighting was intense, several companies were stuck, and NVA mortar fire was blocking attempts to link up. Company L was cut off and unsure of its exact location, precluding fire support. Its captain had been killed and communications were gone. After a bitter, bloody struggle the battalion managed to consolidate at midnight. The North Vietnamese had slipped back out in the meantime. Shortly before noon on December 28, 1967, after a nightlong aerial and naval bombardment, the Marines entered the demolished village.

Several NVA attempts to shove large units south of the DMZ had been defeated in heavy combat. The Con Thien section of the barrier—designed to prevent such incursions—had been renamed PROJECT DYE MARKER and had been emplaced at great cost. Defense Secretary McNamara envisioned the barrier's installation in successive stages with an air barrier projected across Laos and the first land stages stretching from Cua Viet to Dong Ha, thence westward. However, the barrier was never realized. The system's ultimate doom was sealed by the loss of western Route 9 after the fall of Lang Vei and the abandonment of Khe Sanh the next year. The results of the massive scientific effort supplementing the barrier plan, especially in the field of electronic monitoring devices, were later placed to excellent use elsewhere on the Vietnam battleground.

3. The Marine Coastal Campaign

During the DMZ border battles the 1st Marine Division was heavily engaged in the rice plains and coastal sands of the lower three provinces of I Corps Tactical Zone. The Viet Cong stronghold in that area was between Chu Lai and Da Nang in the densely populated, fertile Phuoc Ha Valley, which by 1967 was an old Marine battlefield.[4] Isolated South Vietnamese forces had been consistently cut up trying to outpost the area. The Marines lacked the assets to control the valley and placed a reinforced company (Company F of the 1st Marines) on a critical hill mass overlooking it. On April 21, this company was moving along a ridgeline when it was hit by concentrated volleys of automatic weapons and grenade fire from the 3d NVA Regiment outside Binh Son.

The division responded by air-assaulting two battalions from Da Nang into action the next morning. One of them was airmobiled into a hornet's nest of North Vietnamese infantry and was forced to fight a major action getting beyond its landing zone. The reinforcements reached Binh Son, but combat was so intense all along the front that another battalion was helicoptered in from Chu Lai that evening. Operation UNION, under direction of the 5th Marines, had commenced.[5]

Fighting was heavy through April 25, and then the North Vietnamese began exfiltrating the battlefield. The Marines pursued, but contacts were infrequent. Then, on May 8, the 1st Battalion of the 5th Marines ran into steadily increasing resistance on the northern side of the valley. Hill 110 was taken on

4. Also called the Que Son Valley or Nui Loc Son Basin, this area was the operational confines of both 1965 HARVEST MOON and 1966 COLORADO. It was located just south of the border between Quang Nam and Quang Tin provinces near Tam Ky and became the haunt of the 2d NVA Division.

5. The 5th Marines had gained fame storming the German trenches at bayonet-point in Belleau Wood during World War I. It was activated in June 1917 at the Philadelphia Navy Yard, and had fought in France, Nicaragua, Guadalcanal, New Guinea, New Britain, Peleliu, Okinawa, and Korea. It had been in Vietnam since March–May, 1966. Initially the 1st and 3d battalions, 1st Marines, and 3d Battalion, 5th Marines, were involved in Operation UNION. On April 25, the 5th Marines took over entirely.

May 10, but NVA troops entrenched in nearby caves and sugar-cane fields chewed up several other Marine companies coming to assist. In a fierce daylong battle, marred by accidental aerial rocketing of Marine positions, the battalion pushed the North Vietnamese out of their defensive positions.

Three days later the 5th Marines entered a running battle with NVA companies and platoons in the valley basin. On April 15, the 3d Battalion encountered another fortified bunker area. Marine air strikes and artillery pummeled the complex while the riflemen pushed into assault positions. The fight continued through the evening and then gradually subsided as the Marines overran the main entrenchments around midnight. Two days later Operation UNION was terminated.

Operation UNION II was designed to trap the *21st NVA Regiment* in the same general area, and was initiated with a main heliborne assault on May 26, 1967. Driving south from their landing zone, the Marines ran into the main trenchworks of the North Vietnamese regiment the first day, located on the hillsides north of Thien Phuoc. The 3d Battalion of the 5th Marines charged up the fire-swept slopes to overrun the North Vietnamese lines at bayonet-point. Another large battle developed June 2 in the rice fields and hedgerows outside Vinh Huy, and a day after Maj. Gen. Donn J. Robertson took command of the 1st Marine Division, he was forced to commit an emergency composite battalion into the action. This extra reinforcement tipped the ground firepower scales, and the NVA broke contact. It was the last engagement of the UNION operations.

The Marines continued the campaign against the *2d NVA Division* through airmobile drives closely coordinated with amphibious assaults conducted by the Seventh Fleet's Special Landing Force. However, at this stage strong Army forces were also taking on this same North Vietnamese division in the Chu Lai area, as Task Force Oregon tackled the rugged inland jungle and numerous fortified villages hugging the coast.

Soldiers of the 1st Infantry Division push deep into War Zone D during June of 1967. (Author's Collection)

Soldiers of Lieutenant Colonel Alexander M. Haig's 1st Battalion of the 26th Infantry (1st Infantry Division) mark their forward fighting positions with smoke during the battle of April 1, 1967, in Operation JUNCTION CITY in War Zone C near the Cambodian border. (Author's Collection)

Soldiers of the 3d Battalion, 8th Infantry (4th Infantry Division) guard their perimeter after repelling a North Vietnamese Army attack in the mountains west of Kontum near the Cambodian border. (Army News Features)

Soldiers from the 1st Battalion of the 16th Infantry (1st Infantry Division) collect their dead and wounded on a battlefield near Xom Do in War Zone D during June, 1967. (Author's Collection)

Massed helicopter insertions, such as this one by the 2d Battalion of the 8th Cavalry on October 29, 1967, typified 1st Cavalry Division operations during Operation PERSHING in the coastal provinces. (U.S. Army)

Grim paratroopers of the 173d Airborne Brigade prepare to continue the assault up Hill 875 during the Battle of Dak To in November, 1967. (U.S. Army)

Marines of the 3d Battalion, 5th Marines, take cover as Viet Cong automatic weapons open up on January 27, 1967, in Quang Ngai Province. (U.S. Marine Corps)

This M67 flamethrower tank engages North Vietnamese Army positions with fire as it supports Marine infantry of the 1st Battalion, 3d Marines. (U.S. Marine Corps)

CHAPTER 13.

BATTLE FOR THE COAST

1. A Task Force Named Oregon

In February 1967, action promised to become intense along the DMZ, and MACV decided shock troops like the U.S. Marines should be freed from all coastal security duties. One of the problem areas of the Marine district was the southern half of I Corps Tactical Zone, more specifically, the Viet Cong-infested Quang Ngai Province. The Marines needed more troops on the Demilitarized Zone, where major battles were being waged against North Vietnamese Army regulars.

In February 1967, General Westmoreland decided to throw together three orphan Army brigades into a containing force for southern I Corps, to relieve the Marines of secondary problems in that portion of their zone. The task force was coded Oregon, and with any luck it would provide security in the coastal area, open Route 1 and the railroad, and relieve pressure in northern Binh Dinh Province as well. To replace the Marine presence as well as was possible with Army troops, it was decided to build the framework of this divisional-sized force around elite stiffening. The separate 1st Brigade of the 101st Airborne Division was used for this purpose. In early April, the 196th Infantry Brigade was yanked out of Operation JUNCTION CITY and sent to Chu Lai. The 3d Brigade of the 25th Infantry Division, al-

191

ready in the area under the control of the 1st Cavalry Division, was ordered to Chu Lai by the end of the month. Odds and ends from all over Vietnam were logistically scraped up to support Task Force Oregon, and on April 20, the package was given to III Marine Amphibious Force.

On May 11 the task force launched its first combat operation, MALHEUR, with its airborne brigade near Duc Pho. Supported by generous air strikes, the paratroopers fought eighteen separate firefights and uncovered large food and ammunition caches. Light fighting typified by ambushes and vigorous patrolling continued through July. However, MALHEUR II was concluded August 2 without any success in coming to grips with the elusive VC and NVA forces in the area.

Both the 196th Infantry Brigade and the 3d Brigade of the 25th Infantry Division were in poor condition. The former was filled with green replacements as its initial veterans headed home, and the latter was severely short of sergeants and interpreters. That brigade was hastily beefed up with extra aviation and tanks and then directed to move against Viet Cong main forces cemented in Quang Ngai Province.

Although the 2d ARVN Division was stationed at Quang Ngai itself, the Viet Cong enjoyed free run of this, as well as two adjacent, provinces. In fact, scores of weapons-toting VC were defiantly crossing the fertile rice paddies in broad daylight, much to the chagrin of local MACV advisors. This kind of insolent behavior not only mocked the Saigon government, but also disrupted travel along national Highway 1 and menaced various other activities. Most of these Viet Cong belonged to the combat-hardened *2d VC Regiment*. The 3d Brigade would end up fighting them throughout the year.

The brigade discovered that the regular Viet Cong were highly trained and ready to fight. Their fortified villages contained communications trenches, air-raid tunnels, and fighting bunkers, embellished by booby traps and punji pits. The initial fighting in April was light and sporadic. Relentless pressure by large groups of American infantrymen, usually mechanized or helicoptered in from out of nowhere and accompanied by fierce naval bombardment and pounding B-52 bomber strikes, finally caused many of the regular VC to disperse into the nearby jungle-covered mountains. Afraid and tired, some of the local village Viet Cong began turning themselves in.

Many villages continued to resist. A tank-riding reconnaissance platoon of the brigade was searching the beachside village of An Tho on the breezy, clear morning of August 20, 1967. Shortly after eleven o'clock a resupply helicopter was buffeted by ground fire, and the American tanks rumbled north after two Viet Cong running toward the nearby hamlet of An Thach. There a sixty-man company of the *97th Battalion, 2d VC Regiment* occupied a maze of trenchlines winding among the bamboo thickets and cactus hedgerows, which boxed in small plots of open farmland.

The tanks' steel-encased machine guns opened fire and cut down one of the VC dodging into the sandy brush. Then the hidden trenchline spewed out an uneven racket of automatic rifle fire. Although the Viet Cong had no antitank weapons, they were determined to defend the village with grenades and other weapons. The rest of the combined force at An Tho was swiftly pushed into the skirmish. Suddenly one of the tanks was jarred by an explosion. Although the tank itself was undamaged, its crew had been wounded by the force of the blast. Helicopter gunships hovered above the tanks and infantry as they worked in close conjunction to clear the first trenchline. The crescendo of machine-gun fire was periodically stifled by the boom of tank cannonade slamming point-blank into the hedgerows.

Lt. Col. Norman L. Tiller decided to airlift two more companies of his 2d Battalion, 35th Infantry, into An Thach. The 35th Infantry was particularly well suited to this combat; its regimental shield was emblazoned with a giant cactus and its nickname was the Cacti, derived from its original service along the Mexican border. Now the unit was heavily engaged amidst the bloodstained cacti surrounding An Thach.[1]

The Viet Cong were fighting desperately from bunkers and trenches to hold on to their positions. As they became completely encircled they realized their predicament and decided

1. The 35th Infantry was organized in July 1916 at Douglas, Arizona, for guard duty against Mexico and moved in 1922 to Hawaii. Since then its destiny had been in the Pacific, where it fought through both World War II and the Korean War. It had been in Vietnam since January 1966.

to break for the west. They moved from trench to trench, pausing only long enough to fire a few bursts before moving again. Through the haze of close combat they saw more and more helicopters discharging green-clad, equipment-laden Americans who were closing off all exits. Low-flying helicopters buzzed down the fortified avenues, their machine guns ripping up earth and structures into whirlwinds of dust and smoke. Some Viet Cong clutched their automatic rifles and made frenzied charges against the hated armor-plated monoliths which dominated the square patches of open ground.

The soldiers of the 35th ruthlessly pressed forward as the lopsided battle inevitably deteriorated. The Viet Cong company was broken into smaller fragments under the weight of the tank-infantry assault. Several VC were killed hiding in holes underneath their houses. About two o'clock the gunfire rose to a brief climax as Army riflemen and machines rammed through the last real resistance, a cluster of fourteen soldiers who died in close-quarters combat. Thereafter, the afternoon was punctuated by bursts of rifle fire at ten-minute intervals as surviving VC were flushed out. A flurry of helicopter activity overhead finished eight Viet Cong trying to flee across open rice paddies. Only a single five-man bunker was left by evening. The reinforcing companies had already started shuffling back to their helicopters, which took them to the beach to spend the night.

The Viet Cong company had been annihilated. The day's action was typical of those military victories in Vietnam in which the Army could muster overwhelming power and crush an opponent incapable of meaningful response or flight. This was war as it had existed in every century: uneven, cruel, and reduced to a ritual of slaughter. The warriors' success was measured by violent destruction, in which prompt and systematic elimination of the enemy meant the loss of fewer comrades. The terror and shock of bayonet-point battlefield reality remained the ultimate finishing school of first-class soldiers.

The 1st Brigade of the 101st Airborne Division was searching for the Viet Cong inland through saturation patrolling and ambushing. Companies were air-assaulted into multiple landing zones and, once on the ground, patrolled in three or four areas which were within mutual striking distance in case reinforcement was required. To allow the companies to fade into the tropical rain forest, up to seven days' rations were issued before operations. The brigade seldom moved at night since controlled movement through the jungle became very difficult. During hours of darkness, the paratroopers settled into ambush positions along trails that they had found during the day.

Task Force Oregon was being transformed by mid-August. The 3d Brigade of the 25th Infantry Division was redesignated as the 3d Brigade of the 4th Infantry Division, and this change of title brought it a step closer to rejoining the latter division in the Central Highlands. With the 1st Brigade of the 101st Airborne Division looking forward to recuperating at its Phan Rang home base, only the 196th Infantry Brigade was left without a sponsor. Although the 23d Infantry Division (Americal) had its genesis in Task Force Oregon, only the 196th served both. Daily contacts between small opposing groups continued under a variety of code names well into November. During that time, however, Task Force Oregon was becoming a legitimate Regular Army division.

On September 22, 1967, Task Force Oregon was redesignated the Americal Division. The name Americal was chosen partially in deference to Marine Corps-Army working relationships. The old Americal Division of World War II had been formed from Army units on New Caledonia to support the Marine offensive on Guadalcanal. The name was derived by combining the words American and Caledonia, and it became official. The name Americal had another connection. It was the only division during World War II to be formed outside United States territory, an act being repeated in Vietnam by the conversion of Task Force Oregon.[2]

The Chu Lai security 196th Infantry Brigade initially had to serve as the backbone of the new division. Resulting problems that the Americal Division experienced stemmed mostly from

2. The military in Vietnam also was attracted to the notion that it was the Army's only named division, but this was not strictly the case. The Department of the Army had assigned it the numerical designation 23 after World War II, and Americal was now only an agnomen which could be placed in parentheses. MACV conveniently ignored this officialese whenever it could, and the division was simply known in Vietnam as the Americal Division.

the two poorly trained brigades added as soon as they landed in Vietnam. The 198th Infantry Brigade, another castoff intended for police duty in the Dominican Republic, was given to the Americal Division after it was nixed for duty on the Caribbean island. The 11th Infantry Brigade arrived to join the division in late December. The brigade had been formed to reconstitute the Pacific reserve on Hawaii. The unit was not fully trained or equipped when it suddenly received orders for deployment to Vietnam. This extremely tight scheduling precluded smooth transition to a battlefront role. Predeployment inspections revealed over thirteen hundred men incapable of deploying. Many filler personnel were hastily added to the brigade to meet these shortfalls, and in fact replacements continued to arrive up until the very date of departure. The turmoil and confusion were detrimental to both its predeployment preparation and its ultimate combat performance.

On Thanksgiving Day of 1967, as paratroopers and infantrymen were scrambling up Hill 875 in the Central Highlands, the 196th Infantry Brigade was fighting another fortified position in Quang Tin Province near the South China Sea. The morning was overcast with light misting rain as the 4th Battalion, 31st Infantry,[3] moved out against Hill 63. The hillock island, rising from the flat rice paddies, was covered with thick brush and jumbled boulders. Numerous small houses on these hillocks were surrounded by dense ten-foot high hedgerows dividing vegetable plots.

The hill was defended by soldiers of the *2d NVA Division* entrenched in foxholes and hedgerows. Sudden bursts of close-range submachine-gun fire started cutting down the advancing armor-vested infantrymen. Tanks from the 1st Squadron, 1st Cavalry and armored personnel carriers from Troop F, 17th

3. The 31st Infantry was known as the "Polar Bears," a title gained after service in the ill-fated Siberian expedition of 1918–19. Formed in the Philippine Islands in 1916, it had surrendered to the Japanese 14th Army on Bataan early in World War II. Reorganized in Korea after the war, where it stayed until inactivation in 1957, the regiment did not set foot in the United States until 1965 when it was reformed in Massachusetts as part of the 196th Infantry Brigade. The 4th Battalion had been sent overseas again, to Vietnam, less than a year later. Large, menacing polar bears still decorated the unit's distinctive insignia.

Cavalry, plowed forward. A rocket-propelled grenade struck the ammunition box on one vehicle and a spectacular explosion rocked the area. By noon the fighting had become general and more infantry and armored reinforcements were committed. Some tanks became mired in the monsoon mud.

The battle degenerated into a deadly game between infantry and bunkered positions. The foot soldiers encountering a bunker fired tracer rounds into it, showing the tank commanders where to aim. The tanks resorted to firing two rounds per bunker: a high explosive round with a delayed fuse to kill the NVA inside, followed by another high explosive "superquick" shot to open up the bunker's sides. Their tracked tonnage crushed in many defensive works. One particular bunker held out for over an hour. Finally, some soldiers tied eight pounds of TNT to a twelve-foot bamboo pole and shoved it in the rear entrance. The blast caved the bunker in on its occupants.

Fifteen tons of bombs and ten tons of napalm plastered the surrounding countryside, as the infantrymen were taking fire from across the rice paddies also. The next day dawned cloudy and humid, and the mission was expanded to clear the rest of the islands. Early that morning heavy automatic weapons fire ripped into the armored-infantry teams, announcing the NVA's continued presence. Artillery and air strikes saturated the area, in an attempt to block all avenues of escape. Sweeps across many islands failed to disclose all the hidden positions. Bypassed NVA gunners would fire point-blank into the backs of soldiers moving beyond them. By November 25, the North Vietnamese had been pushed out of the area, and the battle was over. The 196th Infantry Brigade and the new Americal Division would continue to face a determined, resilient foe for the duration of their efforts in Vietnam.

2. Battle for the Bong Son Plains

Maj. Gen. John Norton's 1st Cavalry Division (Airmobile) had been fighting against the *3d NVA Division* in lush, densely populated Binh Dinh Province since early 1966. As 1967 opened, the cavalry was engaged in Operation THAYER II, part of a continuing series of maneuvers designed to maintain pressure in that coastal province. Reinforced by a 25th Infantry Division brigade, it continued to comb the rice and sugarcane fields around the Bong Son lowlands and its adjacent valleys. The North Vietnamese and main force Viet Cong were highly elusive, and contact was difficult. As a result, opposition remained light during the operation, and the only notable action occurred on January 27. The 2d Battalion of the 12th Cavalry air-assaulted into a hornet's nest four miles northwest of Bong Son while conducting a reconnaissance sweep. Its descending helicopters came under fire from two battalions of the *22d NVA Regiment*, and the rest of 2d Brigade leaped into action. However, the North Vietnamese quickly fled the battlefield before blocking forces could reach the scene.

On February 11, during the Tet 1967 holidays, Major General Norton kicked off Operation PERSHING, with the avowed purpose of finishing off NVA forces in northern Binh Dinh Province. Reinforced by swarms of news camera teams, his division began sweeping hamlets and flushing the VC out of tunnels, wells, and hidden bunkers. Light skirmishing also flared along the high ground to the west of the Bong Son plains. During the first week of March, the 2d Brigade tangled twice with the *18th NVA Regiment* in the Crescent Mountain area. On March 19, the 1st Battalion of the 8th Cavalry clashed unexpectedly with a large North Vietnamese force, and two battalions of the 5th Cavalry joined the three-day battle before the North Vietnamese slipped away.

All three brigades of the 1st Cavalry Division (Airmobile) were concentrated in Binh Dinh Province on Operation PERSHING soon after Maj. Gen. John J. Tolson III took command of the division on the first day of April. With the exception of one detached battalion, the entire division was together for the first time in over a year. At the same time the attached brigade from the 25th Infantry Division was freed to join Army Task Force Oregon. During the next month the cavalry's 3d Brigade pushed north into the former Marine trouble spot of Quang Ngai Province. Embedded in the jungled, cave-studded hills it found Viet Cong strongholds which often covered the flat, open rice paddies with grazing fire.

The 2d Battalion of the 8th Cavalry air-assaulted into the

Viet Cong bastion of Song Re Valley on August 9.[4] Following a brief artillery barrage, one company of cavalrymen helicoptered onto a ridgeline which turned out to be bristling with camouflaged North Vietnamese fortifications. Immediately upon touchdown they were greeted by a combined onslaught of heavy automatic weapons, mortar, and recoilless rifle fire which blasted several helicopters out of the sky. Close combat raged for more than four hours before the troopers were able to pull back far enough to call in supporting air strikes. After forty-six tactical Air Force sorties and concentrated aerial rocket fire, the NVA withdrew. Cavalry reinforcements were unable to regain contact.

During September, a number of firefights erupted in both the Bong Son and An Lao valleys. The newly arrived mechanized 1st Battalion of the 50th Infantry was attached to give the 1st Cavalry Division some armored firepower. By November, Operation PERSHING was reduced to a holding action as the division channeled forces in to bolster the Battle of Dak To. During the last month of the year the division returned to win an important victory over a fortified village complex near Tam Quan, along the seacoast of Binh Dinh Province.

Scout helicopters from the 1st Squadron, 9th Cavalry, spotted a radio antenna sticking out of the ground near Tam Quan on December 6. When the flight leader fired rockets at it, he was answered by machine guns. One of the squadron's aerial rifle platoons was landed at once astride Highway 1. It reached the edge of Tam Quan village before being pinned down by accurate fire from trenchlines interlaced with spider holes which were covered by logs and dirt. The hamlet was situated on a large paddy island covered by palm trees and dense bamboo thickets separated by numerous hedgerows, and the trench network was constructed along the edge of this island. Another rifle platoon was air-assaulted into an adjacent rice paddy, but it also

---

4. The 8th Cavalry was one of the Army's post–Civil War regiments raised at the Presidio of San Francisco to tame the West. It fought Apaches, Comanches, and other Indians, most notably in Arizona. After twelve years of Texas duty to 1888, it served in Cuba and the Philippines and fought in both World War II and in Korea with the 1st Cavalry Division.

became pinned in place as night was approaching.

The 1st Battalion of the 8th Cavalry was air-assaulted into the maelstrom to extract the two platoons just prior to dark. As the cavalrymen moved out, the Viet Cong suddenly opened fire from well-concealed spider holes. Company B consolidated on its landing zone as night fell, and armored personnel carriers from the 1st Battalion, 50th Infantry, were added around its perimeter. Deep ditches around the paddy island had prevented the tracked carriers from getting around resistance. The sky was illuminated by constant flares and aircraft searchlights, and the aerial cavalry scouts were able to pull back under fire to the laager. As standard insurance, continuous artillery fire was used to pound the surrounding area.

The next morning rocket-firing helicopters doused the village with nonlethal riot-control gas, and self-propelled antiaircraft Duster guns lumbered in to use their automatic twin 40mm guns to rip through the thick shrubbery concealing the defenders. Artillery fire softened up the objective. The 40th ARVN Regiment pushed south of Dai Dong to complete the encirclement. At nine o'clock the 1st Battalion's cavalrymen, bolstered by several armored personnel carriers, charged across the marshy rice paddies. They were battered and repulsed by fierce interlocking defensive fires. More artillery bombardment was directed into the fortifications. That afternoon two flame-throwing armored personnel carriers arrived, and the battalion was sent in again to dislodge the entrenched Viet Cong.

The cavalrymen went forward with two companies on line and armored personnel carriers interspersed through their ranks. Recoilless rifle fire and rocket-propelled grenades slammed into the advancing troops. One carrier exploded, but a gush of smoke from the backblast of the Viet Cong antitank rifle exposed the weapon site. A burst of flame from one of the special armored personnel carriers scorched the position. As the troopers closed in to the first line of bunkers, dozens of grenades bounced off the rumbling vehicles. Many VC were crushed by the grinding mechanized tracks clanking over the trenches. Combat engineer bulldozers churned into the area to throw a causeway over the soggy battlefield, bury trenchlines, and clear areas for aerial medical evacuation.

That same afternoon a company of the mechanized infantry tried assaulting the nearby village of Dai Dong. They crossed a wide rice paddy but were quickly bogged down in the dikes around the hamlet. The battle raged for the next several days, the Americans pulling back each evening to night laagers ringed with armored vehicles. Reinforcements were urgently required, and the 1st Battalion of the 12th Cavalry had to be airlifted into the fight all the way from Dak To. Dai Dong was finally overrun on December 9 as the VC defenders were splintered into small groups that were methodically eliminated in small firefights throughout the area. The battle continued across the Bong Son River where the last organized resistance was crushed at An Ngheip by the 2d Battalion of the 8th Cavalry. This final engagement was marred by the inability of the armored personnel carriers to cross the swift-flowing, mud-banked river.

The Battle of Tam Quan was costly to both sides. Only three Viet Cong surrendered, and hundreds of bodies were uncovered in the charred wreckage of bunkers and collapsed trenchlines. Army and ARVN forces had suffered grievously as well. However, as a result of 1st Cavalry Division efforts during Operation PERSHING, Binh Dinh was one of the least affected provinces in Vietnam during the upcoming NVA/VC Tet-68 Offensive.

PART 4

1968

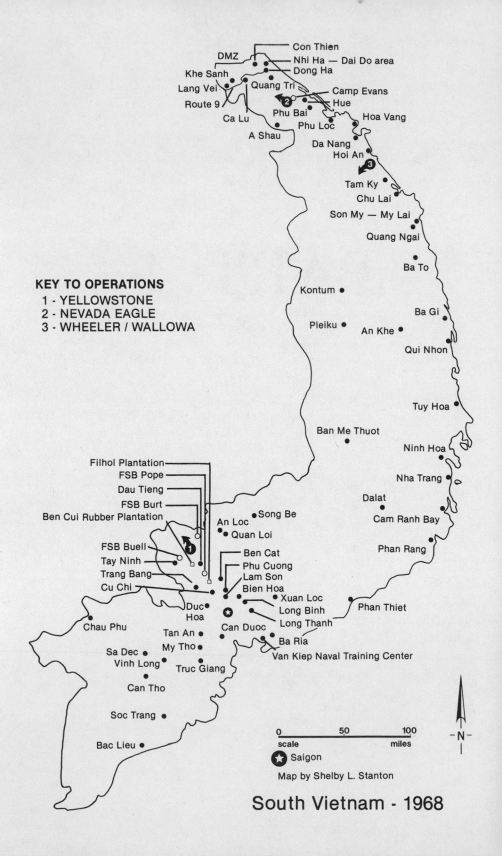

Con Thien
DMZ
Nhi Ha — Dai Do area
Khe Sanh
Dong Ha
Lang Vei
Quang Tri
Camp Evans
Route 9
2
Hue
Ca Lu
Phu Bai
Hoa Vang
A Shau
Phu Loc
Da Nang
Hoi An
3
Tam Ky
Chu Lai
Son My — My Lai
Quang Ngai
Ba To

KEY TO OPERATIONS
1 - YELLOWSTONE
2 - NEVADA EAGLE
3 - WHEELER / WALLOWA

Kontum
Ba Gi
Pleiku
An Khe
Qui Nhon
Tuy Hoa
Ban Me Thuot
Ninh Hoa
Nha Trang
Filhol Plantation
Dalat
FSB Pope
Cam Ranh Bay
Dau Tieng
FSB Burt
Ben Cui Rubber Plantation
An Loc
Song Be
Quan Loi
Phan Rang
FSB Buell
Ben Cat
Tay Ninh
Phu Cuong
1
Lam Son
Trang Bang
Bien Hoa
Cu Chi
Xuan Loc
Duc
Long Binh
Phan Thiet
Hoa
Can Duoc
Long Thanh
Chau Phu
Tan An
Ba Ria
My Tho
Van Kiep Naval Training Center
Sa Dec
Vinh Long
Truc Giang
Can Tho
Soc Trang

0   50   100
scale   miles
⭐ Saigon
—N—

Bac Lieu

Map by Shelby L. Stanton

South Vietnam - 1968

CHAPTER 14.

YEAR OF CRISES

1. 1968: Military Posture in Vietnam

The Vietnam Tet Offensive hit the American military like a thunderbolt. MACV had been expecting trouble, but not on a country-wide scale. On the eve of Tet-68, January 31, the United States had nine divisions, one armored cavalry regiment, and two separate brigades committed to Vietnam. This force totaled 331,098 Army soldiers and 78,013 Marines, concentrated in a hundred infantry and mechanized battalions.[1] MACV also had several strong formations from other countries in Vietnam, most notably the 1st Australian Task Force, a Royal Thai Army Regiment, two Korean divisions (the Capital and 9th), and a Korean Marine Corps brigade.

During January MACV's concerns in Vietnam were riveted on the northernmost provinces, upon which the high command had developed a fixation. The Marine Corps had already invested twenty-one infantry battalions, of its total thirty-six worldwide, into this I Corps Tactical Zone. The 3d Marine Division was defending parts of Defense Secretary McNamara's

1. The U.S. forces and their actual strengths on January 31, 1968, were 1st Marine Division (22,466); 3d Marine Division (24,417); 1st Cavalry Division (18,647); 1st Infantry Division (17,539); 4th Infantry Division (19,042); 9th Infantry Division (16,153); 23d Infantry (Americal) Division (15,825); 25th Infantry Division (17,666); 101st Airborne Division (15,220); 173d Airborne Brigade (5,313); 199th Infantry Brigade (4,215); 11th Armored Cavalry Regiment (4,331); 5th Special Forces Group (Airborne) (3,400).

Project DYE MARKER barrier, and stretched out along the Route 9 trace of strong-points that paralleled the DMZ. The 1st Marine Division was emplaced in Da Nang, Phu Bai, and Quang Tri. One regiment of the 5th Marine Division, the 26th Marines, had garrisoned the western anchor bastion of Khe Sanh.

General Westmoreland had been reshuffling his deck of available combat resources northward for some time. The trend had been set as early as August 1966, when the Korean Marine Brigade had been shipped into Chu Lai. By 1967, major operations in the rest of Vietnam were being curtailed, as field forces sacrificed major units in the rush to shift more Army formations north. Alarming year-end intelligence reports of a major NVA effort brewing in the border province of Quang Tri were followed by events at Khe Sanh. There the frightening results of a mid-January patrol action verified that the Marine combat base was surrounded by at least two dug-in NVA divisions. With the 26th Marines cut off at Khe Sanh, and both 1st and 3d Marine divisions tied down in hard combat, the situation in I Corps Tactical Zone appeared to be fast shaping up as a major disaster unless enough reinforcements could be pushed into the area during January to secure it.

The Army's new 23d Infantry (Americal) Division, charged with taming the two southern provinces of the zone, was still forming and did not carry much offensive clout. Its most recent component was the poorly trained and equipped 11th Infantry Brigade (Light), which had just disembarked in Vietnam in December. Already divisional soldiers were calling it "The Metrecal Division sponsored by General Foods," hardly a phrase reflective of high morale. During the height of the Tet-68 offensive, Marine commanders balked at General Westmoreland's recommendation to use it to reinforce Da Nang.

Airmobile striking power was rammed north when the crack 1st Cavalry Division in Binh Dinh Province was moved to III Marine Amphibious Force control. The 3d Brigade had been helping the Americal Division there since October, and it rejoined the divisional headquarters and 1st Brigade in the Hue-Phu Bai area on January 21, 1968. The division's other brigade did not move north until March, so the 2d Brigade of the 101st Airborne Division arrived as a temporary supplement. The 1st

Cavalry Division immediately began operations around Quang Tri.

If any Army unit could perform airmobile magic, it was this one. Known as the First Team, it was a division forged precisely for the Vietnam style of area warfare. Led by the dynamic Major General Tolson, a paratrooper who had made almost every Pacific jump of World War II, it had been beefed up well beyond average divisional power with lavish amounts of aviation. It was the only division with its own helicopter group, hundreds of assault and rocket-firing choppers that excelled in lifting the veteran skytroopers into the hottest landing zones in Vietnam.

The 1st Cavalry Division not only had dash and experience, but more importantly, its men demonstrated an uncanny willingness to knock heads with the North Vietnamese and Viet Cong. The division enjoyed a reputation for repeated success on the battlefield. Popularly known as Sky Cav, the division staged surprise air assaults so startling that VC mortar crews had been caught firing unarmed rounds, the shipping plugs still inserted, at the cavalrymen pouring out of helicopters. The 1st Cavalry Division's umbrella of aerial war wagons mauled the NVA at Quang Tri, helped crush the opposition in Hue, and leaped into Khe Sanh during the spring of 1968.

However, divisions of the 1st Cavalry Division's caliber were the exception by this time. The famed 101st Airborne Division had recently arrived in Vietnam, but it was airborne in name only and a shadow of its prewar eminence. Drained by years of maintaining its top-notch 1st Brigade in Vietnam, the division's ranks contained a mere sprinkling of parachutists. On January 10, U.S. Army, Vietnam, completed a paratrooper availability study which projected difficulties in retaining even the 173d Airborne Brigade in such a mode. The Army decided to take the 101st off jump status and turn it into a second airmobile attack division, but at the moment requisite aviation and training for such a conversion were lacking. In the meantime, the steady influx of ordinary soldier replacements both in Kentucky and Vietnam had transformed it into a standard division.[2]

2. The Department of the Army redesignated both the 1st Cavalry Division and the 101st Airborne Division on June 27, 1968, as the 1st and 101st Air Cavalry Divisions, respectively. This created a lot of fuss and bother among

The "Screaming Eagles" 101st Airborne Division had initially been programmed as a concentrated shot in the arm for III Corps Tactical Zone. However, it became an early candidate for General Westmoreland's northern buildup. A brigade flew north to reinforce the 1st Cavalry Division in January. At the same time other units of the division searched around Song Be and probed the southern part of War Zone D and the Filhol plantation. On February 19, 1968, the division headquarters and 1st Brigade scurried north to the vicinity of Hue, allowing the 1st Cavalry Division to get into position to relieve Khe Sanh. On that day the Army divisions in the area outweighed the Marine divisions three to two. The big move left III Corps Tactical Zone with only the 3d Brigade, which had been parceled out in several Tet-68 reaction battles.

This 3d Brigade then became the basis for one of MACV's most ambitious surprise moves to bag the North Vietnamese in central South Vietnam. It was alerted to an undisclosed location in the highlands. The anticipated move was so secret that the contingency plans were not mentioned to "foreign" personnel. All divisional patches were ripped off and helicopter and other markings erased. The 3d Brigade deployed to Kontum on May 25, but all its deceptiveness failed to impress or entrap anybody, and in fifteen days it was on its way back south. In October the entire division was put back together in I Corps Tactical Zone.

Due to the accelerated northern buildup, 1968 operations in the central portion of South Vietnam were generally relegated to a holding pattern. During January, "The Herd" 173d Airborne Brigade continued to brush against light opposition in the mountains as it phased into the former 1st Cavalry Division base camp at An Khe. After serving as a general Tet-68 fire brigade, the elite paratroopers scoured the coastal plains of Binh Dinh Province during March. The experienced "Ivy" 4th Infantry Division continued its security of the Central Highlands against light and scattered resistance, broken only by the fierce Tet bat-

---

the traditionalists, and on August 26, 1968, the Army Chief of Staff altered the titles to 1st Cavalry Division (Airmobile) and 101st Airborne Division (Airmobile).

tles at Pleiku and Kontum. The Korean Capital and 9th "White Horse" divisions maintained effective control of the coast from Phan Rang to Qui Nhon.

Two brigades of the "Tropic Lightning" 25th Infantry Division had gone back into War Zone C to locate Viet Cong installations in December of 1967 in Operation YELLOWSTONE. At midnight on New Year's Day, Col. Leonard Daems's 3d Brigade got into a bad scrape at Fire Support Base Burt. The perimeter was defended by the armored personnel carriers and men of the 2d and 3d Battalions, 22d Infantry, against an all-out assault by soldiers of the *271st* and *272d VC Regiments* charging behind a wall of machine-gun, recoilless rifle, and rocket grenade fire.[3]

The fighting was savage and desperate, lasting throughout the night with plenty of Beehive rounds and massive, close-in aerial napalm strikes. Tracked carriers and self-propelled 40mm antiaircraft guns were burning fiercely as the Viet Cong blasted their way into the infantry lines. Reserves rushed from other sides of the perimeter managed to hold the circular wagon wheel defense intact, and at dawn the VC withdrew. Operation YELLOWSTONE ended on February 24, 1968. The division's 2d Brigade was involved in heavy fighting along the Cambodian border south of Tay Ninh during this time.

The "Big Red One" 1st Infantry Division had just driven a wedge between War Zones C and D as it finally succeeded in opening Route 13 to Quan Loi. It would continue to secure this highway and sweep around the Saigon area during the upcoming storm of Tet-68. The "Redcatchers" 199th Infantry Brigade had turned over security responsibilities for the greater Saigon area to the 5th ARVN Ranger Group. The brigade then sortied into War Zone D in Operation UNIONTOWN, a mission which placed it in excellent defensive positions near Bien Hoa and in proximity to the 11th Armored Cavalry Regiment.

3. The 22d Infantry was redesignated in September 1866 in the Dakota territory from units raised at the end of the Civil War. It was a veteran of numerous Indian campaigns from the Dakotas to Montana, later fought in Cuba, and was shipped to the Philippines in February 1899. The regiment missed World War I but served in Europe during World War II. The two battalions had been in Vietnam since October of 1966.

The 9th Infantry Division had shifted to cover the southern approaches to Saigon, while its mobile riverine force had fused with Navy Task Force 117 to cover the northern watershed of the delta. The 1st Australian Task Force commenced its first operation outside Phuoc Tuy Province just east of Bien Hoa on January 24 with Operation COBURG. This incidentally placed it in excellent response positions to several Tet-68 trouble spots. The Royal Thai Army Volunteer Regiment was also operating in Bien Hoa Province.

The extent and fury of the NVA/VC Tet-68 Offensive at the end of January caught the American military off guard, with its resources stretched to the limit by the logistical and tactical strain of the northward shuffle. At the same time eventual success in the northern provinces seemed assured by this large infusion of extra Army assets in the area. MACV responded to the large battles raging there by sending in unprecedented amounts of war materials and additional manpower. Over sixty-five logistical and support units alone were moved north during January and February.

General Westmoreland's deputy and successor, Gen. Creighton W. Abrams, flew to the Hue–Phu Bai vicinity on February 9, 1968, to set up an emergency advance headquarters tagged MACV Forward. He brought an entourage of logisticians, statisticians, and tacticians garnered from the multitude of desks and chart rooms of Pentagon East. The critical situation called for drastic measures, and General Abrams made it clear that it wasn't business as usual, although his loud pronouncements about slicing "nonessentials," such as PX items, beer, and furniture, were mitigated by the provisional company of personal limousines that he brought along for headquarters use.

Front-line losses in the aftermath of the Tet Offensive of 1968 were staggering. United States combat deaths climbed 56 percent in 1968 to 14,592, while total Army and Marine helicopter losses were up 53 percent, with heaviest losses incurred during the intense combat of Tet-68 and Mini-Tet. The number of American deaths was already running twice the number incurred in 1967, the year of the big battles. The magnitude of Tet-68 was also reflected in aircraft destruction, which had doubled over the previous year. NVA/VC determination and combat capability were considered most ominous. The allied combat resources on hand in Vietnam were transfixed by the conflagration. As a result, MACV suddenly made a grab for anything that could be stripped out of the United States. These demands were personally handed to Gen. Earle G. Wheeler, the chairman of the Joint Chiefs of Staff, during his February 22–25 visit to South Vietnam. At the top of the list was a requirement for the immediate deployment of twelve maneuver battalions and eight tactical fighter squadrons. However, in the United States the military cupboards were already almost bare as a result of the spreading quicksand of the Vietnam War.

2. 1968: Military Posture at Home

While the war had escalated into a major conflict, the Defense Department was coping with the possibility of internal insurrection in the United States itself. Increasing racial and civil disturbances at home continued unabated. During the first nine months of 1967, over 150 cities reported disorders ranging from minor demonstrations to the major crises of Newark, New Jersey, and Detroit, Michigan. In most cases the National Guard had been able to handle the situations, but in several incidents federal troops had to be employed.

One of the worst city riots had erupted on July 23, 1967, with its own ironic connection to the raging Vietnam War. A predawn police raid was made on the Blind Pig, an upstairs speakeasy in the black ghetto of Detroit, Michigan, where a party was being hosted for several servicemen, two of whom had just returned from Vietnam. A crowd began pitching rocks at the police, who were putting the club's patrons into police wagons. The rioting quickly spread over eleven square miles, and by the next afternoon Lt. Gen. John C. Throckmorton had forward battalions of both the 82d and 101st Airborne Divisions on the scene. The Detroit riots lasted ten days before the paratroopers unfixed bayonets and withdrew from the fire-swept, sniper-threatened urban ruins. Another five days would pass before the area would completely return to civil authority. It had been a grisly, ugly

confrontation with a great deal of command and control confusion and a high death toll.[4]

Army and Marine troops went into action again during the
Anti-Vietnam Demonstration at the Pentagon in October 1967.
The major attack of the massive demonstration was made by a
two thousand-strong group, some of whom wore gas masks and
were armed with ax handles. They stormed the east side of the
Pentagon behind a barrage of rocks and bottles and crashed
through the lines of the 30th and 504th Military Police Battalions. They were repulsed at the entrance to Corridor 7 of the
Pentagon underneath billowing clouds of tear gas.[5]

The Department of Defense was not only plagued with dis-
sension across the country, but the beginning of January unleashed a wave of military hostilities in Korea. Trouble along its
demilitarized zone had been heating up through 1967, and the
2d Infantry Division north of the Imjin River was suffering heavy
losses as patrols were ambushed, trucks were mined, and North
Korean hunter-killer teams grenaded and machine gunned outposts.[6] On January 23, 1968, the North Koreans captured the
USS *Pueblo* and its crew.

Then Vietnam exploded. Immediately following the NVA/VC
Tet Offensive, General Westmoreland pleaded for additional forces
to stem the tide. Since June of 1966 the Marines had been
struggling to get their newly activated 5th Marine Division in
shape at Camp Pendleton, California. The 26th Marines had been
yanked out first, and now MACV was insisting on another infantry regiment, the newly formed 27th Marine Regimental
Landing Team. The 27th Marines was whisked out of El Toro,

4. At the height of the Detroit, Michigan, riots on July 29, 1967, a total of
15,339 federal and national guard troops were stationed at Detroit, and 9,613
had been committed into action.

5. During the Pentagon Riots of October 21–23, 1967, a total of 10,346 Marine and Army troops were placed in the Washington, D.C., area. Three
battalions were posted inside the Pentagon itself. The United States Strike
Command flew in the 1st Brigade of the 82d Airborne Division from Fort
Bragg, North Carolina.

6. The Joint Chiefs of Staff approved recommendations for combat pay in
certain areas of Korea on February 27, 1968, and the House Appropriations
Committee made it effective from April 1, 1968.

California, on February 17, 1968, and landed at Da Nang. It remained in defense of the key port until withdrawn from Vietnam that September.

The elite, all-volunteer 82d Airborne Division was drilling on the icy pine-fringed lanes of Fort Bragg, North Carolina. It was preparing for another hard year of riot control. With the exception of the 82d, the United States had only two understrength Marine and four skeletonized Army divisions left stateside by the beginning of 1968. The 82d Airborne Division was the sole readily deployable strategic reserve, the last real vestige of actual Army divisional combat potency in the United States left to the Pentagon.[7] It was composed of tough paratroopers who constituted a fanatically reliable formation, which became indispensable to the government during the racial and political revolts of 1968.

Suddenly, in the wake of Tet-68, even the 82d Airborne Division was no longer immune to MACV's incessant appetite. The fiction of paper flags on senior officer briefing maps was fast folding, and the Department of Defense could not spare the most reliable Army division in its inventory. Clearly, the ability of the armed forces to react was being stretched to the breaking point. The Pentagon finally compromised and agreed to release one third. As the 3d Brigade was being jumped on a routine training exercise over Florida on January 22, their orders for immediate Vietnam duty were being stenciled. The entire division was stripped to round out one full-strength paratrooper brigade, and the advance party left a cold, wind-swept Pope Air Force Base next door to Fort Bragg on February 13. On the afternoon of Valentine's Day, the huge emergency airlift of men and equipment went to Chu Lai.

The division had been so rushed to get this brigade to the

7. Forces in the United States in January 1968 were the 2d Marine Division—Camp Lejeune, North Carolina; 5th Marine Division (partial)—Camp Pendleton, California; 1st Armored Division (partial)—Fort Hood, Texas; 2d Armored Division (partial)—Fort Hood, Texas; 5th Infantry Division—Fort Carson, Colorado; 6th Infantry Division (partial)—Fort Campbell, Kentucky; 82d Airborne Division—Fort Bragg, North Carolina; 6th Armored Cavalry Regiment—Fort Meade, Maryland; 194th Armored Brigade (School Support)—Fort Knox, Kentucky; 197th Infantry Brigade (School Support)—Fort Benning, Georgia.

battlefront that it ignored individual deployment criteria. Paratroopers who had just returned from Vietnam now found themselves suddenly going back. The howl of soldier complaints was so vehement that the Department of the Army was soon forced to give each trooper who had deployed to Vietnam with the 3d Brigade the option of returning to Fort Bragg or remaining with the unit. To compensate for the abrupt departures from home for those who elected to stay with the unit, the Army authorized a month leave at the soldiers' own expense, or a two-week leave with government aircraft provided for special flights back to North Carolina. Of the 3,650 paratroopers who had deployed from Fort Bragg, 2,513 elected to return to the United States at once. MACV had no paratroopers to replace them, and overnight the brigade was transformed into a separate light infantry brigade, airborne in name only. Many of those returning would be fighting in Washington, D.C., that April, huddled in burnt-out laundromats and returning sniper fire from open jeeps, as their comrades pushed through dense tropical jungle against bunker lines overseas.

With the February 26 arrival of the 7th Squadron of the 1st Cavalry (First Regiment of Dragoons), a welcome 850-man helicopter search and attack unit from Kentucky, the immediately available military resources in the United States were completely exhausted. Two more major units were still programmed to go to Vietnam, where they were needed to bolster the extreme northern provinces. The 1st Squadron of the 18th Armored Cavalry, a California National Guard unit, was ordered into active federal service at Burbank on May 13, 1968, and scheduled to arrive in Vietnam that August. There was considerable political and antiwar turmoil in California, and MACV canceled the request for the California cavalry on September 25, 1968. The 5th Infantry Division (Mechanized) at Fort Carson, Colorado, was tasked to send its 1st Brigade to replace the 27th Marines. The division became embroiled in the Chicago and Washington, D.C., riots of April, and was hard pressed to get its brigade reorganized and combat-ready. The brigade was rushed to Vietnam's I Corps Tactical Zone on July 25 in order to meet Army scheduling deadlines. It moved to the Quang Tri area but was not deemed combat-ready until September 1, 1968.

Events in the United States slipped from bad to worse. At the end of March, President Johnson announced over national television that he would not campaign for a second term. In April of 1968, seething racial unrest in Washington, D.C., Chicago, and Baltimore flared into major violence following the assassination of Dr. Martin Luther King, Jr. The forces needed to subdue the resulting large-scale riots in all three cities included most of the Regular Army formations left in the United States, as well as massive numbers of National Guard troops.[8] The year also tapped large Army contingents at events such as the Democratic National Convention in Chicago during August, although local authorities quelled the disorders without the need of actual federal intervention.

Changes of the guard were taking place both in Washington and in Vietnam. On March 1, 1968, Clark M. Clifford became the new Secretary of Defense as Robert S. McNamara stepped down. One of the most profound changes of the conflict in Vietnam transpired when General Westmoreland departed as MACV commander to become the new Army Chief of Staff on July 3, 1968. General Abrams would bring far-reaching directional changes to the Vietnam battlefront, primarily in an effort to reduce United States combat losses and get the South Vietnamese Army back into the war's mainstream.

3. Other Vietnam Military Considerations

Military strategy in Vietnam during 1968 was still directed toward sustained offensive operations to defeat the NVA/VC forces, although much of its momentum was in reaction to NVA/VC-initiated events on the ground. City security became a major concern following the battles of Saigon and Hue. Although large offensive operations continued in certain critical areas, these operations were tempered in less essential areas as the military went on the defensive (termed "economy of force"). To compensate for exorbitant American casualty rates in the first six

8. Major Regular Army units involved in April 1968 riot combat were: Chicago—3d Brigade, 1st Armored Division; 3d Brigade, 5th Infantry Division; Baltimore—XVIII Corps Artillery; 197th Infantry Brigade; Washington D.C.—82d Airborne Division; 2d Brigade, 5th Infantry Division; 6th Armored Cavalry Regiment.

months of the year, operational zeal slackened in order to reduce U.S. losses. However, most significant was an April 16, 1968, directive to the Joint Chiefs of Staff announcing that the Defense Department had embarked on a course of gradually shifting the burden of the war to the South Vietnamese military. Although the word *Vietnamization* was not coined until 1969, the planning had already started.

The South Vietnamese armed forces were not militarily self-sufficient, a problem rooted in years of U.S. technical and command control and in America's direct conduct of the war since 1965. The South Vietnamese had started to perk up after it became apparent that the United States might do the lion's share of the fighting. War weariness set in again after the blows of Tet-68, which fell hardest on the ARVN defenders. This condition was manifested by crippling desertion rates and little aggressive battlefield leadership. The South Vietnamese Army was still lacking essential modernization. For example, at the beginning of 1968 only the ARVN Airborne Division, Marine Brigade, 51st Infantry Regiment, and 21st, 30th, 33d, 37th, and 39th ranger battalions were equipped with M16 rifles, which allowed firepower equal to the communist assault rifles.

The South Vietnamese force structure was strengthened as the year progressed. The 11th ARVN Airborne Battalion, which had been cut up by the Tet attacks on Van Kiep Naval Training Center, was declared operational March 30 and sent to Saigon. This completed the expansion of the elite ARVN Airborne Division. On October 1, the dependable and rugged South Vietnamese marine establishment, which had been operating two three-battalion brigades, was given a little extra artillery and redesignated a division.

The ten regular South Vietnamese divisions continued to perform very unevenly during 1968, though in some cases heavy losses accounted for declining abilities. The 1st ARVN Division at Hue maintained its reputation as one of the best. The 2d ARVN Division at Quang Ngai, historically prone to high desertions, displayed so little combat spirit during Tet that it was tagged as a major problem. The Lam Son-based 5th ARVN Division was considered barely effective, a rating shared by the 7th ARVN Division at Can Tho. The 9th ARVN Division posted to Sa Dec was the poorest of all. The trouble-plagued 18th ARVN Division at Xuan Loc remained combat-ineffective despite close command scrutiny. The 21st ARVN Division, located at Bac Lieu, was one of Saigon's better divisions. Both the 22d ARVN Division at Ba Gi and the 23d ARVN Division at Ban Me Thuot had problem regiments (the 41st and 44th respectively), but there had been aggressive assaults on well-entrenched VC positions north of Pleiku city. The 25th ARVN Division at Duc Hoa improved once it was issued M16 rifles and M60 machine guns.

MACV had also been directed to start a civilianization program on September 15, 1967. South Vietnamese workers would be substituted for U.S. military support personnel in certain logistical units. There were many advantages. American manpower could be trimmed as technical expertise was shared. However, MACV was dismayed at the prospect of losing its soldiers in exchange for labor problems and potential sabotage.

Most large construction, and many service, projects in Vietnam were already in the hands of civilian companies. For example, Pacific Architects & Engineers, Inc., handled the repair and utilities support for the Army, and employed over twenty-four thousand civilian personnel. Other examples were the Vinnell Corporation, which built and maintained central power plants and electrical systems, the Philco-Ford equipment yards, and the Alaskan Barge and Transport Company, which provided stevedore, trucking, and intracoastal barge service.

Work stoppages and contractual disputes were already a constant headache requiring frequent Army intervention. As an example, in late 1967 some two thousand Korean employees of the Vinnell Corporation began rioting at the major installation of Cam Ranh Bay. The primary cause appears to have been dissatisfaction with the food served them, particularly the shortage of rice. The Koreans refused to eat their Saturday evening meal on November 18, and went to the Vinnell mess hall where they turned over tables and attacked several Americans. They forced the American project manager to eat some of their food to show him how bad it was. A Vinnell Corporation civilian took out his gun and shot three Koreans. He was then mobbed and severely injured, and a Korean shot another American.

The Army military police stormed the area, but the Koreans

counterattacked with bulldozers and trucks which they rammed into trailers and buildings. Military guards on the vital power ships (converted T-2 oceanic tankers) anchored in the harbor, posted against VC combat-swimmers, managed to repulse Korean attempts to take over the vessels. However, Korean employees in Nha Trang hijacked a number of medium landing craft, and sailed to Cam Ranh Bay harbor in support. The riots were finally broken four days later, following intervention by the Korean Embassy and senior Army officers.

Fighting to retain its level of military authorization in combat service support units, MACV was openly dismayed with civilianization inroads. Much of this attitude stemmed from adverse experiences in Tet-68, during which the majority of the Vietnamese laborers never showed up for work at American installations. By the end of February, radio and television spot announcements were begging the Vietnamese to return to their United States contractors. An important incident occured on May 9, when 90 percent of the 1,046 local employees at the 506th Field Depot in Saigon left work in mid-afternoon without notice. Shortly thereafter (and not so incidentally according to Army reports) the Newport Bridge in Saigon was attacked by the Viet Cong.

The Army was fighting another losing battle. Civilianization was an inevitable by-product of Vietnamization, and as large numbers of Army support units were withdrawn from Vietnam commencing in 1969, civilianization replaced the majority of their functions.

CHAPTER 15.

THE BATTLES OF
TET-68

1. Tet-68: Saigon

MACV had decided as a matter of political feasibility to shift responsibility for Saigon area security to the South Vietnamese. As a result Saigon was only defended by the South Vietnamese 5th Ranger Group, and three regional forces, two service, and two military police battalions. The 1st and 8th ARVN Airborne Battalions, the last South Vietnamese high command reserves, had been programmed to move north to I Corps Tactical Zone on MACV's insistence that the DMZ be reinforced for the Tet period. However, a shortage of aircraft had delayed their out-flights, leaving both parachutist battalions fortuitously in Saigon when the crucial Tet offensive started.

On the night of January 30, 1968, the capital of Saigon was alive with the celebration of the Vietnamese *Tet Nguyen Dan* lunar new year holidays. Throughout the city thousands of traditional firecrackers were noisily popping. The long government wartime ban against fireworks had been lifted to heighten the festivities. Large imported Hong Kong Specials, a favorite with the wealthier Vietnamese, boomed incessantly with a grenade-like din. Chains of smaller linked firecrackers went off in a rattling spectrum of tumultuous sparks that sounded faintly like distant machine-gun fire.

There had been scattered indications of an imminent Viet Cong offensive. However, any reports of major Tet truce violation, much less of attacks on cities, were discounted by South Vietnamese officials. President Thieu departed Saigon on January 29, 1968, to celebrate Tet with his wife's family in My Tho. In view of disturbing intelligence reports, he reluctantly agreed to cancel the truce in the extreme northern part of the country. Even after the tocsin of country-wide attack sounded as Da Nang, Nha Trang, Ban Me Thuot, Kontum, and Pleiku were struck on January 30, alert orders to ARVN units in Saigon were issued without any sense of urgency. Orders canceling leaves either came too late or were simply disregarded. Soldiers on special Tet passes mixed in holiday reunion with their families in Saigon, far from their barracks and weapons.

The people of Saigon reveled in joyous enthusiasm, reflecting boundless optimism as the Vietnamese Year of the Monkey was ushered in. American assistance had brought a great boom in jobs and prosperity. The fortunes of war apparently now favored South Vietnam, and government-distributed gift parcels contained Munchausen horoscopes promising the brightest of futures. War and politics always took a back seat to the excitement of the Tet celebrations, and Saigon itself always seemed aloof from any battlefront.

Just before midnight, fully armed soldiers in palm-leafed helmets and Binh-Tri-Thien black rubber sandals jostled through crowds of jubilant Saigon celebrants, then disappeared down alleys, slinking back into the shadows. The people shrugged, perhaps another coup was under way. The first flashes of gunfire in the early morning of January 31 simply faded into the crashing echo of Tet fireworks. The Viet Cong had achieved complete surprise as they initiated simultaneous rocket, mortar, and ground attacks against buildings and installations throughout the capital.[1]

At two o'clock in the morning a bus came to a sudden stop in front of Gate #5 of the ARVN Joint General Staff compound. A score of VC sappers scurried out. Already their comrades were

1. Initial Viet Cong attacks in the Saigon-Cholon area were conducted by the *1st, 3d, 4th, 5th,* and the *6th, 267th, 269th, 506th Local Force Battalions, 2d Independent Battalion,* and *C-10 Sapper Battalion.*

in supporting positions inside the Long Hoa Pagoda. The gate had momentarily swung open for a South Vietnamese general, but as the sappers dashed across the street to rush the guard-house, a U.S. military police jeep happened along. The Viet Cong opened fire, the jeep spun to a stop, American military police from a nearby building ran out to join the gunfight, and the ARVN sentry slammed the gate and returned fire from his bunker. The botched attack on Gate #5 fizzled into a general exchange of gunshots.

At 9:30 A.M. the *1st* and *2d VC Battalions* knocked down northern Gate #4 with B-40 rockets. They charged into the Joint General Staff compound, a vital installation defended by the ARVN Honor Guard Battalion and a company of tanks. In the initial confusion the Viet Cong could have occupied vital communications and command centers. However, they were confronted with a host of fancy general headquarters signs marking the location of the headquarters support company, which they mistook as the main complex. They dug in to defend their prize, and elements of the 8th ARVN Airborne Battalion arrived to counterattack. Finally, after the paratroopers were reinforced by South Vietnamese marines and more tanks, they cleared the occupied buildings. By 10:30 A.M. on February 1, the Viet Cong had been chased out into the neighboring city blocks.

The *C-10 VC City Sapper Battalion* was composed of Saigon inhabitants, including cyclopousse and taxicab drivers. Nineteen members had been given a most important mission: seizure of the United States Embassy on Thong Nhat Boulevard. The two American flak-vested military policemen managed to close the gate after a taxi opened fire on them, but the Viet Cong breached the ambassadorial wall with satchel charges. They killed the guards, but the heavy teakwood entrance doors slammed shut, leaving the assailants to pepper the main chancery building with rocket-propelled grenades and automatic weapons fire. The company-sized U.S. Marine Saigon Guard Detachment and American government officials held the VC at bay by firing submachine guns and revolvers from open windows.[2]

---

2. The Marine detachment was armed with 9mm Beretta submachine guns, Smith and Wesson .38-caliber revolvers, and 12-gauge Remington shotguns loaded with 00 buckshot shells.

At 5:00 A.M. helicopters from Bien Hoa tried to land a platoon from Company C, 1st Battalion of the 502d Infantry (Airborne), on the embassy roof. Army military police, crouched behind trees across the avenue, watched as heavy gunfire exploded from the courtyard. The helicopters took several hits, a door gunner was wounded, and the airmobile assault was postponed. Finally, at eight o'clock the helicopters managed to make the insertion, and within one hour the entire band of sappers was annihilated.

Another platoon of the same VC battalion, occupying a high-rise hotel under construction on Nguyen Du Street, hit the staff entrance gate of Independence Palace with B-40 rockets and machine guns. The Presidential Security Brigade, national police, two tanks, and a contingent of U.S. military police cordoned off the unfinished building. The minisiege lasted two days before the Viet Cong were flushed out.

The Viet Cong temporarily seized Saigon's National Broadcasting Station,[3] shelled American officer quarters at Splendid Hotel and three other locations, and attacked the Korean Embassy as well as the Vietnamese Naval Headquarters. The Philippine Chancery was held briefly. Two district police stations had fallen in Cholon, the Chinese sector of the capital.

The reinforced 716th Military Police Battalion was charged with antiterrorist security and law enforcement in the greater Saigon–Cholon–Tan Son Nhut metropolitan area. Its duty uniforms consisted of starched fatigues and glossy helmets banded with wide red and white stripes blocking off large "716" numerals. Its main concerns were static guardposts, VIP escorts, traffic accidents, and the Saigon Police Boy Scouts Association.

When the first reports of Viet Cong activity started flooding the switchboards, Lt. Col. Gordon D. Rowe, the battalion commander, implemented the "disaster plan." Tet-68 in Saigon was certainly a disaster, but the plan was designed for emergencies such as riots or isolated bombings. Platoons of twenty-five men with sketch maps were dispatched on open trucks into unknown situations throughout the largest city in South Vietnam. One of

3. The actual transmitting portion of the station was located at Quan Tre several miles away. The power to the Saigon studio was quickly shut down, and broadcasting continued from an alternative studio with prerecorded programs, enabling Radio Saigon to function without interruption.

the first groups was immediately wiped out when their $2^{1}/_{2}$-ton cargo truck was rocked by an explosion, followed by a hail of machine-gun bullets, satchel charges, and grenades hitting the troop benches. On the night of January 30, 1968, the battalion was blasted into the front lines of the Vietnam War.

After the battle began, the 716th Military Police Battalion, already responsible for over a hundred buildings housing Americans scattered all over Saigon, received calls from dozens of unknown government billets, villas, and private dwellings. In many cases the military police took losses just trying to locate and gain entrance to them. The individual occupants, often nervous and under no one's apparent direction, soon produced every conceivable type of weapon in response to perceived threats to their billets. A pandemonium of gunfire erupted everywhere. Indiscriminate shooting was being directed at streets, buildings, rooftops, fellow Americans, military police, most South Vietnamese, and even dogs scrambling down alleys. The military police found it just as dangerous to try to tell the occupants to stop firing as to confront the Viet Cong. This problem was never resolved until the firing died of its own accord several nights later.

The 89th Military Police Group sent two V-100 commando cars to reinforce Saigon, giving the military police their first real firepower. In one instance a VC machine gun in the upper floor of a building had two joint patrol jeeps pinned down. The armored cars "buttoned up," drove around a large traffic circle with rounds ricochetting off their sides, and charged the building with their turreted twin machine guns blazing. As soon as one car was alongside the structure, a crew member popped out of his hatch and fired his M79 grenade launcher directly into the window. The explosion set the room on fire, silencing the machine gun.

The hectic nightmare of city combat eradicated the nocturnal celebrations. By daybreak Viet Cong forces had effectively penetrated much of western and southern Saigon, and were in firm control of several precincts in Cholon. Helicopter gunships greeted the dawn with renewed aerial rocket sorties against suspected VC strong-points. A pall of smoke hung over the smoldering urban sprawl of greater Saigon.

Early that morning the Viet Cong assaulted the Quan Trung

infantry training camp in the urban suburbs between Hoc Mon and Go Vap, and swept through the central police station and the Co Loa artillery base. Although twelve 105mm howitzers were captured, the retreating South Vietnamese had dismantled the firing blocks. By ten o'clock the Armored Command headquarters was also in VC hands. They had brought along specially trained personnel to use the tanks ordinarily stationed there, but all the armor had been removed two months earlier. The 4th VNMC Marine Battalion regained the artillery and armor areas by nightfall. However, the going was tough in downtown Hoc Mon district. There the 1st Battalion of the 27th Infantry was air assaulted into combat during the afternoon, but unable to make much headway against the stiff resistance.

The Phu Tho racetrack had been seized by the *6th VC LF Battalion*. The hub of several main roads, it was a good rallying point for Viet Cong unfamiliar with the city, and its use as a helicopter landing zone was denied to the Americans. It became the focus of another battle. Brig. Gen. Robert C. Forbes's 199th Infantry Brigade (Light) was hard pressed defending the huge Long Binh complex, but he dispatched Company A from the 3d Battalion, 7th Infantry, to regain the racetrack.[4] At eight o'clock on the dismal morning of January 31, eight armored personnel carriers from the brigade reconnaissance troop and several trucks moved the soldiers downtown toward the objective.

Six blocks from the racetrack, heavy automatic weapons fire opened up from rooftops and houses lining the boulevard. The column gingerly went forward another two blocks as the Viet Cong fire intensified. A rocket slammed into the lead tracked command carrier, killing the cavalry platoon leader and two crewmen. Company medics and truck drivers, aided by the battalion chaplain, frantically evacuated dazed and wounded sol-

4. The 7th Infantry was an old frontier regiment organized in 1812 in Tennessee, Georgia, and adjacent territories and known as the Cottonbalers, having once stood behind cotton bales to mow down marching British Redcoats at the Battle of New Orleans in the War of 1812. It was famed for strongpoint assaults at Telegraph Hill during the Battle of Cerro Gordo in the Mexican War, and against the stone wall at the Battle of Fredericksburg in the Civil War. It also served in the Indian Wars and the Spanish-American War, on Samar in the Philippine Insurrection, in Europe in World Wars I and II, and it saw intense action in Korea.

diers out the back side as flames spread through the demolished vehicle, cooking off belts of linked ammunition. Viet Cong small arms, machine-gun, and grenade fire hammered the column as the advance continued. Dismounted infantrymen fought from building to building. Recoilless rifles blasted holes through walls, grenade launchers were fired through the jagged cavities, and then soldiers clambered into the smoking entrances.

Hundreds of panic-stricken civilians fled past the armored carriers as the battle raged on. The column continued to contest the Viet Cong in fierce house-to-house fighting as it pressed closer to the racetrack. Gunships swooped down to blast apart structures with minigun and rocket salvos. By one o'clock that afternoon the company had advanced two more city blocks. Then the Viet Cong withdrew to positions dug in behind concrete park benches, backed up by heavy weapons located in concrete towers on the spectator stands inside the racetrack itself.

The men of Company A reloaded their rifles and machine guns, pushed helmets low over their foreheads, and charged the barricades. A deafening crescendo of machine-gun fire and grenades swept the avenue, leaving it clogged with fallen riflemen and discarded equipment. The first American charge had been repulsed, but the company grimly regrouped to try again. Clustered in squads around their sergeants, they lit cigarettes with bandaged hands. The grueling city fighting had soiled and frayed their jungle fatigues, and cotton ammunition bandoliers sagged heavily across their tunics.[5] Some still had light antitank weapons strapped across their backs, but most of the single-shot, disposable tubes had already been expended.

The company decided to charge the racetrack from the southeast. Gunships and recoilless rifles pounded the VC positions as the sweating infantrymen surged forward. At 4:30 that afternoon the Viet Cong, overwhelmed by this tremendous supporting firepower, fled the field. Just after dark, Companies B and C of the 3d Battalion, 7th Infantry, were airlifted into the

---

5. Soldiers were still experiencing high malfunction rates with their M16 rifles during normal field operations. Many problems could be traced to dirt and mud which accumulated in their ammunition magazine pouches. As a result cotton bandoliers were issued, but these were difficult to obtain in early 1968 and often used beyond the point of serviceability.

Phu Tho racetrack to set up the battalion's forward command post. The next day, February 1, they were reinforced by two companies of the mechanized 5th Battalion, 60th Infantry (from the 9th Infantry Division), and the 33d ARVN Ranger Battalion. This composite group then ventured out to subdue the general racetrack vicinity.

The combined allied force cautiously moved down the city blocks surrounding the racetrack. Company B of the mechanized battalion was moving along a narrow street three blocks away. Suddenly the last three armored personnel carriers were hit by heavy machine-gun fire and rockets from an adjacent graveyard. Two were destroyed and one was heavily damaged and on fire. However, its crew stood at their machine guns firing into the tomb markers until their dead and wounded were removed. Company B backed out of the ambuscade, and joined Company C in response to a frantic call for assistance at the Phu Tho racetrack. A large Viet Cong force was attacking from the west. The added firepower of the two arriving armored-infantry companies broke the counterattack. The fighting around the racetrack ebbed and flowed for several days as the Viet Cong troops continued to attempt to rally there. Eventually personnel from every Viet Cong unit in the Saigon offensive was identified in the area.

Clearing operations in Saigon were originally designed to be a South Vietnamese show, with American units limited to blocking actions and screening operations in the suburbs. By February 5, 1968, ARVN forces had taken the offensive in Saigon coded Operation TRAN HUNG DAO. Action was particularly intense in the densely populated Cholon area assigned to the 5th ARVN Ranger Group.[6] Large fires at the government rice depot at Binh Duong and a paper mill at Phu Lam sent billowing clouds of black smoke across the city, hindering aerial observation and fire support.

The 3d Battalion of the 7th Infantry had been pulled out of

6. By February 3, 1968, principal ARVN forces in the Saigon area were the 30th, 33d, 35th, 38th, and 41st Ranger Battalions; 1st, 2d, 3d, 4th, and 6th VNMC Battalions; and 1st, 3d, 6th, 8th, and 11th Airborne Battalions. At this time the U.S. Army had one military police, seven infantry battalions (one mechanized), and six artillery battalions engaged.

the Phu Tho racetrack in accordance with South Vietnamese desires. By February 9, the South Vietnamese high command was calling for its reinsertion, and the battalion returned to the racetrack and the Cholon battlefront. On February 12 this unit, acting on ARVN intelligence, found the main Viet Cong command post in the Phu Lam communal temple. Surrounding it, the battalion destroyed the VC defenders and claimed to have killed a top communist general.[7]

Although a renewed Viet Cong assault was made February 17–18, with fifty-seven rocket shellings and ten firefights erupting inside Saigon and Cholon, the second wave effort quickly sputtered out. The Tet-68 Battle for Saigon ended after a final fierce battle between ARVN rangers and main force Viet Cong in the Cholon sector on March 7. The Vietnam War had come to Saigon with a vengeance, and it would be hit again that May on a smaller scale. This latter Mini-Tet counteroffensive would be defeated almost exclusively by South Vietnamese capital defense forces.

2. Tet-68: Capitol Command Battles Beyond Saigon

The Long Binh area fifteen miles north of Saigon was a crucial American military logistical and headquarters complex, containing the command posts of both II Field Force, Vietnam, and the III ARVN Corps. The 199th Infantry Brigade (Light), backed by a mechanized battalion from the 9th Infantry Division in reserve, was in charge of the area's defense.[8] At 3:00 A.M., January 31, the Viet Cong attack was heralded by an intense rocket and mortar barrage directed against the infantry and field force headquarters. A half hour later the mechanized reserve was ordered forward. The 275th VC Regiment launched a ground as-

7. Supposedly they had killed General Tran Do, the communist political chief who was in command of all Viet Cong forces attacking Saigon. A subsequent fingerprint check on the body proved this to be untrue, but the results were never made public to avoid dampening ARVN spirits. See Col. Hoang Ngoc Lung, The General Offensives of 1968–69, U.S. Army Center of Military History, Washington, D.C., 1981, p. 74.

8. The 2d Battalion of the 47th Infantry (Mechanized) near Bear Cat was the mechanized battalion. During the actions described, Company A swept Ho Nai village, Company B secured the ammunition storage area, and Company C was sent to the relief of III ARVN Corps headquarters.

sault through Ho Nai village across Highway 1 against the northern perimeter of Long Binh. At the same time *U-1 VC LF Battalion* engaged the eastern perimeter in order to divert attention from sappers who penetrated the main ammunition dump.

The Long Binh bunker line returned fire, and the 199th Infantry Brigade counterattacked both on foot and from armored personnel carriers. Helicopter gunships (from the 3d Squadron, 17th Cavalry) blasted Viet Cong foxholes and crew-served weapons in front of the soldiers. The VC were also attacking in other areas, but were slowed by thick bamboo between the compound and the ammunition dump, and defeated in an attempt to overrun the runway of the 12th Aviation Group.[9] Meanwhile, tracked vehicles of the mechanized reserve, escorted by military police gun-jeeps, protected the main Long Binh compound. However, sappers had infiltrated the ammunition dump there. Army explosive ordnance disposal (EOD) teams frantically worked under the cover of armored carrier machine guns to strip demolition packages off the ammunition pads. Despite their efforts four bunkers in the one hundred-pad storage area detonated at eight o'clock that morning.

Company B of the 4th Battalion, 39th Infantry, was forced to make a helicopter assault under fire on the grassy helipad across from the II Field Force, Vietnam, headquarters building. The infantrymen quickly cleared the area and moved against an adjacent village which was taken after a daylong struggle. Aside from Viet Cong resistance in the hamlet, the battle at Long Binh was concluded as daylight ground sweeps were accompanied by aerial and artillery bombardment. With the arrival of the 11th Armored Cavalry Regiment that evening, after a twelve-hour forced road march, the Long Binh area was secured from further danger.

At the same time Long Binh was first struck, the Bien Hoa air base received twenty-five rockets followed by a mortar-supported ground attack. The *274th VC Regiment* charged into the east bunker line, which was manned by a platoon of South Vietnamese and the U.S. Military Police base reaction force. The

9. MACV later had Rome plow dozers destroy the bamboo grove "to remove the concealment offered near friendly installations." Ironically, this bamboo had slowed the momentum of the Viet Cong attack during Tet-68.

Viet Cong breached the perimeter wire, but did not get onto the airstrip. At daybreak the 2d Battalion, 506th Infantry, arrived by helicopter to reinforce the strategic airfield. The battalion attacked out the east gate to clear the surrounding area.

The nearby III ARVN Corps headquarters was under attack by the *238th VC LF Battalion*, and armored personnel carriers of the reserve mechanized battalion were dispatched into the battle. The column fought right through the middle of the *275th Regiment* astride Highway 1 and plowed into the flank of the *274th Regiment* attacking Bien Hoa air base. Heavy machine guns on the armored personnel carriers sent blazing paths of tracered light careening into the Viet Cong, who fought back with rocket-propelled grenades. Explosions and flares ripped through the darkness as the tracked cavalry roared onto the battlefield.

Meanwhile another mechanized cavalry troop of the 9th Infantry Division fought a running battle past roadblocks and exploding bridges down Highway 1 into Bien Hoa. The mechanized cavalry inflicted and suffered heavy losses, but managed to link up with the 2d Battalion of the 506th Infantry. The latter battalion then teamed up with the 11th Armored Cavalry to sweep Ap Than, adjacent to the air base, against the blocking positions of the South Vietnamese 58th Regional Force Battalion. The village was taken house by house in heavy fighting on February 1. This cleared the last pocket of organized VC resistance between Bien Hoa and Long Binh.

At the same time Long Binh and Bien Hoa were hit, the Viet Cong *D16* and *267th Battalions* and a battalion from the *271st Regiment* occupied the Vinatexco textile mill directly across Highway 1 from the sprawling Tan Son Nhut airbase. They emplaced heavy weapons in the doors and windows and posted flak guns on the roof. At precisely 3:21 A.M. they attacked the airfield. While secondary assaults were hurled against eastern Gate #10 and northern Gate #58, waves of Viet Cong stormed the fence line at western Gate #51. Rockets slammed against the bunkered guardhouses and smashed down the gateway. The massed assault force poured into the breach. Surging past the wreckage of wire and concrete, three full VC battalions spilled into the airport and raced toward the main runway.

The commander of the Tan Son Nhut "Sensitive Area" desperately scratched together one of the oddest battle groups ever fielded, and shoved it forward to defend the airstrip.[10] After furious fighting, this heterogeneous defense began to fall back under the sustained Viet Cong onslaught. At 4:15 A.M., Tan Son Nhut requested urgent reinforcement, but most of the ARVN airborne strategic reserve had already been parceled out in other emergency firefights throughout the city. Only two companies of the 8th ARVN Airborne Battalion were left, and they were ordered to counterattack immediately.

The South Vietnamese paratroopers charged over the open expanse of the runway right into the onrushing Viet Cong. Grenade blasts and streams of bullets tore gaping holes in their ranks. Dozens of men pitched forward as their weapons clattered across the concrete. Then the frenzied countercharge closed the VC lines. The black uniforms of Viet Cong and bright green camouflage of the paratroopers clashed in a vortex of hand-to-hand combat. Losses were extremely heavy, but the momentum of the Viet Cong attack was blunted. In the meantime, just as any American Western pulp novel would have it, the U.S. Cavalry was on the way to the rescue.

Lt. Col. Glenn K. Otis's 3d Squadron of the 4th Cavalry was the armored reconnaissance unit of the 25th Infantry Division. Just before dawn, he ordered Troop C, stationed at Cu Chi fifteen miles away, forward at once. It raced down Highway 1 as Colonel Otis flew overhead in his command helicopter dropping flares and guiding it around possible ambush sites. The tanks and armored personnel carriers suddenly crashed right into the rear of the Viet Cong at Gate #51. Rocket-propelled grenades and machine guns raked the steel-hulled vehicles, and the column screeched to a halt. The thunder of multiple explosions jarred the front vehicles. Crewmen leaped out as flames shot into the air, and hastily cut loose with automatic weapons fire from roadside ditches. Four tanks and five armored carriers were lost and one third of the column destroyed. However, they had

10. The Tan Son Nhut battle group was composed of the U.S. Air Force 377th Security Police Squadron, two platoons of U.S. Army Vietnam headquarters guards, and a mixed bag of South Vietnamese units including national police, the 52d Regional Force Battalion, the 2d Service Battalion, and Vice-President Ky's bodyguard.

succeeded in cutting off the trailing VC battalions from their source of weapons and ammunition in the mill. This proved to be the deciding action which defeated the main Viet Cong assault on the Tan Son Nhut air base.

As the morning light flooded the smoldering battlefield an armada of low-flying helicopter gunships darted through the skies to rocket and strafe targets throughout the area. Run after run was made on the Vinatexco plant, leaving it in shambles. Troop B of the cavalry squadron arrived to finish off the Viet Cong around it. Shortly past noon an American master sergeant rallied a mixed contingent of U.S. and South Vietnamese soldiers and led a final counterattack against the decimated Viet Cong inside Tan Son Nhut. As the contingent reached Gate #51, the battle for the air base ended.

3. Tet-68: I Corps and Hue

The Tet-68 Offensive swept the length of South Vietnam like a cyclone, ripping through cities and military installations in a three-day cataclysm of furious proportions. The national capital, 36 of 44 provincial capitals, 5 of 6 autonomous cities, and 64 of 242 district capitals were hit by its violence. South Vietnamese units, assigned defensive duties near populated areas as part of "pacification," bore the brunt of this onslaught. Due to the Tet holidays they were universally undermanned, averaging 50 percent understrength.

The very shock of such a massive Viet Cong *coup de main* produced incredulity before rational response. When one of the first Tet hammer blows struck Da Nang shortly after three o'clock in the morning of January 30, South Vietnamese Col. Nguyen Duy Hinh frantically telephoned Lt. Gen. Hoang Xuan Lam, the commander of I ARVN Corps. General Lam kept interrupting him over the phone, "Baloney! Baloney!"

Da Nang had been pelted the night before with 122mm rockets, and the Marble Mountain Marine air base had been mortared. Now elements of the *2d NVA Division*, spearheaded by the *402d Sapper Battalion*, were striking the I ARVN Corps command building. A Marine combined action platoon and the headquarters duty staff were forced to defend alone until reinforced by a smattering of South Vietnamese and Marine military police. The sappers were driven back in a chaos of gunfire and individual combat. Two Marine battalions (3d Battalion, 5th Marines, and 2d Battalion, 3d Marines) intercepted other division elements before they could reach the amorphous firefight.

Hoi An, the provincial capital of Quang Nam nineteen miles to the south, was held only by the determined resistance of the 102d ARVN Engineer Battalion in the early morning darkness of January 30. A tumultuous seesaw battle ensued. The 1st Battalion, 51st ARVN Regiment, pushed the Viet Cong out, but the VC regained and lost the town again on February 5. Other I Corps clashes on the eve of Tet occurred at Hoa Vang and Chu Lai. Lunar New Year's Day was spent in prompt repulse of these intrusions, but Tet night on January 31, 1968, brought another, more forceful wave of Viet Cong attacks.

Quang Ngai, Tam Ky, and Quang Tri were successfully defended. In the latter town, the 1st ARVN Regiment and 9th ARVN Airborne Battalion waged a fierce city battle against the *812th NVA Regiment* and *10th VC Sapper Battalion*. Col. Donald V. Rattan's 1st Brigade of the 1st Cavalry Division (Airmobile) took advantage of the worsening situation to execute a swift, classic airmobile counterthrust. He airlifted two battalions, the 1st Battalion, 5th Cavalry, and the 1st Battalion, 12th Cavalry, out of dense fog to smash into the rear of the attackers the next day, and the battle was over by noon on February 1.

A bizarre spear-rifle attack was mounted February 1 on the Ba To district headquarters by some seven hundred Viet Cong, about half of whom were only armed with spears and knives. The camp strike force from Special Forces Operations Detachment A-106 joined the Regional Forces defenders, but they were unable to prevent the breach of the town perimeter. After destroying the province chief's home and several bunkers, the VC withdrew, leaving behind twenty spears, thirty-five knives, and one carbine.

The third largest city in South Vietnam, the ancient walled imperial capital of Hue, was infiltrated and seized just after the Tet New Year midnight rites. Unlike the struggle for most Tet objectives, the battle for Hue was protracted from January 31 through March 2, 1968. Two North Vietnamese Army regiments and two Viet Cong sapper battalions would be pitted against eight American and thirteen South Vietnamese infantry battalions in one of the most savage battles of the Vietnam War.[11] Although the NVA/VC realized their hold on Hue was subject to ultimate defeat by vastly superior forces, the gamble to make a battleground of Hue was well reasoned, and based on the knowledge that great propaganda value would accrue to that force able to seize and hold, however temporarily, the cultural and religious center of the nation. The furor of the Tet-68 Offensive would become symbolized by the catastrophic destruction incurred in this grim city struggle.

The determined North Vietnamese and Viet Cong soldiers were in excellent condition, backed by prodigious stockpiles of ammunition and supplies already in place. Large elements appearing in Hue on January 31 had been there for some time, while others were surreptitiously infiltrated into the city, masked by the normal Tet crowds. The well-coordinated plan achieved complete tactical surprise. Key positions were simultaneously taken within the city, as more reinforcements entered under the early-morning mortar attack signaling the assault.

As in all Tet-68 attacks, timing coincided with the holiday leave of the bulk of ARVN troops and national police. Within Mang Ca compound inside the northeast corner of the city, Brig. Gen. Ngo Quang Truong's 1st ARVN Division headquarters staff and the elite Hac Bao (Black Panther) reconnaissance company were at less than half strength. The 3d ARVN Regiment, which would fight harder than almost any other unit and absorb crippling losses in the upcoming battle, was located five miles to the northwest, similiarly undermanned.

In a matter of hours after the first volleys reverberated through the city, the NVA/VC controlled all of the Citadel (with the exception of 1st ARVN Division headquarters), and that part of Hue below the Perfume River, which contained the MACV compound, the provincial administration facilities, public utilities, the university complex, and a densely packed residential section. Well armed with mortars, rockets, and automatic weap-

11. The initial NVA/VC forces employed at Hue were the *4th* and *6th NVA Regiments*, and the *12th VC* and *Hue City VC Sapper Battalions*. Additionally, a total of 2,500 prisoners were released from the local jail, and over 500 of these joined the Viet Cong ranks.

ons, and confident other coordinated attacks throughout the country would inhibit any rapid allied countermove, the NVA/VC consolidated their gains and waited for major reinforcement. They were clearly prepared to stay, and at eight o'clock that morning raised the flag of the National Liberation Front on the stately Midday Gate's majestic flagpole.

The defense of Hue, like that of most cities, was a South Vietnamese responsibility, and General Lam initially intended to recapture it with ARVN forces. A South Vietnamese response force convoy fought its way to the battlefront through a major ambush at An Hoa. Badly battered, a troop of the 7th ARVN Armored Cavalry Squadron and two airborne battalions, the 2d and the 7th, managed to reach sector headquarters that afternoon. Half of the 3d ARVN Regiment was safely off-loaded at riverside piers toward evening after being ferried down the Perfume River, but its other two battalions traveling by road were decimated fighting their way out of an encirclement.

III Marine Amphibious Force was concerned about the immediate danger to the MACV compound, and rushed two rifle companies from the nearest Marine base at Phu Bai by helicopter and truck. These were joined by tanks and went into combat under the control of the headquarters of 1st Battalion, 1st Marines.[12] They cleared the MACV compound area and then tackled the adjacent Truong Tien Bridge extending across the Perfume River into Hue. In spite of heavy losses, the Marines secured the bridge at 4:15 P.M. The city was enclosed by the Citadel wall, twenty feet thick and thirty feet high, surrounded by a water-filled zigzag moat. Past this barrier was an inner brick wall. Attempts to gain these fire-swept earthen stone ramparts were repulsed, and the Marines turned over their hard-won bridge sector to South Vietnamese troops. They returned to southern Hue at twilight. Plans were made to attack at dawn,

12. The 1st Marines was one of the most illustrious regiments in the Marine Corps, having battled tropical fortifications and ambushes from the Caribbean Banana Wars to the Pacific in World War II. It was activated at Philadelphia, Pennsylvania, in November 1913, being first designated as the 1st Marines in 1930. It fought in Vera Cruz, Mexico, Haiti, and the Dominican Republic from 1914–1924; in Guadalcanal, Eastern New Guinea, New Britain, Peleliu, and Okinawa in World War II, and throughout the Korean War.

destroy the citadel defense, and recapture the city by nightfall the next day.

At first light on February 1, the combined American–South Vietnamese counterattack against Hue was launched. The two South Vietnamese airborne battalions and the 7th ARVN Cavalry Squadron recaptured the Tay Loc airfield. Two Marine companies attacked southwest to secure the areas south of the Perfume River, while South Vietnamese forces moved into the Citadel from the north. Fierce resistance from well-selected fortified positions during the initial hours of the assault soon vaporized illusions of any speedy reconquest. More Marine reinforcements would be required immediately. During the next two days heliborne arrivals increased Marine strength to battalion size, and this force was doubled again within another forty-eight hours. South Vietnamese stakes were raised by two more airlifted battalions.[13] On February 4, the 1st Battalion of the 3d ARVN Regiment stormed the An Hoa gate, taking the northwest wall.

As the misting drizzle turned into a cold, soaking downpour, the four Marine rifle companies maintained the momentum of an attack measured in yards. They grimly advanced house by house down lanes choked with demolished brick, timber, and wreckage toward the provincial headquarters and jail. Many homes in the residential area were surrounded by barbed wire–laced hedgerows, covered by sinister crew-served weapons jutting out of windows and doorways. Backed up by mortars and recoilless rifles, the riflemen maneuvered to isolate them and finish them off with grenades and rapid M16 bursts. By February 6, they had recaptured the Thua Thien sector headquarters, prison, and hospital. However, that night a North Vietnamese counterattack using grappling hooks drove the 4th Battalion, 2d ARVN Regiment, off the breastworks on the recently recaptured southwest wall.

13. Company A, 1st Marines, and Company G, 5th Marines, entered combat at Hue on January 31. Companies F and H, 5th Marines, arrived February 1 and 2. By February 4, the command group of Col. Stanley S. Hughes's 1st Marines, the 2d Battalion of the 5th Marines, and Company B, 1st Marines, were also present at Hue. South Vietnamese reinforcements on February 2 included the 9th ARVN Airborne Battalion from Quang Tri, and the 4th Battalion, 2d ARVN Regiment, from Dong Ha.

Soldiers of the 716th Military Police Battalion maneuver closer to the United States Embassy during the Viet Cong attack on Saigon, January 31, 1968. (U.S. Army)

Military Police move forward behind a V100 Commando Car to clear Viet Cong out of a bachelor officer barracks during the fighting in Saigon on January 31, 1968. Note the open cargo truck which had been ambushed while carrying U.S. reinforcements. (U.S. Army)

The formidable Viet Cong defensive bastion at the Phu Tho racetrack in Saigon had to be frontally assaulted by the 3d Battalion of the 7th Infantry during Tet-68. (U.S. Army)

Soldiers of the 199th Infantry Brigade, having captured the Phu Tho racetrack in Saigon, grimly sweep the densely populated areas around it on February 5, 1968. (U.S. Army)

A gutted M48 main battle tank stands as mute testimony to the fury of combat during the Battle of Hue on February 16, 1968. (U.S Marine Corps)

A Marine rifleman prepares to assault through a blasted wall during heavy action in the Battle of Hue on February 4, 1968. (U.S. Marine Corps)

Lieutenant Colonel Daniel Schungel presents an interim Bronze Star Medal for Valor to Sergeant Allen on February 24, 1968, as the survivors of the Lang Vei battle are honored. (Author's Collection)

The Army Special Forces camp at Lang Vei the morning after being overrun, showing one demolished North Vietnamese tank outside the ruined command bunker where several Special Forces soldiers held out. (Author's Collection)

The Marines resorted to tank guns, aerial rockets, and aircraft 20mm cannon strafing, but initial restrictions ruled out heavier firepower, since General Lam had requested city destruction be minimized. The use of artillery, bombs, and napalm during the first three days of the battle was precluded, but any sentiments of forbearance were soon abandoned. Beginning on February 5, the awesome warship guns of the Seventh Fleet were used in sledgehammer blows to pound Hue with an average of two hundred shells a day. Marine naval gunfire spotters radioed targets as armor-piercing rounds fired up to fourteen miles away zoomed overhead like express trains to obliterate defensive bunkers virtually impervious to other weapons. By the end of the battle 4,780 naval shells and 48 Marine aircraft attack sorties would be used.

The 1st Cavalry Division's 3d Brigade helicoptered into blocking positions to the west of the city on February 2. The foot cavalry sloshed through muddied paddy water as they advanced east toward Hue. The 2d Battalion, 12th Cavalry, was given the mission of making a forced march through the chilly, fog-shrouded night of February 4 behind Viet Cong lines to seize a critical hill.[14] Exhausted and many shaking with fever, the cavalrymen reached the hilltop the next day. From its summit four miles west of Hue they could see the entire valley before the city, and all major VC infiltration routes feeding the raging battle.

On February 7, the 5th Battalion of the 7th Cavalry smashed into the first of a series of Viet Cong trench networks. The 2d Battalion of the 12th Cavalry was called forward, passed through the 7th Cavalry's lines, and charged into fortified Thong Bon Tri. At daybreak on February 21, the 12th Cavalry men renewed the assault in the La Chu area as the brigade advanced on a four-battalion front behind air strikes, naval gunfire, and

14. The 12th Cavalry was organized February 8, 1901, at Fort Sam Houston, Texas, and had cut its teeth on Moro kampilan knives and war clubs during the Philippine Insurrection, returning to those islands in World War II as part of the 1st Cavalry Division. Inactivated in 1949, it missed the Korean War, but was reactivated in 1957 with the same division. Two battalions had been in Vietnam since September of 1965.

heavy artillery which pulverized VC defenses. By dark they were three miles from the city, and still facing strong opposition.

In the meantime, the Marines had reclaimed southern Hue by February 9. On the north side of the Perfume River, attacking South Vietnamese units controlled three fourths of the Citadel. The NVA/VC forces were still in firm possession of the southeastern portion of the Citadel, including the key Imperial Palace, and manned a series of strong-points along the west wall. The Marines began firing CS tear gas rounds, and the NVA responded with their own mortar-delivered CS. Hue was one of the few battles in the Vietnam War in which both sides fought wearing gas masks. Streets were barricaded by overturned trucks and piles of household furniture. Civilians had been impressed into service digging fighting holes and bunkers, and local cadre wearing red arm bands directed North Vietnamese regulars scurrying through the maze of alleys and residential courtyards. Additional replacements were funneled into the city by traversing the waterways and fortified hamlets to the west. Although this area was covered by the advancing 3d Brigade of the 1st Cavalry Division (Airmobile), these reinforcement and supply avenues were never effectively sealed off.[15]

The defenders constantly lashed back against the attackers. In one spectacular night attack Viet Cong combat-swimmers used floating mines to drop two spans of the Truong Tien Bridge. On February 10, a strong counterassault was made against the 1st ARVN Division, effectively destroying one of its battalions. Two days later the 1st and 5th VNMC battalions were moved from the fighting at Go Vap in Saigon by naval transport and unloaded at the Bao Vinh landing in Hue. The South Vietnamese Marines moved into line and relieved the mauled airborne battalions. The same day the 1st Battalion of the 5th Marines was landed by helicopter and river-assault craft at the Citadel, joining ARVN forces pushing through the staunchly defended heart of metropolitan Hue.

The 3d ARVN Regiment and Hac Bao (Black Panther) Com-

15. Fresh units infiltrated into Hue during the battle included elements of the *416th Battalion, 5th NVA Regiment,* and *324B Division.*

pany were placed in the center and given the signal honor of recapturing the Imperial Palace. In order to appease South Vietnamese concerns over the sacred "Throne of Kings," U.S. Marines were prohibited from entering the palatial grounds. The Marines moved on the left into the Citadel's tough eastern sector, and the South Vietnamese Marines were assigned the right, western flank. Attacking generally to the southwest, the combined force encountered fierce resistance at every turn, from gateways to schoolhouses. The 4th VNMC Battalion arrived from the Battle of My Tho in the Delta to reinforce the allied drive on February 16. Marine eight-inch howitzers, Ontos recoilless rifle vehicles, and aircraft were supporting all South Vietnamese attacks.

The Marines moved forward through rain and fog, fighting at bayonet-point as they assailed ruined houses and stark, smoldering city parks. Marine medium tanks, holed several times and driven by replacement crews, lumbered forward in the urban shadows as flak-vested riflemen, crisscrossed by ammunition bandoliers, followed in their wake. Machine-gun fire and rocket-propelled grenades ripped into the grime-caked machines and cut down drab green-uniformed men as they clawed their way forward a block at a time. Flamethrowers snuffed out NVA strongpoints with tongues of liquid fire. Marine scout-sniper teams waged individual contests to the death against accurate NVA snipers nested on both the Citadel and palace walls.

The swift, dependable Ontos, mounting twin triple-tubed recoilless rifles, proved crucial in close city assault. Suddenly appearing in debris-clogged streets, the sturdy little vehicles would instantly blast bunkered positions with their six-gun volley, then dash behind corners. The NVA developed a respectful distaste for their bold direct-fire tactics, and the Ontos became prime targets. Sometimes return rocket fire would catch these stinging self-propelled weapons. One Ontos of Company A, 1st Antitank Battalion, was detracked by a chance round and hit by eleven more B-40 rockets. It stood its ground before finally disappearing in a tumultuous explosion.

The carnage of close combat was typified by the casualties taken among the platoon leaders of the 1st Battalion, 5th Marines. The battalion had been continuously committed in the

Phu Loc area twenty-four miles south of the city since December 29, when it was thrown into the Hue fighting on February 12. It assaulted the rows of shattered buildings held by the *6th NVA Regiment*. Nine days later its ten rifle platoons were being led by three second lieutenants, one gunnery sergeant, two staff sergeants, two buck sergeants, and two senior corporals.

Each overmastered bunker took its toll. The forward edge of the battle line relentlessly pressed on through the shambles. Slain attackers were aligned in poncho-draped rows across muddy street puddles. Medical collecting points were reduced to triage. The Marines reached the inside wall and water-filled moat of the Citadel on February 21. General Lam had first authorized bombing of the Citadel on February 5. On February 22, he decided air strikes would have to be used against the Imperial Palace. Early that morning, a massed NVA charge had surged out of the southwest wall and caught the leading South Vietnamese contingents before a storm of artillery fire tore it apart. By the end of that day, the Marines had terminated organized resistance in their zone of action, and the 21st and 39th ARVN Ranger Battalions arrived to sweep the island across Dong Ba Bridge and Eastern River.

The following night soldiers of the 2d Battalion, 3d ARVN Regiment, made a surprise attack along the citadel wall at a dead run. Although the North Vietnamese quickly recovered, the charge sallied past their weapons pits. Fighting hand to hand in the light of wild tracer streams, flares, and explosions, they reached the imperial courtyard. At 5:00 A.M., February 24, 1968, the battered battalion tore down the Viet Cong banner and raised the South Vietnamese flag over the Citadel.

That afternoon the Hac Bao (Black Panther) Company successfully assaulted and seized the Imperial Palace. At the same time the South Vietnamese Marines compressed the last defending remnants into the southwest corner of the Citadel, and the Army's 2d Battalion, 7th Cavalry, advanced to link up. Mopping up continued, but Hue was declared secure on February 25. For another week, until March 2, Marine, Army, and South Vietnamese troops continued to crush isolated pockets of stragglers in the general vicinity. Once the most beautiful city in Vietnam and previously unscarred by the war, Hue had been blasted into corpse-strewn rubble. The battle became one of the fiercest city actions the American military had fought since World War II.

4. Tet-68: Countrywide

The critical central twelve provinces of South Vietnam were under the military control of I Field Force Vietnam, where ten major ground attacks of the Tet Offensive rolled through seven provincial capitals, the autonomous city of Dalat, and the two key military towns of An Khe and Ninh Hoa. With the exceptions of Phan Thiet and Dalat, all were cleared during the first week of fighting.[16]

At Tuy Hoa a battalion of the *95th NVA Regiment* attacked the airfield, the provincial prison, and American artillery positions. By dawn on January 30, 1968, a paratrooper company from the 4th Battalion, 503d Infantry (Airborne), reinforced by a battalion of the Korean 28th Regiment, had reached the scene of action. In a sharp twenty-four-hour firefight they surrounded and destroyed most of the North Vietnamese soldiers. Two battalions of the ARVN 47th Regiment moved against the remaining North Vietnamese stronghold in the center of Tuy Hoa on February 5 and captured it the next day.

At Ban Me Thuot the *33d NVA Regiment,* supported by the *301E VC LF Battalion*, attacked the 23d ARVN Division headquarters, the MACV compound, both airfields, and numerous other targets including the bank. Initially they were only opposed by local South Vietnamese militia (a Regional/Popular Forces training center was located there) and Special Forces Operations Detachment B-23. By midday on January 30, the 8th ARVN Cavalry Squadron and the 45th ARVN Regiment were also engaged. The house-to-house fighting was so intense that the 23d ARVN Ranger Battalion was committed February 1. The rangers were quickly consumed by the slaughter, and the next

16. The order of the city battles in II Corps Tactical Zone and their dates were *Tet Eve, January 30—Ban Me Thuot (Jan. 30–Feb. 6), Kontum (Jan. 30–Feb. 4),* Nha Trang (Jan. 30–Feb. 1), Ninh Hoa (Jan. 30–Feb. 4), Qui Nhon (Jan. 30–Feb. 5), *Pleiku (Jan. 30–Feb. 4), Tuy Hoa (Jan. 30–Feb. 6); Tet Night, January 31—*An Khe and Bong Son (attacks on installations only), *Phan Thiet (Jan. 31–Feb. 23); Second Tet Night, February 1—Dalat (Feb. 1-11).* The italicized battles are summarized in this section.

day American paratroopers of the 1st Battalion, 503d Infantry (Airborne), were flown in from Pleiku. Four major NVA assaults were hurled against Ban Me Thuot during the course of the battle, but by February 6 the town was cleared. Over one third of the city had been reduced to smoking rubble.

Pleiku was stormed by the Viet Cong *15H LF* and *40th Sapper Battalions*, crossing an expanse of open field at great cost. Heavy fighting raged around the Pleiku sector headquarters, the MACV compound, 71st Evacuation Hospital, the prisoner-of-war compound, both airfields, and a Montagnard training center. The 3d ARVN Cavalry Squadron and the 22d ARVN Ranger Battalion, backed up by a company of medium tanks from the 1st Battalion, 69th Armor, responded immediately. Two mobile strike force companies from Company B, 5th Special Forces Group (Airborne), were added to the street fighting. Finally the 4th Engineer Battalion doubled as infantry, grabbed machine guns, and hastened into the inferno of close combat. By February 3 this amalgamated force was mopping up.

Kontum was also struck early on January 30 and the *24th NVA Regiment*, the *304th VC Battalion* and the *406th Sapper Battalion* crashed into the MACV compound, post office, airfield, and 24th ARVN Special Tactical Zone headquarters. Some of the most ferocious combat of Tet-68 transpired in Kontum city. The initial assault was met by two Montagnard scout companies, which were rapidly brushed aside, and the 2d Battalion of the 42d ARVN Regiment, which fell back. The compound of Special Forces Operations Detachment B-24 was penetrated at several points. At noon the Americans rustled up the ground crews of the aerial 7th Squadron, 17th Cavalry, fused them with the 1st Battalion of the 22d Infantry, and gave them tanks from Company C of the 1st Battalion, 69th Armor. This composite task force was shoved into the heart of the city, but the fierce tempo of urban fighting was sustained five more days.

The city perimeter of Phan Thiet in lower Binh Thuan Province was assaulted by the Viet Cong *482d LF* and *840th MF Battalions* just after 3:00 A.M. on January 31, 1968. The MACV compound, water point, and sector headquarters were all hit. The 3d Battalion, 506th Infantry, and two battalions of the 44th ARVN Regiment were soon forced to counterattack in various other sectors as well. Several school buildings in the northern part of the city and a large pagoda in the western portion became focal points of extended fighting. The heaviest fighting was over by February 4, but sporadic skirmishing flared over the next six days. A renewed VC assault carried the city prison on February 18. After another grueling week of block-by-block combat the Viet Cong were ejected from the town.

The final city to be struck in the region was the innocuous mountain resort town of Dalat, nestled in the pine forests of Tuyen Duc Province. The Viet Cong *145th* and *186th Battalions* attacked one hour after midnight on February 1. They quickly entered Dalat and took the central marketplace. Two armored cars, two regional forces companies, engineering cadets, and a helicopter gunship repelled the VC, who then retreated to fortified positions in the Pasteur Institute. Combat was renewed when the depleted 23d ARVN Ranger Battalion arrived February 5. It was backed by the camp strike force company of Special Forces Operations Detachment A-233 from Trang Phuc. A week later the 11th ARVN Ranger Battalion also arrived. Dalat was finally declared secure on February 11. By that date only Hue and Saigon were still embroiled in continuing Tet combat.

In the lower half of South Vietnam the Tet-68 Offensive had hit numerous other localities in addition to the Capital Military District. Major ground attacks in the surrounding provinces of III Corps Tactical Zone were initiated against Ben Cat and Duc Hoa on January 31, 1968. On February 1, the Viet Cong launched three more attacks, against the engineer school at Phu Cuong, and the towns of Cu Chi and Ba Ria. The latter locality was retaken by various South Vietnamese elements spearheaded by the 3d Battalion of the Royal Australian Regiment on armored personnel carriers. That afternoon a Viet Cong assault on Xuan Loc, headquarters of the 18th ARVN Division, was broken up by concentrated artillery fire and air power. The next day another, similiar attack on Xuan Loc was defeated the same way.

On the night of February 3, the *273d VC Regiment,* already battered from an unsuccessful attack on Thu Duc the previous day, attempted to blow up the large Newport Bridge linking Saigon and Bien Hoa. The Viet Cong were able to overrun a number of bunkers and took the eastern end of the bridge. A relief force composed of elements of the 720th Military Police Battalion, fighting as infantry and backed by a mechanized company of the 5th ARVN Cavalry Squadron, counterattacked the key structure. At 2:50 A.M., in heavy combat lighted by a brilliant cross fire of tracers and burning houses reflected in the lampblack waters, Newport Bridge was recaptured.

Tay Ninh city was targeted for February 6, but by that date the Viet Cong were expected. Their advancing columns were ambushed and the survivors stung by orbiting helicopter gunships. They fled the field, leaving it strewn with parade banners for the victory march. The second wave of Tet attacks, which befell Saigon and Cholon, also struck Song Be, Tan An, and An Loc. They were feeble by comparison to the first round of Tet attacks.

The 1st Brigade of the 101st Airborne Division (Airmobile) was operating in the Song Be area when the *211th* and *212th VC Infiltration Groups* captured the western portion of the city. The 31st ARVN Ranger Battalion, assisted by the 2d Squadron, 17th Cavalry (Armored), and 1st Battalion, 506th Infantry, defeated the Viet Cong in acrid combat fought block by block through the hovel-choked town. Song Be was practically destroyed in the process.

The defense of the low, marshy plain known as the Delta had always been the primary responsibility of the South Vietnamese. Although devoid of NVA troop support, the Viet Cong Tet-68 Offensive was most extensive in this area. Within the Delta region thirteen of the sixteen province headquarters were attacked within the first forty-eight hours.[17] The main highway in the Delta, Route 4, was interdicted at sixty-two locations and six bridges were dropped. It wasn't until a final mud roadblock was cleared on May 15 that Route 4 was reopened along its entire length.

At My Tho in the upper Delta region the Viet Cong employed their *261st, 263d,* and *514th Battalions* to pin the 32d

17. Major attacks in IV Corps Tactical Zone were made on the night of Tet, January 31, at Cai Be, Cai Lay, Can Tho, My Tho, Soc Trang, Truc Giang, and Vinh Long. Other attacks the same night or shortly thereafter were conducted at Chau Phu, Moc Hoa, Phu Vinh, Quan Long, Rach Gia, Sa Dec, and Tri Ton.

ARVN Ranger Battalion outside town and enter the city. There they fought to within two hundred yards of the 7th ARVN Division command post before being beaten back. Navy Task Force 117 landed the 2d Brigade (Riverine) of the 9th Infantry Division on the southern edge of My Tho on the morning of February 1. The South Vietnamese lashed back in conjunction with the 3d Battalion, 47th Infantry. The mobile riverine troops were subjected to the harsh house-to-house fighting that typified Tet-68. Supported by massed artillery fire and air strikes, they advanced room by room and from door to door under intense machine-gun and rocket fire. By nightfall the western half of the city had been cleared to the main canal. The following day the 3d Battalions of both the 47th and 60th Infantry attacked north astride the city reservoir. At 6:00 P.M. on February 2 they had linked up with South Vietnamese forces, and My Tho was once again in allied hands.

Truc Giang was attacked on Lunar New Year's Day by the *516th* and *518th VC Battalions,* which took the town and surrounded its MACV compound. The reinforced 3d Battalion of the 39th Infantry airmobiled into a landing zone south of the city on the night of February 1, and broke through to the besieged American camp. The Viet Cong were eliminated inside the city two days later, but Truc Giang's environs were not cleared until the middle of the month.

The 9th ARVN Division guarding Vinh Long was considered a weak division, with two of its regiments rated as only marginally combat-effective. On January 31 the Viet Cong *306th, 308th* and *857th Battalions* attacked Vinh Long city and its airfield. Both South Vietnamese reinforcements and the 2d Brigade (Riverine) of the 9th Infantry Division were required to regain the area. On February 4 the mobile riverine force anchored north of town on the Mekong River. The 3d Battalion of the 47th Infantry conducted river-assault probes while the 3d Battalion of the 60th Infantry conducted an airmobile assault south of the city. Two days later, two companies of this battalion, supported by helicopter gunships and assault patrol boats, made beach landings on the banks of the Rach Cai Cam. After heavy combat, the city was retaken on February 8.

The 21st ARVN Division was busy defending both Can Tho

and Soc Trang. A major four-day engagement, in which Company D of the 5th Special Forces Group took an active part, shattered Can Tho. On February 5, the Viet Cong were routed out of the university buildings, and the battle was terminated. Chau Phu, a provincial capital on the Cambodian border, was infiltrated by small groups of Viet Cong who established themselves in key locations. They were opposed by some of the roughest allied combatants in Vietnam, who were posted there on special missions. The counterattack was made by small but lethal teams from Detachment B-42 of the Army Special Forces, a provincial reconnaissance unit of Project PHOENIX, and a Navy SEAL contingent. The fight lasted a tough thirty-six hours; mass civilian casualties resulted and a fourth of the city was burned to the ground, but the Viet Cong were utterly defeated.

The country-wide NVA/VC Tet-68 Offensive achieved a positive psychological effect and worldwide publicity, but only transient success on the ground. The Viet Cong had performed most of the assaults and took such heavy losses that they were largely destroyed as an effective military menace to the South Vietnamese government. Thereafter, VC activities would be confined to minor ambushes and raids, and main force Viet Cong formations had to be completely rebuilt using regular North Vietnamese replacements. All chances of "liberating South Vietnam from within" were thoroughly defeated with the bloody military reverses suffered by the Viet Cong in Tet-68.

The South Vietnamese forces had taken the brunt of the Tet-68 attacks and had been shaken and cut up by its unexpected violence. Although a considerable number of soldiers returned to their units as soon as practicable, desertions in February skyrocketed. The superb South Vietnamese Airborne and 1st Divisions, as well as the 11th, 21st, 23d, 37th, and 39th Ranger Battalions, had so many casualties that they were out of commission for most of the year. Throughout the ARVN military, losses in key officers and sergeants had been severe. However, the South Vietnamese armed forces had performed well considering the intensity of combat and confusion resulting from the surprise. In many regions of the country it had been the heaviest combat ever experienced. Tet-68 thrust the ARVN back into the forefront of the war, and a General Mobilization Law promulgated on June 19, 1968, allowed the army to slowly regain its cohesion.

The American forces had wreaked absolute havoc on the North Vietnamese and Viet Cong attackers, bringing superior armaments and mobility to crush entire units. Although Tet-68 had been a great military victory, most of its potential as such was lost, since the American public never got over its initial shock at the apparent ability of the Viet Cong to strike and hold targets throughout Vietnam. The battles fought during those hectic weeks had been vicious and costly, but the strategic possibilities raised by their successful conclusion were lost to a government dazed by the surface carnage. As a result, great pressure was brought against the military to curtail further casualties. This command desire to cut further losses inhibited any chance of a ruthless follow-up campaign aimed at finishing off the VC remnants and discouraging future NVA activity in South Vietnam.

CHAPTER 16.

SIEGE AND
BREAKTHROUGH

1. Khe Sanh: The Siege Begins

The ambush of a platoon from Company I, 3d Battalion, 26th Marines, on January 19, 1968, on a ridgeline just south of Hill 881 North, was like a recurring nightmare of the previous year's ambuscade in the same area, which had touched off The Hill Fights around Khe Sanh. This time, however, both reinforced *304th* and *325C NVA Divisions* were in the immediate vicinity. Instead of the localized firefights of 1967, the resulting battle for Khe Sanh would become the highest strategic military concern of the United States government.

Colonel David E. Lownd's 26th Marines defending the key Marine combat base of Khe Sanh were thinly spread, protecting both the main bastion and several nearby hills deemed critical to its survival.[1] These hill strong-points had been carved out of the tree-splintered, upchurned earth left by the massive American bombardments used in taking them the previous spring. The trees had been so riddled with metal shrapnel shards that

---

1. The 26th Marines had been forged in the heat of World War II at Camp Pendleton, California, in January 1944, and its heritage consisted of only one battle, Iwo Jima. There the regiment's valiant performance on Nishi Ridge earned it fellowship with older Marine units. It had been deactivated in March 1946 and called back to the colors to fight in Vietnam, where elements had been quickly lifted into Khe Sanh.

engineers attempting to cut them for bunker timber only ruined their chain saw blades. The Marines had ringed Khe Sanh and its hills with triple rows of wire, deep trenches, and sandbagged mortar-proof bunkers. The men struggled through torrential monsoon rains which washed away barrier obstacles, collapsed trenches, and caved in bunkers. They toiled under sniper fire to string barbed wire and razor-sharp German wire, emplace mines and personnel detectors, and shore up fortifications. They sent out daily patrols into the jungled ravines and elephant grass in constant sweeps that often brought sudden death, and then sent other patrols to retrieve the bodies and avenge the fallen.

The six hilltops guarding Khe Sanh were themselves exposed islands of resistance tenuously connected by helicopter airlift only. Already their slopes were cluttered with aircraft wreckage. Helicopters alighting on the elevated landing zones dumped cargo and lifted out seriously injured Marines in seconds, as intense mortaring bracketed them with geysers of dirt. Casualties were run out on stretchers carried by Marines who sometimes had to be evacuated with the wounded, as the helicopter-evoked shellings inevitably injured the litter bearers as well. When the hilltops were buried in cloud cover they were totally isolated, sometimes for weeks.

In the night mists of January 20, the North Vietnamese attacked up Hill 861. Sappers ran bangalore torpedoes into the defensive barriers, and soldiers poured through the gaps. Mortar explosions tore into the packed groups of onrushing men as the Marine defenders flayed them with red tracer-lined streams of machine-gun fire. *Fougasse* barrels splattered the attackers with burning concoctions of diesel fuel and gasoline. Twisted fencing and barbed wire were piled high with smashed bodies riddled by hot steel, hideously lighted by brilliant flashes of detonating shellfire. More NVA infantry dashed up the slippery mud as explosions erupted along the entire slope, and jumped into the trenchlines of Company K, 26th Marines.

The Marines desperately fought back in close-quarters combat, knifing and clubbing the North Vietnamese in a melee of individual fighting. Some bludgeoned assailants were flung over the sides of the ditches and rolled to their deaths down the fire-swept hill. Other Marines, relying on their flak vests, simply dropped grenades as the attackers swarmed over them, and curled up to absorb the shrapnel fragments in their legs and armor. Marine mortar tubes on supporting hills were overworked until they glowed red in the dark. Finally the North Vietnamese attack broke, and Hill 861 remained in Marine hands.

At dawn on January 21, the North Vietnamese plastered Khe Sanh airstrip with a barrage of rockets and mortars. Almost everything above ground at the base was flattened or damaged by the combination of the shelling and the destruction of the main ammunition dump, which burned furiously for two days. The 1st Battalion of the 9th Marines was flown to Khe Sanh the following day. On January 27, the 37th ARVN Ranger Battalion arrived at the camp, a symbolic gesture from the South Vietnamese government.[2] These five battalions would endure the siege of Khe Sanh, along with artillery, five tanks, two Ontos platoons, and a CIDG company with their Special Forces advisors.

The bleak situation had many of the overtones of Dien Bien Phu, the great communist battlefield victory which had closed the curtain on French rule in Indochina and created the two Vietnamese states. There was widespread fear that this Marine base might be overrun also, giving North Vietnam a similar military and political triumph. Although the situation was not a carbon copy of the former siege, since the Marines at Khe Sanh were entrenched on a small plateau and controlled adjacent high ground, the parallels were certainly there. The Marine predicament at Khe Sanh was extremely precarious. They were surrounded by at least two crack North Vietnamese divisions, one of which was the home guard *304th NVA Division,* which had fought at Dien Bien Phu (and was destined to conquer Da Nang

2. Concerning the commitment of the 37th ARVN Ranger Battalion, Col. Hoang Ngoc Lung states, "Not until the fighting had been in full progress did the RVN decide to deploy one ARVN Ranger battalion to the base, more for political than tactical reasons, evidently." (*The General Offensives of 1968– 69,* U.S. Army Center of Military History, Washington, D.C., 1981, p. 11). General Westmoreland was more blunt: "To assure ARVN participation in what I deemed to be an important fight, I insisted that the South Vietnamese contribute an ARVN Ranger Battalion." (*A Soldier Reports,* Doubleday & Company, 1976, p.339).

on March 30, 1975). Since Route 9 had been cut, the base had to subsist entirely on aerial resupply, a chancy business in the monsoon season.

Hill 861A was assaulted in the morning darkness of February 5. Exploding bangalore torpedoes ripped through the wire and the North Vietnamese surged up the slope. Captain Breeding's Company E of the 26th Marines unleashed an unrestrained torrent of machine-gun, claymore mine, and grenade fire to annihilate the first groups storming through the sapper lanes. Then the NVA gained the summit and took the northernmost trench-line. They stopped momentarily to loot the dead Marine defenders, giving the rest of Company E a chance to reform and counterattack. The assault was so sudden that the North Vietnamese had no time to react. The savage fighting was hand to hand as searing grenade blasts lighted the fisted blows, kicks, and knifings in white-hot, blinding flashes. The fury of the assault ejected the North Vietnamese from the redoubts.

Two days later, the North Vietnamese would overrun an Army Special Forces camp only six miles to the west along Route 9. This time they would use tanks for the first time in Vietnam.

2. Khe Sanh: The Pressure Mounts (Lang Vei)

The Special Forces camp of Lang Vei, located along Route 9 only a mile and a half from the Laotian border, was just southwest of the Khe Sanh base. Although the camp was not part of the Marine defenses, it was tied into Marine artillery and re-action forces for support. Lang Vei was the last Special Forces border surveillance camp along the northwestern Vietnam border, and its loss terminated fixed American presence in that critical region. Its destruction by North Vietnamese armor also marked the final transition of the war from one of guerrilla tactics to a classic, conventional struggle between national armies.

The camp was unexpectedly reinforced by the 33d Laotian Volunteer Battalion (Elephant) on January 24, 1968. They had been overrun the previous day at Ban Houei San in Laos. Although there had been disturbing reports of North Vietnamese tanks, Capt. Frank C. Willoughby, the commander of the Lang Vei Special Forces Detachment A-101, did not expect the armor actually to attack the camp except in a fire support role from the jungle. As a result training with the hundred light antitank weapons was limited to a dozen Americans and ten indigenous troops, leaving seventy-five of the one-shot, disposable weapons on hand.[3]

Special Forces Lt. Col. Daniel F. Schungel had been posted to the camp on February 6, after the Laotian colonel there refused to listen to lower-ranking Americans. He arrived to experience an intense camp mortaring at six o'clock that evening. One hour before midnight two North Vietnamese PT-76 amphibian tanks escorted by infantry from the *66th NVA Regiment* rumbled over the outer wire. Their headlights swept the ground in front of them as they fired their cannon and machine guns at the camp defenses. CIDG riflemen shot out the lights, and a Special Forces-manned 106mm recoilless rifle swiveled around to destroy each tank in turn. Three more tanks then swung into view, roared around the disabled vehicles, and rolled over the camp's ramparts.

Lt. Col. Schungel led bands of Special Forces troopers, armed with light antitank weapons, chasing after the clanking tanks. They exploded one tank and gunned down three crewmen clambering from the smoking hatches. However, more tanks were now appearing on the road leading into camp, and the antitank rounds were either misfiring or scoring direct hits with little effect. A fourth tank was destroyed by the 106mm recoilless rifle position. It then fired three rounds of Beehive ammunition before being knocked out. By 2:00 A.M. the sole remaining recoilless rifle position was also destroyed. Special Forces and indigenous troopers were desperately climbing the sides of the fifteen-ton steel vehicles and trying to pry open hatches to grenade them. Most were killed or wounded by North Vietnamese shock troops following behind them and firing assault rifles. NVA sappers were using satchel charges, tear gas grenades, and flamethrowers to tear into the inner compound.

The outer fringes of the camp were overrun despite a tough

3. On February 7, 1968, Lang Vei Special Forces camp had 1,007 troops: 24 Special Forces, 14 LLDB, 161 Mike Force, and 282 CIDG Bru tribal soldiers, 6 interpreters, 520 Laotian Ca tribal soldiers, and 2,200 Laotian civilians. Not counting the Laotians (the reports are blank as to their fate), the camp forces suffered 219 killed (10 U.S.) and 77 wounded (13 U.S.).

defense (with the exception of the Laotian Ca tribal soldiers, whose commander wanted to "wait to fight until morning"). The cloud cover and rolling ground fogs combined with communications difficulty to preclude accurate air support. Sergeant First Class Ashley, five other Special Forces sergeants, and fifty CIDG soldiers kept low to the ground as the tanks lumbered past them and then escaped outside the wire to hide in bamboo clumps and dry creek beds. When the Special Forces troops tried to organize a counterattack from the outside, using the throngs of panicked indigenous soldiers now streaming out of the camp, no one stopped at their orders.

Lieutenant Colonel Schungel and several Special Forces and LLDB personnel ran back to the main bunker looking for more light antitank weapons. They were surrounded by sappers. The LLDB troops dodged into the bunker, but Lieutenant Colonel Schungel's Americans manned positions behind dirt- and stone-filled fifty-five-gallon drums around the fortification. A tank rumbled to a stop in front of the barricade. The Americans fired a light antitank round, but it bounced off. The tank blasted back with its 76mm main gun. The force of the explosion knocked Schungel down, tossed a barrel on top of a lieutenant, and blinded another Special Forces soldier with flying gravel. The men pulled back to sandbags at the bunker entrance. An LLDB officer nearby realized that the bunker was a prime target and that defending it was hopeless. He dashed off looking for a better place to hide. The lieutenant colonel and the lieutenant tried to follow, but the tank prevented their movement.

It was 3:00 A.M. The tank began clanking around the bunker and shooting at the abandoned observation tower, which refused to collapse. Schungel pitched two grenades under the tank. The explosions did not harm it, but the tower structure fell over. At that point someone hit the tank with a light antitank weapon, and its turret hatch suddenly popped open. A hand appeared, and then slipped back inside as flames started shooting out the hatchway.

Lieutenant Colonel Schungel and the lieutenant, both badly wounded, then killed a five-man sapper squad and managed to crawl underneath the dispensary. They hid for the rest of the night under a blanket of sandbags, while a platoon of North

Vietnamese set up positions overhead. Meanwhile, Captain Willoughby and the small group of Americans and LLDB in the underground level of the main bunker now believed they were the only ones left alive. They had no communications, as all their outside antennae were cut down by the victorious North Vietnamese swarming over the compound. The men, covered with splinters and rubble, positioned themselves behind overturned furniture.

The NVA kept pitching incendiary and riot gas grenades into the bunker, and the defenders either had to put on gas masks, handkerchiefs, or vomit. Then they shouted out in Vietnamese, "We are going to blow up the bunker, so give up." At this command the LLDB captain and his four LLDB soldiers in the bunker walked out with their hands up and were summarily executed. Although the NVA kept tossing grenades in the doorway, they never stormed the bunker interior. Captain Willoughby, seriously wounded, lost consciousness at 8:30 A.M., still holding a flak jacket in front of him.

Meanwhile Sergeant Ashley and two other Special Forces troopers were walking up Route 9 pleading with fleeing Laotians and CIDG Bru tribesmen to counterattack the camp. They finally mustered sixty Laotian volunteers and twenty CIDG, got in touch with aircraft by radio, and attacked. The Bru native warriors bolted after receiving machine-gun fire and had to be coaxed back. Sergeant Ashley's composite contingent assaulted three different times attempting to reach the main bunker. Each time they were repulsed. Fighter-bombers were raking the inside of the camp with rockets and cannon fire.

At 9:30 A.M. Schungel and the lieutenant decided that the NVA had vacated the dispensary because there was no longer return fire against the air strikes hitting the camp. They painfully hobbled out and saw two blackened tank hulks, apparently hit by aircraft, standing just outside the doorway. Both men walked out the east gate of the camp. A half hour later the main bunker reestablished outside communications, and at eleven o'clock Captain Willoughby, whom everyone had thought dead, regained consciousness. By this time Sergeant Ashley's group was in its fourth try to break through. Between each assault the Americans had to round up the reluctant CIDG soldiers, and each attack stalled as the indigenous soldiers ran off again down the road. On the fifth and final assault, Sergeant Ashley was hit in the chest and mortally wounded.

The camp survivors were now ordered to evacuate the compound, which was only lightly held after hours of blistering air attacks. The bunker group stumbled out of its position in a move closely coordinated by radio with Skyraider fighters, which were making final bombing and strafing runs. Captain Willoughby's dazed and bloodied column reached the main gate at Route 9. There the LLDB officer was waiting in a jeep. He had been captured by the North Vietnamese, had escaped, and had then run all the way to old Lang Vei (450 yards from the present camp) where he had found the vehicle.

The Americans, South Vietnamese, and Bru and Laotian Ca warriors assembled on the old Lang Vei landing strip for aerial extraction. The Marine helicopters landed, but attempts at orderly evacuation were rendered impossible when the Laotians and indigenous soldiers mobbed the Marine helicopters. However, the Marine aircraft managed to get the wounded and the Americans on board. They flew back, suffering considerable damage from ground fire despite continuous overhead fighter cover.

The rest of the Laotians and a horde of civilians, some six thousand strong, descended on Khe Sanh itself at eight o'clock on the morning of February 8. They had walked the entire distance along the road. Behind them the North Vietnamese enjoyed full possession of Lang Vei, a critical Route 9 location.[4]

3. Khe Sanh: Siege and Relief

At daybreak on February 8, 1968, the *101D NVA Regiment* attacked Hill 64, held by Second Lieutenant Terence R. Roach, Jr.'s platoon of Company A, 9th Marines. They rolled over the barrier wire on top of canvas and rushed the western trenches. Using liberal air and tank support, the rest of Company A recaptured the hill in vicious fighting later that morning.

---

4. Army Special Forces reports were sharply critical of Air Force and Marine response, which was hampered by weather and larger tactical considerations as well as the ambush-prone nature of Route 9 connecting Khe Sanh to Lang Vei.

The siege then became an extended standoff as the North Vietnamese began constructing entrenched approach works, snipers patiently waited for careless targets, constant shelling continued, and Marine aircraft struggled to keep the base supplied. The weather and hostile fire mandated a total of 679 supply drops, as landings were prohibited. The air space above Khe Sanh was always crowded with droning cargo planes, whirling helicopters, darting light observation Birddogs, propellered Skyraiders, thundering Spooky aircraft, and shrieking jet fighter-bombers. The earth constantly rumbled with the distant mass explosions from B-52 bombers flying beyond sight and sound. The lush green hillsides, which had once supported the finest Southeast Asian coffee plantations, had been reduced to charred ochre slopes of cratered mud.

Action intensified late in the month when Khe Sanh endured the heaviest barrage of the siege on February 23, and the loss of two patrolling squads from Company B, 26th Marines, by ambush two days later. The 37th ARVN Ranger Battalion, defending the southern outer perimeter of the main base, was hit by a major ground assault on the night of February 29. The North Vietnamese infantry launched two assaults from three trenchlines in front of the ranger barrier wires. Both attacks were obliterated by the response to frantic South Vietnamese calls for protective fire which sent a devastating firestorm of artillery shells exploding over the entire front. This massive artillery barrage annihilated three waves of NVA soldiers before they could get past the barbed wire. Airbursts created an equally lethal hailstorm of shrapnel, which also swept throught the trenches and killed many of the soldiers before they could "go over the top."

In March, blue skies replaced the monsoon clouds above Khe Sanh, bringing a consequent increase in air activity. The Marines and the South Vietnamese rangers began vigorously sweeping the base perimeter. An upbeat mood prevailed with the change in weather and the decline of North Vietnamese pressure. The military looked forward to relieving the siege of Khe Sanh. Provisional Corps Vietnam, the precursor of XXIV Corps, had been activated at Phu Bai on March 10, 1968, under Lt. Gen. William B. Rosson, to continue the missions of MACV Forward. Although planning was stymied by a major interservice squabble over tactical aircraft direction and Army-Marine problems of coordination, it continued to direct the elimination of the Hue pocket, control the additional Army formations inserted in "Marineland," stockpile war supplies, and prepare a breakthrough to Khe Sanh.

General Westmoreland, dissatisfied with Marine air support arrangements for certain Army formations, demanded that the Seventh Air Force provide all tactical aircraft direction. A major high-level squabble erupted in the midst of the Tet Offensive, the Battle of Hue, and the Siege of Khe Sanh. The proposal became a focal point of Pentagon, Pacific Command, and MACV–III MAF bickering. Doctrinal debate exploded, General Westmoreland considered resignation, and its final resolution (Air Force management of fixed-wing missions) came on March 8, 1968, as all three engagements were ending. Actual Air Force control was not implemented until April 1, 1968.

The long-awaited allied drive on Khe Sanh, Operation PEGASUS/LAM SON 207, began at 8:00 A.M. on April 1, 1968. The jump-off point was the supply-packed staging fortress of Ca Lu, fifteen miles away from the Marine combat base. Columns of armor-vested, helmeted riflemen of the 2d Battalions of the 1st and 3d Marines trudged along both sides of Route 9 through thick morning ground fog. Behind them roared Marine dozers, trucks, and cranes of the 11th Engineer Battalion, which would have to build culverts, emplace bridges, and carve out bypasses. The heavy construction vehicles and equipment of the Navy Seabees followed.

To the rear of the moving frontage of men and vehicles was Landing Zone Stud, which the Seabees had turned into a major airfield. Although wrapped in foggy haze that delayed flight operations, it was a hub of hectic activity. Rows of helicopters were parked the length of the airstrip. That afternoon, crammed with battle-hardened troopers of the 7th Cavalry, they soared into the low-hanging clouds. Throngs of Marines marching along the roadway lifted their heads as the throbbing pitch of helicopters resonated over the clatter of equipment and the noise of vehicle engines. Waves of 1st Cavalry Division Hueys were racing overhead. In one spectacular hop the 3d Brigade launched a massive three-battalion heliborne assault directly into the critical terrain midway between Ca Lu and the Khe Sanh combat base. The landings were virtually unopposed.

The airmobile pace of Major General Tolson's 1st Cavalry Division quickened on April 3, as three battalions of the 2d Brigade helicoptered southeast of Khe Sanh. Again there was little resistance. The only firefights resulted from the North Vietnamese determination to retain certain high ground positions north of Route 9, in order to cover the withdrawal of their major forces to the south and west.

At daybreak on April 4, Lt. Col. John J. H. Cahill's 1st Battalion of the 9th Marines attacked Hill 471, a critical piece of real estate two miles south of Khe Sanh that overlooked much of the valley. It had been occupied by NVA forces since January, but the Marines were on top of it by late afternoon. They found only a few bodies of those killed by the artillery and air strikes delivered prior to the assault. The next day a battalion of the *66th NVA Regiment* made a predawn attempt to retake the hill. After two hours of fighting on the slopes, the Marines mounted a savage, artillery-supported counterattack which repulsed this effort. Enjoying excellent fields of observation and fire from Hill 471 covering the advance of the cavalrymen, the Marines continued to attack to the northwest.

Actions were delayed April 6, as the 2d Battalion of the 7th Cavalry fought west along Route 9 in a continuous day of combat against the North Vietnamese. The 1st Battalion of the 5th Cavalry ran into a strong-point at the Old French Fort, the last obstacle between the Army and the Marines at Khe Sanh. The position fell to the 5th Cavalry's 2d Battalion the following day. South Vietnamese paratroopers of the 3d, 6th, and 8th ARVN Airborne Battalions airmobiled to the west of Khe Sanh near the Laotian border on April 7. Meanwhile, the 2d Battalion of the 26th Marines cleared bunkered resistance between the combat base and the northwestern outposts on Hills 861 and 881 South. Another objective was secured April 10. On that day the 1st Battalion, 12th Cavalry, swept into the ruins of the Lang Vei Special Forces camp.

During the second week of April, the North Vietnamese launched only one major attack, an early morning attempt on April 8 to overrun the ARVN command post five miles south of

Khe Sanh. Supported by artillery and Marine fighter-bombers, the South Vietnamese paratroopers fought off the battalion-sized assault. The same day, the relief of the Khe Sanh combat base was formally accomplished as the 1st Cavalry Division helicoptered Colonel Campbell's 3d Brigade command post inside the Marine compound. As the 11th Engineer Battalion closed the base on April 12, it marked the first time since September 1967 that an operational traffic lane existed over the forty-two road miles connecting Dong Ha to Khe Sanh.

Wide-ranging air cavalry units continued to uncover large supply caches and other evidence of hasty withdrawal into neighboring Laos. The final battle occurred on Easter Sunday, April 14, in the same saddle between Hills 881 South and North, where the Battle of Khe Sanh had begun in January. Preceded by an extensive air and artillery bombardment, the 3d Battalion, 26th Marines, attacked at first light and, after heavy fighting up the fortified slopes of Hill 881 North, secured the summit at 2:28 P.M. Through the end of April, the Marines continued to clear the Khe Sanh vicinity in numerous slow and difficult company- and battalion-sized operations. These sweeps uncovered abandoned North Vietnamese weapons and many dead, and generated sporadic contact with NVA stay-behind units. The forces that remained in western Quang Tri were small but well armed, and derived substantial combat advantage from the hundreds of well-prepared positions located throughout the Khe Sanh area.

The siege had lasted seventy-seven days, during which time staggering amounts of war materials had been expended. Between January 20 and the end of April, 110,022 tons of bombs had been dropped, 142,081 rounds of artillery fired, and over 14,000 tons of supplies had been air-delivered. However, the end of the siege marked the end of Marine interest in retaining Khe Sanh. General Westmoreland deferred the touchy decision to his successor, Gen. Creighton W. Abrams. When he nodded approval, the Marines had already been dismantling the base for some time. By July 5, it was razed to the ground, and all the recently refurbished bridges along Route 9 were systematically destroyed.

Its abandonment created a storm of military debate and public furor. This was a natural consequence of the officially stated military reasons for its defense in the first place, which had been put out largely as propaganda during a wartime siege. The real basis for its abandonment was the demise of Defense Secretary McNamara's barrier dream. The Marines, a mobile shock force by design and tradition, had an ingrained distaste for static defense, which was heightened by the Khe Sanh experience. While the destruction of Khe Sanh eradicated a strong-point of McNamara's extended DYE MARKER plan, it also promised a return to Marine mobility. However, by mid-1968, although limited tactical offensives abounded, the United States military participation in the war would soon be relegated to a strategic defensive stance. The South Vietnamese forces would shortly be directed to carry the burden of offensive combat.

CHAPTER 17.

COUNTEROFFENSIVE

1. Into the A Shau Valley

Following the Tet-68 onslaught of shock attacks, MACV moved to sweep and secure the regions adjacent to cities and installations that had been targeted, and also launched several counteroffensives into suspected NVA/VC base camps along the border. The devastating Battle of Hue convinced General Westmoreland of the need to strike deep into the North Vietnamese Army staging area of A Shau Valley, on the westernmost fringes of Thua Thien Province, in order to preempt the massing of further attacks on the crucial city. The highly mobile 1st Cavalry Division, just north of the valley as a result of its spectacular Khe Sanh relief, was chosen as the sword of vengeance.

The remote A Shau Valley was one of the most rugged and inaccessible regions straddling Vietnam's haunting western frontier. The valley itself was a flat strip of bottomland, masked by trackless, man-high elephant grass and deep, verdant tropical rain forest. It had been carved out of the jungle-wrapped, misting mountain ranges towering five thousand feet on either side of the Rao Loa River, which flowed past the bones of the overrun A Shau Special Forces camp at its southern end to loop at Ta Bat and then west into Laos. This corner of highland wilderness had been a haunt of the North Vietnamese since early 1966, and MACV was unsure of the extent of fortification there or whether the NVA would stand fast and defend it. Since the valley's rocky outcrops and steep slopes were reinforced with batteries of heavy antiaircraft guns, the division would be facing the most concentrated air defense encountered in South Vietnam up to that time.

Aerial scout teams of the 1st Squadron, 9th Cavalry, started working the area in mid-April. Scores of glassy, bubble-light observation helicopters, sleek Cobra gunships, and slender Huey aerial workhorses darted alongside the valley walls in three days of excellent flying weather. Behind their whirling cameras and flashing machine guns came hundreds of Marine and Air Force jet fighters spilling napalm and bombs. B-52 stratofortresses pummeled the valley with a high-altitude heavy bombing blitz.

The intensity of unsuppressed antiaircraft fire in the central valley caused Major General Tolson to shift his opening assault to the northern end with his division's 3d Brigade. On an overcast April 19, troop helicopters filled with riflemen of the 1st and 5th Battalions of the 7th Cavalry helicoptered over the jagged peaks of several Chaine Annamitique ridgelines, and swung toward two landing zones being rocketed and strafed by last-minute air strikes and rocket runs. The helicopters veered into their final approaches, abruptly dipping like runaway roller coaster cars. The cavalrymen felt their stomachs flutter as they held onto the lurching aircraft and flipped their rifles onto firing mode. Many squad privates were raw stateside recruits; the division had absorbed some 6,104 replacements since the beginning of February as a result of hard fighting at Hue and Khe Sanh.

These first air assaults of Operation DELAWARE/LAM SON 216 planted the airmobile infantry near a valley trail on a nearby hillside. Explosives and engineer tools flattened trees and vegetation, and soon the red earth was pitted by foxholes and littered with piles of sandbags and munitions boxes. Then the NVA gunners suddenly opened up with their accurate 37mm and 23mm antiaircraft guns as more aircraft descended through the lowering clouds. Flak bursts and machine-gun fire laced the thick humid air. Ten helicopters were shot down and another thirteen damaged. As drizzling rain set in, the division aborted the lift-in of a second artillery firing battery. That night the 7th Cavalry's 5th Battalion spotted a large convoy of nearly a hundred trucks near their landing zone, and took it under fire with light artillery.

General William C. Westmoreland from June 20, 1964 to June 1968 (U.S. Army)

General Creighton W. Abrams from July 2, 1968 to June 1972 (U.S. Army)

President Lyndon B. Johnson bids farewell to paratroopers of the 3d Brigade, 82d Airborne Division, as they are rushed as emergency reinforcement into Vietnam from Fort Bragg, North Carolina. (Author's Collection)

Soldiers of the 2d Battalion, 47th Infantry, 9th Infantry Division advance on the Y-Bridge during the Mini-Tet Offensive in Saigon on May 11, 1968. The flak-vested soldier in the center carries the M79 grenade launcher, while the soldier on the far right carries an M60 machine gun. Others are armed with M16 rifles. (U.S. Army)

Soldiers of the 101st Airborne Division rappel into broken jungle as the Army takes the post-Tet offensive into Vietnam's border regions. (101st Airborne Division Information Office, Vietnam)

Wounded troops of the 101st Airborne Division are rushed to medical evacuation helicopters as mopping up operations continue south of Hue. (Author's Collection)

Armored Personnel Carriers of the 1st Brigade, 5th Infantry Division (Mechanized) cross over sixty-foot span of an Armored Vehicle Launched Bridge near Khe Sanh. (U.S. Army)

The flexibility of the Mobile Riverine Brigade of the 9th Infantry Division is demonstrated as soldiers of the 3d Battalion, 60th Infantry, land from Armored Troop Carrier vessels in Kien Hoa Province of the Delta. (U.S. Army)

For the next four days a late-season monsoon front passed through, bringing vile weather which jeopardized the entire operation. Dense fog and intermittent thundershowers obscured the rain-soaked jungle, and clouds blanketed the valley. Helicopters leaving Camp Evans with supplies and reinforcements climbed through the murky mist on instruments, leveled out above the clouds, and then flew to the mountain peaks rising above the overcast like craggy islands. The young aviators of the 11th Aviation Group then descended through the clouds and antiaircraft fire, and groped through the gloom at near zero visibility to seek out American troop positions. Flights into the valley became impossible past noon of each day. In this harrowing manner the rest of the brigade was airlifted into the valley by April 23. Finally, when the weather improved, the low daytime ceilings never lifted above two or three thousand feet, covering the higher elevations.

Meanwhile, the foot cavalry pushed out from their landing zones and began finding ammunition stocks and abandoned antiaircraft guns mounted on flatbed trucks. The 7th Cavalry's 1st Battalion made a cross-country trek to secure an abandoned airfield outside A Loui, enabling the 1st Brigade to land there on April 25. The North Vietnamese soldiers were slipping away with as much material as possible, using their mobile flak guns to discourage close airmobile pursuit, and the cavalrymen were rapidly frustrated by these evasive tactics. A brief, indecisive skirmish on April 26, the result of a 5th Battalion company from the 7th Cavalry accidentally brushing against departing NVA infantry, was the first solid ground contact of the A Shau Valley sweep.

Three days later the Americans secured Ta Bat in the middle of the valley. The 3d ARVN Regiment was flown in to this site on the first day of May. They started moving along the Rao Loa River toward the old A Shau Special Forces camp, uncovering fresh stocks of ammunition, spare parts, and communications equipment. The 1st Cavalry Division continued to reconnoiter the area and find more caches. The 8th Engineer Battalion repaired the A Loui airfield for use by fixed-wing cargo planes, but daily thunderstorms washed it out by May 11. The division was forced to evacuate the valley the same way it entered, by helicopter alone.

As the rains increased, the division began destroying its fire bases and preparing to leave. The first in were the first out, and the 3d Brigade departed May 10 followed by the South Vietnamese. The 1st Brigade's aerial extraction was completed by the middle of the month. Operation DELAWARE was over, and the Army quickly claimed a resounding success by citing bundles of captured war materials, including one PT-76 light tank. The actual results were less satisfying. The cavalrymen were exposed to intense North Vietnamese rocketing and heavy artillery shelling, and the helicopters had suffered grave losses due to weather and severe flak. Again the NVA had chosen not to fight, being content to offer only token resistance as the cavalrymen freely roamed the valley. By willingly giving up a quantity of military stores, they had gained the advantage of maneuvering their fighting forces elsewhere while the highly mobile 1st Cavalry Division was occupied in the A Shau Valley.

Major General Melvin Zais's 101st Airborne Division was ordered into the A Shau Valley next. MACV hoped to bag North Vietnamese troops reentering on the heels of the cavalry raid. The planned operation, SOMERSET PLAIN/LAM SON 246, was delayed three days by unsuitable weather, but on August 4 the clouds cleared enough for the division's 1st Brigade to airmobile in. They were guided by a troop from the ubiquitous 1st Squadron of the 9th Cavalry, and brought along the 1st ARVN Regiment. The air assaults had to run the gauntlet of intense antiaircraft fire. Four gunships, one observation helicopter, and one Phantom fighter-bomber were shot down, and another four gunships and seven troopships were heavily damaged. The soldiers were dropped off in the old northern and central cavalry sectors around A Loui and Ta Bat. The NVA resorted to delaying and harassing tactics, but did not carelessly leave many large weapons or ammunition caches behind. General Zais's divisional long-range reconnaissance team had to be content with emplacing booby-trapped mines and sensor devices. The allied force boarded outbound helicopters August 18–19.

Both operations were feats of airmanship and logistics conducted over some of the world's most difficult tropical terrain. They were entirely air-supported and stand as milestones in evolving airmobile tactics. However, neither neutralized the targeted area, since North Vietnamese forces in neighboring Laos quickly moved back into the valley upon allied departure. The ephemeral excursions continued throughout the next year as MACV kept up the pressure against a permanent NVA return to the valley. Each operation was highly dangerous because of the unpredictable weather and the uncertainty of NVA reaction. Although the North Vietnamese usually retreated, American commanders could never be sure what reception their airmobile infantry would receive, and in 1969 the NVA chose to fight.

2. Action Along the DMZ

Throughout 1968 the Marines continued to seal the Demilitarized Zone, blocking NVA movement south across it by counterattacking out of their fixed bases along Route 9. Since the American rules of engagement still permitted Marine sorties up to the demarcation line itself, the 3d Marine Division was getting ready to slam into the DMZ as part of MACV's Tet-68 counteroffensive effort. Before the Marines could strike, the North Vietnamese hit first.

The advancing *320th NVA Division* was detected only four miles from the major Marine base at Dong Ha on April 29, 1968. The 2d ARVN Regiment became enmeshed in a six-day road fight with elements of the division, but other North Vietnamese troops pushed around that battle and got into Dai Do village, over two miles closer to Dong Ha, on April 30. The NVA were then able to block an important logistical channel, the Cua Viet River, with mortar and rocket fire as well as long-range artillery from North Vietnam. A Marine battalion, sent to reinforce the Dong Ha area, was battered by a major ambush. The Marines attacked Dai Do with another battalion (2d Battalion, 4th Marines) from road and riverbank, supported by tanks and amphibious tractors.

On May 1, the Army's 196th Infantry Brigade (Light), on loan as an emergency reserve from the Americal Division, airmobiled its 3d Battalion, 21st Infantry, into blocking positions northeast of the battlefield.[1] The battalion prepared to seal off the northeastern exits of the battleground, but became involved in a protracted battle at the fortified hamlet of Nhi Ha. They pressed their attack for two days through trenches and bunkers, supported by plenty of Marine aircraft. Nhi Ha fell May 4, but soon after the Americans left the NVA reoccupied it and constructed new blockhouses and entrenchments.

The Marines fighting near Dai Do began to make better headway after air observers put Marine jets on top of an NVA artillery spotting team on the morning of May 1. The riflemen rolled a barrage through the village, charged in behind it, and dug in positions on the northern side. The North Vietnamese soldiers counterattacked the Marines in force late in the afternoon, running forward behind a shield of artillery and mortar support. The Marines answered with machine guns, rifles, grenade launchers, and tank cannons, and desperately called for air strikes and heavy shelling. During the height of the action almost every American artillery tube in northeastern Quang Tri Province was either firing counterbattery concentrations or creating a wall of final protective fires in front of the Marines. The NVA assault ploughed through the fiery detonations and into the Marine lines, where it was defeated after a four-hour melee of hand-to-hand combat.

The *320th NVA Division*'s thrust toward Dong Ha was checked at Dai Do on May 2. That afternoon the NVA mounted a second counterattack against Dai Do. Artillery was active on both sides, and Marine aircraft made fourteen sorties. The Marines repulsed the charge and followed in pursuit. The North Vietnamese troops suddenly turned and made a third counterattack, the most violent of the battle. The 4th Marines fell back into a hasty perimeter as rocket and mortar explosions ripped through their ranks. Supporting air strikes were brought in as close as possible as napalm and cluster bombs tore through the

1. The 21st Infantry soldiers were known as the Gimlets. The regiment had been formed in occupied Virginia after the Civil War, and had fought its way west from Arizona in the Indian Wars, across the Zapote River in the Philippine Insurrection, in Luzon in World War II, in Korea, and finally into Vietnam.

jungle. The battalion held its ground through the evening in furious combat waged at close quarters. The following day the 1st Battalion, 3d Marines, relieved them and continued the drive, meeting only fragmented opposition. The last major firefight occured on May 5, when the Marines took final organized NVA positions in a daylong engagement. Although mopping up operations were characterized by several sharp company-sized actions against rear-guard detachments, the *320th NVA Division* successfully broke contact.

Two weeks later, after refurbishment, the *320th NVA Division* returned and began advancing toward Dong Ha again. Aerial reconnaissance spotted North Vietnamese troops on May 25, 1968, and a Marine company was sent to investigate. The Marines were stopped cold by the entrenched forces which had renewed the defenses at Nhi Ha. A classic frontal assault, made behind a rolling artillery barrage, carried the strong-points, but most of the defenders were able to escape through the swampish bogs. The South Vietnamese had also run into units of the same division less than two miles from Dong Ha. Commencing May 26, the 3d and 9th Marines drove against each flank of the division, and after a week of bitter fighting the North Vietnamese abandoned their Dong Ha approach.

The fixed Marine base camps guarding the Demilitarized Zone were frequently shelled but never to the extent that Con Thien had been during September 1967. However, daily patrols resulted in frequent skirmishing, and the Marines were looking forward to a promised mail-fisted Army brigade, being mustered in the United States to muscle up the eastern DMZ sector.[2] The open, grassy plains were ideal tank country, and Col. Richard J. Glikes's arriving 1st Brigade of the mechanized 5th Infantry

2. The 1st Brigade, 5th Infantry Division (Mechanized) was stationed at Fort Carson, Colorado. It had just commenced reorganization for Vietnam duty on March 25, 1968, when it was assigned riot control tasks during Operation GARDEN PLOT April 7–13. After hurried combat training a flotilla of C-141 Starlifter transports flew the entire brigade to Da Nang by July 31, where other aircraft immediately moved it to Quang Tri. The brigade shipped a total of 1,072 vehicles from its home base, and once in Vietnam it was given 140 armored personnel carriers and 8 mortar carriers from Fort Hood, Texas; 25 M48 medium tanks from Fort Knox, Kentucky; and 42 M48 medium tanks from the Letterkenny Army Depot at Chambersburg, Pennsylvania.

Division contained one tank battalion and two infantry battalions, one of them mounted on armored personnel carriers. His formidable armored shock force was envisioned as an excellent deterrent to invading formations of North Vietnamese light infantry, and was moved to the front lines during August.

The Marines were also delighted with the offshore arrival of the sixteen-inch-gunned battleship USS *New Jersey* (BB-62) on September 29, 1968. Her nineteen-hundred-pound shells could reach twenty-four miles, practically to Camp Carroll. On October 4, the 2d Battalion of the 26th Marines ran into bunkers north of the Rockpile. The battleship rendered its first fire mission in direct support of ground combat in Vietnam. The bunkers were flattened.

The mechanized brigade got into real action about the same time. Although some elements started shooting on August 12, the unit was still completing shakedown. This had been complicated by the September monsoons, which washed out the main bridge along the line of communications to Cam Lo, temporarily cutting the unit off except by aerial resupply. When the tankers and soldiers of the 5th Infantry Division began sustained combat operations, their impact was immediate. The North Vietnamese in the DMZ vicinity had never battled true armored formations that combined mechanized momentum. Their experiences were limited to fighting Marine infantry who used occasional tank support. Initially the NVA tried to stand fast in their earthen fortifications, which led to violent firefights and certain destruction.

One of the roughest encounters took place northeast of Con Thien in response to a reconnaissance report on October 25. The 1st Battalion of the 61st Infantry (Mechanized) found itself opposed by a North Vietnamese bunker complex.[3] The mechanized infantrymen dismounted their carriers and blasted their way into the trenches under a hail of machine-gun and rocket

3. The 61st Infantry was formed in June 1917, at Gettysburg Park, Pennsylvania, and had served in World War I with the 5th Infantry Division, where it made a distinguished crossing of Meuse River near Dun in November of 1918. Afterward it had been axed in the peace cuts and never served in World War II or Korea. Elements were reactivated as part of the combat arms regimental system in 1962.

fire. In a seven-hour struggle, tanks of Company B, 1st Battalion of the 77th Armor, crushed the trenches and finished off bunkers at point-blank range.

The North Vietnamese Army had suffered some serious defeats along the Demilitarized Zone in 1968, but late in the year gained several advantages regardless. On November 1, 1968, all U.S. offensive operations were ordered discontinued inside the DMZ, with the exception of squad patrols (with platoon backup in case extraction assistance was required), which were permitted in the southern portion until December 4, 1968. The NVA formations had also learned to avoid pitched battles with the mechanized brigade. The pace of warfare slowed to the patrol and sweep actions typical of the rest of the country. Bold as ever, the mechanized soldiers began spreading their tracked vehicles out on line and covered the gaps with small four-man fire teams. They hoped to block continued NVA infiltration through the tropical savannah by such picketing, and depended on the speed of nearby armored carriers to bail out any team in trouble. The DMZ campaign had slowed to an indefinite stalemate, which was only broken by the American withdrawals later in the war.

3. Incidents on the Northern Front

Throughout South Vietnam, MACV's counteroffensive was typified by hundreds of battalion-sized operations and literally thousands of small unit actions conducted each week attempting to locate and destroy NVA/VC units. After the Battle of Hue, the 1st Marine Division initiated mobile sweeps in Thua Thien and Quang Nam provinces, taking advantage of the newly arrived 27th Marines reinforcing Da Nang. The division swept the provincial borders and secured the razor-backed Hai Van Mountain Pass area of Highway 1. The North Vietnamese were still able to get several combat units within the Da Nang area by August 18, 1968. On that day sapper and rocket attacks blasted several localities as the Marines were suppressing a major three-day riot in the III MAF detention compound. A lively action followed on August 23 when the *402d VC Sapper Battalion* seized one half of Highway 1's key bridge leading into Da Nang. They had been stopped by the Marine 1st Military Police Battalion, and the city garrison's 1st Battalion of the 27th Marines drove the Viet Cong out.

The 101st Airborne Division (Airmobile) commenced Operation NEVADA EAGLE on May 17, 1968, in Thua Thien Province. Several days later, just after midnight on May 21, the division base camp five miles southeast of Hue was pounded by an intense mortar and rocket barrage. The helicopters quickly scrambled into the air, and an NVA battalion stormed the length of the 1st Brigade perimeter. They broke through the outer perimeter wires with exploding bangalore torpedoes and demolition charges. As the North Vietnamese soldiers rushed the bunker line, the Americans frantically replied with machine-gun, helicopter, and direct Beehive artillery fire. The attack was thrown back by first light.

The division's field activities were typified by infrequent contact and increased booby-trap losses, punctuated by sharp clashes during airmobile assaults in the nearby mountains. Emphasis was placed on protection of rice, scattered ambushing of suspected Viet Cong pathways, and offensive sweeps along roads. This tempo of fighting would continue into the next year.

As American airmobility became commonplace in the northern provinces, the Viet Cong and North Vietnamese soldiers were adapting to the tactics. By the middle of June, the level of air activity and the NVA/VC response was a far cry from the dazzling 1st Cavalry Division intrusion of January. American helicopters were no longer readily picking on opportune targets. The NVA started using small groups of men as bait. When attacked, these men would entice the gunships to fly over well-concealed sections of deadly antiaircraft machine guns. The Americal Division air commanders retorted by calling in massed artillery alongside any close air support. Helicopter losses were mounting in all units, but many of the crews survived the crashes. Often their lives depended on the speed and luck of units attempting to retrieve them.

A 101st Airborne Division OH-6A light observation helicopter was overflying Thua Thien Province on the morning of October 4, 1968, on a visual reconnaissance mission southeast of Phu Loc. In addition to the warrant officer pilot, an artillery captain was aboard. The helicopter was following a ridgeline which was crowned with four clusters of thatched dwellings. Farther down the slope the captain thought he saw a bunker with overhead cover, and several well-used trails connecting all the structures. While turning back to fly over the area and adjust artillery fire on the huts, the little helicopter was suddenly peppered by four rounds of AK47 automatic rifle fire. The bullets all hit the engine compartment, and the craft nosed over to crash upside down on a nearby hillside.

The pilot had been knocked unconscious by the crash, which had broken his right leg, and was wedged in the helicopter's smashed cockpit. The artillery captain was in terrible pain with a fractured left leg and a right leg burned by hot gasoline from a ruptured fuel line. The captain pulled the pilot out of the wreckage, and after the latter had regained consciousness they crawled two hundred yards from the aircraft. They hid under a log in some thick underbrush, armed with only their .45-caliber pistols. As the tropical sun's torrid heat sapped their strength, they cut banana stalks and sucked out the scant moisture.

Throughout the day, close artillery shelling and air strikes kept the Viet Cong away from their hiding place. After dark the two men crawled to a nearby stream and fell asleep on its banks. At various intervals throughout the night, they heard the faint noise of a hand-cranked generator being used to power a radio using morse code. With the coming of daylight the wounded pilot and observer crawled sixty more yards downstream and hid in a hollow under the mud ledge of the streambed. Later that morning the warrant officer saw a helicopter flying back and forth in the sky and crawled out into the open and waved his handkerchief and map in the air. He then hobbled back and dragged out the captain so the helicopter could see both of them.

That afternoon gunfire erupted at a distance. They realized it was an American patrol fighting on the ridgeline. They stayed hidden in the streambed and counted the distinct noises of light machine guns and a few crackling rifles, guessing that only one VC delaying squad was involved. Nightfall descended and they moved to a flat area ten yards away and fell into a broken, exhausted sleep.

At nine in the morning on October 6, they heard a group of Vietnamese voices. A half hour later they waved again at another helicopter and then crawled back to their sheltered position by the stream bank. The morning passed slowly. Then firing started again in the afternoon along the ridgeline, accompanied by rifle shots from a downstream direction. At 5:00 P.M. another helicopter guided riflemen of the 2d Battalion, 505th Infantry, to their location. Both officers were put on a medical evacuation helicopter and flown directly to the 22d Surgical Hospital at Phu Bai.

Maj. Gen. Samuel W. Koster's American Division was actively patrolling the southern two provinces of I Corps Tactical Zone, including the beautiful but dangerous, cave-studded Phuoc Ha Valley. The division's primary operation was the yearlong WHEELER/WALLOWA, but there were several others. These sweeps were characterized by light, scattered contacts with a high rate of sniping, mine, and booby trap incidents. Villages were found to be fortified and deadly, but it was difficult to pin down the elusive Viet Cong. Battalions in the field encamped their artillery and headquarters on high ridges. From such fire bases their rifle companies would venture into the surrounding jungle, carrying a single 81mm mortar and always keeping within range of the fire base artillery. This was called "reconnaissance in force." If the companies ran into resistance they called in as much artillery, helicopter gunship, and Air Force tactical support as possible. The battalion commanders usually arrived over trouble spots in command helicopters within five or ten minutes to direct actions personally, and the troops began calling them "flying squad leaders." Usually operations ceased at dark and contact with the NVA/VC was broken off as quickly as possible. The companies either returned to the fire base or set up in place. Each man in a company carried eight empty sandbags, and these were filled and pooled at night into three-man positions. In this way, field fortifications of sorts were constructed rapidly, with less digging required. Small combat outposts would then be emplaced by company patrols, which were euphemistically labeled "ambushes."

The Americal Division suffered from grave command and control problems, stemming from poor training and a lack of leadership, from division down to platoon level, which permitted civilian mistreatment. Some elements of its 11th Infantry Brigade (Light) were little better than organized bands of thugs, with the officers eager participants in the body count game. In March the brigade conducted a series of atrocities along the coast of Quang Ngai Province in Son My village, which the division and brigade staffs covered up by suppressing information or conducting sham investigations. When the rape, torture, and slaughter of civilians in what became known as the My Lai incident were finally exposed, it marked the first of a string of disasters that would blight the Americal Division's combat record. Meanwhile, in the field the 11th Infantry Brigade had already been ordained the Butcher Brigade by the soldiers.

The Army discovered serious problems that stabbed at the very heart of the disciplined war machine that had initially gone into Vietnam. Within the Americal Division, dereliction of duty, ignored regulations, and hoodlum activity were more commonplace than the Army had ever imagined. Although the official Army board of inquiry came up with a list of thirty persons, mostly officers (including the division's commanding general), who had known of various war crimes, the military submitted charges against only fourteen of them. Additionally, four of the officers and nine more enlisted men were charged with war crimes or crimes against humanity. All had their charges dismissed or were acquitted, with the exception of the most junior officer, 1st Lt. William L. Calley, Jr., who was found guilty of murdering at least twenty-two civilians. His platoon alone was estimated to have killed some two hundred innocent women, children, and old men.

Actually, the My Lai massacre itself reflected the stark terror of a war of attrition, in which military success, for lack of terrain objectives, was measured statistically by counting corpses. While casualty counts are valid measurements of war, in Vietnam they unfortunately became more than yardsticks used to gauge the battlefield. Rather than means of determination, they became objectives in themselves. The process became so ghoulish that individual canteens were accepted as authorized substitutes if bodies were too dismembered to estimate properly. Guidelines were even issued by MACV on factoring additional dead based on standard percentages by type of encounter and terrain. This appalling practice produced body counts that went largely unquestioned, and were readily rewarded by promotions, medals, and time off from field duty. For example, General Westmoreland had issued a special commendation to the 11th Infantry Brigade based on its claim of 128 enemy killed at My Lai.

4. Mini-Tet and Beyond

Following the Tet-68 Battle for Saigon, American and South Vietnamese forces started scouring the countryside around Saigon in eleven separate operations. MACV consolidated all these ongoing operations under the TOAN THANG (Complete Victory) Campaign, which started April 8, 1968, and would become the mainstay of all allied activity in that area for the duration of American combat presence in Vietnam. The major goal of TOAN THANG was the prevention of future armed incursions into Saigon, and a huge ring of units was formed around the capital. Some forty-two American and thirty-seven South Vietnamese infantry and tank battalions were immediately assigned to the task, and this initial investment was soon increased.

When American and North Vietnamese negotiators announced forthcoming peace conversations in Paris on May 3, defense of Saigon was heightened. The 3d Brigade of the "Old Reliable" 9th Infantry Division was given the screening responsibility for the southern approaches in Long An Province, a job which it held until departure from Vietnam years later. The "Tropic Lightning" 25th Infantry Division was operating as usual to the west of Saigon in the Cambodian border provinces. The 199th Infantry Brigade "Redcatchers" patrolled beyond Bien Hoa to block movement from War Zone D, and the "Big Red One" 1st Infantry Division guarded the northern approach. The 1st Australian Task Force at Long Thanh patrolled the eastern front. The South Vietnamese forces were deployed within the Capital Military District Command itself. With few exceptions, all the American troop assignments remained permanent until final redeployment back to the United States.

The jarring explosion of a taxi filled with a hundred pounds of TNT outside the Saigon television and radio station on May 4, 1968, signaled the next Viet Cong onslaught against Saigon, which became known as Mini-Tet. That night several bombardments were followed by attacks on the key Saigon–Bien Hoa Highway Bridge which connected the two vital centers. South Vietnamese marine units repulsed these efforts throughout the next day. On May 6, the 25th Infantry Division and air cavalry formations trounced attacks on two villages near the Tan Son Nhut air base. All eyes were riveted on VC intentions in Saigon itself, and the following day another intensive struggle began in Cholon. The *267th VC LF Battalion,* well equipped with flak guns and antitank rifles, seized a vital crossroad in Phu Lam district and dug in. The 38th ARVN Ranger Battalion would spend days of hard fighting trying to pry it out. The nearby Binh Tay Distillation Plant and the bridge at Binh Tien were also taken by the Viet Cong, and the 35th ARVN Ranger Battalion required several days of tough combat to clear the built-up area.

Two Viet Cong local force battalions attacked the critical **Y**-Bridge over the Kinh Doi Canal, which separated downtown Saigon from the urban Nha Be district. The 9th Infantry Division sent two mechanized battalions, the 2d Battalion of the 47th Infantry, and the 5th Battalion of the 60th Infantry, into harrowing city combat to counter this dangerous situation.[4] Every day the house-to-house fighting raged, and upgunned armored personnel carriers slowly churned through the debris-strewn streets. Entire blocks of buildings were in ruins and the four-lane bridge itself severely damaged. The infantrymen struggled forward under heavy machine-gun cross fire to take out one strong-point at a time. The Viet Cong defenders occupied multi-story buildings and strategic choke points in the rubble. They used great quantities of accurate B-40 rockets, but the American mechanized-infantry assault slowly crushed defensive positions. The tracked carriers fired their topside recoilless rifles in direct support of the advancing infantry assault teams. This methodical, determined assault finally cleared the well-defended city blocks around the bridge site, allowing it to be recaptured. The successful six-day battle to regain the **Y**-Bridge marked the

4. Both the 47th and the 60th Infantry had been organized in June 1917 for World War I service, and they had both served with distinction in the St. Mihiel and Meuse-Argonne offensives. Later the two regiments fought side by side from French Morocco and Algeria to the heartland of Germany in the second World War.

toughest city combat American troops encountered during the Mini-Tet Offensive.

The South Vietnamese Battle for Cholon was renewed May 25 after the third wave of Viet Cong attacks on Saigon. In the violent inner-city clashes progress was measured in yards, and VC counterattacks often canceled hard-won gains. In the midst of this raging battle, on June 2, a technical mishap caused an American helicopter gunship to misfire two rockets which then struck a large group of senior South Vietnamese officers watching the battle from positions in the Thuong Phuoc high school. Among those killed were the commanders of the Saigon police and of the 5th ARVN Ranger Group. Several other key personnel were seriously wounded. At the time there was widespread belief among the South Vietnamese that the rockets had deliberately cut down these officers, who were all confidants and appointees of Vice-President Ky, in order to allow President Thieu to fill the slots with people of his own choosing. The unfortunate incident marked a new low in the Vietnamese public image of American assistance that was not easily erased. The battle continued into early June in some old familiar sectors, including the Phu Tho racetrack vicinity, before South Vietnamese units finally crushed all remaining resistance. The combined victories in the capital fighting during the spring of 1968 assured the security of downtown Saigon from all but rocket attacks for the next seven years.

Mini-Tet had been, like the main Tet Offensive before it, a dismal failure for the participating NVA/VC ground troops. Much of the impact of Mini-Tet was negated by the success of American formations in interdicting and destroying many Viet Cong elements before they could reach their targets. The Saigon incursions had been decisively defeated in the Cholon sector by South Vietnamese troops with minimal American support. Most other localities in the country suffered only rocket or mortar barrages, some 433 being recorded nationwide, since the VC no longer had the strength to mount widespread ground attacks. In fact the VC tactics displayed during Mini-Tet reflected their major Tet losses. Units broke down into small groups rather than risk large assaults with attendant casualties, and avoided direct attacks on American installations altogether. This second practice reaped a certain communist advantage, as it further strengthened popular Vietnamese suspicions that the United States and North Vietnam were negotiating behind South Vietnam's back. The South Vietnamese leadership was already disdainfully calling the war "talk-fight."

In August, the 9th Infantry Division's 1st Brigade fought several major battles. These culminated in an encirclement action fought by the 2d Battalion, 39th Infantry, on August 12 southwest of Can Duoc. Massive air strikes and artillery firepower were used to annihilate a battalion of Viet Cong. The 25th Infantry Division was engaged in several fire base defensive battles during the same month, notably at Fire Support Base Buell on August 18, and on August 24 at a battalion night defensive position west of Dau Tieng. These battles were all fought in conjunction with the last NVA/VC offensive of 1968, a weak thrust made in mid-August which was only a shadow of Tet or Mini-Tet. Fifteen ground attacks were managed, but only two of them involved battalion-sized units. Again, there was heavy reliance on rocket bombardments, with ninety-five initiated throughout the country, but Saigon was rocketed on just one day, August 22.

The 9th Infantry Division had dedicated its 2d Brigade as the Army's unique mobile riverine force. This force was designed to work the canals and waterways of the upper Mekong Delta. Most of the regional villages were clustered along the banks of these twisting brown streams, and the dense forests and swampland were usually VC territory. Land traffic was impossible during rainy periods and the Viet Cong used the water channels for movement of supplies and troops. The Army mobile riverine force was conceived and tailored to use this same water system to reach the Viet Cong, and to bring American military presence into these untamed areas.

Dredges were put to work pumping mud from the bottom of the My Tho River into adjacent rice paddies, and soon a six hundred-acre division base was established in the tropical delta swales. The riverine force itself was housed on Navy barracks ships, which provided air-conditioned billets and operations centers, topped with helicopter platforms. Barges tied alongside were used to deploy the soldiers on and off the host of smaller craft which actually took them on operations. They were transported along the network of waterways by armored troop carrier "tango" boats, and escorted by assault-support patrol boats and monitors. These gunboats sported exotic armaments ranging from howitzers and 40mm guns to twin flamethrowers. Riverine artillery, Army 105mm howitzers mounted on barges and landing craft, also reinforced naval gun power. Some strategists questioned these operations as expensive Army experimentation. The floating brigade seemed to offer little advantage over airmobile infantry in reaching objectives. Others saw such a concept as potentially more rewarding with Marine Corps assets.

While these land and river battles were being waged, smaller firefights prevailed throughout the year. Action in the Ben Cui rubber plantation west of Dau Tieng in August was representative of these fierce skirmishes. A mechanized infantry company of the 1st Battalion, 5th Infantry, was sent into the plantation to sweep along the southern side of Route 239, the main supply road to Tay Ninh. It left the base camp and crossed the Saigon River with fourteen armored personnel carriers. As the company advanced through the rubber trees, the battalion's scout platoon and composite American–South Vietnamese Combined Reconnaissance-and-Intelligence Platoon, with a self-propelled 40mm Duster flak gun, moved down the road itself.

Upon entering the dense rubber plantation's undergrowth, the troops dismounted and fanned out in a classic V formation, led by a three-man scout dog team. The armored personnel carriers were arranged in a formation that gave the best support with their shielded machine guns to the walking infantry. Suddenly at 8:30 A.M., the scout dog on the point alerted, and his handler informed the captain of nearby VC personnel. The commander halted the formation and relayed the information to a senior battalion staff officer overflying the unit in an observation helicopter. The helicopter then dropped down to conduct a low-level reconnaissance. The company lobbed several rounds of mortar fire into the suspected area as a precaution and then continued the advance.

As the mechanized infantry force continued west they saw a red star cluster rising over one of the villages. They had been in constant radio contact with the scout and recon platoons, which had moved through the villages a short distance away. The road group radioed that they had found no Viet Cong but had discovered several buildings used recently as sleeping quarters, and a classroom for combat instruction. One contained a drawing of an armored personnel carrier with two antennae. Shortly before noon the company started receiving sporadic rifle fire, which quickly increased in tempo. Then the forward troops began to see VC dodging from tree to tree and firing as they advanced. The company radioed immediately for helicopter fire support.

The infantry fell back to the protection of the armored carriers as the company swung into defensive positions. Firing was now at a high level, but there were difficulties getting clearance to fire artillery due to the proximity of populated villages. The company marked its positions with purple and yellow smoke for helicopter recognition, but combat elsewhere delayed aerial support. The unit held its initial position for thirty minutes. After three armored personnel carriers were knocked out by point-blank rocket-propelled grenade fire the company began a fighting withdrawal. Only eight vehicles made it to the new defensive positions. The infantry were desperately shooting off magazines as the remaining tracked carriers spit out concentrated heavy machine-gun fire. The dual antiaircraft gun was firing from the roadway across the company front with direct rapid-cannon fire. This withering firestorm had allowed the mechanized company to regroup. Finally, heavy artillery rounds started falling on top of the advancing VC.

The Viet Cong pressed their assault and three more armored personnel carriers were exploded by direct hits. These detonations caused the loss of the company commander as well as both artillery and mortar forward observers. A lieutenant took over as helicopter gunships appeared overhead to begin strafing and rocketing in front of their lines. The unit then retreated out of the rubber and into a clearing where it was joined by the road element. The concentrated artillery and aerial firepower forced the VC to break off the attack rather than pursue.

Several battles erupted in the southern provinces of III Corps Tactical Zone during the fall. On September 3, the 3d Brigade of the 101st Airborne Division ran into a tough fight at a hot landing zone just east of Trang Bang which developed into a three-day engagement. Fire Support Base Pope of the 25th Infantry Division was assaulted and successfully defended on September 1. Late in the year, III Corps Tactical Zone and the Saigon area were reinforced by the addition of two important American formations. The 3d Brigade of the 82d Airborne Division arrived in October to tighten the protective ring around the capital, followed a month later by the powerful 1st Cavalry Division. This airmobile division deployed south to take up duties facing the Cambodian border.

The United States military began tagging its efforts as the Accelerated Pacification Campaign on November 1, 1968. As peace negotiations got underway in Paris, MACV increased its efforts to maximize the number of villages under Saigon control and to develop the South Vietnamese armed forces. Ground combat operations were becoming concentrated on pacification through village cordons and area security, and by keeping the North Vietnamese and Viet Cong main force units out of populated areas by a "protective shield of containment." The strategy of attrition was abandoned as the American Army's conduct of the war took a new direction.

PART 5

1969

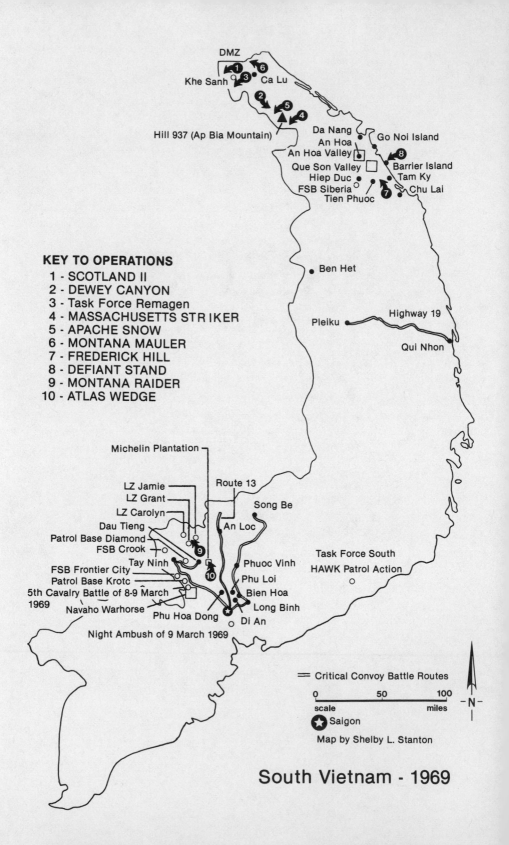

DMZ

1
3
Khe Sanh   Ca Lu
6

2
5
4

Hill 937 (Ap Bia Mountain)

Da Nang
An Hoa   Go Noi Island
An Hoa Valley
Que Son Valley   8
Hiep Duc   Barrier Island
FSB Siberia   Tam Ky
Tien Phuoc   Chu Lai
7

Ben Het

Highway 19
Pleiku

Qui Nhon

KEY TO OPERATIONS
1 - SCOTLAND II
2 - DEWEY CANYON
3 - Task Force Remagen
4 - MASSACHUSETTS STRIKER
5 - APACHE SNOW
6 - MONTANA MAULER
7 - FREDERICK HILL
8 - DEFIANT STAND
9 - MONTANA RAIDER
10 - ATLAS WEDGE

Michelin Plantation

LZ Jamie   Route 13
LZ Grant   Song Be
LZ Carolyn
Dau Tieng   An Loc
Patrol Base Diamond
FSB Crook   9
Tay Ninh   Phuoc Vinh   Task Force South
FSB Frontier City   10   Phu Loi   HAWK Patrol Action
Patrol Base Krotc   Bien Hoa
5th Cavalry Battle of 8-9 March   Long Binh
1969   Di An
Navaho Warhorse
Phu Hoa Dong
Night Ambush of 9 March 1969

=== Critical Convoy Battle Routes

0   50   100
scale   miles   - N -

⭐ Saigon

Map by Shelby L. Stanton

South Vietnam - 1969

CHAPTER 18.

ONE WAR

1. One War and Vietnamization

In early 1969 General Abrams decreed that the largely separate war of the big battalions would be fused with pacification and territorial security in the One War concept. Both the MACV 1969 Combined Campaign Plan and Pacification and Development Plan were consolidated into this One War plan, which became effective on February 1, 1969. In actuality, MACV control over battlefield strategy was already subordinated to the powerful Washington triumvirate composed of President Richard Nixon, Defense Secretary Melvin Laird, and National Security Advisor Henry Kissinger. They speedily implemented the Nixon doctrine and its new Asia approach, which hinged on a rapid buildup of the South Vietnamese military so that American forces could be quickly withdrawn. An active political campaign of appeasement and negotiation was simultaneously conducted with North Vietnam.

During the year, MACV's highest priorities shifted away from U.S. combat operations against the NVA/VC, and toward Vietnamization—the accelerated improvement and development plan for the South Vietnamese armed forces. The broad program governed the conduct of the war through the Army's final phaseout from the country. The transition year of 1969 intensified this trend as plans for further American divisional withdrawals were hastened and joint training operations with South Vietnamese units accelerated.

On the battlefront, critical priority was shifted to provincial protection for territorial pacification programs, and city security, a concern added as a result of the Tet-68 confrontations. Concentrated offensives were to be mounted against NVA/VC troop and supply bases, with heaviest pressure directed toward the DMZ and the border regions of Cambodia and Laos. American formations were given orders to heighten border surveillance and reaction operations, and paired off with assigned ARVN units to perform combined operations. In the field these ARVN units were familiarized with American battle techniques, especially fire support. Beginning in 1969, the South Vietnamese military was to be given prime responsibility for maintaining the "protective shield of containment" within their country.

The One War plan largely limited American military participation to a mobile defensive stance while preparing the South Vietnamese forces to take over their areas of responsibility. To do this job, MACV had a total of 359,313 Army soldiers and 80,716 Marines in Vietnam on January 1, 1969. They were divided into 110 infantry and tank battalions.[1] On June 10, in line with low NVA/VC activity and the apparent success of both South Vietnamese pacification and mobilization efforts, President Nixon announced the start of U.S. troop withdrawals. The initial military response to the redeployment directives was slow, forcing Defense Secretary Laird to insist on daily troop reduction charts to meet deadlines in view of high public pressure in the United States.

The first Army unit home was the 3d Battalion of the 60th Infantry from the 9th Infantry Division. On July 8, it was flown to McChord Air Force Base outside Seattle, Washington, paraded through town, and sent to Fort Lewis where it was immediately folded up. The bulk of the 9th Infantry Division fol-

1. Major U.S. forces in Vietnam on January 1, 1969, were the 1st and 3d Marine, 1st Cavalry (Airmobile), 101st Airborne (Airmobile), 1st, 4th, 9th, 23d (Americal), and 25th Infantry Divisions; 1st Brigade of the 5th Infantry Division (Mechanized) and 3d Brigade of the 82d Airborne Division; 173d Airborne and 199th Infantry Brigades; 11th Armored Cavalry Regiment; 5th Special Forces Group (Airborne); and three separate battalions: the 1st and 2d Squadrons of the 1st Cavalry, and 1st Battalion, 50th Infantry (Mechanized).

lowed, being inactivated in either Hawaii or Washington. A further troop pullout was announced by President Nixon on October 16. This time most of the units were simply inactivated in Vietnam, although larger elements usually sent flag escorts home for ceremonial purposes. By the end of the year most of the 3d Marine Division was also out of Vietnam.

The Vietnamization program was initially intended to build up the South Vietnamese military to the point where it could fight VC insurgent activities, once the major North Vietnamese and allied armies had left the country. After the June 1969 Midway Conference, Washington informed the Pentagon that the Saigon regime would be given responsibility for all aspects of the war, even if current NVA/VC levels persisted. As a result, Defense Secretary Laird revised all Vietnamization goals toward producing a self-sufficient South Vietnamese military capable of coping successfully with the combined NVA/VC threat.

These were tall orders, since the war-weary South Vietnamese armed forces were still wracked with alarming leadership, morale, and desertion problems. Authorizations for new units, to expand the size and power of the ARVN, only offered paper solutions.[2] During the year there were over 107,000 deserters, a manpower loss equal to ten divisions. VNMC desertions were the highest, while ARVN desertions remained at crippling levels, especially in the Delta (IV CTZ) where they faced the Viet Cong largely alone without American combat presence. The South Vietnamese still lacked the technical know-how and logistical sophistication necessary to absorb and properly use the massive quantities of American equipment now being thrust upon them.

MACV thoroughly diagnosed the state of the South Vietnamese military during the year in a series of in-depth studies. It found that the South Vietnamese Army's fighting spirit was

2. Major South Vietnamese combat units as of July 1969 were the Airborne, Marine (six VNMC battalions), 1st, 2d, 5th, 7th, 9th, 18th, 21st–23d, and 25th Divisions; 42d and 51st Regiments (Separate); sixteen armored cavalry squadrons; and twenty ranger battalions. By the end of June 1970, the Marine Division would be brought up to full strength at nine battalions. Total maneuver battalions (including divisional armored cavalry squadrons) increased from 173 in 1968 to 185 in 1969, and to 189 in 1970. Artillery battalions climbed from 30 in 1968 to 47 in 1969, and to 58 in 1970. During the expansion, the biggest gains were in Air Force and logistical units.

low, a fact reflected in the devastating desertion rates. Lack of aggressive leadership remained prevalent, and combat staff support, planning, and coordination was practically nonexistent. Promotion was slow and imbalanced. Most company commanders were lieutenants, and battalions were still led by captains. Desertion losses forced trainees directly into the front lines as replacements. While some junior officers were confident of the ARVN's ability to replace U.S. troops, most of the experienced generals expressed open pessimism over South Vietnam's chances of survival without substantial American combat support. Most officers were only concerned about their welfare, and the enlisted men were discontented and discouraged. Neither expressed much interest in either Vietnamization or the larger conflict.

By 1969, the Vietnamization of the capital military district was essentially complete. All U.S. troops had been withdrawn except for a small number of radar and generator operators. In the northern I CTZ, the 1st and 2d ARVN Divisions and 51st ARVN Regiment were already initiating multibattalion operations independent of American support. In the Central Highlands, South Vietnamese forces had assumed responsibility for Kontum Province. For example, the Battle of Ben Het in that province had been fought by ARVN ground troops supported only by some U.S. combat support and service elements.

The results of Vietnamization on the battleground were mixed during the year but held promise. Large-scale issuance of M16 rifles and M2 carbines was made in an attempt to upgrade the regional and popular militia forces (RF/PF), long held in utter disrepute. This gave them firepower equal to the Viet Cong, but their combat ability remained uneven. At the same time, RF/PF assumed an increasing share of pacification security. With fewer security missions, ARVN units could get into the field on combat operations. Likewise, a number of formations that had been problem units or that had reputations for chronic poor performance, namely the 2d, 5th, 9th, 18th, and 23d ARVN Divisions, showed some improvement.

The 1st Logistical Command became almost totally dedicated to redeployment matters, technical schooling of ARVN logisticians, and equipment transfer to the South Vietnamese military. While the majority of the equipment required to outfit the new ARVN units came directly from the United States, many American units (especially artillery and engineer units) were promptly relegated to fulfilling this need. As Vietnamization came to dominate U.S. efforts, more and more units were identified in a phased process to provide specialized training and turn over their material. After the units had been stripped, their flags were flown home.

The American Army was subordinated to a supporting role, in which it provided much of the required material, technical experts, and advisors. The job of actually fighting the war was rapidly turned over to ARVN units, and U.S. forces were either given diminished combat assignments or began standing down for redeployment. A reevaluation of advisory assistance efforts led to a direct increase in the number of sergeants and officers assigned and to a reorganization of their tactical advisory elements. This further eroded the capabilities of those American units that remained in the field.

2. The 1969 Post-Tet Offensive

The North Vietnamese Army had taken advantage of the U.S. Presidential decision that had halted all bombing on November 1, 1968, to rush supplies south for a renewed offensive. MACV made sure that a powerful group of units ringed Saigon to prevent a repeat of the Tet-68 episode. This effort involved three and a half American divisions matched by an equal number of South Vietnamese military assets. These formations were kept in the field seeking military caches and sweeping known avenues of infiltration from Cambodia. There were only a few skirmishes in January and early February, since both sides were restricting combat activity to extensive reconnaissance.

The NVA/VC offensive was finally initiated, as predicted by allied intelligence, on February 23 and consisted largely of a week-long series of scattered rocket and mortar shellings across the country. In III CTZ only two significant ground attacks, against Long Binh and Bien Hoa, were made by the 9th and

5th VC Divisions, respectively.[3] Both were handily defeated. On March 6, a more powerful NVA tank-supported thrust was made toward the Ben Het Special Forces camp, near Kontum in II CTZ. The fighting at Ben Het lasted until July, when the attackers were forced to withdraw.

The 1969 Post-Tet Offensive was primarily aimed at disrupting the allied support network. This strategy was designed to retard the South Vietnamese Army rearming process, as well as deny combat units some of their mobility and reaction potential. As a result, attacks were concentrated on logistical installations and supply lines. The NVA/VC avoided major confrontations with allied troops, as the swift response and firepower of American tactical forces had defeated their Tet-68 attempts. The Post-Tet Offensive consisted mainly of attacks on shipping, convoy ambushes, pipeline interdiction, ground sapper assaults, and rocket barrages. It resulted in minimal damage to MACV support sites and caused light casualties. However, it did place many American logistical troops once again on Vietnam's front lines.

Beginning in 1969, more service units found themselves having to defend their own areas as the American combat drawdown gathered momentum. Most soldiers in supply and service organizations were specialists inexperienced in tactical operations, and the 1st Logistical Command initiated crash training programs to prepare them for combat contingencies. Provisional security units were hastily formed, but the situation only worsened during the years of declining American presence in Vietnam. Too often the rear-echelon guards manning bunkers and perimeters were unqualified to operate the machine guns, rifles, and grenade launchers they were armed with. The increased exposure of once-secure logistical support sites, coupled with a rising inability to properly defend them, was a problem faced by rapidly retreating armies throughout history.

---

3. The Viet Cong divisions were largely filled by regular North Vietnamese soldiers, since mounting wartime losses culminating in Tet-68 had left them VC in name only. The few actual Viet Cong forces involved were main force units, since most local force guerrilla organizations had been destroyed at this stage of the war.

3. Convoy Battles

The 1969 Post-Tet Offensive singled out logistical targets for attack and renewed the convoy battles. In II CTZ the most frequently ambushed route remained the Qui Nhon–Pleiku Highway 19 axis, while in III CTZ the Long Binh–Tay Ninh/Dau Tieng road net received the most attention. On April 15, on Highway 19 west of Cha Rang, a Korean convoy going west and a 54th Transportation Battalion convoy heading east were ambushed while passing each other. Two weeks later a 48th Transportation Group convoy on Highway 13 south of An Loc was hit hard by rocket-propelled grenades and automatic weapons.[4]

At the beginning of the Vietnam campaign, American wheeled logistical convoys offered lucrative targets with minimal risk to the Viet Cong and North Vietnamese. The ambuscade expertise of the NVA/VC threatened most overland lines of support. The United States had not encountered this type of warfare to any extent either during World War II or the Korean War. In those more conventional wars the vast majority of Army convoy operations had been conducted behind the front lines in relative safety.

MACV considered military traffic and road security critical. Most inland installations depended on convoy supply, and their disruption hampered ongoing field operations. Truck movement provided most of the support for more than a million Army troops dispersed over sixty-six thousand square miles. Airlift was only capable of emergency and temporary high-priority cargo delivery. Convoy protection had to be improvised, as the military police that the Army assigned were too few in number to give adequate security. Early efforts were marked by a variety of transportation security measures, including attempts to make convoys too costly to attack and reliance on mobile reaction forces, which were geared to the MACV red-amber-green road classifications. Red lanes required infantry and engineer support to

4. The 48th Transportation Group ambush of April 28, 1969, was particularly fierce. Five fuel tankers, an ammunition truck, one armored car, an armored personnel carrier, and a gun-jeep were destroyed. Numerous other vehicles were damaged. Two helicopters were also lost, one of them a Cobra gunship and the other a medical evacuation chopper. The 2d Battalion, 2d Infantry, reinforced the scene of combat and broke the attack.

open them; amber lanes were frequented by NVA/VC activity and demanded high security; and green lanes could be used by vehicles during daylight hours with less caution.

Beginning in September of 1967, the 8th Transportation Group took heavy losses from repetitious large-scale ambushes along Highway 19 connecting the port of Qui Nhon with the rugged interior city of Pleiku. It cleared large amounts of brush and undergrowth along the roadway and resorted to the "hardened convoy": cargo trucks were fitted with side and frontal armor plating and sandbagged, while even the beds of the larger ones were floored with armor. The ideal support ratio was one gun truck for every ten cargo vehicles. These specially fitted gun truck escorts were jerry-rigged with heavier armor and featured exotic combinations of weapons systems and quadruple machine-gun mounts. The gun trucks changed positions in the convoys daily and were supplemented by V-100 armored cars of the 18th Military Police Brigade. Normally only two of these excellent scout cars were available per convoy, since the military police were stretched thin throughout the country. This limited amount of standard protection was insufficient to cover convoys which were normally broken down into three or four serials to avoid road congestion. Gun truck conversions also effectively meant a loss of one light truck company per transportation group. Assignment of transportation personnel as *ad hoc* infantry further diminished operational manpower.

Helicopters added a new dimension to available transportation protection, but it was impossible to overfly every convoy. Helicopter gunships were normally placed on ground alert at their airstrips, but communication difficulties often prevented their timely appearance. Convoy commanders under fire were hard pressed to maintain continuing radio control of their convoy, direct counterambush measures with their gun trucks, and give precise locational data for helicopter and artillery support.

The internal order of the convoy was rearranged to minimize losses. Trucks loaded with subsistence items were put up front. This enabled the refrigerated "reefer" trucks to avoid convoy dust and allowed them more off-loading time at destination. Trucks loaded with clothing, construction materials, and miscellaneous items were placed next in the column. Trucks carrying petrol, oil, and ammunition were put in the rear. In this manner explosive cargo detonations did not block other vehicles on the highway.

The Viet Cong used ambush tactics against the Americans that had been perfected during the French-Indochina War. Initial fire was concentrated on several vehicles within a convoy in order to destroy them and block further traffic. Trucks in the center were the preferred targets. Once segments of the convoy had been brought to a standstill by the swift and violent attack, mortar and rocket fire were directed against immobilized individual vehicles. Road ditches and adjacent brush were often mined to cause losses among dismounting troops trying to gain better defensive positions. Sometimes ground attacks were staged to overrun trapped portions of a convoy. Drivers were told to keep moving through sniper fire and to contact security forces at the first sign of trouble, but the military was working on better convoy defensive weapons.

When Troop A of the "Blackhorse" 11th Armored Cavalry's 1st Squadron prepared to make a sweep down Route 13 past An Loc on January 11, 1969, its six armored personnel carriers were secretly reinforced by a seventh machine just introduced to Vietnam; the Vulcan. This particular stretch of road was well known as an ambush alley, but this time the regiment intended to unleash a surprise of its own if the column was bushwhacked.

Midway down the highway, the troop's vehicles were suddenly hit by a storm of automatic weapons fire from both sides of the lane. Within the first fifteen seconds rocket-propelled grenades slammed into five of the square-hulled carriers. They skidded to uncontrolled stops under the onslaught of rapid fire and detonations hammering against their tracks and armor-plated sides. Several burst into flames, and none were firing back. The entire column was pinned by the gauntlet of VC attack.

The third vehicle in line started churning jerkily around its immobilized sisters. It stopped to spin its sinister six-barreled gun to the rear. Aiming back down a drainage ditch, the weapon flashed continuously with devastating bursts of concentrated 20mm cannon fire. Inside the beleaguered armored personnel carrier Lieutenant Wright radioed headquarters that they were under attack. He knew another Vulcan was stationed there and could provide timely ammunition resupply. The ultimate fate of the stranded column depended on the singular ability of his weapon to break the ambush.

He continued to fire the new Vulcan, designed for antiaircraft work, at the "slow" rate of one thousand rounds per minute, the recommended dosage for ground use. Within fifteen minutes the other Vulcan appeared down the road. Already Viet Cong fire from the ambush positions along the ditch had ceased. Other fire peppering the stricken column was becoming sporadic. Both Vulcan carriers moved back to back. The Vulcan gun turret on Wright's vehicle was elevated to 45 degrees and traversed over the driver's hatch, silent for the first time. As the second Vulcan flared into action and spit out a constant stream of packed steel, rear ramps were dropped and spare ammunition belts were rushed over to Wright.

The Viet Cong ambush force was silent. Crippled and shocked by the intense volume of return fire from a previously unknown weapon, it had fled. This innovative weapons system had promising convoy security potential, since the introduction of the powerful Vulcan rapid-fire antiaircraft gun could ensure a high degree of vehicular firepower. Its slow and tedious development seemed worth the wait, but it remained strictly experimental and was never made available for general use in Vietnam. The soldiers angrily suspected that the Army was simply using the battlefield as a testing ground, afraid to expose critical weapons to possible loss or capture in a war which, by 1969, was obviously dwindling in national importance.

Convoy ambushes, sniping, and mines plagued 1st Logistical Command supply efforts throughout the year. The last major attack occurred on November 22, when a three-hundred-vehicle mixed engineer–48th Transportation Group convoy traveling north from Long Binh to Song Be was struck. However, attacks against Army convoys continued until the U.S. pullout absented them from the roads of Vietnam. The bravery of the long-haul drivers became so commonplace that MACV recognized a special, unofficial Line Haul tab which was worn proudly over their 1st Logistical Command patches. One sergeant of the 48th Transportation Group earned the Medal of Honor during a late-1968 ambush near Ap Nhi. The convoy battles, which ranged from catastrophic defeats of entire convoys to botched failures to hit a single vehicle, became a legacy of American security and support in a frontless war.

4. Decline of an Army

Vietnamization had a profound impact on American troop morale. The U.S. soldier was poorly indoctrinated with respect to changing national goals and generally did not understand his continued exposure to combatant conditions during the long withdrawal period. Since no one wanted to be the last killed on the way out, an understandable reluctance to engage in continued front-line activity developed.

The state of the American Army was showing other signs of stress and combat fatigue as well. The Selective Service system had produced a working class army heavily weighted toward the lower income groups, since it permitted easy draft avoidance by the more privileged members of society. Such serious and inequitable flaws caused resentment among active-duty soldiers. Project One Hundred–Thousand, a social experiment designed to shove people of low intelligence into the armed forces (where most ended up as riflemen in Vietnam), and the willingness of many judges to send misfits and criminals into the Army for "rehabilitation," created severe disciplinary problems. The fact that a disproportionate number of ethnic minority members were drafted increased racial strife.

The reserve components were largely filled with personnel avoiding active duty, and there was trouble when forty-three Reserve and National Guard companies and detachments were finally ordered to Vietnam for one-year tours. The units proved to be unsatisfactory upon alert and required extensive retraining. Several, such as the 1002d Supply & Service Company, challenged the legality of their call-up. Although Justice William O. Douglas held up the unit's deployment to Vietnam in September of 1968, the Supreme Court ruled the mobilization legal and it arrived in country on October 20. Once in Vietnam, where they remained through most of 1969, most of these components rendered a good account of themselves.

The officer corps, which had been comprised mostly of West Point or college Reserve Officer Training Course (ROTC) graduates when the war started, had lowered standards in response to Vietnam escalation. The unpopularity of the war among university students caused a drastic reduction in ROTC enrollment and led to the outright expulsion of thirty-eight ROTC units from 1969 through 1972. To fill the void, the Army resorted to increased outputs from the Officer Candidate Schools (OCS), which tapped persons of generally lower educational background.

The noncommissioned officer corps had suffered an alarming quality decline in the rush to produce enough junior sergeants to fill expanding needs. Stateside "Shake 'n' Bake" courses rushed promising privates directly through twenty-one weeks of advanced training and slapped from three to four stripes on their uniforms upon completion. These young buck and staff sergeants had considerable difficulty leading combat troops, and tended to be lax in efforts to win over their men. However, there were still not enough sergeants to go around, and many squads in Vietnam were simply led by specialists, fourth class— a rank many enlisted men achieved either before or shortly after they arrived in country.

By 1969 the U.S. soldier in Vietnam usually represented the poorer and less educated segments of American society. He was often being led by middle-class officers and inexperienced sergeants, creating a wide gap between attitudes, abilities, and motivation. This combined with increased idleness—the result of lowered combat activity—and overall frustration with obscure national goals, to produce severe morale problems. Continuing personnel turbulence, resulting from the combat-tour rotational policy, destroyed any of the stiffening that wartime unit cohesion traditionally offered. Once America began to pull its troops out of Vietnam, the average soldier simply wanted to get home alive and cared little for the ultimate fate of his formation or the accomplishment of the country's mission. Medals lost their gloss, officers forced to falsify after-action reports in order to preserve their careers or favorably reflect unit activities lost their confidence, soldiers lost interest, and the Army lost its fighting edge. The decline of the American Army was well under way by the end of the year.

CHAPTER 19.

ONE WAR IN THE NORTHERN PROVINCES

1. Guarding Borders

At the beginning of 1969, some of America's toughest fighting units were lined up inside the hotly contested northernmost provinces under Lt. Gen. Richard G. Stilwell's XXIV Corps. It contained the crack 3d Marine Division along with the tank-spearheaded 1st Brigade of the 5th Infantry Division (Mechanized) and the helicopter-endowed 101st Airborne Division (Airmobile). With this force MACV felt confident that General Stilwell could guard the DMZ while conducting major excursions deep into NVA base camp areas along the remote western fringes of the country.

In late January, Maj. Gen. Raymond G. Davis's 3d Marine Division picked up the pace of combat near the rugged Laotian border. The 4th Marines stalked the Khe Sanh region in Operation SCOTLAND II, and the 9th Marines initiated Operation DEWEY CANYON against a main North Vietnamese supply route which crossed into Vietnam and curved through both the upper Da Krong Valley and the A Shau Valley just below it. Since the DEWEY CANYON operational area consisted of high mountain plateaus covered by dense double-canopy jungle, the reinforced 9th Marines planned to jump off from two fire support bases on its northern rim and move south in a three-pronged advance.

When they reached the limit of artillery support coverage, they would build new fire support bases and keep moving south.

On January 22, 1969, the 2d Battalion of the 9th Marines air-assaulted into the upper valley, followed by the 3d Battalion three days later. Opening moves were relatively easy, and two landing zones were hacked out only four miles from the Laotian border. Shortly after the Marines moved into the jungle, nine days of foul monsoon weather locked the valley in. The Marine pilots depended on sheer flying heroics to keep the operation going despite thunderstorms and dense cloud cover. On the ground, squads maneuvered in the steaming jungles as the torrential downpours continued. The advance was stepped up once the weather cleared. On February 10, the 1st Battalion was committed in the center of the line, and the Marines pushed farther out from their fire bases toward the Laotian border.

MACV intelligence had indicated that the North Vietnamese had ringed deeper landing zone sites with sophisticated antiaircraft weapons. A foot approach would be slow and laborious but it would negate the fearsome NVA flak advantage. The Marines began a tortuous overland trek, sticking to the ridgelines and toiling through the primeval rain forest overgrowing each jagged tor. The relentless tropical heat began taking its toll of the marchers, as men dropped from stroke and exhaustion. The Marine advance continued inexorably forward.

Only two ground attacks were mounted on the Marine fire bases. In these actions, the North Vietnamese sappers used bamboo mines and satchel charges to blast through the perimeter wire, but both attacks were quickly repelled. Action intensified on February 17 as the Marines stumbled into vicious local counterattacks and fixed defenses. The 1st Battalion was halted by an extensive bunker system on February 23. Artillery and air strikes saturated the defenders with fire and shards of razored steel, and then Companies A and D seized the fortifications in heavy combat. The Marines were in no mood to condone privileged NVA movements. On the night of February 21, Company H, 9th Marines, moved across the twisting Laotian border and bushwhacked a truck convoy on Route 922. General Abrams granted authority two days later for further limited Marine operations across the boundary, and the 9th Marines continued search and destroy missions on both sides of the border through early March.

Marine perseverance was rewarded with some of the largest caches captured during the Vietnam War. Over 525 tons of weapons and ammunition were uncovered, including twelve large 122mm cannons—the first ever seen inside South Vietnam and probably brought down during the bombing halt imposed by President Nixon the previous November. That cessation of bombing had taken effect at the beginning of the dry season, enabling tremendous quantities of material to be moved unhindered and stockpiled throughout the NVA infiltration network. The Marines had surmounted great logistical difficulties attempting to destroy some of the buildup. Over thirteen thousand sorties had been flown under severe weather conditions. These often necessitated the use of special Marine-devised radar-guided parachute supply drops. When the operation ended on March 18, the 9th Marines could justifiably claim a major setback had been meted out to the North Vietnamese.

Lieutenant General Stilwell's XXIV Corps sent a mechanized task force to check out Route 9 as far as the Laotian border, which would also protect the northern flank of allied forces in the Da Krong and A Shau valleys. The 1st Brigade (Mechanized) of the 5th Infantry Division formed Task Force Remagen around the 1st Battalion, 77th Armor, and swung it out of Ca Lu down the dirt roadway toward Khe Sanh on March 16.[1]

The task force was led by an engineer-reinforced scout platoon which gingerly picked its way through antitank mines on the upward-winding road. The tracked vehicles built bypasses around washouts, clanked up the narrow defiles, and spanned streams with their armored vehicle-launched bridges. Since there were no extra soldiers to guard the passes and the unfordable streams, the bridges were mechanically lifted back onto their

1. Task Force Remagen was composed of two mechanized infantry companies, a tank company, a self-propelled 105mm artillery battery, armored engineers, and self-propelled antiaircraft guns. Later the 1st Battalion, 77th Armor, was replaced by the 1st Battalion, 61st Infantry. Remagen was named in honor of the March 7, 1945, crossing of the Remagen Bridge over the Rhine River by the 9th Armored Division, which spearheaded the breakthrough into Germany during World War II.

carriers after the column crossed. This isolated the advancing task force from overland resupply; causing it to be completely fed, fueled, and equipped by helicopters. Major repairs and overhauls were accomplished under arduous field conditions and eventually included replacing twelve engines, eighteen sets of tracks, and seven transmissions. Army and Marine cargo helicopters airlifted all material. Precious fresh water was placed in containers ranging from "lug-a-lug" three-gallon collapsible drums to empty shell casings.

Four days later, Task Force Remagen reached the abandoned Khe Sanh Plateau. They encamped for the night, and then the tanks and armored personnel carriers rumbled west through the abandoned Special Forces campsite at Lang Vei on March 20. The column reached the Vietnamese border and looked across at the sinister Co Roc, a granite ridge running along the Laotian side of the boundary and overlooking the Khe Sanh Plains. The task force prowled around the region until the end of April. Only light resistance was encountered, but the mechanized infantry was continually harassed by accurate mortar fire directed from the Co Roc ridge.

In February, MACV Intelligence had reported another flurry of bunker and way station construction in the forbidding A Shau Valley. The "Screaming Eagles" 101st Airborne Division (Airmobile) built two fire bases on the valley's edge, emplaced artillery, and waited for a break in the weather. On March 1, 1969, the day Operation MASSACHUSETTS STRIKER commenced, rain and fog prevented airmobile assaults. However as the clouds cleared, a company of the 1st Battalion, 502d Infantry, helicoptered into an immediate fight. The firefight promised good hunting in the A Shau Valley, but the hunting proved too good before the year was out. The 2d Brigade lifted four more battalions into the southern end of the valley. The first major items the soldiers discovered in the heart of the jungle were thirteen trucks on jacks. The engines and tires were removed and buried nearby. Further searches revealed a major depot stocked with everything from signal equipment to cod-liver oil.

Throughout April, Maj. Gen. Melvin Zais's 101st Airborne Divison (Airmobile) kept finding more caches and evidence of considerable North Vietnamese logistical investment. On May

1, the 1st Battalion of the 502d Infantry uncovered a well-supplied field hospital and a heavy-machine repair shop. When Operation MASSACHUSETTS STRIKER was concluded on May 8, MACV decided to mount a bigger expedition into the North Vietnamese stronghold. Two days later the division's 3d Brigade teamed up with the 9th Marines and 3d ARVN Regiment to go back into the northern part of the valley under Operation APACHE SNOW.

On May 10 a classic helicopter assault was made into the thickly jungled mountains along the Laotian border west of the A Shau Valley. The division also established a fire support base at Ta Bat, an abandoned village in the valley's center. There were only scattered bursts of gunfire the first day as the troops began sweeping eastward through the valley.

The next day Company B of the 3d Battalion, 187th Infantry, was pushing toward a series of ridges cloaked in lush, tropical forest. Platoon leaders checked their maps and found it marked Hill 937, known to the Vietnamese as Ap Bia Mountain. The soldiers took advantage of the orientation stop to readjust the straps of their rucksacks, which were loaded with canteens, ponchos, trip flares, and smoke grenades. Soldier slang would shortly dub the prominent terrain feature Hamburger Hill.

The sergeants waved the men forward, and the soldiers pressed their M16 rifles close to sagging ammunition bandoliers as the advance resumed. The careful approach march up the tree-covered slopes was suddenly shattered by a fusillade of concentrated machine-gun fire. It erupted from unseen bunkers, ripped through a snarl of vegetation, and cut down dozens of men in the lead ranks. Rucksacks were dropped as the soldiers fired back with light antitank weapons and rifles. They desperately dragged out their seriously wounded comrades as officers ordered them away from the hillside. Fortified positions would be doused with aerial and artillery bombardment first. The ten-day battle for Ap Bia Mountain had begun.

Heavy artillery began its merciless pounding of the hillsides, and through the clouds of grayish smoke, jet fighters unleashed a rain of incendiary and high explosive bombs. Hour after hour through daylight and darkness the terrific shelling continued. Meanwhile, the soldiers of the 187th Infantry "Rakassans" grimly prepared to attack up the mountain again.[2] On May 13, two companies of the 187th Infantry's 1st Battalion stormed the northwest ridges of the mountain. They were repulsed by rocket and heavy automatic weapons fire from the tenacious bunker occupants of the *7th* and *8th Battalions* of the *29th NVA Regiment*. They had built their practically indestructible fortifications flush to the ground with deep overhead cover and had designed them to mutually converge and interlock their fire. During the night and early morning, artillery and aircraft again pummeled the ridgeline with high explosives and searing napalm.

The full battalion was sent up against the entrenchments on May 14, but the lead company commander was wounded and the radio silenced. The soldiers again retreated and called for heavy shellfire. At that point the 187th Infantry's battalion was reinforced by two other divisional battalions (1st Battalion, 506th Infantry, and 2d Battalion, 501st Infantry). A battalion of the 3d ARVN Regiment was also grabbed and thrown into the fight, and these forces were posted around the hill to seal it off. On May 18, after thirty-six straight hours of artillery barrage and tactical air strikes, two battalions frontally assaulted the heavily fortified North Vietnamese positions still controlling the mountain slopes.

The 187th "Rakassans" pushed up the southeastern side and the 506th took on the northern slope. By mid-afternoon some platoons had reached the summit but a thunderstorm drenched the hill, visibility dropped to zero, and the soldiers were unable to keep their footing in the mud. A fourth withdrawal was then ordered. Finally, on May 20, after intensive cannon and aerial rocket bombardment, all four battalions attacked and the North Vietnamese were driven off the mountain fortress.

2. The 187th Infantry had a proud heritage of amphibious assaults on the Philippines during World War II, and parachute assaults in Korea. The 187th Glider Infantry was activated for World War II service in February 1943, at Camp Mackall, North Carolina. It had been reorganized as the 187th Airborne Infantry in 1949 and had made spectacular parachute drops at Sukchon and Munsan-Ni in the Korean War. Part of the 101st Airborne Division since 1956, its battle groups had been considered some of the finest components of the Screaming Eagles.

CH47 Chinook helicopter brings ammunition, sandbags, food, and other supplies to the 173d Airborne Brigade in the Central Highlands of Vietnam during January of 1969. (173d Airborne Brigade Information Office)

A UH1D Huey helicopter rests upside down on Ap Bia Mountain after being hit by machine gun fire while attempting to carry reinforcements into the May 1969 battle. (Author's Collection)

Typical Fire Support Base, this one named Lorraine I *northwest of Saigon, as seen from the air. Note all-around defenses and artillery howitzers positioned in the center of the complex.* (U.S. Army)

Standard fighting bunker at a typical fire support base, this one named Picardy, northwest of Saigon, has frontal berm to deflect direct fire, firing ports, full overhead cover, and a low silhouette. The sleeping quarters were dug in directly behind the position. A water trailer is in the background. (Author's Collection)

Weary soldiers of the 3d Battalion, 187th Infantry (101st Airborne Division), search through the debris on top of Dong Ap Bia Mountain ("Hamburger Hill") after the Battle of May 20, 1969, in the A Shau Valley. (U.S. Army)

Machinegunner of the 3d Battalion, 187th Infantry, of the 101st Airborne Division (Airmobile) during the fighting in the A Shau Valley. (Author's Collection)

A XXIV Corps fire support base on Hill 88 in Thua Thieu Province contains self-propelled artillery and aviation assets. (U.S. Army)

Colonel George S. Patton's 11th Armored Cavalry Regiment attacks toward the Michelin Rubber Plantation in Operation ATLAS WEDGE during March of 1969. (Author's Collection)

The Battle of Ap Bia Mountain, or "Hamburger Hill," ignited a storm of public controversy over military objectives and tactics in an increasingly unpopular war. The soldiers had fought bravely and had suffered heavy losses for an objective that was abandoned soon after being taken. The entire action seemed senseless and irresponsible, and many in the division could not understand their sacrifice. Zais claimed a tremendous victory, but his explanation sounded hollow:

> The only significance of Hill 937 was the fact that there were North Vietnamese on it. My mission was to destroy enemy forces and installations. We found the enemy on Hill 937, and that is where we fought them.

Soon after the battle, disgruntled soldiers placed a $10,000 reward offer in an underground division newspaper for the assassination (or fragging) of officers giving orders for such attacks. Actually, the battle was part of the 1969 campaign to keep up mobile pressure against NVA staging bases, by destroying materials and defenses in these strategic areas. Lacking the assets to physically occupy the terrain, MACV had hoped that the South Vietnamese would take over such chores as their muscle increased. Five days after the fall of Ap Bia Mountain, Maj. Gen. John M. Wright, Jr., assumed command of the division, and Major General Zais was promoted to command XXIV Corps. The rest of Operation APACHE SNOW consisted of extensive reconnaissance and search operations extending to the Laotian border. There was little action, and it was brought to a close on June 7, 1969.

Action along the Demilitarized Zone itself was generally light during the first three months of the year, with the usual smattering of mortar and rocket rounds delivered nightly against defensive positions and landing zones. In late March, Col. James M. Gibson's "Red Devil" 1st Brigade, 5th Infantry Division (Mechanized), began meeting heavy NVA resistance just west of Con Thien as part of Operation MONTANA MAULER. The brigade was under 3d Marine Division control and served as a response force in case North Vietnamese forces were encountered in Quang Tri Province after crossing the DMZ. Its 1st Battalion of the 11th Infantry was the airmobile reserve.[3] On March 26, the battalion became involved in sweltering fighting against well-defended trench networks, uprooting North Vietnamese fortifications in temperatures of 105 degrees. Supporting air strikes were subjected to heavy automatic weapons fire as the battle went into its second day.

A costly dawn assault cleared some bunkers, but a company that had air-assaulted north of the defenses was blocked by mortar fire and heavy resistance on Hill 208. A full armored cavalry squadron (3d Squadron, 5th Cavalry) had to be sent against the hill to assist the stranded company. The other battalion infantrymen frontally assaulted more trenchlines that afternoon, but as each trench was taken a fierce counterassault was immediately hurled back against the newly won ramparts. By that evening one of the attack companies had lost all its officers and was being led by the artillery observer. The next day the infantrymen settled for destroying some of the bunkers that had already been isolated.

The 2d ARVN Regiment agreed to airlift a battalion to the battlefield on March 29. That proved to be the last day of heavy fighting. Bunkers were taken at rifle-point and lead platoons were chopped off by sudden NVA charges. Hasty reinforcements and plenty of air support assured eventual American success. The South Vietnamese changed their landings to safer spots, meeting only sporadic rifle fire as the action ended.

The DMZ front remained stable, although punctuated by scattered firefights. The level of combat dropped dramatically as bad weather set in during the last quarter of the year. During the second week of November, the 5th Infantry Division's 1st Brigade got into another scrape southwest of Con Thien. In the meantime the old DMZ frontier guardians, the 3d Marine Division, departed Vietnam and redeployed to Camp Courtney,

3. The 11th Infantry had broken Santana's Kiowan arrows during its Western Indian fighting in 1874, and matched Filipino bolo knives in the Visayas during the Philippine Insurrection of 1900. It had been consolidated in 1869 from several previous units of Civil War vintage, spent seven years fighting Commanches in Texas and Indian Territory, and then served a decade in Dakota and Montana. The regiment fought in Cuba, the Philippines, and Europe in World Wars I and II.

Okinawa. However, the overall level of combat activity remained very low and continued to taper off through December.

2. Guarding the Coast

The northern coastal regions were being garrisoned by two American divisions, the 1st Marine and Army Americal, which were engaged in small-unit patrolling and security operations. The NVA/VC Post-Tet Offensive of February 23, 1969, initiated the first real combat of the year. The Post-Tet Offensive, composed of a hundred rocket and mortar attacks scattered across the country, was not a large effort. However, the allied fuel and ammunition dumps at Da Nang were largely destroyed.

Maj. Gen. Charles M. Gettys's Americal Division, based at Chu Lai, reacted to several Post-Tet Offensive incidents with its 196th Infantry Brigade and excellent armored cavalry elements. Some of the heaviest fighting transpired as a result of the *3d NVA Regiment*'s attack upon Special Forces Detachment A-102's compound at Tien Phuoc, considered the most threatened 5th Special Forces Group camp in I Corps Tactical Zone. The 1st Battalion of the 52d Infantry was dispatched into attack positions along the Song Bon River, southeast of Tien Phuoc.[4] It slugged its way forward against cleverly concealed North Vietnamese bunkers built to cover the high ground. Bitter fighting continued for eight days. On March 6, the 3d Battalion, 21st Infantry, was sent in to help. After three more days of intense combat, two more battalions were helicoptered in to the battle area, and the 196th Infantry Brigade took command.

The battle was like many unwelcome affairs in Vietnam. Combat was waged under the direct fire of skilled NVA gunners dug into carefully selected positions with plenty of overhead cover and connecting trenches. The 196th Infantry Brigade responded with predictable American backup in the form of massive tactical air strikes and artillery. The 1st Battalion of the 46th In-

4. The 52d Infantry was known as the Ready Rifles, a regiment raised at Chickamauga Park, Georgia, in June 1917 for service in World War I, where it had fought in Alsace. It was broken up into the 27th, 52d, and 60th Armored Infantry Battalions in October 1943 and fought in Europe during World War II with the 9th Armored Division. The 1st Battalion had been in Vietnam since February of 1968.

fantry joined the fight to take the place of the 52d's worn battalion and made a hasty river crossing in an attempt to block NVA escape routes.[5]

The main attack was pressed in advances that were met with intense fire from strong-points which held their fire until the soldiers were only ten yards distant. Combat engineers and infantrymen with flamethrowers crawled forward to demolish one bunker at a time. The Americal infantry methodically reduced the critical positions, and after the key terrain was captured, the North Vietnamese soldiers began withdrawing in small groups. Contact became sporadic, and by March 22 only snipers remained. The immediate threat to Tien Phuoc had been eliminated and the Americal Division pulled its units out.

The Americal Division also saw heavy fighting in the Tam Ky vicinity where it had posted its attached 1st Squadron, 1st Cavalry, to clear VC in the wake of the Post-Tet Offensive.[6] The armored cavalry squadron fought another battle in the Tam Ky vicinity on May 12–19, 1969, during Operation FREDERICK HILL. It was ordered to move against a hilltop where the *1st VC Regiment* had overrun a critical militia outpost. When initial counterattacks failed, the 3d Battalion of the 21st Infantry, old hands at destroying fortifications in the Demilitarized Zone, was air-assaulted into the battlefield. After air strikes and artillery literally blew the top of the hill off, the mixed armored-infantry force made several assaults up the fire-swept slopes and finally recaptured it.

5. The 46th Infantry was known officially as the Professionals. Like the Ready Rifles, it was another tough old armored infantry veteran of World War II, having crashed through Normandy, the West Wall, and the Hurtgen Forest. It was organized at Fort Benjamin Harrison, Indiana, in June 1917, but missed World War I. In September of 1943 it had been broken up as the 15th, 46th, and 47th Armored Infantry Battalions of the 5th Armored Division for World War II service. The 1st Battalion had been in Vietnam since October 1967.

6. The 1st Cavalry was organized in 1833 as the Regiment of United States Dragoons from the Mounted Rangers of the Black Hawk War. It had fought through Mexico, the Civil War, almost every Indian War, the Spanish American War, the Philippine Insurrection, and World War II (as the 1st Armored Regiment and later 1st Tank Battalion). It was still technically part of the 1st Armored Division, having been detached from Fort Hood, Texas, for Vietnam service as a boost for Pacific theater armor assets in August 1967.

Combat in the American Division sector was light during the summer months as Maj. Gen. Lloyd B. Ramsey took command of the division. He established common brigade-regimental tactical areas with the 2d ARVN Division and colocated their command posts at the same base camps. The division began conducting combined operations and joint protection of supply lines. The American Division was transformed into a training security division and remained in this capacity until it was closed down in Vietnam.

The few heavy actions fought by the division during the rest of the year transpired in the Hiep Duc sector. There the 196th Infantry Brigade was matched up with the 5th ARVN Regiment in Operation FREDERICK HILL. On August 18, the 4th Battalion, 31st Infantry, ran into strong VC trench networks east of Hiep Duc in two separate firefights. The battle became more than a grisly contest to capture dug-in positions. As the ground action was raging, a command helicopter carrying the battalion commander, Lt. Col. E. P. Howard, and several other key personnel including an Associated Press correspondent, was hit by heavy machine-gun fire, exploded in midair, and crashed.

Two companies of the battalion immediately combat-assaulted near the downed helicopter site but were blocked from reaching it by interconnecting machine-gun nests. The soldiers were pinned down until the evening of August 20. The following day several companies from 1st Battalion, 46th Infantry, and elements of the 2d Battalion, 7th Marines, were airmobiled into the battle. Two more days of fierce fighting ensued as the soldiers and Marines pushed forward through heavy resistance. At 8:25 A.M. on August 24, the Viet Cong fire began to slacken, and Company C of the 21st Infantry battalion found the downed aircraft and recovered the bodies. Fighting continued for five more days before the battlefield was cleared.

The American Division's last major engagement of the year occurred in the FREDERICK HILL sector on September 11, 1969, the day after the communist cease-fire honoring the funeral of Ho Chi Minh ended. The 4th Battalion, 31st Infantry, repulsed a *60th VC Main Force Battalion* attack on Fire Support Base Siberia outside Hiep Duc. Afterwards, the level of combat dropped dramatically as Typhoon Doris brought heavy rains and severe flooding.

Maj. Gen. Ormond R. Simpson's 1st Marine Division covered the approaches to the vital city of Da Nang during 1969. This brought the Marines into considerable combat in the An Hoa and Que Son valleys and mandated extensive sweeps in the "rocket belt." The belt area, guarded by the 1st and 5th Marines during the year, was the strip of territory within NVA rocket range of Da Nang. Over a span of time incessant patrolling of the booby-trapped fields and villages produced a lot of casualties. Fighting in the valleys was more conventional.

On April 21 a reconnaissance team from the 1st Battalion of the 7th Marines spotted a large Viet Cong force crossing the Vu Gia river northwest of An Hoa. The squad ambush held its fire as they called in artillery. Several fire support bases responded in quick succession, and an onslaught of concentrated steel suddenly descended on the river crossing, catching the VC in sampans and on foot as they waded through the stream. The ambush position joined the slaughter by firing automatic weapons into the confused mass of men and churning water. Hundreds of Viet Cong were killed by fire or drowned in the swift current.

Later that month a grass fire touched off the entire ammunition supply point at Da Nang, demolishing thirty-eight thousand tons of munitions and twenty thousand drums of fuel. This dealt a major blow to operational stocks, but the 1st Marine Division was soon relegated to guarding rice harvests in the An Hoa basin. The operation was marked by only a few skirmishes. Ground action soon dwindled to extensive patrolling and occasional reconnaissance attacks by both sides.

The Marines also worked over some islands that were havens for Viet Cong activity along the coast south of Da Nang, islands suspected of being rocket crew refuges. In these tedious searches they were assisted by Korean Marines and South Vietnamese troops. On May 26, the Marines joined forces with the 51st ARVN Regiment and the 2d Korean Marine Brigade to storm Go Noi Island, only twelve miles from Da Nang. The region was ringed and traversed by a maze of rivers and streams combined with a labyrinth of tunnels, caves, and trenches. Previous operations in the area had been unsuccessful at eradicating the Viet Cong installations and materials on the island. This time the Marines sent in engineer land-clearing equipment which razed 6,750 acres, geographically transforming the whole island.

The Seventh Fleet made its final combat landings on Vietnamese soil on another island—sandy, squalid Barrier Island, thirty-four miles south of Da Nang. The 1st Battalion, 26th Marines, had the landing force duty and attacked the island three times during the year, in early May, in June, and in September. Again joint amphibious exercises were conducted with the Korean Marines and the ARVN forces to attempt clearance. This last operation, DEFIANT STAND, transpired on September 7. This time the big amphibian tractors churning through the surf toward the beaches were carrying a battalion of Korean Marines. The last of sixty-two Seventh Fleet Special Landing Force operations in Vietnam was also the first amphibious assault conducted in the twenty-year history of the Korean Marine Corps. The Special Landing Force air-assaulted inland while patrol craft cut off escape routes. The Viet Cong offered only light resistance and stayed low during the massive sweep. The next time U.S. Marines would use the Seventh Fleet offensively in Indochina would be to evacuate American, Vietnamese, and Cambodian citizens as the capitals of Saigon and Phnom Penh fell in the spring of 1975.

CHAPTER 20.

ONE WAR IN THE SOUTHERN PROVINCES

1. Guarding the Cambodian Frontier

In Vietnam's southern provinces the Army's formations were increasingly engaged in joint training operations with the South Vietnamese Army as the year progressed. Along the Cambodian frontier this mission was tempered with the additional task of garrisoning the border areas and preventing large NVA incursions. The 4th Infantry Division screened the Central Highlands portion of the Cambodian front, while the 173d Airborne Brigade was fragmented under its Pair-Off mission between the 22d and 23d ARVN Divisions in II Corps Tactical Zone. The 1st Cavalry and 25th Infantry Divisions were committed along the Cambodian border in III CTZ, and by the end of the year both were primarily dedicated to combined static security roles. Border defense remained a top MACV concern and produced some significant battles in the first half of 1969.

Maj. Gen. George I. Forsythe's 1st Cavalry Division (Airmobile) had been stationed northwest of Saigon across three provinces, and most of its line battalions were strung along the Cambodian border. Their triplex mission entailed covering the NVA infiltration routes, destroying forces encountered, and protecting the vital Saigon–Bien Hoa area from westward attack. The 1st Brigade had one of the toughest areas, coded NAVAJO WARHORSE, a stretch of dry rice fields covered by six cavalry battalions on one side squared off against several secure North Vietnamese divisions on the other. The brigade posted its battalions in Indian-fighting style, safeguarding the frontier with screening patrols backed up by fire support base strong-points in lieu of wooden stockades. This was why Capt. David L. Parker's Company B of the 2d Battalion, 5th Cavalry, was positioned near the southern tip of a protrusion of Cambodian territory jutting into Vietnam known as the Angel's Wing.

Major trouble started brewing on March 5, 1969, and from that date the battalion area sparked with sudden ambushes, light skirmishing, and fresh sightings of NVA soldiers. Three days later Company D had a tough run-in with the *272d VC Regiment* north of Phuoc Lu, and a warning was flashed to all cavalrymen in the sector to expect combat, especially at night, with well-armed, fresh, aggressive North Vietnamese infantry coming out of Cambodia.

Lt. Col. Jerry J. Burcham, commanding the 5th Cavalry's 2d Battalion, told his company commanders to keep roving ambushes moving at night and to change company locations after dark. It was hoped that night movement and deception would combine with ground radar to give his cavalrymen a continued advantage, one which could be rapidly reinforced by rocket-firing helicopters, lots of artillery, and fighter-bombers. Foot mobility in the open paddies was rapid, and the companies would select their overnight positions during the day. They would move away from them, have hot chow flown in, rest, and then march to the predetermined locations at dusk.

At sundown on March 8, Company B moved into its night perimeter and started breaking up. The 3d and Weapons Platoons began digging in and siting their ground radar and mortar. They also had brought along a big 90mm recoilless rifle with Beehive and high explosive rounds, and counted their firepower better than average. Unfortunately, neither radar nor recoilless rifle had been checked, and both proved inoperable.

The 1st and 2d Platoons, with twenty-seven men each, moved out in different directions to their roving ambush sites. As the troopers prepared to leave the company lines they checked gear. Each carried twenty full magazines for his M16, two hand grenades, one smoke grenade, three heat tablets, and one trip flare.

The nine squad claymore mines were divided among the men. Each of the platoons also had three machine guns with nine hundred rounds each, three grenade launchers, two radios, and one starlight scope. The cavalrymen slowly moved through the heavy ground haze to the sites and dug chest-high foxholes. The haze lifted at midnight and a cool, pleasant tropical breeze wafted through the starry darkness. Under the full moon even distant paddy dikes were stark and visible.

Both platoons radioed the company headquarters that they were set up, but the 1st had great difficulty making the report because its radio was cranky. First Lieutenant Powell of 2d Platoon made his first spotting report a half hour after midnight; six suspects were approaching his lines. He called in a salvo of forty artillery rounds, and five North Vietnamese soldiers ran from the explosions right toward his position. A trip flare was thrown for illumination and the platoon fired for a solid minute. Then all was quiet, and the troops guessed that they had killed some but that others might have gotten away. The men decided not to change their position for the rest of the night so they could get a body count at first light.

At 2:45 A.M. a private scanning the horizon from the anthill in 1st Platoon's perimeter spotted another five-man group that seemed to be coming out of a tree line. He awoke his commander, First Lieutenant Stevenson, who looked across the field. He saw the entire tree line moving, a huge mass of troops coming right at them. They quickly radioed for Blue Max, the rocket helicopters, and heavy artillery. A moment later they got a response. The helicopter was refused because they were not yet in contact. The cavalrymen watched breathlessly as the large force, numbering over two hundred men, stopped at a road and sent out scouts to secure a crossing. Suddenly a crashing wall of artillery rounds began exploding between the platoon lines and the NVA.

The forward observer at the company site began walking the salvos into the North Vietnamese, who were now scrambling to get out of the shellfire. He tried to keep the artillery between the outlying platoons and the NVA. Then NVA mortar rounds began falling on the ambush platoons, and the forward observer made a desperate gamble. He shifted the artillery to try to knock out the NVA mortar tube. Five minutes after the second urgent call for Blue Max, the armed helicopter was hovering overhead and requesting the platoons to mark their locations. For some unknown reason the helicopters were not on the right frequency, and radio contact was impossible. It was another one of those details bound to go wrong in a battle, a phenomenon often expressed as Murphy's Law. The howitzers had to stop firing as soon as the rocket helicopter was on station to avoid hitting it.

Lieutenant Colonel Burcham got in his helicopter and was overhead also. He could see the platoons were not marking their postions well, and radio trouble was cropping up again. A Spooky aircraft was also in the air but having difficulty seeing the battlefield for another reason. The lingering haze was reflecting the illumination. Colonel Burcham ordered the Spooky aircraft miniguns to suppress machine-gun fire being aimed at the Cobra gunships.

Five minutes after the helicopter had arrived, the 1st Platoon was pinned by heavy mortar and rocket-propelled grenade fire. Several men were seriously wounded and the radio was knocked out for good. Lieutenant Stevenson and his platoon sergeant used the protection of the anthill to see a battalion's worth of flickering lights coming at them: machine guns, rockets, and assault rifles. Then two NVA suddenly ran at a foxhole and were brought down inside the perimeter. An instant later a B-40 rocket hit the lieutenant's foxhole and disintegrated the occupants. Platoon Sergeant Martinez took over and told the men to conserve their ammunition and to fire only at NVA who actually breached the perimeter. That was all he had time to say; the first mass assault was hurled against the platoon as NVA radio traffic echoed eerily through the fiery half-light of night battle.

The troopers fired off their claymores and took well-aimed shots at the incoming waves of charging soldiers. Every time they flipped on automatic, a fusillade of B-40 rockets would strike in their direction. The NVA were obviously trying to knock out any automatic weapons. Sergeant Martinez was desperately trying to get the Spooky's attention, but the trip flares were three feet outside the foxholes. The men squirted insect repellent on the ground and lit it with matches, but this effort was met with such intense fire that it had to be abandoned.

As the North Vietnamese moved steadily closer, setting up new rocket and firing positions, Sergeant Martinez and three men moved to new locations. Two were killed and the sergeant was severely wounded. The remaining man dragged him back. By now everyone in the platoon had been killed or wounded. The North Vietnamese were slipping in and overrunning foxholes. Two troopers were unable to return fire at one such attack because of a berm. They heaved grenades which landed short on the berm just as the North Vietnamese popped up to emplace a heavy machine gun. The grenade blasts wiped the NVA crew out.

Two assaults were made before daybreak. Both were repulsed by steady, deliberately aimed defensive fire. Frequently NVA soldiers simply walked forward in groups, and at other times they charged wildly. In the midst of the battle a crazy incident happened. A group of North Vietnamese soldiers suddenly ran across the battlefield, yelling and laughing at each other. The Americans watched in amazement as NVA officers tried to reach out and get them back in line. Firing stopped on both sides for a few seconds. At daybreak the North Vietnamese pulled back and broke off contact. The platoon expended all its ammunition and was down to the last magazines taken off the dead.

The 2d Platoon underwent an equally vicious assault. There the men were badly hit in the opening mortar explosions and made a mad scramble for a drainage ditch that seemed to afford better protection. This sudden retreat abandoned the claymore mine protection as well as the trip flares which might have marked their positions. One machine gun was then destroyed by another mortar round. However, they suffered no wave assault. The NVA were using advance-by-bounds techniques, firing and moving in the manner of professional drill sergeants at Fort Polk. The platoon sergeant kept crawling up and down the ditch, giving encouragement and assisting the growing number of wounded.

Then the cavalrymen hit upon a marking solution. They began stripping, taking off their shirts first and pouring insect repellent over them. After setting them afire, they heaved the burning clothes into the air. Each time a flaming shirt left the ditch, a B-40 round screamed in on the man who threw it. However, the trick worked. Cobra gunships began strafing in front of their lines and broke the attack.

With dawn the North Vietnamese began to withdraw. The battlefield was a smoking shambles. While losses had been very heavy, both platoons had managed to hold by sheer determination and calm marksmanship. Many of the things that had gone wrong were serious, but errors and gremlins always pop up in the heat of battle. The cavalrymen were experienced enough to expect serious difficulties and innovative enough to work around them.

Later it was discovered that the 1st Platoon had some unintentional help in holding its perimeter. The North Vietnamese had also committed a grave blunder. The group attacking the 2d Platoon was advancing in a direction uncoordinated with the other group. Rockets that sailed over the target were ripping into the other soldiers advancing on 1st Platoon. It was perhaps the only time in the war when an American platoon was receiving effective direct support from NVA gunners. Battlefield reality remained a bloody constant throughout the prolonged American withdrawal from Vietnam.

In mid-April, two brigades of the division initiated a series of operations commencing with MONTANA RAIDER against the *1st* and *7th NVA Divisions* in the heavily fortified jungle of central War Zone C, while the 3d Brigade sortied into War Zone D against the *5th VC Division*. Patrols and ambushes were overshadowed by larger field operations as Maj. Gen. Elvy B. Roberts assumed command in May. These operations were designed to follow in the wake of massed B-52 bombing runs, as infantry was air-assaulted into the stricken areas to seek out North Vietnamese supply and assembly points. These raids were part of the 1969 One War plan to maintain pressure on NVA base areas, and the 1st Cavalry Division was considered MACV's premier mobile attack formation for these offensive assignments.

Several NVA attempts were made to overrun isolated helicopter landing sites, most notably at LZs Carolyn, Grant, and Jamie, in May, as the cavalry spent the wet, humid summer searching through trackless, arboreal wilderness. There well-fortified strong-points tested the fortitude of the American front-line soldier. The bunker sets were invariably constructed in thickly vegetated bamboo groves and often bypassed due to their perfect camouflage. When the bunker gunners abruptly opened up, leading company elements were often only able to break contact by exploding bangalore torpedoes dropped from helicopters. These ripped apart enough foliage to allow accurate counterfire with machine guns and light antitank weapons used for bunker suppression.

Immediate retreat was required to save casualties, and men pulled back under heavy automatic weapons fire, dragging seriously wounded and dying troopers with them. Positions were marked with all available smoke and white phosphorus, creating smoke screens which both covered the withdrawal and enabled aircraft to spot locations. Helicopters raked targets with rockets and riot gas bomblets. Then artillery shelled the area until Air Force fighters arrived with napalm and 750-pound bombs. After intensive bombardment the foot cavalrymen would have to go back in and assault the charred, blasted ruins at rifle-point.

The 1st Cavalry Division enjoyed an excellent reputation for aggressive conduct under fire, but it too was in a transitional stage. By the end of the year II Field Force, Vietnam, had mated the ARVN airborne regiments with the division's brigades. The elite South Vietnamese parachute division was paired up with the crack 1st Cavalry Division to gain experience utilizing its large number of helicopters and sophisticated airmobility doctrine. This task placed the 1st Cavalry Division in a sponsor capacity, which overshadowed its combat role as MACV'S mobile response force. Battlefield incidents became increasingly sparse as the year closed out.

Maj. Gen. Ellis W. Williamson's 25th Infantry Division was also entrusted with a share of the Cambodian border duty. His division was paired with its adopted sister, the 25th ARVN Division, west and north of Saigon in Tay Ninh and Hau Nghia Provinces. The "Tropic Lightning" division was engaged in some heated rubber-field fights, convoy skirmishes, campsite battles, and extensive riverine operations along the Saigon and Vam Co rivers. However, its main task was identical to that of the 1st

Cavalry Division: security of the western approaches to Saigon.

Throughout the early part of 1969, the division's 1st and 2d Brigade border area patrol bases weathered several attacks. These started with the Post-Tet Offensive attack on Patrol Base Diamond I, occupied by the 2d Battalion of the 27th Infantry, on February 23. It was subjected to ten minutes of mortaring followed by a massive ground assault. In spite of tons of aerial bombs, rockets, and artillery shells, the North Vietnamese blasted their way through the perimeter wire and took three bunkers. Direct fire from artillery within the camp finally broke the assault. Elements of the same battalion again employed plenty of artillery, air strikes, and aerial rockets to break up a North Vietnamese Army probe against Patrol Base Diamond II on April 5.

Capitalizing on the proximity of the Cambodian border to produce combat, the division established its fifth patrol base within two miles of the border. Patrol Base Frontier City was a well-entrenched company-sized outpost built in a flat, open area where observation was only hindered by two small wooded areas and a stream lined with dense brushwood, located over five hundred yards away. It was manned by Company C of the 9th Infantry's 4th Battalion.[1] MACV had resorted to giving every inhabited area of Vietnam a report card called the MACV Hamlet Evaluation System Report, based on loyalty to the Saigon ime. In the latest report the nearby village of Long Khanh had only gotten a C. The division was looking forward to trouble.

Work on the base began on the morning of April 24, and all defensive preparations were completed by dark. One dozer was brought in by a CH-54 Flying Crane, and the other was floated down the Vam Co River and the Rach Bao Canal on a raft, and then driven into camp. The position of the base was

1. The 9th Infantry's motto Keep up the Fire! commemorated the marksmanship and guts demonstrated by the regiment at the Wagon Box Fight near Fort Kearney, Wyoming, on August 2, 1867. Thirty 9th Infantry soldiers had repulsed a mounted charge by 2,000 Sioux, killing several hundred Indians while suffering only three casualties. It was first organized at Fort Monroe, Virginia, in March 1855, and participated in the Civil and Indian wars, fought in Cuba, the China Relief Expedition, the Philippine Insurrection, World Wars I and II, and the Korean War. The 4th Battalion had been in Vietnam since April 1966.

selected and an engineer stake was driven at the center. A 130-foot rope was tied to the stake and walked around to form the circular trace of the bunker line. Twenty-four standard packages were helicoptered in and dropped off around the perimeter. Each contained a shaped demolition charge, two sheets of pierced steel planking, and a bundle of sandbags. After the explosives created the initial bunker holes, the infantrymen tackled the hard job of squaring off the hole and using the packaged materials to build their nine-foot bunkers. All twenty-four were completed in nine hours.

As the bunkers were being completed, the dozers were pushing up berms of dirt between them. Other soldiers were busy clearing fields of fire, stringing rows of triple concertina wire, and setting up three hundred claymore mines. A prefabricated twenty-foot observation tower was flown in and set up in the middle of the patrol base. The tower was sandbagged and crowned with both a radar and starlight scope. Finally, two howitzers were flown in. Twenty-one sorties of Chinook helicopters had been used to bring in the fortification packages, crew-served weapons, and ammunition. By sundown all barriers, mortar and howitzer pits, ammunition bunkers, troop positions, and the observation tower were ready for combat.

Late in the night of April 25, the observation tower radar began to detect movement southwest of the base. As the movement increased, the defenders called for artillery fire on the woods southwest of the patrol base. Three Air Force Spooky and one Shadow minigun aircraft, twenty-two Cobra and Huey helicopter gunships, and four fighter-bombers arrived and started bombing, napalming, and rocketing all suspected approach routes to the American position. The NVA responded with a barrage of rockets, mortars, grenades, and antiaircraft fire. Illumination rounds blossomed into bursts of light over the battlefield as flares drifted through the clear night.

One hour after midnight, a battalion of the *271st NVA Regiment* charged across the open ground. Helicopters of the 25th Aviation Battalion rolled in to strafe the attackers as AC-47 fire support aircraft decimated targets marked with white phosphorous rounds fired from the base mortars. Waves of North Vietnamese soldiers were mowed down, but eleven made it to the wire, threw in a bangalore torpedo, and started to cross. The defenders then set off their claymore mines and took them under fire with a 90mm recoilless rifle and two machine guns. The attackers were killed in the hailstorm of combined weapons fire. Patrol Base Frontier City was receiving only sporadic rounds as the slaughter subsided. The 9th Infantry had only suffered one casualty, a man lightly wounded by shrapnel.

The 25th Infantry Division had been experimenting with improved battlefield surveillance devices and armed Night Hawk helicopters equipped with night observation devices and xenon searchlights. These were put to the test during the all-out North Vietnamese Army assault against Fire Support Base Crook, defended by the 3d Battalion, 22d Infantry, on June 6–7, 1969. It was located northwest of Tay Ninh city about four miles from the Cambodian border in a flat but forested area. While dense jungle surrounded its northern and eastern sides, abandoned rice paddies extended in other directions. All approaches were covered by sensor devices made available by the abandonment of McNamara's DMZ barrier, as well as radar mounted on the observation tower. These detected large movement in the tree line around the base on the night of June 5. Artillery was immediately fired into those areas, and things quieted down until three o'clock in the morning, when the base began taking a heavy concentration of rocket and mortar fire. Most of the rockets simply sailed over the base and went off outside the wire on the other side. One soldier was killed by a mortar round as a listening post was pulled in, but within the base there were only minor injuries and little damage.

The *272d NVA Regiment* then charged the base from the south and east. The defenders answered with intense machine-gun fire as the base howitzers fired directly into the North Vietnamese attackers with lowered gun tubes. Heavier artillery pounded the woods and pathway of the assault. This concentration of explosions and bullets dropped dozens of soldiers, but a sixteen-man group managed to breach the outer wire with bangalore torpedoes before being killed by claymore mines and rifle fire. Although the charge had faltered, the majority of the NVA remained on the field and kept firing their assault rifles and rocket-propelled grenades. One hour after the attack started AC-

47 and AC-119 aircraft came overhead and started circling Crook's perimeter, lacing it with devastating direct minigun and cannon fire. Helicopter gunships and fighter-bombers also arrived and annihilated the remainder of the exposed North Vietnamese troops, who had remained defiantly in the open.

The next night the radar and seismic sensor devices detected an identical pattern of activity. The Americans were bewildered at the prospect that the North Vietnamese would try a second time after the overwhelming destruction of the first attempt. However, they grimly manned their bunkers as mortar and direct howitzer fire slashed into the tropical forest again. At two o'clock in the morning a Night Hawk helicopter detected large groups of soldiers moving toward the base on a road, and artillery was shifted to shatter this formation. An hour later a renewed barrage hit Fire Support Base Crook at the rate of 150 rockets and mortar shells a minute. Three U.S. soldiers were wounded by this initial volley. For the next hour and a half the barrage kept up, but at a diminished pace. Then two battalions of the *88th NVA Regiment* attacked from two tree lines in the north. As the North Vietnamese troops appeared out of the trees, they were strafed immediately by helicopters which had been hovering overhead.

The base defenders replied with heavy automatic weapons fire and antipersonnel cannister fire from the lowered howitzer tubes. Again AC-119 aircraft blasted the area with minigun fire, as heavy artillery sent a torrent of rounds slamming into the path of the attack. One wave of attackers was broken up short of the wire, but the other force got into the first wire barrier before the last attacker was stopped. A retreat was attempted, but the violence of automatic weapons and bursting munitions chopped through the survivors while they were still in the open. By 5:30 A.M., those NVA soldiers that could had withdrawn, leaving the fields strewn with hundreds of dead.

Then the unbelievable happened. On the night of June 7, an artillery barrage testing the same woods around the base prompted the North Vietnamese to make a third try. This halfhearted attack was quickly eradicated, and Fire Support Base Crook remained secure. Vietnam had reconfirmed the old World War I axioms governing the futility of charging fixed defenses without strong armored or firepower backup. However, as the experiences of the 1st Cavalry Division had demonstrated during the spring, American tactics were premised on tremendous quantities of aerial rockets, bombing, and shellfire as a preface to assaults on far less sophisticated, earthen bunker systems.

The 25th Infantry Division was fully engaged in the Dong Tien Progress Together program with its counterpart 25th ARVN Division by the latter part of the year. Combat fizzled out across the Cambodian frontier front as this joint training and operations effort consumed the division's resources. Plans were underway to accelerate U.S. withdrawal schedules, and the 25th Infantry Division was tagged for return to Hawaii the following year. However, MACV was already drafting operational orders for a final, massive strike across the border to destroy the NVA staging bases inside Cambodia. It would take place in the spring of 1970.

2. Guarding the Saigon Approaches

While the 1st Cavalry Division and the 25th Infantry Division held down the western border approach, the remaining Saigon approaches were guarded by other large American formations. The three provinces directly north of the capital were covered by the "Big Red One" 1st Infantry Division, reinforced by the bulk of the "Blackhorse" 11th Armored Cavalry Regiment and the 5th ARVN Division. The southern approach through Long An Province was watched by the 3d Brigade of the 9th Infantry Division, which employed small-unit reconnaissance and special night patrols to saturate its sector throughout the year. In the meantime the rest of the 9th Infantry Division departed Vietnam, and the 25th Infantry Division absorbed control of the separate 3d Brigade. The eastern approaches to the city were covered by the 18th ARVN Division, the 1st Australian Task Force, and the Royal Thai Army Volunteer Force. Major General Warren K. Bennett's 199th Infantry Brigade was heavily engaged in upgrading the 18th ARVN Division and pacification projects. It also conducted daily operations with South Vietnamese territorial militia and warded off small-scale attacks against hamlets and "Ruff-Puff" outposts northeast of Saigon.

All maneuvers in III Corps Tactical Zone revolved around

Operation TOAN THANG II. This security operation had been going on since June of 1968 when it replaced the first serial by that designation. The 1st Infantry Division, the 3d Brigade of the 9th Infantry Division, the 199th Infantry Brigade, and the 11th Armored Cavalry Regiment were all dedicated by MACV to its support. The operation entailed static defense of designated tactical areas of responsibility, as well as limited reconnaissance expeditions to discourage NVA campsites and rocket positions within striking distance of Saigon.

The biggest unit in the area was Maj. Gen. Orwin C. Talbott's 1st Infantry Division. During most of the year, combat was relatively light, and he focused on joint field operations with the 5th ARVN Division. The division watched over suspected hamlets as part of the pacification-imposed population control around Di An and Phu Loi. In mid-January the "Big Red One" became heavily involved in road clearance, as the 1st Brigade began an engineer-backed effort to open the route from Phuoc Vinh to the provincial capital of Song Be. The road had been closed for three years due to Viet Cong activity, necessitating the airlift of all supplies to several critical towns and bases. The division covered combat engineers as they cut 250-yard-wide swaths out of the vegetation on each side of the dry-weather single-lane pass, while other road construction engineer crews transformed it into a major highway. This was accompanied by extensive infantry patrolling in the Iron Triangle. When the herculean effort was completed six months later in mid-June, it marked one of the division's major achievements in Vietnam.

In March, Col. George S. Patton's 11th Armored Cavalry was alerted that the *7th NVA Division* was infiltrating toward Saigon through the Michelin rubber plantation. While the Michelin plantation was a typical rubber tree area, a lot of scrub brush had grown up between the trees since its abandonment. It was surrounded by thick jungle, but the month of March was hot and dry and the regiment took advantage of the excellent tank weather to initiate Operation ATLAS WEDGE on March 17, 1969. Colonel Patton's observation helicopters were sent up in the clear blue skies and looked down to see large groups of North Vietnamese troops bicycling through the rubber. They made little or no attempt to hide and were clearly in a march formation, not expecting battle.

Throughout the rest of this first day the low-flying light observation helicopters dodged return fire to bring artillery and
tactical air strikes down on the soldiers. On the morning of March
18, the helicopters returned but only spotted squads moving below. Closer examinations were met by intense antiaircraft fire,
which wounded one observer. Armored personnel carriers of the
1st Squadron moved off Fire Support Base Holiday Inn and drove
west through the "great swath" cut by Rome Plow dozers, leading from Highway 13 into the Michelin plantation. The 3d
Squadron followed right behind. The vehicle movement was
slowed at a ford as combat engineers carefully checked for mines.

The tracked carriers and tanks were soon skirmishing in the
marshy woods as they responded to helicopter sightings. Troop
H was hit by delaying antitank teams which hit two of its battle
tanks with rocket-propelled grenades. One tank blew up in flames
and had to be abandoned. Troop L was hit in midstream, but
the NVA antitank gunners did not have clear fields of fire, and
most of the rounds exploded in the trees. In the process of maneuvering around this position two troopers were wounded, and
a landing zone had to be cleared for their evacuation. The North
Vietnamese concentrated intense fire on this site as the medical
evacuation helicopter arrived. A lieutenant was killed and nine
others were hit. As darkness fell, Troop L established a night
defensive position at the landing zone. Troops B, C, D, and M
also ploughed through underbrush in sharp action during the
first day's drive, and laagered overnight next to their landing
zones.

Under an umbrella of Cobra gunships and observation helicopters, the armored vehicles moved out on the morning of March
19, a day marked by tedious fighting against bunker complexes
which had to be destroyed one by one. The action continued
into the night, fought in the glare of headlights and aircraft spot-
lights. The battle intensified the following day. Troops L and
M of the 3d Squadron became involved in a pitched battle after
an aero rifle platoon became pinned down in two bomb craters
by a large horseshoe-shaped fortification complex of the *320th
NVA Regiment*. A number of medium battle tanks arrived on
the scene and began churning through the bunker-studded woods
in a wide circle. The platoon leader's tank was suddenly hit by
a rocket-propelled grenade which sent shrapnel over the turret

and blinded the lieutenant. The tank lurched into a large B-52 bomb crater on the far side of the bunker line, where it was stranded. Three more tanks were quickly destroyed by close-in rocket-propelled grenade fire.

The one remaining tank no longer had a working radio. The squadron commander, Lt. Col. Lee D. Duke, landed his helicopter and dashed over to order a last attack in the lengthening afternoon shadows. He directed the armored personnel carriers to go on each side of the tank and placed the infantry in line to the rear of the vehicles. The colonel then mounted the rear deck of the tank and with a wave of his arm the advance began. His center tank, flanked by tracked armored carriers, rumbled right into the midst of the North Vietnamese bunkers. A grenade was heaved on the tank's engine compartment, where it exploded and wounded Colonel Duke, but he continued to direct the mechanized infantry force through the bunkers and then back again. They passed the burning hulks of the tanks that had already exploded and one that was still blazing furiously as its ammunition cooked off. It was close to evening and the troopers pulled back to a night defensive position, recovered the tank in the bomb crater, and called in medical evacuation helicopters.

The 1st Squadron took over the attack on March 21. By now only three light observation helicopters remained flyable and Huey troopships were being used for scouting. The fresh armored cavalry unit took over the job of destroying the remaining bunkers in the base complex encountered the previous day. For the next five days, the 11th Armored Cavalry continued to thrash through the Michelin plantation, but the battle was over. It also marked the last big operation for Colonel Patton, as that April he turned over the reins of the regiment to Col. James H. Leach.

Maj. Gen. Albert E. Milloy took over the 1st Infantry Division in August. It was heavily involved in upgrading the 5th ARVN Division, and most combat operations were of a combined nature. They consisted of small-unit ambushes, and ground reconnaissance, airmobile, and water operations along the Saigon, Thi Tinh, and Song Be rivers. Operations were typified by the cordon of Phu Hoa Dong during September 15–26 in southern Binh Duong Province. The 2d Brigade joined forces with the 7th ARVN Regiment and South Vietnamese field police to completely seal off the village and conduct night ambushes and reconnaissance throughout the area. Each house was thoroughly searched as aerial broadcasts were made from helicopters, leaflets were dropped, and ground speakers set up to blare down the streets. For eleven days the villagers were confined to one of the four hamlets. During that period the Americans served 2,200 noon rice meals, distributed sixteen bags of flour and four bags of meal, gave away 475 school kits and 3,200 bars of soap, and passed out fifty patriotism packages. The vilagers sat through fifteen hours of movies, sixteen hours of band music, two magician shows, and a lottery in which nine pigs were given away. The children were carted off on three trips to the Saigon zoo. Since there had been an opening firefight trying to get into the village, which had destroyed several homes, the Americans also dumped sheets of tin and plywood off before leaving. Whether or not such pacification projects succeeded became irrelevant within five years. North Vietnam gained control over the south through military invasion, and population sympathies—"the hearts and minds" long deemed central to all allied (and Viet Cong) efforts —were in the end of no consequence to either side.

The "Big Red One" was alerted to begin a new operation, KEYSTONE BLUEJAY, on December 15. On that date, Major General Milloy received official word that his division was going home. KEYSTONE BLUEJAY was the first welcome operation in four years of combat. It governed equipment turnover and plane scheduling for return to the United States by April 15, 1970.

3. 1969 Army Field Performance

The One War plan produced fewer large-scale operations and more small-unit patrolling and reconnaissance. The Vietnam conflict had always demanded a higher level of tactical capability than most conventional wars, since mobile area warfare doctrine broke normally massed formations down into independently operating battalions, companies, and platoons. The real tempo of the battlefield was at the platoon level, and Army proficiency was primarily measured in bands of five-man squads mustered into twenty-man platoons. The advent of Vietnamization introduced combined operations, and by mid-1969 most purely American combat missions became small-unit ambuscades.

One of the better line units in the Army was the 25th Infantry Division's "Wolfhounds": its two battalions of the 27th Infantry. The 2d Battalion was using scattered patrol bases to detect and ambush North Vietnamese Army elements crossing the border from Cambodia. Company B had been operating its three rifle platoons on a staggered three-day cycle which consisted of a daytime reconnaissance followed by a night ambush, a day of defending the local militia outpost, and a day of rest and training.

On October 12, the nineteen-man 1st Platoon was alerted that some action against Patrol Base Kotrc seemed imminent, and they spent the day reconnoitering the muddy rice paddies and scattered hedgerows for prospective ambush sites. The soldiers then returned to their outpost for supper, grabbed three South Vietnamese Popular Force militiamen, and grudingly set out into the darkness at seven o'clock that evening. Morale was low because the platoon had been making nocturnal sorties for months without contact against its highly elusive North Vietnamese adversaries.

The platoon soldiers moved through the countryside just off a trail that they knew by heart. They had been in the area so long that they navigated by moonlight, spotting the familiar silhouettes of fish screens and traps. The lieutenant set up the ambush north of the planned location because the soldiers had found a wide dry area near the trail with several rice dikes converging on it. The platoon set up in a rough triangle composed of the three squads, with machine guns in the corners sited to cover the dike approaches. Claymore mines were set up in a circle at fifteen paces, and by ten o'clock that night the platoon was silently in position.

One hour later one of the machine-gun crews saw six North Vietnamese running along the rice dike leading directly into the position. The Americans waited breathlessly until the ammunition bearer cut loose with his M16 at a distance of only six yards, chucked out the spent magazine, and shoved another one in the rifle. He went through fifteen magazines back to back. The machine gun clattered into action at the first shot, and grenadiers joined the action by firing illumination rounds into the sky. Claymore mines were detonated at once. The M60 jammed after going through 150 rounds, but the gunner quickly realized that the ammunition belts had become crossed. He unscrambled the tangled bullet chains and had his machine gun firing again in seconds. He fired continuously for two minutes.

Four of the North Vietnamese soldiers fell in the initial fusillade, and the last two soldiers ran off in different directions. Two of the fallen had been wounded and hobbled away. For another eight minutes the platoon fired in the direction of the escaping survivors. The grenadiers switched from illumination to regular high explosive rounds, as the rest of the platoon was sending up dozens of star clusters and parachute flares. A "Night Hawk" helicopter arrived overhead and flicked on its powerful searchlight. Its door gunner began blazing away at the ground. In fifteen minutes a shower of howitzer shells plummeted into the flat, open fields.

The helicopter then radioed the platoon to check and see if the NVA soldier they had targeted was still alive. The lieutenant organized a "killer patrol" of five men who sallied from the platoon ambush site, passed the two broken bodies near the dike, and turned north. About a hundred yards out they saw one of the soldiers trying to crawl away, opened fire with everything they had, and quickly killed him. Another platoon "killer patrol" had gone south into the rice paddies and followed the helicopter's searchlight to another wounded soldier. They went over and found that he had been shot in the chest and landed the helicopter to perform a medical evacuation. The evacuated prisoner later died from his wounds.

After breakfast the next morning, the company commander led 3d Platoon into the area, along with several volunteers from the ambush platoon. They found the three bodies that had been located the night before and a fourth dead soldier. They also picked up homemade grenades, assault rifles, and ten bamboo field launcher tripods for 122mm rockets. The six who had been ambushed were part of an ammunition supply party. The 27th Infantry claimed a totally successful ambush. There had been no U.S. casualties. In fact, not one shot had been fired in return.

In late 1968 the Army had established a new composite unit to guard the boundary of II and III Corps Tactical Zones called Task Force South. One battalion of the rugged 173d Airborne Brigade was detached to join it, and the paratroopers brought their concept of hunter-killer HAWK operations with them.

HAWK teams of squad size or larger were designed to search for and attack targets within their capability, while smaller teams sought out information or captives. Companies or platoons were assigned areas, which they patrolled with HAWK missions, backed with reaction forces. These teams were essentially night ambush positions.

On March 29, 1969, the twenty-five-man 1st Platoon of Company B, 3d Battalion, 503d Infantry (Airborne), led by an experienced paratrooper platoon sergeant, was given a routine HAWK assignment. It had two rifle squads and a weapons squad with two machine guns, as well as a command section. Additionally it had a forward observer from the battalion mortar platoon, a senior aidman, and a scout dog team. However, the handler had just acquired a new dog and was not yet familiar with him.

The platoon members swept the jungle for seven days without contact. On April 5, the dog put them onto twenty Viet Cong moving along a trail, dressed in brand new uniforms and carrying new rucksacks. They called in artillery and began following the trail, hoping to catch them. That night the platoon split into two HAWK teams, but there was no combat.

The next day they continued to follow the trail. At noon they discovered an old base camp and a shallow grave. They destroyed all the bunkers and then advanced. The scout dog was very nervous and kept alerting them, but they could see no one. The handler reasoned that the canine was agitated simply because of the old base camp. Early in the afternoon, a soldier in the rear of the unit suddenly spotted a uniformed Viet Cong and both opened fire at each other. Nobody was hit. By mid-afternoon the platoon found itself on a well-traveled pathway. After stopping for water, the sergeant moved back to the ridge to establish a night position along the trail.

The following day they were due to be resupplied, so he decided to maintain the platoon in one defensive perimeter. The paratroopers constructed four bunkered positions and several foxholes well before dark, making plenty of noise as they dug in. This was not in line for HAWK procedure, which was to move into smaller clandestine ambushes as silently as possible. The bunkers had no overhead cover, and no listening posts were set out beyond the perimeter. Two machine guns were placed in two separate positions covering the trail, and five men were assigned to each emplacement. The two rifle squads were put in two positions on the other side of the trail. The platoon sergeant and the others set up a command section in the center and set up trip flares and claymore mines beyond the perimeter.

The scout dog was beside himself by this time, and the handler had trouble trying to calm him. The dog's behavior made the troops nervous, but they decided not to fire illumination rounds. It rained off and on during the night, and several paratroopers thought they heard voices around them. At first light, the platoon sergeant made his rounds of the position through the dense morning fog that had rolled over the hill. The dog began to growl and the sergeant ordered some of his men to check beyond their lines. At this instant a trip flare went off, and the Viet Cong surged out of the jungle. They were wearing red bandanas and fresh uniforms, firing assault rifles and heaving grenades as they charged. They tried to rush the machine-gun position but were cut down. Then more VC began attacking the entire position. The forward observer called for artillery, but South Vietnamese howitzers were in support and could not follow his directions to adjust their round impacts. Throughout the battle, the ARVN artillery fell off in the distance. The observer was killed still trying to shift fire. Although there were three radios in the platoon, no one ever bothered trying to regain communications contact.

As the attack continued, the paratroopers began to run out of ammunition. One of the machine guns ran out completely, and the other was hit by a B-40 rocket. The platoon sergeant ordered a retreat to the north. He was gunned down as he tried to muster the men. Another staff sergeant took over as grenades and automatic weapons fire laced the thick tropical vegetation with shrapnel and bullets. In the meantime the battalion commander had been alerted to the action by the artillery liaison section, and scrambled into a helicopter to locate them and determine a landing zone site for reinforcement. It was now twenty minutes since the action had started and all communications with the HAWK platoon had been lost.

One half of the position was overrun, and the new platoon sergeant retreated down the ridge to the stream with the rest.

Only thirteen wounded men and the dog were left alive, and as they withdrew, the Viet Cong stopped their attack and broke contact. One of the wounded was unable to keep up and was left on the trail. Since the VC were not following, the Americans later found him still alive where he had collapsed.

The battalion commander spotted the platoon remnants from the air when they began pitching smoke grenades, and immediately landed. He wanted to counterattack at once, but everyone was out of ammunition. He agreed to use the helicopter instead to lift out the seriously wounded. At eight o'clock that morning Company C was landed and moved back to the overrun American positions. They found most of the dead still in their foxholes. The rucksacks had all been quickly ransacked, but many valuable items had been left. Both machine guns and their crews were found where they had been close assaulted. One machine gun was covered with spent brass and had clearly gone out of ammunition. The other one still had 150 rounds left to fire.

Numerous searches of the area by the battalion over the next several days failed to locate any Viet Cong, although they uncovered some grave sites and a camp area with hot coals still glowing. It had been a hard lesson in the unsoundness of mixing conventional tactics with ambush practice. The ambush derived its security from secrecy, whereas the defensive position derived its security from strength and defensibility. By attempting to combine the two, the platoon leader had sacrificed the security afforded by either. In appropriate ceremonies, the dog was later awarded the Purple Heart for wounds received in action.

The Army was also sending patrols into the rice fields near Saigon. The 1st Battalion of the 2d Infantry was one of the Army's oldest and proudest formations and, by March of 1969, was considered an old timer by Vietnam standards—having arrived in October 1965, with the "Big Red One" 1st Infantry Division.[2] However, the 1st Infantry Division was in its last year of Viet-

2. The 2d Infantry originated in Pennsylvania in 1808, fought in both the War of 1812 and the Mexican War, garrisoned in California in the 1850s, battled from Bull Run to Petersburg in the Civil War, engaged Indians ranging from Seminoles to Nez Perces, fought in Cuba during the Spanish American War, in the Philippine Insurrection, and during World War II, when it occupied Iceland and then fought from Normandy to Czechoslovakia.

nam service and, like most Army formations of that year, was
war-weary. The draftees in its ranks were already calling it the
"Big Dead One." The commander of its 3d Platoon of Company
D was an experienced and dependable first lieutenant who had
served a previous Vietnam tour as a staff sergeant in the 1st
Cavalry Division. When his outfit was selected to pull night ambush duty in the Delta countryside outside the capital, nothing
unusual was expected.

The platoon helicoptered in and began a grueling march, aggravated by bizarre tides and tropical riverbanks, toward the selected area, the junction of four streams in unknown territory.
This trek through knee-deep and waist-deep mud was so difficult that a rubber boat was flown to the twenty-nine men. The
soldiers finally reached the site that evening and chose a pinch
of land jutting out into the Rach Giong tributary which was covered with scrub and dominated by a lone tree. The lieutenant
and his platoon sergeant, a national guardsman, took three radiomen and a medic and planted themselves under the tree.
Surrounded by rice paddies and painfully aware of being in the
middle of "Viet Cong country," the men settled into a tight egg-
shaped ring of six fighting positions. Tired as they were, some
soldiers nervously tried to differentiate between the sounds of
lapping water and possible human movement along the water's
edge. There, under a full moon, the platoon passed a restless
but uneventful night.

Early in the morning a Landing Craft, Mechanized (LCM),
picked up the platoon and ferried it over to the rest of Company
D.[3] The recombined company patrolled until noon, when it split
up again. Directed back to its night ambush spot, the platoon
sloshed across the river at low tide and spent the afternoon patrolling near a sandy graveyard behind its old positions. Several
soldiers excitedly dug up graves and stuffed bones into their
packs, an act which infuriated their officer. He ordered the graves
covered up and, with several hours of daylight left, ordered the
men into their previous area. During this time someone found
a Sony transistor radio, tuned to a Vietnamese station, dangling
from a bush.

3. The LCM were used widely by the Army for lighterage and inland water-
way traffic. The Army had approximately 150 of these 113-ton aluminum vessels in Vietnam at the time.

One of the platoon's radiomen, a Specialist Fourth Class, mentioned the tree as they hunkered back down beside it. As was standard practice on ambush, no one dug in, but rather crouched or lay behind shrubs. "Well, you're right," the lieutenant replied. "It's sort of an aiming stake." But no one moved. Due to tidal conditions, protective claymore mines were only placed facing one direction, across the stream. The two machine guns were sited as before, with one covering the water and the other right next to the command post at the base of the tree. The exhausted men relaxed in their compact grouping. The last perimeter check the lieutenant made was a half hour before midnight, and he found several soldiers sleeping on guard.

The Viet Cong had carefully surveyed the vicinity during the platoon's absence, and now took advantage of tall grass and bushes for their approach early in the morning of March 9. They also found the singular tree a most convenient reference point, and signaled the attack by slamming a rocket-propelled grenade into it. Hand grenades and automatic rifle fire ripped through the American positions at close range.

"What was that?" the radio specialist on watch exclaimed as the first round exploded against the tree trunk. Dazed, he blurted out again, "What was that?" By now the firing was intense and the lieutenant scrambled past him, telling him to get away from the tree. The specialist could not get to his radio; it was being peppered by enemy bullets. He then noticed that everyone in the command post was either dead or wounded.

The sergeant in charge of rear security was a "shake 'n' bake," like all the squad leaders in the platoon.[4] The blasts of several explosions jarred him awake, and he yelled to return fire. His seven-man squad blazed away with their M16 rifles and M79 grenade launchers, but no one actually saw any Viet Cong. The intensity of the action lasted only ten minutes. It was later obvious to him that the Viet Cong had preselected their targets and had come up so quickly and quietly that the platoon never stood a chance.

The platoon leader awoke to the deafening explosion in the tree, which showered fragments through men and vegetation.

4. "Shake 'n' Bake" was the term popularly describing a sergeant who earned his rank quickly through noncommissioned officer schools or other means with little time overall in the service.

Several grenades sailed into the position, and the platoon sergeant lunged to hurl one back as it spun around on the ground. Still trying to regain his senses, the lieutentant stumbled over to the rear security squad sergeant, whom he noticed was returning fire. He checked another squad next, but most of the men were seriously wounded, including the platoon's Kit Carson scout. Both machine guns were out, and this surprised him, since these were manned by particularly good soldiers with over six months of combat experience behind them.

Then he heard a loud "No, don't!" from the direction of one of the silenced machine gun positions. Hollering at the top of his voice, the lieutenant dove forward and was hit immediately. For fear of hitting possible American survivors, he did not return fire. The Viet Cong had gone forward to finish off the crew before slipping away with the captured weapon. After being hit a second time, he retreated back to a radio and called for helicopter gunships which were overhead in minutes. A later count showed nine M16 rifles also missing.

The attack had lasted only fifteen minutes. The Viet Cong melted away with the approach of rocket-firing, fire-spitting support helicopters. Nine U.S. soldiers lay dead and eleven were wounded, and medical evacuation aircraft worked the next two hours taking them out. The 3d Platoon of Company D was shattered as a combat-effective organization, and the 2d Infantry's 1st Battalion had suffered a sharp reverse. No casualties had been inflicted on the Viet Cong, who were credited with pulling off another classic raid on an ambush position.

When the action was analyzed by Army staff, the lessons were only too clear: the selection of the same site two nights in a row with plenty of opportunity for VC observation in the interval, a command post situated under an obvious point of reference, the bunching of positions exposed to concentrated fire. The real problem was much more ominous—the same mistakes and complacency indicative of untried troops were being made late in the war by experienced officers and men of good, solid American units. Although realistic Vietnam-oriented stateside training had fused with rigorous in-country unit combat courses to produce efficient jungle soldiers by 1969, field performance was being hampered by lowered morale, lack of motivation, and poor leadership.

PART 6

1970–1973

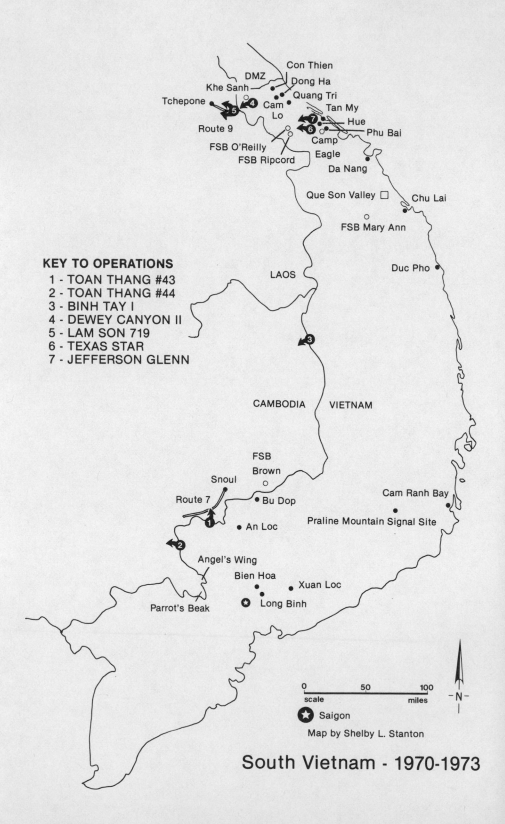

KEY TO OPERATIONS

1 - TOAN THANG #43
2 - TOAN THANG #44
3 - BINH TAY I
4 - DEWEY CANYON II
5 - LAM SON 719
6 - TEXAS STAR
7 - JEFFERSON GLENN

Con Thien
DMZ
Dong Ha
Khe Sanh
Quang Tri
Tchepone
Tan My
Cam Lo
Hue
5   4
Route 9
6   7
Phu Bai
FSB O'Reilly
Camp Eagle
FSB Ripcord
Da Nang

Que Son Valley
Chu Lai
FSB Mary Ann

LAOS
Duc Pho

CAMBODIA   VIETNAM

3

FSB Brown

Snoul
Cam Ranh Bay
Route 7
Bu Dop
1
An Loc
Praline Mountain Signal Site
2
Angel's Wing
Bien Hoa
Xuan Loc
Parrot's Beak
Long Binh

0   50   100
scale   miles

-N-

★ Saigon

Map by Shelby L. Stanton

South Vietnam - 1970-1973

CHAPTER 21.

A CHANGING WAR

1. Cross Border Attack

The year 1970 was marked by the headlong rush to get the South Vietnamese Army into big actions, and the American formations out of the country. Even with U.S. forces withdrawing as rapidly as possible, the actual flow of the war expanded as major offensives were flung into Cambodia and planned for Laos. United States military goals in Vietnam for 1970 were fixed in sharp contrast to those set out in 1965. The top objective, Vietnamization of the war, was seconded by a duty to lower the number of U.S. casualties. Third in importance was the continued withdrawal of forces on schedule, while at the bottom were American combat operations. These were only conducted if designed to "stimulate a negotiated settlement." There was no more mention of military victory. The first two goals were actually intertwined since the casualty rate dropped as the Army became less active due to Vietnamization. The year was to be highlighted by the combined American–South Vietnamese cross-border operations into Cambodia, but characterized elsewhere by decreased and smaller contacts with the NVA/VC.

MACV still possessed a powerful striking force of 330,648 Army soldiers and 55,039 Marines in Vietnam as 1970 began. These were concentrated in eighty-one Army infantry and tank battalions. However, many of these were either preparing to leave the country or expected to in the near future. As a result

335

many units were not actually available for combat during a great part of the year.[1]

By the spring, MACV had several U.S. divisions poised in short range of the Cambodian border, which had been drilling their counterpart ARVN formations in combined offensive maneuvers for over a year. With the exception of the 1st Cavalry Division, these American formations were already programmed to depart Vietnam. The allied command felt ARVN line units were now capable of sustained operations and was willing to put Vietnamization to the crucial test of open battle against the North Vietnamese Army on its own ground.

Several large NVA/VC divisional base areas and support depots were located across the flat expanses of the Cambodian frontier within equally short striking distance of Saigon. They had been used as immune staging and supply points for NVA and VC activity in the south for years, and continued to pose a dangerous threat to South Vietnam's security. Intelligence reports verified recent stockpiling, and it was obvious North Vietnam anticipated renewed employment of these strategic locales in future invasions after American military departure.

MACV believed that a massive joint U.S.-ARVN "spoiling attack" would destroy the bases, gain maximum utilization of American combat assets prior to redeployment, and put Vietnamization to the ultimate test of battle. The American units were envisioned as cracking the tough early-on resistance, making the big depot finds, and providing the necessary support the ARVN forces would initially need. The large South Vietnamese formations that participated in the cross-border assault would be able to savor victory on a grand scale, since the Americans—including advisors—were only going in nineteen miles (thirty kilometers), on a limited time schedule. The ARVN forces would

1. Major U.S. forces in Vietnam in January of 1970 were the 1st Marine, 1st Cavalry (Airmobile), 101st Airborne (Airmobile), 1st, 4th, 23d (Americal), and 25th Infantry Divisions; 1st Brigade, 5th Infantry Division (Mechanized), and 3d Brigade, 9th Infantry Division; 11th Armored Cavalry Regiment; 173d Airborne and 199th Infantry Brigades; 5th Special Forces Group (Airborne); 1st Battalion of the 50th Infantry (Mechanized); 1st and 2d Squadrons of the 1st Cavalry, and 3d Squadron of the 5th Cavalry.

stay and continue to operate as long as required to accomplish the mission.

The primary goal of the Cambodian venture was the eradication of the sanctuaries and destruction of the NVA/VC regular forces defending them. This would free much of South Vietnam from future military danger once the U.S. combat forces had left. Additionally, it had the potential of favorably demonstrating the South Vietnamese Army's ability to challenge even the most critical NVA strongholds. The resulting favorable psychological impact promised great rewards in cementing a new foundation of pride and accomplishment for the South Vietnamese Army. As a collateral bonus, American units would have a tangible objective which would invigorate morale and a sense of mission.

Time was of the essence. The Cambodian border region was a low area, and its grassy fields and rice paddies were subject to swift inundation by monsoon rains. At the beginning of April the scattered, majestic palm trees lining the paddy dikes were starting to bake under the tropical sun. The large NVA headquarters, rest areas, and supply centers were nestled into the jungles, light, leafy forests, and brackish swamps. Mobile operations capable of reaching them could only be conducted in the dry period during April and May.

The South Vietnamese kicked off a preliminary three-day offensive in mid-April against the Angel's Wing. On April 29, several ARVN battalions went into the Parrot's Beak, the tip of the Cambodian land protrusion, located only thirty-five miles from the capital. The results were reminiscent of the frustrating searches through the old Vietnamese lettered war zones, and the NVA proved elusive and cagey. MACV consoled itself with the belief that the large number of overflights and reconnaissance missions, which had preceded the drive, had tipped them off to allied intentions. However, it also served notice that the Cambodian border was no longer inviolable to conventional attack, and the North Vietnamese were quick to pack up in the face of potentially overwhelming offensives.

At daybreak on May 1, 1970, heavy artillery boomed across the Cambodian border as the last bomb from six B-52 bombing runs crashed into the earth. Then the tanks and armored personnel carriers of Maj. Gen. Elvy B. Roberts's 1st Cavalry Division (Airmobile), clanked onto Cambodian soil. Task Force Shoemaker's Operation TOAN THANG #43 had as its objective nothing less than the field command headquarters for all communist activities in South Vietnam.[2]

Overhead the sky was filled with scout helicopters of the 1st Squadron, 9th Cavalry, buzzing over the patches of jungle and rolling landscape. First blood was drawn once they had spotted and destroyed several vehicles below. To the west, fighter-bombers zoomed through plumes of smoke drifting over the grassy plains. An armada of troop helicopters was already ferrying South Vietnamese paratroopers and American cavalrymen of the line battalions inland to pop ahead of the racing armor. Their landing zones were blasted out by colossal, earth-shattering Commando Vault fifteen-thousand-pound bombs. The troops landed and consolidated their positions. All along the front the only resistance was scattered rifle and desultory automatic weapons fire.

The initial impression that Operation TOAN THANG #43 would bring the NVA into open battle soon gave way to the realization that the North Vietnamese were evading again. Large groups of fleeing North Vietnamese troops were spotted by aerial observers throughout the day, and Cobra gunships raced to rocket and strafe them. However, they were already too far ahead to be caught by the allied infantry. The expectations of crushing battlefield victories vaporized as the long-awaited Cambodian incursion became a matter of seizing and destroying massive abandoned supply dumps. The sizes of the depots being uncovered were beyond belief. One depot complex contained so many military stores and foodstuffs that it was promptly dubbed the City. The large storage areas were packed with incredible amounts of

2. Participating forces in Operation TOAN THANG (Total Victory) #43 were the 11th Armored Cavalry (Regiment) and 3d Brigade, 1st Cavalry Division reinforced by the 2d Battalion, 34th Armor (25th Infantry Division), and 2d Battalion, 47th Infantry (9th Infantry Division). The 1st ARVN Armored Cavalry and 3d Brigade, 1st ARVN Airborne Division, composed the South Vietnamese portion of the operation. The task force was named after its commander, Brig. Gen. Robert H. Shoemaker, who was the deputy commander of the 1st Cavalry Division.

new supplies and cargo trucks, neatly arranged and obviously abandoned in a hurry.

Major General Roberts's 1st Cavalry Division had reinforced its commitment to the operation with another brigade, and had thirteen tank and infantry battalions rolling across Cambodia within a week. Col. Donn A. Starry's 11th Armored Cavalry passed through the ARVN lines and attacked straight up Route 7. The tanks and armored personnel carriers raced past a string of rubber plantations at speeds up to forty miles an hour. In the mechanized trek they bridged three unfordable streams, the last after Colonel Starry found a suitable vehicle-launched bridging site by personal reconnaissance. The 2d Squadron smashed into the grubby town of Snoul on May 5 and came under .51-caliber antiaircraft and rocket-propelled grenade fire on the local airstrip. The 3d Squadron joined the battle against the flak positions, which were soon captured after a spectacular battle marred only by the accidental rocketing of forward armored cavalry elements by a Cobra gunship.

Maj. Gen. Edward Bautz Jr.'s 25th Infantry Division advanced its 2d Brigade over the border on May 9 against fragmentary opposition. North Vietnamese rocket and mortar attacks, accompanied by some ground probing, were launched in greater intensity against night defensive bases about a week later. The NVA had regrouped, but overall action remained low because U.S. forces were not going farther than nineteen miles beyond the Vietnamese border. The captured stocks were inventoried and carried out or destroyed, and by June 30 the operation was over. Although finds had been significant, the major communist headquarters had not been neutralized.

The 25th Infantry Division prepared to cross its 1st Brigade into Cambodia on May 6 under Operation TOAN THANG #44. Tactical air power pummeled the border regions, and huge Air Force Commando Vault bombs were again used to blast out helicopter landing zones in the dense jungle. Two battalions were air-assaulted, one into the heart of the base area and one just across the shoreline boundary of the Rach Beng Go River. A float bridge was quickly thrown across and the 2d Battalion, 22d Infantry, roared into Cambodia the next day. Helicopters of the 3d Squadron, 17th Cavalry, were busy gunning down the retreating NVA soldiers as the division advanced west. The only ground action consisted of brief but violent skirmishes between small groups of fast-moving riflemen, and the operation was terminated on May 14.

On May 6, the 1st Cavalry Division leaped into Cambodia on its second thrust by air-assaulting two battalions northeast of Bu Dop. Another huge depot was uncovered, and engineers had to build an overland road so the materials could be hauled out. It took nine days to empty and contaminate this supply area, which was nicknamed Rock Island East. Fire Support Base Brown was attacked May 12. It was defended by the 5th Battalion, 12th Infantry (199th Infantry Brigade), which repelled the determined ground assault, suffering only one fatality. The cavalry division had sent every battalion into the front by the first week in June, and supplies were still being found faster than troops could be provided to eliminate them. Another fire support base was hit by a ground attack in the second week of June. Rocket and mortar bombardments of American positions became general, and on June 20, the 1st Cavalry Division began pulling out.

On May 6, Operation BINH TAY (Tame the West) I, carried out by Maj. Gen. Glenn D. Walker's 4th Infantry Division, reinforced with the 40th ARVN Regiment, marked the third MACV wave of Cambodian assaults. Six devastating B-52 bombing runs preceded the thrust, but the 3d Battalion, 506th Infantry (attached to the division), was driven away from its intended initial landing zone by heavy fire. Other units of the 4th Infantry Division also met fierce receptions at their opening landing zones and were forced to retire. The 3d Battalion of the 8th Infantry ran into trouble after it had put only sixty men on the ground. One helicopter was shot down and two more damaged before the landing could be completed.

In the face of more hot LZs, the division either landed at alternative sites or simply postponed the insertions. Once on the ground there was only one significant firefight, and the soldiers searched out numerous caches. However, after only ten days the Americans bailed out and left the South Vietnamese to continue the operation on their own. There had been a noted lack of divisional aggressiveness in following through with airmobile assaults if opposed by any ground fire. While the division was under the usual MACV restraints on avoiding U.S. losses, the "Funky Fourth" seemed to be suffering from almost total combat paralysis.

All American units were out of Cambodia by June 29, 1970, although several South Vietnamese operations continued. The operation had been militarily successful despite the fact that NVA/VC main force units simply eluded the advancing allies. Large amounts of war booty had been captured or destroyed, buying as much as a year in South Vietnam's survival. Vietnamization was enhanced, but not to the degree that would have been achieved by a solid combat victory. Behind the facade of renewed South Vietnamese military confidence and morale were laid the seeds of South Vietnam's ultimate defeat. Most South Vietnamese units performed in a timid and cautious manner, and overall command and control was still lacking. Much of this lack of ardor could be attributed to its being a new army still unsure of itself on the battlefield. Victory was still directly premised on the ready availability of an umbrella of American air power, something that the ARVN forces would not have in the spring of 1975.

Vietnamization was still proceeding at a rate so rapid that the problems manifested during the Cambodian incursion were virtually ignored. Such deliberate disregard of lessons learned would invite disaster during the following year's Laotian incursion. This crash program to mold the South Vietnamese military overnight into an image of the self-sufficient, highly technical U.S. armed forces was doomed to failure. While MACV insisted on complex units in the ARVN inventory, such as long lines signal battalions, South Vietnamese field units were still experiencing difficulties in basic artillery support coordination.

The Cambodian campaign gave the American Army a welcome relief from routine operations and put a capstone on the service of several units scheduled for pending departure from Vietnam. While American aviation and armor played a vital and aggressive role, many infantry companies avoided combat and were hesitant in moving out to new locations. This was the last combat operation for many participating American units, and there was a considerable effort to minimize losses. Ironically, Maj. Gen.

George W. Casey, who had taken over the 1st Cavalry Division on May 12, was flying on July 7 to visit wounded soldiers when his helicopter crashed, killing all aboard.

2. War at Large

While Cambodia grabbed the headlines, the northern five provinces of the country situated underneath the Demilitarized Zone in Military Region 1 were considered the most dangerous and contained the largest numbers of American troops.[3] On March 9, 1970, the III Marine Amphibious Force was subordinated to the XXIV Corps, since the twenty-five Army maneuver battalions in the region outnumbered the nine remaining Marine battalions. Maj. Gen. Edwin B. Wheeler's 1st Marine Division guarded the greater Da Nang area. During the summer the division lashed out again at the Que Son Valley, silencing it until Marine departure from Vietnam.

While combat continued to decrease through 1970, there were still many violent actions in the region, but they mostly involved South Vietnamese units. The North Vietnamese Army tenaciously defended its mountain fortresses and waged battles throughout the lowlands. Rocket and mortar attacks against cities and isolated fire support bases were common. Fierce fighting flared against an American unit on April 3 when the 1st Brigade of the 5th Infantry Division was hit in defensive positions southwest of Con Thien. The attacks were repulsed with air support. The next morning the night defensive position of the 3d Squadron, 5th Cavalry, near Cam Lo was hit by rocket-propelled grenades and automatic weapons fire. The firefight lasted nearly three hours before the NVA broke off the action. A Sheridan tank and two armored personnel carriers were destroyed, and several other vehicles were damaged.

The Americal Division was engaged in security operations in Quang Ngai Province, and was taking a frustrating number of losses from booby traps and mines, including 250-pound bombs rigged as antitank mines. Just after Maj. Gen. Albert E. Milloy took over the division on March 22, one of the nastier surprise

---

3. On July 2, 1970, the I–IV Corps Tactical Zones were redesignated Military Regions 1–4.

traps was set off. On the afternoon of April 15, a soldier from the 4th Battalion, 3d Infantry, tripped a 105mm artillery shell converted into a booby trap just south of Duc Pho. The resulting explosion caused two 81mm mortar rounds to explode, which in turn caused claymore mines in some of the soldiers' packs to detonate, killing fourteen and wounding another thirty-two.

American military strategy in Vietnam by 1970 hinged on fire support bases, which were self-contained islands of artillery firepower located on critical terrain features. Army units became so reliant on their security that they ceased to operate at any great distance from such artificial fortress islands, a condition dubbed "fire base psychosis." Army mobility and operational flexibility were generally lost as a result.

The fire bases were deceptively efficient. They not only backed up infantry operations but served as ideal observation posts, and were often deliberately set up in remote areas to command approach routes or likely avenues of infiltration. They relied completely on helicopters for their construction, sustenance, and evacuation. Fire support bases were often set up, occupied for a while, and then left. Departure from a fire base was commonly dictated by weather conditions, requirements for resources elsewhere, or NVA activity that exerted more pressure than the fire base was worth. Fire bases closed down were often reopened at later dates, especially if their closures had been determined by monsoon cycles. In some cases they were built with only future occupancy in mind and called Howard Johnsons by the troops. Mobile area warfare required a fluid, flexible system of interlocking fire bases that could be set up or left as circumstances warranted.

Once the site for the future fire support base had been chosen and planned out, the combat engineer party was the first to be inserted. These rugged teams contained six to ten men armed with power saws, demolitions, and other tools. If a helicopter could not set them down, they rappelled in or used rope ladders. In most cases an infantry platoon was assigned as protection. As the force touched down the foot soldiers moved into covering positions, and the engineers fanned out to cut defensive fields of fire and blast out foxholes. Immediately afterwards they would clear a rough landing zone and crater the gun pit areas with explosives to ease future dozer work. Next a Flying Crane helicopter would bring in a mini-dozer, and a Chinook followed, carrying the dozer blade and a drum of diesel fuel. The sweating engineers and infantry would manhandle the blade onto the dozer, which then began clearing the hilltop of debris and carving out the first gun pit. Meanwhile, a combined mini-scooploader/backhoe was helicoptered in to start construction of the earthen ammo berms.

Waiting helicopters were radioed in once the gun pits were dug. The aircraft brought in the first cannoneers with their shells, artillery pieces, and fire direction equipment. The howitzers were set up and often ready to fire within five hours after the assault engineers had first arrived. As the howitzers were emplaced, the mini-dozer and scooploader were busy improving the landing zone, constructing bunkers, and digging trench networks. Soldiers and engineers joined together to string wire and set out mines. Soldiers stationed at a fire base were always toiling at the never-ending job of upgrading the habitability and defensive protection of their fortifications.

Fire Support Base Ripcord was built in April 1970 by the 101st Airborne Division (Airmobile) about twenty-five miles west of Hue in Thua Thien Province. It was a key forward artillery base in the division's summer offensive plans against the A Shau Valley. Like most fire bases, Ripcord was built as part of a network of individually isolated posts which garnered mutual protection because they were within artillery range of each other. On March 13, after delays due to foul weather, Company A of the 2d Battalion, 506th Infantry, air-assaulted onto the future Ripcord hill. As soon as the unit landed, it was struck with intense mortar, automatic weapons, and recoilless rifle fire. The company evacuated the hillsite two days later. On April 1, after another period of bad weather Company B of the same unit air-assaulted onto the hill and was greeted with the same hostile reception. It moved off the hilltop and rejoined the battalion, which was operating close by.

The 506th Infantry's 2d Battalion teamed up with the 1st ARVN Regiment to sweep the vicinity around Fire Support Base Ripcord for the next week. Then Company C went to the top of the hill on April 11. On the same day engineers and the battalion command post were helicoptered in. For five days rain and clouds prevented helicopters from delivering the artillery.

After the guns were brought to the hill, the battalion constructed a fire support base. They worked unmolested until July 1, when daily mortaring and rockets began to bombard them. By that time the positions were solid and impervious to all but the heaviest artillery.

That day the base received a light peppering by mortars, but the next day a nearby night defensive position of the battalion was hit hard by elements of the *803d NVA Regiment,* which used assault rifles, rocket propelled grenades, and satchel charges. It was a bitter firefight with high losses to both sides. Increased barrages and ground movements quickly disclosed North Vietnamese interest in knocking the base out. Fire Support Base Ripcord became the center of attention in Military Region 1 during July.

On July 18, a Chinook helicopter carrying a sling load of howitzer ammunition was shot down by antiaircraft fire while approaching the base. It crashed into the ammunition storage area, triggering an inferno which touched off a series of awesome explosions. Six 105mm howitzers of the 2d Battalion, 319th Artillery, were destroyed and thousands of shells went off. Two recoilless rifles and the counter-mortar radar were lost as well. In the meantime American patrols around the hill were taking considerable losses in a number of sharp skirmishes. It was obvious by July 22 that the NVA were all around Ripcord in force, and another Khe Sanh-like siege was imminent.

Maj. Gen. John J. Hennessey, commanding the 101st Airborne Division (Airmobile), had no choice but to fold up the fire base. Further defense of an artillery post set up to cover a summer operation was foolish in view of the North Vietnamese buildup. Area warfare doctrine called for extraction. During the night of July 22–23, over 2,200 rounds of artillery pounded the adjacent hills and valleys. Navy, Air Force, and Marine fighter-bombers began flying seventy strikes commencing at daybreak on July 23. Fourteen Chinook helicopters dashed in to begin lifting out the 2d Battalion, 506th Infantry.

Everything went smoothly at first, but at 7:40 A.M. antiaircraft fire scored against one of the helicopters. It crashed into the fire base and began to burn and explode, preventing the other helicopters from lifting out the rest of the artillery and heavy equipment. The infantry was being slowly pulled out by Huey helicopters. The heavy mortaring forced them to dart in one at a time to pick up the soldiers. The Ripcord extraction claimed four more Chinooks, shot up so badly they had to be scrapped, and another four were heavily damaged. Fire Support Base Ripcord was left abandoned to the North Vietnamese at 2:07 P.M., July 23, 1970.

Just northwest of Fire Support Base Ripcord was Fire Support Base O'Reilly, which was on top of a critical mountain in Thua Thien Province eleven miles west of Hue. Beginning on August 6, 1970, NVA rockets and mortars increased the tempo of their attacks on O'Reilly, and by September 13 the fire base had sustained ninety-two barrages. The hilltop resembled a moonscape. Since this was the area of operations of the 1st ARVN Regiment, it had a battalion guarding the American howitzers. The North Vietnamese attacked uphill on September 9 on a probing mission. Four days later another assault was launched.

At this time a tactical emergency was declared, and 137 tactical air missions were flown to pulverize the area around it. Nineteen B-52 bombing missions were flown to pound the North Vietnamese further off. Soon four battalions of South Vietnamese infantry were flown in to the hilltop, but bad weather commenced on September 15. Dense clouds and thunderstorms could easily cut off the fire support base, and already a number of nearby fire bases were being closed down due to the monsoon storms. Fire Support Base O'Reilly was abandoned accordingly on October 7, 1970. Typhoons Kate and Louise wreaked havoc in the latter part of the year, and heavy monsoon rains curtailed activities throughout Military Region 1 during the last two months of the year.

3. An Army in Transition

Withdrawal during 1970 accelerated at a dizzying speed, taking out formations that had served so long in Vietnam that they seemed an indelible part of that tropical landscape. Now at last they were coming home. The "Big Red One" 1st Infantry Di-

vision left the 5th ARVN Division in charge of its territory north
of Saigon and went back to Fort Riley, Kansas. There it swapped
pennants with the 24th Infantry Division to fill up again with
new soldiers, draftees who would probably never see combat.
The shadow of the "Ivy" 4th Infantry Divison never fell again
over the woods it had left in Washington state. It turned over
the Central Highlands to the 22d ARVN Division, and by December had assumed a new posting near the foot of the Rockies
at Fort Carson, Colorado.

The "Tropic Lightning" 25th Infantry Division gave its Cambodian border sector to the 25th ARVN Division and went back
to its halcyon Hawaiian station. There Schofield Barracks patiently waited for its return from the latest of three overseas
wars. The 199th Infantry Brigade, formed in the dust and heat
of the big Vietnam buildup, reappeared at Fort Benning, Georgia, like a denizen. Its flag was folded up and its combat journals, faded with the sun and mildew of a thousand days of patrolling the rice paddies around Saigon, were sent to the
underground records vaults at Suitland, Maryland.

The last brigade of the 9th Infantry Division returned and
passed into temporary oblivion. Later the Army would reraise
the 9th at Fort Lewis, Washington, but time had molded a new
Army filled with volunteer men and women on the leading edge
of modern warfare concepts. The 9th would become an advanced test bed as the first Army High Technology Light Division. Its Vietnam days of riverine combat and sniper teams
seemed as ancient as the Union riverine expeditions of the
Cumberland River during the Civil War. The 7th and 26th Marine Regimental Landing Teams also came home in 1970, the
latter to be scrubbed and the former to assume a new role in
national defense. It relocated to Panama in mid-1972 as the first
Marine regiment outside the United States in the post-Vietnam
era.

For those units that remained, the war was typified by protective security and static defensive missions as levels of combat
throughout the country dropped off and more South Vietnamese
units assumed offensive field operations. These military tasks included guarding installations, towns, and roads. However, many
troop units were still actively engaged in high-intensity combat

sweeps and mobile reconnaissance efforts to detect NVA/VC forces before they could reach such areas. Infantry and tank forces were backed up by an array of artillery, tactical airpower, and massed B-52 bombing raids which could deliver overwhelming concentrations of firepower on any threatened battlefield.

The American Army of 1970 in Vietnam was unraveling like the war around it, and morale and discipline were steadily deteriorating. With the loss of offensive combat missions, units were withdrawn into enclaves on the coast or into populated areas where they began processing for return to the United States. Boredom and corruption manifested themselves in increased crime rates, drug use, and racial tension. The Army tried to ease problems with a more tolerant attitude toward troop concerns. The previous seven-day rest and recreation (R & R) vacations to selected Oriental and Australian cities, permitted once during a combat tour, were extended to two weeks and included visits to the United States.

The front-line soldiers of the 1970 Army in Vietnam were still tough, young, and lean. The Army did not experience breakdowns in unit cohesion until the final withdrawal period of 1971–72. The Cambodian incursion, as predicted, gave a renewed sense of purpose to the soldiers. There they could be seen advancing with M60 machine guns strapped over their shoulders to hang at hip-level, their jungle fatigue shirts open in the sweltering heat to expose fashionable peace beads or religious chains dangling across chests caked in dust and polished with sweat, with cut-down "bush hats" crunched over long hair that was tolerated as a front-line privilege. Line units were composed of men in excellent fighting trim, who exhibited great courage, resourcefulness, and dedication. Their insular unit scoffing (Electric Strawberry instead of Tropic Lightning, or Puking Buzzards instead of Screaming Eagles) turned to fierce fraternal pride when they were confronted by outsiders. Since Vietnam was a "frontless" area war, many soldiers outside the traditional combat branches shared the deep pride of battle-tested loyalty, from truck drivers in the long-haul convoys to signalmen on remote mountaintop relay sites. Perhaps some of the most dangerous duty during the war was that performed by advisors, combat engineers, and explosive ordnance disposal teams.

However, overall Army combat efficiency was continuing to slip compared to its record of performance prior to 1969. Added to the adverse impact generated by personnel discontinuity and loss of battle experience as a result of the one-year tour limit, was the ugly stain of combat disobedience. In the elite 1st Cavalry Division (Airmobile), a unit carefully nurtured by the 90th Replacement Battalion to represent the better side of soldiering, there had been thirty-five instances during 1970 of refusal to fight. Some had involved entire units.

The ingredient necessary to check the Army's decline, good leadership, was conspicuously absent. Senior officer attention was on the latest buzzword: Vietnamization. During the years of troop buildup and big battles, the prestige and promotions inherent in American unit assignments had taken many good officers and sergeants away from advisor duty. By 1970, however, the emphasis was back on the advisory role as the crucial instrument of Vietnamization. Army advisors were being assigned in increasing numbers to modernize all facets of the ARVN structure, from line battalions to logistical training schools. The American Army was competing for the same leadership resources, but coming in second behind the Army of the Republic of Vietnam.

The site of the Viet Cong raid on the ambush position set out by the 1st Battalion, 2d Infantry, on March 9, 1969. (Author's Collection)

Aerial view of Phu Hoa Dong village which was cordoned off by the 1st Infantry Division during September 15–26, 1969, and discussed in Chapter 20. (Author's Collection)

Armored Personnel Carriers from the 11th Armored Cavalry push toward Snoul inside Cambodia, spearheaded by M551 Sheridan reconnaissance vehicles. (U.S. Army)

The 11th Armored Cavalry Regiment rolls into Snoul against scattered resistance on May 5, 1970. (U.S. Army)

Fire Support Base Ripcord, the beleaguered 101st Airborne Division artillery base finally abandoned to the North Vietnamese Army on July 23, 1970. (Author's Collection)

Typical late-war fire support base of the 101st Airborne Division in Military Region 1 of Vietnam's rugged interior. These came to represent the final static bastions of American combat presence in that country. (Author's Collection)

Buddhist religious rites bless new 175mm guns before they are added to the arsenal of the 1st ARVN Division on November 15, 1971. (Author's Collection)

United States Army instructors supervise basic training of South Vietnamese Regional Force soldiers at Cat Lai. (U.S. Army)

CHAPTER 22.

AN ARMY DEPARTS THE WAR

1. Into Laos

The destruction of the Cambodian dumps had already paid handsome dividends in lowered NVA activity level throughout Military Region 3, and MACV was now planning a Parthian shot at an even bigger prize. In order to gain the most combat mileage from remaining American formations, a hasty plan was thrown together using American aviation and artillery resources to bolster a South Vietnamese drive into the Laotian panhandle before withdrawal made the U.S. supporting assets unavailable. A staged series of attacks would bring a powerful combined force to the Laotian border. From there the South Vietnamese would drive across to destroy stockpiles of war materials being staged in the Tchepone vicinity.

The chance for success seemed bright, and a swift blow to NVA war stocks accumulated in Laos would also bring increased combat experience and confidence to the South Vietnamese military. Planners were optimistic that this thrust, like the Cambodian incursion, would be lightly opposed. Since vehicles and aircraft required dry season conditions, and American withdrawals would leave little left by next dry season, nothing could be postponed. The rush impelled by impending American departure, coupled with the desire for secrecy, gave units extremely

350

short fuses for planning purposes. When the South Vietnamese went onto Laotian soil, for the first time American advisors would not be on the ground with them. Since the advisors were the conduits of essential air support, Vietnamese military interpreters were placed in each forward air control team and center.

The plan called for the Americans to open Route 9 to the border. A South Vietnamese armored drive would then roll down Route 9 toward Tchepone. Inside Laos, the dirt road followed the east-west Xe Pon River through a narrow valley littered with boulders and rocky outcroppings and hemmed in by high, jungled mountains. The flanks of the road advance were to be covered by a number of airmobile, leapfrogging fire support bases to be established by South Vietnamese paratroopers helicoptered on the north side, and airmobile infantry paralleling the road to the south. An abundance of American airlift and aerial fire support, as well as the reinforced 108th Artillery Group, was made available.[1]

While no specific mention was made of termination dates, it was generally understood that the ARVN troops would scour the area and clean out caches until the start of the rainy season in early May. Tchepone was only an intermediate objective, because a further advance would be necessary to actually reach the main North Vietnamese logistical complexes. Serious resistance was not expected; if fighting was required, the terrain past Tchepone meant pushing uphill through dense jungle and thorny bamboo thickets against probable bunker lines.

The preliminary phase was the American Operation DEWEY CANYON II, designed to make Route 9 passable for heavy traffic all the way to the Laotian frontier. In the predawn darkness of January 30, the mechanized 1st Brigade, 5th Infantry Division, moved an armored cavalry-engineer task force down the roadway toward Khe Sanh. A dozer led the column with its head-

1. The U.S. ground forces engaged in direct support of LAM SON 719 were the 108th Artillery Group (four battalions); 45th Engineer Group (two battalions); 101st Airborne Division with 3d Brigade reinforced with an engineer task force, and 1st Brigade in reserve; 101st Aviation Group (six battalions); 1st Brigade of the 5th Infantry Division reinforced with two mechanized, one cavalry, one tank, and one airmobile infantry battalions; and the 11th Infantry Brigade of the Americal Division with two infantry battalions.

lights on full beam. The column soon had large numbers of 14th Engineer Battalion soldiers tearing out obstacles and toiling over bridges and culverts. The brigade's infantry helicoptered into the Khe Sanh area after daybreak, while armored personnel carriers of the 1st Squadron, 1st Cavalry, raced up to reconnoiter the border. By February 5, the road was secured behind them.

The engineers were also active hacking a secondary pioneer road from mountainside cliffs paralleling Route 9, which was nicknamed Red Devil Road. The brigade protected the tracked, self-propelled long-range guns of the 108th Artillery Group, which began moving toward their forward support sites. The 101st Airborne Division (Airmobile) launched a feint assault into the dreaded A Shau Valley. The preliminary stage of the offensive was going extremely well, and signs were bright for a splendid confirmation of Vietnamization on the Laotian venture.

At 7:00 A.M. on a misting February 8, 1971, after a massive artillery bombardment and eleven B-52 bombing missions, the cross-border attack began. The South Vietnamese armor rumbled into Laos against light resistance, churning around the ditches and craters in the roadbed. American helicopters ranged the mountains destroying guns and vehicles. Helicopters of the 158th Aviation Battalion with paratroopers of the ARVN Airborne Division set down at their first landing zones, as the 223d Aviation Battalion carried in a regiment of the 1st ARVN Division. Poor weather usually ruled out morning airlifts, but the drive was only lightly opposed, casualties were few, and the westward road march seized many of the initial objectives.

Air cavalry in the meantime was inflicting massive damage on staging depots, weapons sites, and moving troop columns, but the nature of the territory and weather impeded target destruction. The highly mobile and modern North Vietnamese antiaircraft system was very active and was causing considerable difficulties. Helicopter missions flew in the face of intensive air defense fire which demanded that even single resupply helicopters be escorted by armed gunships. Lt. Col. Robert F. Molinelli's 2d Squadron of the 17th Cavalry was soon spotting so many tanks that it was running out of ammunition before it could strike them all. On February 18, his helicopters exploded two giant petroleum pipelines, sending balls of flame shooting high into the air.

Then the outer flanks of the advance started to come under counterattack. The 39th ARVN Ranger Battalion was mauled in a savage battle on February 19, and fire support bases were subjected to heavy antiaircraft, artillery, and rocket fire. Tank-supported North Vietnamese infantry stormed Fire Support Base Delta in another violent attack on February 25, and all dreams of easy conquest quickly faded. It was going to be a hard fight. South Vietnamese morale was still high as the offensive continued to grind toward Tchepone. With ARVN troops grimly hanging on to the outer fire bases, and combat sharply escalating, it was decided to slam into Tchepone before momentum was lost. On March 3, a battalion of the 1st ARVN Division was air-assaulted into a landing zone near Tchepone with the loss of eleven helicopters shot down and forty-four more hit by ground fire. Three days later the 2d ARVN Regiment airmobiled into the ruined ghost town of Tchepone, but there was only sporadic gunfire.

Good flying weather and further discoveries of several supply caches presented good reasons for the ARVN units to search out the area, but they were ready to leave on March 7. The determined North Vietnamese defense ruled out further advances toward the supply belt of the Ho Chi Minh Trail. Sustained artillery barrages were already threatening the continued existence of several fire support bases, and there were signs of more NVA reserves massing to counterattack. Since Tchepone had been reached, President Thieu could claim political victory.

One of the most difficult tactical maneuvers in war is orderly withdrawal under heavy enemy pressure. This is the true mark of a professional army, but the quickest undoing of an unfinished one. Vietnamization had come too fast, with too little foundation, ever to give the South Vietnamese military a chance at executing an organized pullback under such perilous circumstances. The withdrawal became a disorderly retreat, and finally collapsed into an uncontrolled rout. The fate of rear guards was typified by the early experience of a 1st ARVN Infantry Regiment battalion annihilated along the river while engaged in a covering assignment. As spirits plunged, other units fought less well, or simply ran away.

The March 19 ambush of an armored convoy on the road set panic in motion. Tanks, engineer equipment, and artillery howitzers were abandoned. Helicopter gunships were desperately called in to destroy the vehicles before they fell into North Vietnamese hands. The Vietnamese armor was too restricted by terrain to maneuver adequately, and suffered the devastating consequences. The next day U.S. fighter-bombers, B-52 strategic bombers, and helicopter gunships made thousands of sorties into the skies to lend all possible support. One battalion of the 2d ARVN Regiment was lifted out, but twenty-eight of the forty helicopters were damaged in its extraction. Plans to lift out another regimental battalion were aborted when the first helicopter was exploded making the approach.

The VNMC battalions were hanging on to several fire bases by their fingernails, and only the heroics of Army helicopters of the 14th Aviation Battalion kept them supplied with ammunition. Route 9 was now littered with abandoned vehicles, and the fleeing armored force had to break jungle to get back into Vietnam. The "elite" ARVN Airborne Division, the showpiece of Vietnamization, performed so miserably that it not only lost key fire bases, but utterly failed in its flank security mission on the way out. The Vietnamese Marines abandoned several critical areas after halfhearted resistance, and were unable to control their elements. Panic seized several marines and paratroopers defending bases to the rear, and Army helicopters became mobbed.

Only the bold, decisive use of American air power enabled the South Vietnamese forces to reach Tchepone and get back. Helicopters provided cover overhead, resupplied ammunition, and retrieved survivors by flying through a wall of flak. In the process, ninety-two aircraft were lost and over six hundred damaged. Twenty-five Commando Vault bombs were used to break up NVA troop concentrations and to cut landing zones.

For the Saigon regime, the projected victory of LAM SON 719 turned out to be a sour defeat, exposing grave deficiencies in planning, organization, leadership, motivation, and operational expertise. The absence of calm, reasoned leadership canceled the tactical proficiency and gallant service of some individual ARVN units. Operation LAM SON 719 was a dismal failure that boded poorly for future encounters with the able NVA light infantry and tanks. Vietnamization had not brought the South Vietnamese military to the point where it could safely challenge NVA-defended base territory.

2. "Dynamic Defense"

The Laotian offensive of 1971, like the Cambodian incursion of 1970, dominated the military history of the year. MACV contained fifty-four American infantry and tank battalions when the year started, but most of these would shortly stand down in an exit posture.[2] Most of its 330,648 Army soldiers and 25,394 Marines would spend the year helping prepare their units for the KEYSTONE series of redeployment operations. Only the unit flags were being sent home in most cases; a lot of closeout paperwork and equipment and property to be transferred to the South Vietnamese remained.

Throughout 1971 there was little action inside South Vietnam as the withdrawal continued. Some hunting expeditions were managed by the 101st Airborne Division (Airmobile) against NVA forces in the rugged Vietnamese frontier regions, but the latter remained too evasive for meaningful contact. The NVA units were still suffering from the combined Cambodian-Laotian shocks and making only a few highly selective rocket and mortar attacks. In Military Region 3, American contacts with the NVA were fleeting, except for encounters against bunker complexes, and it was obvious the NVA was avoiding Americans as a matter of policy.

MACV stretched remaining combat assets through the final years of American redeployment by implementing another important strategic change. The area warfare concept of "tactical

2. Major U.S. forces in Vietnam in January 1971 were the 1st Cavalry Division (Airmobile), 23d Infantry (Americal) Division, 101st Airborne Division (Airmobile), 1st Marines, 5th Marines, 1st Brigade of the 5th Infantry Division (Mechanized), 2d Brigade of the 25th Infantry Division, 173d Airborne Brigade, 11th Armored Cavalry Regiment, 5th Special Forces Group (Airborne), and three separate battalions: 1st Squadron, 1st Cavalry; 3d Squadron, 5th Cavalry; and 1st Squadron, 10th Cavalry.

areas of responsibility" was modified. These had always diluted available U.S. assets by requiring constant sweeping and patrolling of large slices of countryside. The campaign plan of 1971 gave American commanders "tactical areas of interest" instead, which allowed them to focus on specific trouble spots. Vietnamization enabled territorial forces and ARVN line units to assume wider defense responsibilities in the larger regions assigned to the remaining Army and Marine units. The American soldiers noticed the change as their formerly far-ranging patrols were scaled down, and more South Vietnamese troops became visible stalking the brush.

After the LAM SON 719 campaign, the 101st Airborne Division (Airmobile) gradually disengaged from direct contact with North Vietnamese Army units in the jungled western regions, in consonance with the decreasing combat role of U.S. units. The division was actively engaged in Operation JEFFERSON GLENN, a long-term effort which had begun in September of 1970. Three battalions established a series of fire bases around the coastal lowlands of Thua Thien Province. At the end of July, the operation was renamed OPORD 13-70, and it was terminated on October 8, 1971, as the last major American ground combat operation.

The main scope of ground activity for U.S. units was concentrated in patrolling and sweeping the rocket belts of various critical installations. Rocket belts were strips of land from which the NVA/VC could launch barrages into the cities. This security role was dubbed "dynamic defense" by the Army, and by the end of the year all U.S. formations had been phased into this new mission near critical installation complexes.

In early March, the 5th Special Forces Group (Airborne) officially returned to Fort Bragg, North Carolina. Most of its personnel actually remained in South Vietnam. They were absorbed into a number of special units raised quickly to train the latest foreign army (from Cambodia), and continued conducting reconnaissance missions and raids under MACV's special operations group.

The "Blackhorse" 11th Armored Cavalry Regiment began preparations to leave South Vietnam in the first week of February and departed during March. The 14th Armored Cavalry

Regiment, on German frontier duty, was retitled as the new 11th, now oriented toward "modern" urban and mechanized warfare. By 1971 the Army had begun readjusting all its training and emphasis back toward the traditional European battlefield. It was rapidly extricating itself from Southeast Asia and seeking a return to the former worldwide responsibilities and status it had enjoyed prior to the big Vietnam buildup in 1965. However, the disengagement was made with great difficulty.

The Army had become extremely permissive as it tried to cope with changing societal attitudes, and standards of soldiering eroded proportionately. In Vietnam serious disciplinary problems resulted in disintegrating unit cohesion and operational slippages. In the field, friendly fire accidents became more prevalent as more short rounds and misplaced fire were caused by carelessness. There was an excessive number of "accidental" shootings and promiscuous throwing of grenades, some of which were deliberate fraggings aimed at unpopular officers, sergeants, and fellow enlisted men. Redeploying units gave vent to years of frustration as their speeding army vehicles tore down the frequently ambushed highways, shooting and hurling rocks, cans, and insults at the Vietnamese alongside the roads.

Widespread breakdowns in troop discipline forced the military police into a front-line role serving as assault troops against other soldiers. These actions were typified by two instances. Composite military police Whiskey Mountain Task Force was engaged in a rather spectacular standoff on September 25, 1971. Fourteen soldiers of the 35th Engineer Group had barricaded themselves in a bunker and were holding out with automatic weapons and machine guns. A homemade explosive device was exploded in the rear of the bunker, and all fourteen surrendered and were treated for wounds. Chinook helicopters had them in Long Binh Stockade the next day. A month later, on October 27, 1971, another military police strike force air-assaulted onto the Praline Mountain signal site near Dalat. Two fragmentation grenades had been used in an attempt to kill the company commander two nights in a row. Initial escorts had proved insufficient protection, and military police had to garrison the mountaintop for a week until order was restored.

MACV launched its Drug Abuse Counteroffensive in the

summer of 1971. On June 17, President Nixon announced that the military effort in the drug program, as part of the national effort, would include the identification of heroin users in Vietnam. By early July, Army sampling surveys disclosed high usage rates in many Vietnam-based units. Drug Treatment or Rehabilitation centers were established in all regions. On July 7, the Army began testing units rotating back to the United States, and on August 1 expanded the testing to cover amphetamines and barbiturates. A secure drug abuse holding center was placed into operation at Long Binh on September 24 for recidivist drug abusers.

The military police were soon stretched thin guarding the facilities. For example, on June 21, the 6th Convalescent Center established a Drug Treatment Center at Cam Ranh Bay. By mid-August, the 97th Military Police Battalion had to be reinforced, and finally the separate 127th Military Police Company was permanently assigned. It was charged with protecting the lives of volunteer patients and medical staffers, preventing the entry of drugs and other contraband, stopping unlawful exits prior to detoxification, and maintaining order at the center. Static guard posts had to be manned along all fence lines, and police armaments at gate entrances were increased to shotguns and submachine guns. The company guarded messing areas, occupied patient wards at night, and built a separation ward with one- and two-man cells.

Lowered troop morale and discipline were manifested in increased crime, racial clashes, mutinous disregard of orders, antiwar protests, and monetary corruption in black market currency exchanges, as well as drug use. At the same time, some units tightened control and actually improved combat efficiency. The separate 2d Brigade, 25th Infantry Division, and the two withdrawing brigades of the 1st Cavalry Division (Airmobile), continued to function brilliantly from February through March, up to the very day of their withdrawal from the jungle to their base camps for stand-down. In the last nine days before stand-down, with every man in the battalion knowing the exact date, the 1st Battalion of the 5th Cavalry fought fifteen skirmishes with the NVA.

The 2d Brigade of the 25th Infantry Division rejoined its

parent division on Hawaii in April, the same month that the bulk of the 1st Cavalry Division (Airmobile) departed for Fort Hood, Texas. There the famed First Team was transformed into a test "triple capability" (Tricap) division composed of a mix of armor, helicopters, and infantry. The division left behind the very large seven thousand-man 3d Brigade in Vietnam, which became separately assigned to II Field Force, Vietnam, on the last day of March (passing to direct U.S. Army, Vietnam, control on April 14, 1971). It was charged with operational security of northeastern Military Region 3, encompassing the arc of Binh Tuy, Long Khanh, and Phuoc Tuy provinces around Xuan Loc.

The NVA was already stepping up activity in Military Region 1. A devastating 122mm rocket bombardment pulverized Fire Support Base Charlie 2 in Quang Tri Province, causing a large number of U.S. losses. Three separate attacks were made against Da Nang during the first week in June, accentuating the reduced security following the final departure of the 1st Marine Division. The first major Army unit to deploy from the region was the 1st Brigade of the 5th Infantry Division (Mechanized), at Quang Tri just south of the DMZ. It was notified on June 12, 1971, that it was going home and immediately began the difficult job of disengaging while still subject to front-line action against the NVA. Hard work and close scheduling enabled it to make a smooth break from combat and to transfer over one hundred miles to Da Nang for exit from Vietnam by the end of August. The new 3d ARVN Division, formed in October, took over its sector. The brigade rejoined its parent division, which had moved to Fort Polk, Louisiana.

The unfortunate Americal Division was folded down in Vietnam at the end of November, still in disgrace over its latest fiasco, the Fire Support Base Mary Ann incident, with its commanding general and several other officers being recommended for punitive action. Fire Support Base Mary Ann had been hit on March 22, 1971, southwest of Tam Ky in Quang Tin Province. The 196th Infantry Brigade's 1st Battalion of the 46th Infantry failed to safeguard the perimeter, enabling fifty North Vietnamese Army soldiers to overrun the outpost. They roamed through the fire base, destroying one 155mm howitzer and damaging another, throwing satchel charges in the command bunker, knifing Americans in their sleeping bags, and wrecking the communications equipment. They killed and wounded nearly half the 250 soldiers there, who got only ten in exchange because they were cringing in their bunkers. After the defeat, the acting battalion commander flew into a rage and had five NVA bodies burned in the trash dump. General Westmoreland personally took over the investigation and found there was clear dereliction of duty, lax defensive posture with officers not in charge. Army Secretary Resor took formal disciplinary action against six officers, including the division and assistant division commanders.

For most of the year the Americal's 11th Infantry Brigade continued dynamic defense operations in conjunction with the 2d ARVN Division. During August it attempted to locate the Quang Ngai VC provincial headquarters without success. At the same time, the division's 198th Infantry Brigade was placed in a dynamic defense status inside the rocket belt area around Chu Lai. The 196th Infantry Brigade was selected to occupy the area adjacent to Da Nang, which had been vacated by III Marine Amphibious Force early in the year.

The Americal Division was so jinxed that it could not even turn over its huge Chu Lai base to the 2d ARVN Division without severe damage. The base camp took the brunt of Typhoon Hester on October 23. The surprise storm was the worst experienced by Vietnam in twenty-seven years. It flattened half the buildings and destroyed the airfield "typhoon-proof" hangars, along with most of the divisional helicopters. These had been desperately needed by the 11th Aviation Group. Once the Americal Division was shut down, XXIV Corps chose to retain the 196th Infantry Brigade as a separate dynamic defense guard force for the Da Nang rocket belt.

In Military Region 2, "The Herd" 173d Airborne Brigade, left the country in August and was inactivated in January of 1972. This elite formation, retained as a fully qualified paratrooper unit throughout its Vietnam service, had long represented the best in American fighting spirit. It had been the first Army combat brigade into the country, and its departure hastened the realization that the American Army was in full retreat from the Vietnam War.

3. An Army Retreats

A major three-pronged, six-divisional North Vietnamese invasion was made into South Vietnam at the end of March 1972, and became known as the Nguyen Hue Offensive. It raged through Quang Tri Province, smashed into Kontum, and stabbed toward Saigon. The Battle of Quang Tri itself commenced on April 27, and by May 1 most U.S. advisors were evacuated by helicopter, although eighteen elected to stay with their South Vietnamese units. Quang Tri was taken later that evening, and the entire province was in NVA hands the following day. While U.S. Marine and Army helicopters saw extensive action, and American installations at Da Nang were severely rocketed, U.S. ground forces were prohibited from participation. The 196th Infantry Brigade was rushed up to reinforce Phu Bai and Tan My, but it was not in good disciplinary shape. Morale was low, and on April 12 a company of its 2d Battalion, 1st Infantry, refused to conduct a patrol into the hills around Phu Bai. Finally, after a lot of pleading and cajoling, the company conducted its mission.

The shattered 3d ARVN Division was rebuilt at Phu Bai as the 1st ARVN Division counterattacked into Quang Tri Province on May 5. The ARVN Marine Division conducted amphibious and airmobile insertions, and by the first week in July the ARVN Airborne Division had reached Quang Tri city. A prolonged battle ensued, with organized NVA resistance inside the Quang Tri Citadel finally crushed by South Vietnamese paratroopers and marines on September 15. The North Vietnamese had still gained a considerable chunk of territory south of the DMZ and retained possession of Dong Ha and the old Marine Route 9 defensive lines.

The North Vietnamese also won a major victory in the Kontum Battles and entrenched their forces in the northern Central Highlands. The NVA offensive northwest of Saigon had been blunted during the three-month siege of An Loc. The main assault on An Loc, May 10–15, was broken by massed American B-52 and tactical air strikes and helicopter gunships. Losses had been heavy, and Brig. Gen. Richard J. Tallman was killed by artillery there July 9, while visiting to finalize plans for relieving the 5th ARVN Division with the 18th ARVN Division.

The U.S. Army continued to pull out throughout the midst of the Nguyen Hue Offensive, and it was apparent that Washington now considered the war a Vietnamese affair. The "Screaming Eagles" 101st Airborne Division (Airmobile), began its redeployment from Vietnam in November of 1971 and closed rapidly out of Da Nang just prior to the NVA invasion. The division formed a self-sufficient security force to cover its own withdrawal. This "roll-up force" turned over Camp Eagle and outlying protective firebases to the 1st ARVN Division and hurriedly passed through Phu Bai. The division was reduced to one color-bearing battalion-sized increment, which departed Vietnam in March and returned to Fort Campbell, Kentucky.

Most of the men from the 101st Airborne Division were actually sent south to the separate 3d Brigade of the 1st Cavalry Division. During January and February that brigade absorbed an average of five hundred soldiers a week and pushed them through its Combat Training Center, regardless of "bush time," for shipment to field units. The unit was still seeing some scattered action. On January 3, 1972, in a skirmish northeast of Xuan Loc, the airmobile cavalry reaction force, gunships, and medical evacuation helicopters all received heavy fire. Later that month the brigade was tapered to five thousand men and relinquished control of its operational area to the 18th ARVN Division. The 1st Cavalry Division's 3d Brigade was assigned the dynamic defense mission of securing the critical Bien Hoa–Long Binh–Saigon rocket belt.

The United States had been engaged in secret negotiations to end the war since August 1969, a period marked by increased governmental stress on the urgency of disengagement and the general decline of the American Army. President Nixon made these negotiations public on January 25, 1972, and remaining Army combat elements were hastened out of Vietnam. The 3d Brigade of the 1st Cavalry Division departed on June 26, only a week past the resumption of the Paris discussions to end the war. The 196th Infantry Brigade in the northern part of the country was closed down three days later. Both left small garrison battalions which redeployed that August. The 3d Battalion of the 21st Infantry and the 1st Battalion of the 7th Cavalry, which departed within a day of each other, thus happened to be the last American infantry battalions to serve in Vietnam.

The 1st Battalion of the 7th Cavalry remained in Vietnam until August 22, 1972. On that day the battalion colors were carefully furled and placed on an outbound plane for Texas. The flag was draped with campaign streamers harking all the way back to a hot summer day in June of 1876 when its troopers had fallen at the Little Big Horn River during Custer's Last Stand. Intermingled with the dazzling array of multi-colored ribbons representing its service in a half dozen wars, were five silken blue Presidential Unit Citation streamers awarded for highest valor on the battlefield. One was embroidered simply PLEIKU PROVINCE, 23 OCTOBER–26 NOVEMBER 1965. The band of silk represented the terror-filled, searing tropical day when Lt. Col. Harold G. Moore's cavalrymen hurled back wave after wave of NVA infantry at Landing Zone X-Ray in the Ia Drang Valley of the Central Highlands—one of the first big battles fought so valiantly by a rising American Army.

The Paris Agreement, designed to settle the war, was signed January 27, 1973. Accordingly, all American Army presence in Vietnam was terminated at the end of March. Two years later a major NVA invasion overran the south, and the Republic of Vietnam ceased to exist as a nation on April 30, 1975.

4. Conclusion

In 1965, twenty years after the great allied victories of World War II, and just ten years after checking the advance of a hostile army into South Korea, the United States committed its regular ground forces to safeguard an ally in Southeast Asia.

The Regular Army and Marine Corps of 1965 represented the active tip of a much larger potential national ground military machine. Behind this battle-ready crust of front-line forces were the National Guard and Reserve components, which had been programmed to provide the necessary round-out and backup in case of war. While the latter did not represent the instant fighting capability of the main force armed forces, they were counted on to serve as a training base in case of required expansion and to provide certain critical support elements.

The United States government, for domestic political reasons, never mass-mobilized its reserves to fulfill this intended role. The country's active armed forces were sent into Vietnam and forced to expand quickly to meet the increasing requirements for more troops. The resulting rapid expansion placed such severe strain on limited technical, logistical, and leadership personnel, that the American Army became seriously impaired in its ability to carry out its combat missions.

The American Army of 1965 was headstrong with confidence, sharply honed to a lethal fighting edge by years of service on the brink of global war and national crises, and well equipped with modern weapons. Spearheaded by an elite Special Forces and advisory effort on the forefront of international "New Frontier" policies, it was eager to field-test its newly acquired wings of airmobility. When the armed forces were sent to South Vietnam they had the relatively limited, simple objective of providing a shield of protection while the South Vietnamese Army was rebuilt. This initial military objective was fulfilled, and in 1968 and 1969 a rejuvenated ARVN reentered the main battlefield.

Once in Vietnam, the American Army began to pursue a policy of defeating the NVA and VC forces throughout the country. This objective was hampered by the territorial confines of the war, since United States ground forces were prohibited from striking outside South Vietnam's borders. The NVA and main force VC were able to escape battlefield annihilation and retain intact supply channels through their access to cross-border maneuver. This self-imposed restraint effectively negated any possibility of conventional military victory.

America's military objective in Vietnam was now directed toward defeat of the NVA/VC through combat attrition. This required more and more battalions, which the armed forces could not provide without increased draft calls. In the meantime, the government failed to declare a war, minimizing the real emergency, or explain its goals in Vietnam to the American public. The draft system safeguarded the affluent from the burden of military service, and the Army increasingly came to represent the poorer and more disadvantaged segments of society. The Army's own expansion and its insistence on the luxury of elite units diluted available leadership resources. Although logistically it never lacked for material goods, the inefficiency and cost surrounding their acquisition and distribution further sapped the Army's strength.

Although the American Army was still winning battlefield victories, combat was bitter and difficult against what proved to be a resolute, determined opponent. The American military was fighting well below its potential as a result of several factors, one of which was the one-year combat tour policy. This led to constant unit discontinuity and lack of combat proficiency. During 1967, the year of the big battles, the war was a standard contest being waged between national armies using conventional tactics. At the same time, policy planners in Washington continued to misread battlefield reality. They remained mesmerized by "counterinsurgency," which had effectively been terminated with the large-scale introduction of NVA and U.S. divisions to the battlefront in the previous year.

As a result of Tet-68, the American Army finally won a crushing ground victory and largely eliminated the local force VC as an effective military threat. However, the shock of the communist offensive further dismayed the American government and public, and the reaction against the war more than offset any allied military gains. General Abrams, the new MACV commander, gave up attrition and pursued a policy of phasing South Vietnamese units into American tactical areas of responsibility. With the exception of a few selected attack divisions, this fixed U.S. units in place and canceled responsive mobility.

By 1969, the American Army had been ordered to start withdrawing its combat forces from the war. Vietnamization was introduced, a concept designed to turn the war over completely to the South Vietnamese. This process was accelerated regardless of the consequences, and America's military sword—which had been thrust so quickly into Southeast Asia—became dulled and eroded. Morale and discipline caved in on an escalating basis, and combat performance declined. In 1970, by the time America had finally decided to penetrate NVA/VC sanctuaries in Cambodia, concern over losses brought a halt to aggressive Army tactics.

Vietnamization proceeded at a breakneck pace, and the South

Vietnamese Army was abandoned before it had a chance to properly assimilate American equipment and military doctrine. In the last years of the Army's retreat, its remaining forces were relegated to static security. The American Army's decline was readily apparent in this final stage. Racial incidents, drug abuse, combat disobedience, and crime reflected growing idleness, resentment, and frustration. Already the Army was looking toward a "modern volunteer army" to ease the many problems it placed squarely on the country's draft system. Actually, the draft—for all its faults—was not the culprit. Public dissatisfaction with the war was simply evident in its war machine, which was still a democratic institution reflecting national attitudes.

The military was faced with a terrible nightmare, an army pinned in the muddy, fiery jungled rim of Asia which consumed its own uniformed masses from every one of its ramparts and bastions. In an effort to fuel wartime operations with the Regular Army and Marine Corps alone, the preparedness of the pre-Vietnam Army to meet its overriding security obligations was sliced to the thinnest margins of national safety. Deprived of the anticipated skilled manpower base that the reserve components represented, the Pentagon swelled its thin ranks of regular troops beyond their ability to absorb the drafted multitudes, and undermined the overall readiness posture of the military.

More and more battalions were fed into the Vietnam cauldron until, by mid-1968, the entire United States armed forces were reduced to nearly worldwide combat ineffectiveness outside the Vietnam theater itself. By that year in Europe, only 39 percent of the 465 reporting units had a personnel readiness equal to even their deliberately diminished assigned capability. Within the eight major combat units posted to Germany, rapid personnel turnover and shortages of experienced officers and sergeants prevented four divisions from meeting minimum combat standards. The 3d Armored and 3d, 8th, and 24th Infantry Divisions were all woefully undermanned. Even more chilling was the secret December 31, 1968, pronouncement by United States Army Europe, that none of its major combat units had met their operational training readiness conditions for the second straight year. Yet the state of European defenses worsened with the withdrawal of the entire 24th Infantry Division, during

1969, in a desperate effort to reconstitute the Army strategic forces in the United States.

The Korean front in 1968 sparked with flashfires of combat, but the 2d and 7th Infantry Divisions stationed there were desperately short of soldiers. The former had to hold its assigned section of the Demilitarized Zone, but reinforced with the Korean 98th Regimental Combat Team, a Special Forces A-Detachment, and a brigade from the 7th Infantry Division. I Corps had only five helicopters available for either training or operations. The 7th Infantry Division, bolstered by a rotational company of Royal Thai troops, was rated by the Army as only marginally combat ready.

In the United States itself, the Vietnam war had reduced all active military formations to understrength holding containers for Vietnam returnees, or tropical combat schooling mills. Additionally, all units were tasked with either actual riot duty or preparation. In June of 1968, the Joint Chiefs of Staff were forced to flunk every division and brigade on the continent with the lowest rating possible in all categories—including personnel, training, and logistics, with the exception of the 82d Airborne Division (which had a brigade in Vietnam). The 1st and 2d Armored Divisions, 5th and 6th Infantry Divisions, and 6th Armored Cavalry Regiment were deemed unsuitable for combatant deployment. Army response had been stretched to the breaking point. The previous month a limited reserve mobilization brought the 29th and 69th Infantry Brigades onto active duty in Hawaii and Colorado respectively. Both had to be extensively retrained, verifying the length of lead time and orderly processing required to transform reserve components into satisfactory line units.

The dangerous drawdown on American global military capability was a calculated risk which also impacted on the Vietnam battlefield. The rapid deployment of fresh brigades, formed in haste without the proper training base that mobilization could have provided, directly impaired their combat performance. Most notably, the 11th, 196th, 198th, and 199th Infantry Brigades and 27th Marines had all suffered from inadequate preparation. Alarming personnel turbulence, critical shortfalls in leadership quantity and quality, and erosion of fighting skills were further manifestations of the same basic problem: the Regular Army and Marine Corps were extended far beyond their ability to wage and control a distant, full-scale war.

The United States soldiers and Marines in Vietnam fought through some of the most difficult terrain in the world, and won some of the toughest encounters in American military history. However, they fought without benefit of the country's larger military machine programmed for their support in case of war. The Reserves and National Guard were notably absent in the Vietnam conflict. The magnificent courage and fighting spirit of the thousands of riflemen, aircraft and armored crewmen, cannoneers, engineers, signalmen, and service personnel could not overcome the fatal handicaps of faulty campaign strategy, incomplete wartime preparation, and the tardy, superficial attempts at Vietnamization. An entire American army was sacrificed on the battlefield of Vietnam. When the war was finally over, the United States military had to build a new volunteer army from the smallest shreds of its tattered remnants.

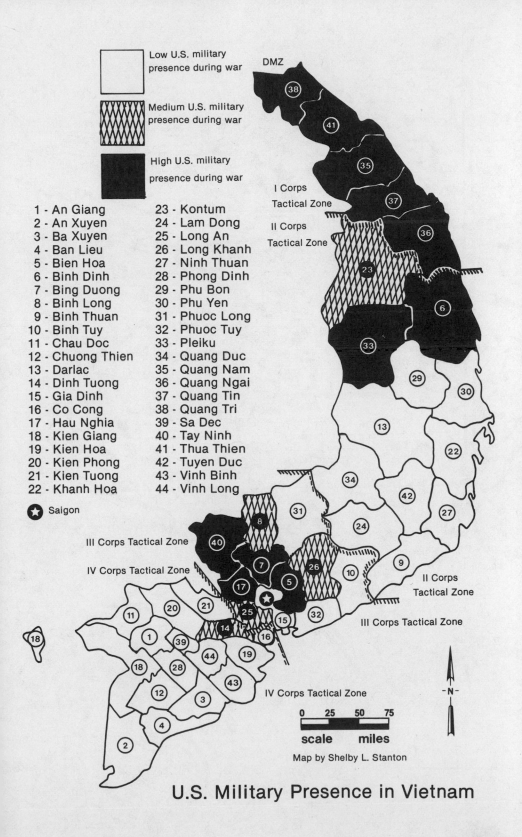

Low U.S. military presence during war

Medium U.S. military presence during war

High U.S. military presence during war

1 - An Giang
2 - An Xuyen
3 - Ba Xuyen
4 - Ban Lieu
5 - Bien Hoa
6 - Binh Dinh
7 - Bing Duong
8 - Binh Long
9 - Binh Thuan
10 - Binh Tuy
11 - Chau Doc
12 - Chuong Thien
13 - Darlac
14 - Dinh Tuong
15 - Gia Dinh
16 - Co Cong
17 - Hau Nghia
18 - Kien Giang
19 - Kien Hoa
20 - Kien Phong
21 - Kien Tuong
22 - Khanh Hoa

23 - Kontum
24 - Lam Dong
25 - Long An
26 - Long Khanh
27 - Ninh Thuan
28 - Phong Dinh
29 - Phu Bon
30 - Phu Yen
31 - Phuoc Long
32 - Phuoc Tuy
33 - Pleiku
34 - Quang Duc
35 - Quang Nam
36 - Quang Ngai
37 - Quang Tin
38 - Quang Tri
39 - Sa Dec
40 - Tay Ninh
41 - Thua Thien
42 - Tuyen Duc
43 - Vinh Binh
44 - Vinh Long

★ Saigon

DMZ

I Corps Tactical Zone

II Corps Tactical Zone

III Corps Tactical Zone

IV Corps Tactical Zone

II Corps Tactical Zone

III Corps Tactical Zone

IV Corps Tactical Zone

0   25   50   75

scale   miles

-N-

Map by Shelby L. Stanton

U.S. Military Presence in Vietnam

DMZ

Ben Hai River

LAOS

NORTH VIETNAM

SOUTH VIETNAM

Bo Ho Su

Helicopter Valley

Ngan River

Nui Cay Tre
("Mutter's Ridge")

The Rockpile

Route 9

Camp Carrol

Red Devil Road
(built January 1971)

Ca Lu

Hill 861   Hill 861 A

Hill 881 N   Hill 558

Dong Tre
Mountain

(Landing Zone

Stud)

Hill 881 S

Khe Sanh
Combat Base

Old French Fort

Hill 471

Route 9

To Tchepone

Lang Vei Special Forces camp

N

LAOS

Da Krong Valle

scale   miles

Xe Pon River

0   5

Map by Shelby L. Stanton

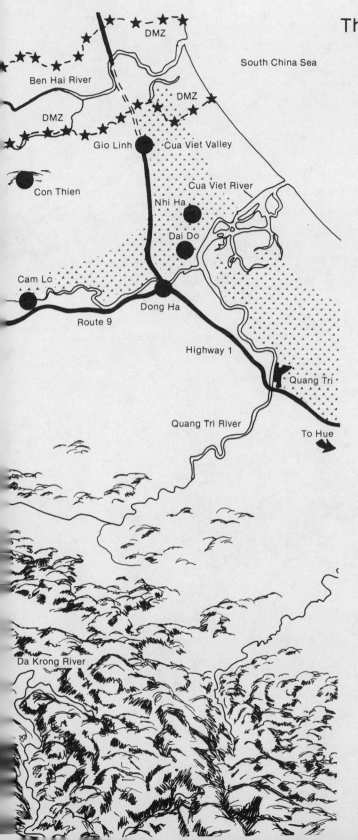

The DMZ Front

South China Sea

DMZ

Ben Hai River

DMZ

DMZ

Gio Linh

Cua Viet Valley

Con Thien

Cua Viet River

Nhi Ha

Dai Do

Cam Lo

Dong Ha

Route 9

Highway 1

Quang Tri

Quang Tri River

To Hue

Da Krong River

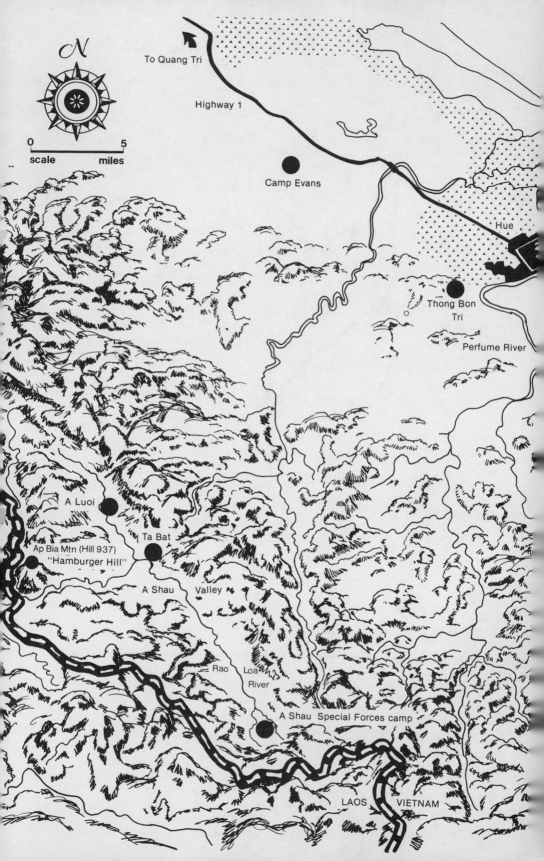

N

scale
0 _____ 5
miles

To Quang Tri

Highway 1

Camp Evans

Thong Bon
Tri

Perfume River

A Luoi

Ta Bat

Ap Bia Mtn (Hill 937)
"Hamburger Hill"

A Shau   Valley

Rao   Loa
River

A Shau Special Forces camp

Hue

LAOS   VIETNAM

1 - MACV Compound
2 - Mang Ca Compound
3 - Imperial Palace

South China Sea

Hue and the A Shau Valley

Truong Tien Bridge

Phu Bai

Phu Thu
Peninsula

Huong Thuy

Highway 1

Map by Shelby L. Stanton

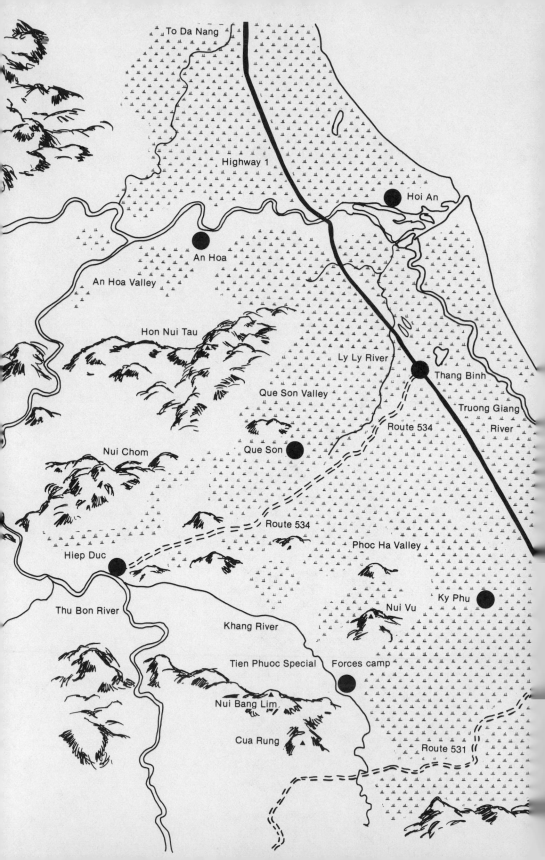

Phuoc Ha-Que Son An Hoa Valleys

Hon Giai

South China Sea

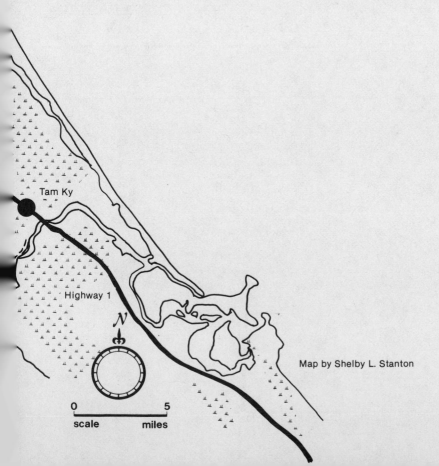

Tam Ky

Highway 1

N

Map by Shelby L. Stanton

0   5
scale   miles

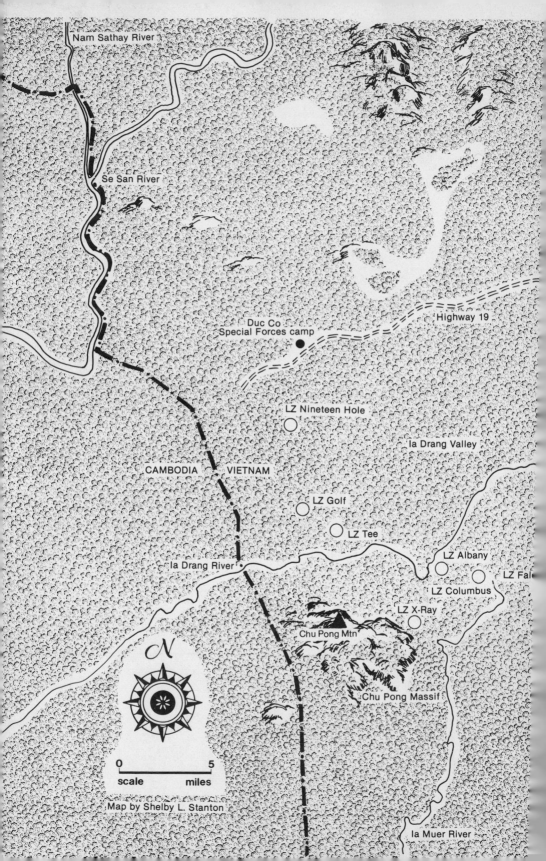

Nam Sathay River

Se San River

Highway 19

Duc Co
Special Forces camp

LZ Nineteen Hole

Ia Drang Valley

CAMBODIA   VIETNAM

LZ Golf

LZ Tee

LZ Albany

Ia Drang River

LZ Fal

LZ Columbus

LZ X-Ray

Chu Pong Mtn

Chu Pong Massif

N

0   5
scale   miles

Map by Shelby L. Stanton

Ia Muer River

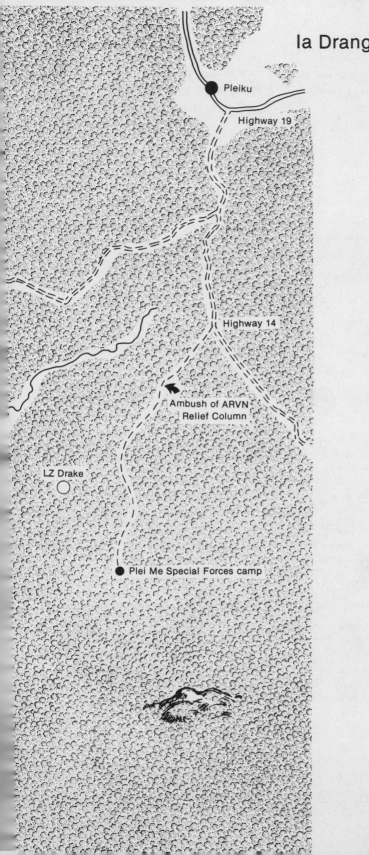

Ia Drang Valley

Pleiku

Highway 19

Highway 14

Ambush of ARVN
Relief Column

LZ Drake

Plei Me Special Forces camp

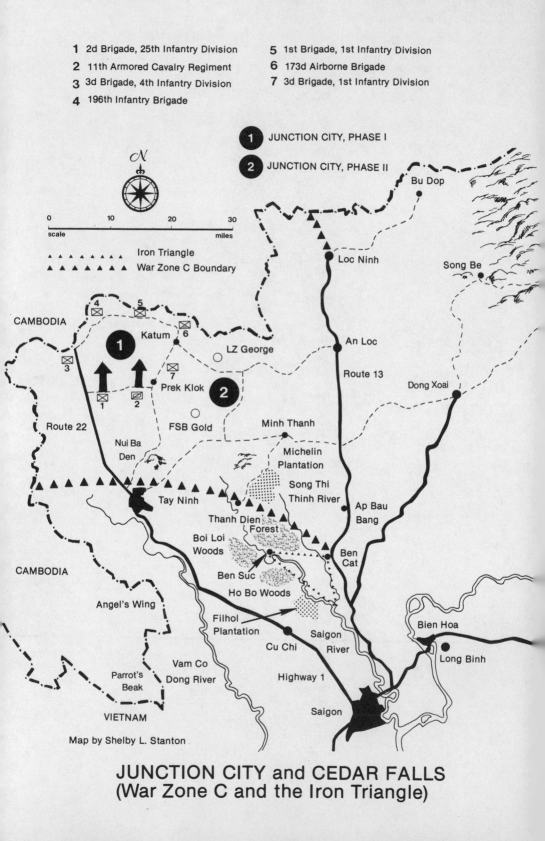

**JUNCTION CITY and CEDAR FALLS
(War Zone C and the Iron Triangle)**

1 2d Brigade, 25th Infantry Division
2 11th Armored Cavalry Regiment
3 3d Brigade, 4th Infantry Division
4 196th Infantry Brigade
5 1st Brigade, 1st Infantry Division
6 173d Airborne Brigade
7 3d Brigade, 1st Infantry Division

1 JUNCTION CITY, PHASE I
2 JUNCTION CITY, PHASE II

scale
0   10   20   30
miles

▲▲▲ Iron Triangle
▲▲▲▲▲▲▲ War Zone C Boundary

CAMBODIA

Bu Dop
Loc Ninh
Song Be
Katum
LZ George
An Loc
Route 13
Dong Xoai
Prek Klok
FSB Gold
Minh Thanh
Route 22
Nui Ba Den
Michelin Plantation
Song Thi Thinh River
Ap Bau Bang
Tay Ninh
Thanh Dien Forest
Boi Loi Woods
Ben Cat
CAMBODIA
Ben Suc
Ho Bo Woods
Angel's Wing
Filhol Plantation
Cu Chi
Saigon River
Bien Hoa
Long Binh
Parrot's Beak
Vam Co Dong River
Highway 1
VIETNAM
Saigon

Map by Shelby L. Stanton

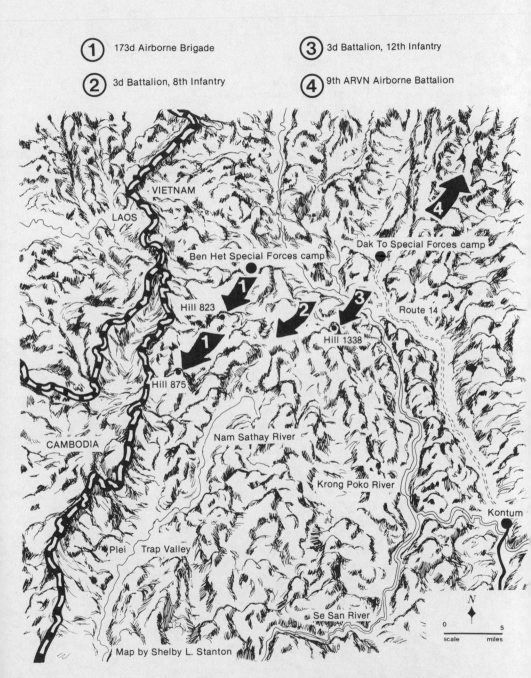

① 173d Airborne Brigade   ③ 3d Battalion, 12th Infantry

② 3d Battalion, 8th Infantry   ④ 9th ARVN Airborne Battalion

VIETNAM

LAOS

Ben Het Special Forces camp

Dak To Special Forces camp

Hill 823

Hill 1338

Route 14

Hill 875

Nam Sathay River

CAMBODIA

Krong Poko River

Kontum

Plei   Trap Valley

Se San River

Map by Shelby L. Stanton

N

0   5
scale   miles

The Dak To Battlefield - 1967

N

0   1   2
scale   miles

Map by Shelby L. Stanton

Di An

Hoc Mon

Highway 1

Thu Duc

To Cu Chi

Tan Son Nhut Airbase

Go Vap

Newport
Bridge

MACV Compound

Textile Mill

Vietnamese Joint General Staff Compound

Radio
Station

SAIGON

United States Embassy

Independence Palace

Phu Tho Racetrack

Nha Be River

Phu Lam

Y-Bridge

Cholon

The Saigon-Bien Hoa-Long Binh Area

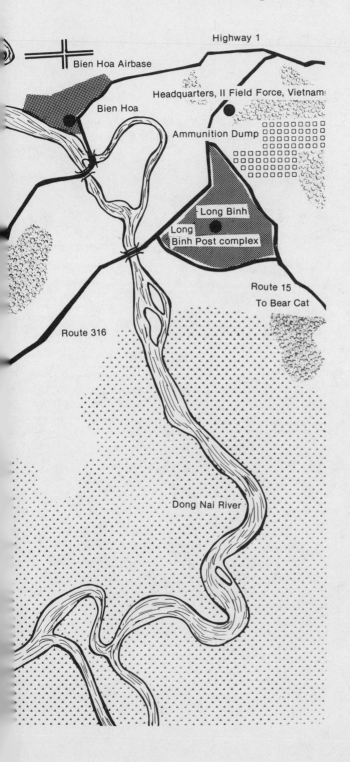

Khe Sanh Area and Lam Son 719 Offensive

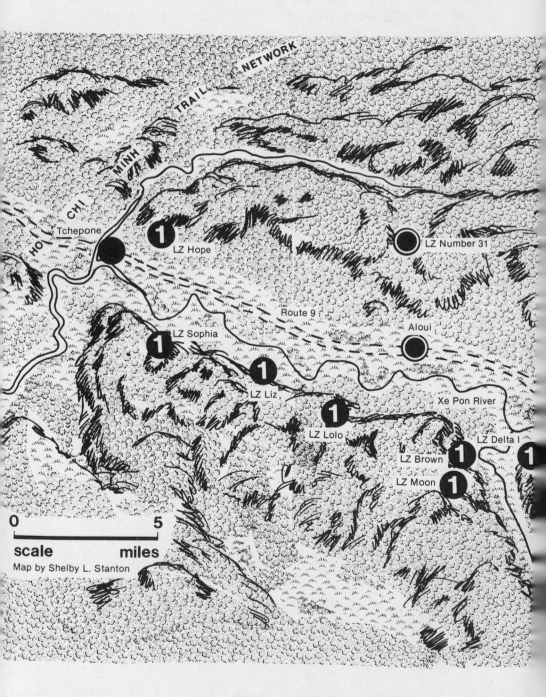

HO
CHI
MINH
TRAIL NETWORK

Tchepone

LZ Hope

LZ Number 31

Route 9

LZ Sophia

Aloui

LZ Liz

Xe Pon River

LZ Lolo

LZ Delta

LZ Brown

LZ Moon

0   5

scale   miles

Map by Shelby L. Stanton

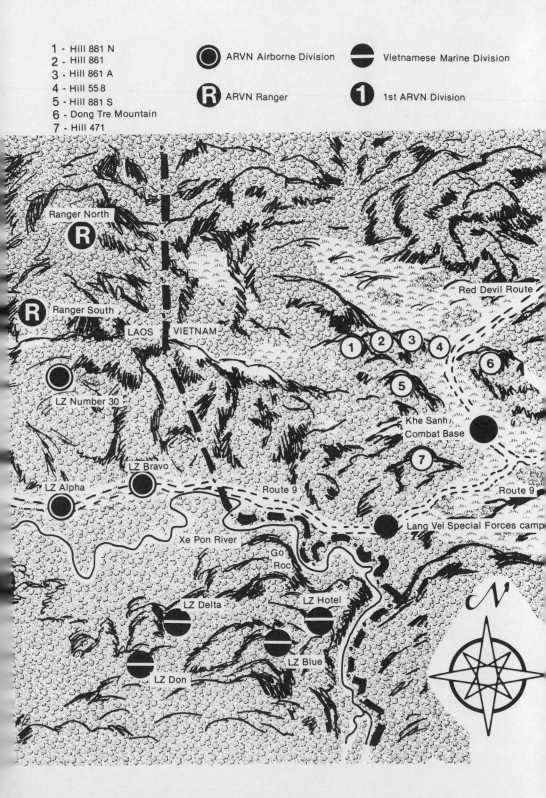

1 - Hill 881 N
2 - Hill 861
3 - Hill 861 A
4 - Hill 55 8
5 - Hill 881 S
6 - Dong Tre Mountain
7 - Hill 471

ARVN Airborne Division

Vietnamese Marine Division

ARVN Ranger

1st ARVN Division

Ranger North

Red Devil Route

Ranger South

LAOS   VIETNAM

1 2 3 4

6

5

LZ Number 30

Khe Sanh
Combat Base

7

LZ Bravo

LZ Alpha

Route 9

Route 9

Lang Vei Special Forces camp

Xe Pon River

Go
Roc

LZ Delta

LZ Hotel

LZ Blue

LZ Don

N

Guide to Unit Organization and Terms

This section briefly discusses the general pattern of United States ground force organization during the Vietnam War as a basic guide to some of the unit terms found in this book.

The squad, which usually fielded five to ten soldiers in Vietnam and was led by a sergeant, was the basic building block of the military infantry machine. Squad weapons ordinarily consisted of M16 rifles, pistols, and M79 grenade launchers. Weapons squads contained machine guns or heavier weapons, such as recoilless rifles.

Ideally, there were four squads in each platoon (one of them a weapons squad), which was led by a lieutenant. Three rifle platoons and a weapons platoon composed the infantry company, which was commanded by a captain or a lieutenant. Army rifle companies in Vietnam were authorized 164 men, but most operated at half this strength. As an exception to title, cavalry units retained the use of "troop" instead of "company," and artillery used the word "battery."

The Army infantry battalion in Vietnam was usually composed of four line companies (Companies A–D), a slightly smaller headquarters company, and one combat support company (Company E). Battalions were commanded by lieutenant colonels and were authorized a total of 920 men. Most of the time they were lucky to have an assigned strength of five hundred, and not all of these would be present in the field. Again, cavalry retained the traditional title of "squadron" instead of "battalion."

Marine battalions were part of regiments commanded by colonels, each regiment having three battalions. With one exception (the armored cavalry regiments, consisting of three squadrons) there were no operational regiments in the Army during the Vietnam War. Army combat arms battalions had regimental associations, which permitted a continuation of heritage, but the regimental designation in their titles was a matter of honorary "paper" distinction.

Army battalions were grouped into brigades, commanded by colonels. Brigades had from three to four battalions under them. Three Marine regiments or three Army brigades composed a division, although there were several separate brigades, independent in their own right, which were commanded by brigadier generals.

The division was commanded by a major general. It had nine or ten battalions of infantry, four battalions of artillery, a reconnaissance cavalry squadron, a combat engineer battalion, and division support and aviation. Some divisions had brought their tank battalions with them to Vietnam; others had not. Divisions in Vietnam varied in size from fifteen to twenty-two thousand personnel, but most had around seventeen thousand soldiers. However, since only a fraction were actually line riflemen, their "foxhole strength" was very low in comparison.

The two Army field forces, III Marine Amphibious Command and XXIV Corps, were the higher headquarters that controlled these tactical formations in their respective regions of South Vietnam. They were commanded by lieutenant generals, and had large artillery and support assets under them.

The U.S. Army Special Forces had a very complicated, unique structure in Vietnam. Basically its organization was tailored around a flexible combination of twelve-man (later fourteen-man) Operations Detachments A, or "A-teams," all the team members usually being sergeants or officers.

Sources and Bibliography

Primary Sources

The majority of material for this book was compiled from the original documents of Vietnam-based American units, which are now housed in the Washington National Records Center, Suitland, Maryland, by the General Archives Division of the U.S. National Archives and Records Service. The quarterly operational reports, combat staff journals, command chronicles, and after action reports of major Army and Marine units were examined. These are contained in Records Group 338 (Vietnam War: MACV/USARV records). To facilitate further research by interested readers, those original records used as principal sources are identified by their individual document accession codes and arranged by chapter and section. Published works listed below are also fully cited in Section 2, General Sources. Additionally, the mass of interviews and working papers prepared by the author during the course of research for his *Vietnam Order of Battle* (Washington: U.S. News Books, 1981) was extensively utilized. These notes and tapes are identified as *Original Papers, Vietnam Order of Battle Project*.

Chapter 1. Section 1

Principal sources used were Gen. Cao Van Vien et al., *The U.S. Advisor*, Indochina Monographs (Washington: U.S. Army Center of Military History, 1980); U.S. Military Assistance Command Vietnam RCS J3 Advisory Detachment, *After Action Reports* from Son Tinh District and III Corps Tactical Zone Senior Advisor, 1965; Department of the Army Pamphlet 550-55, *Area Handbook for South Vietnam* (Washington: Government Printing Office).

Section 2

Principal sources used were the 5th Special Forces Group Operational Briefing Narrative, "The Role of U.S. Army Special Forces in Vietnam," dtd 31 December 1965; Memorandum dtd 22 April 1968, "Development of the CIDG Program, 1964–1968," contained in 5th Special Forces Group, *Operational Report*, dtd 15 May 1968, OACSFOR-OT-RD 682179; Col. Francis J. Kelly, *U.S. Army Special Forces, 1961–1971*, Vietnam Studies (Washington: Department of the Army, 1973).

Section 3

Principal sources used were 5th Special Forces Group, *Command Report,* dtd 15 January 1966, OACSFOR-OT-RD 65008, and Detachment B-52 Memorandum dtd 15 November 1965, Subject: Sequence of Events for Plei Me Operation for Period 20–28 October 1965.

Chapter 2. Section 1

Principal sources used were 1st Logistical Command, *Command Report,* dtd 15 July 1965, OACSFOR-OT-RD 650063; USARV, *The Logistics Review, 1965–1969,* Volumes I–VIII; Joint Logistic Review Board, *Logistic Support in the Vietnam Era* (Washington: Deputy Secretary of Defense, 1970), Volume II and Monographs 1–13; Lt. Col. William R. Fails, *Marines and Helicopters* (Washington: U.S. Marine Corps, 1978), Chapters 2, 5, and 6; *Original Papers, Vietnam Order of Battle Project.*

Section 2

Principal sources used were the Basic Study and Annexes A–J of Volumes I–IV, *Army Strategic Mobility Requirements* (Washington: Department of the Army, 1965); Thomas C. Thayer, editor, *A Systems Analysis View of the Vietnam War* (Washington: Southeast Asia Intelligence Division, 1975), Volume 2; Office of the Deputy Chief of Staff for Personnel, *Study of the 12-Month Vietnam Tour,* dtd 29 June 1970; USARV Report, *Summary of Lessons Learned,* Volumes I and II, dtd 30 June 1966; Maj. Gen. George S. Eckhardt, *Command and Control,* Vietnam Studies (Washington: Department of the Army, 1974), Chapter 3; Russell Weigley, *The American Way of War* (New York: Macmillan Co., 1973); BDM Corporation, *A Study of Strategic Lessons Learned in Vietnam* (McLean, Virginia: BDM, 1980), Volumes III and VII; Gen. William C. Westmoreland and Adm. U.S.G. Sharp, *Report on the War in Vietnam (As of 30 June 1968)* (Washington: Government Printing Office, 1968); Deputy Chief of Staff for Personnel, *U.S. Army Training Base, 1945–1971* (Washington: Department of the Army, 1971).

Chapter 3. Section 1

Principal sources used were *A Chronology of the United States Marine Corps, 1965–1969* (Washington: U.S. Marine Corps, 1971), Volume IV; Jack Shulimson and Maj. Charles M. Johnson, *U.S. Marines in Vietnam: The Landing and the Buildup* (Washington: U.S. Marine Corps, 1978), Part I.

Section 2

Principal sources used were Jack Shulimson and Maj. Charles M. Johnson, *U.S. Marines in Vietnam: The Landing and the Buildup* (Washington: U.S. Marine Corps, 1978), Part I; Defense Department, *United States–Vietnam Relations, 1945–1967* (Washington: U.S. Government Printing Office, 1971), Volume 4.

Section 3

Principal sources used were Jack Shulimson and Maj. Charles M. Johnson, *U.S. Marines in Vietnam: The Landing and the Buildup* (Washington: U.S. Marine Corps, 1978), Chapter 5; Fleet Marine Force Pacific, *U.S. Marine Corps Forces in Vietnam*, Volume I.

Section 4

Principal sources used were Jack Shulimson and Maj. Charles M. Johnson, *U.S. Marines in Vietnam: The Landing and the Buildup* (Washington: U.S. Marine Corps, 1978), Chapters 6 and 7.

Chapter 4. Section 1

Principal sources used were Headquarters, Field Force Vietnam, *Command Report*, dtd 14 January 1966, OACSFOR-OT-RD 650116; 173d Airborne Brigade, *Operational Report for Period Ending 31 January 1966*.

Section 2

Principal sources used were Headquarters, 1st Brigade, 101st Airborne Division, *Operational Report for Period Ending 31 January 1966*; Lt. Col. Albert N. Garland, editor, "Infantry in Vietnam" (Fort Benning: *Infantry Magazine*, 1967), pp. 131–141; Field Force Vietnam, *Command Report*, dtd 14 January 1966; OACSFOR-OT-RD 660116.

Section 3

The principal source used was Headquarters, 1st Cavalry Division, *Quarterly Command Report*, dtd 1 December 1965, OACSFOR-OT-RD 650110.

Section 4

Principal sources used were Headquarters, 1st Cavalry Division, *Quarterly Command Report,* dtd 10 January 1966, OACSFOR-OT-RD 650109; and MACV Operations Report, *Lessons Learned 3–66: The Pleiku Campaign,* dtd 10 May 1966.

Chapter 5. Section 1

Principal sources used were USARV, *Operational Report,* dtd 1 July 1966, OACSFOR-OT-RD 660114; USARV, *Operational Report,* dtd 7 September 1966, OACSFOR-OT-RD 660546; USARV, *Operational Report,* dtd 10 February 1967, OACSFOR-OT-RD 660522; USARV, *Operational Report,* dtd 28 February 1967, OACSFOR-OT-RD 670243; Jack Shulimson, *U.S. Marines in Vietnam: An Expanding War* (Washington: U.S. Marine Corps, 1982), Parts I and VII; MACV, *Command History, 1966.*

Section 2

Principal sources used were Jack Shulimson, *U.S. Marines in Vietnam: An Expanding War* (Washington: U.S. Marine Corps, 1982), Chapter 1; Marine Corps History and Museums Division, *The 1st Marine Division and Its Regiments* (Washington: U.S. Marine Corps, 1981).

Section 3

The principal source used was 4th Infantry Division, *Operational Report,* dtd 22 December 1966, OACSFOR-OT-RD 6604506.

Section 4

The principal source used was Headquarters, 199th Infantry Brigade, *Lessons Learned, Operational Report for Quarterly Period Ending 31 January 1967,* dtd 14 April 1967, OACSFOR-OT-RD 670222.

Section 5

The principal source used was Headquarters, 25th Infantry Division, *Operational Report on Lessons Learned for the Period 1 January 1966–30 April 1966,* OACSFOR-OT-RD 660120.

Section 6

The principal source used was 11th Armored Cavalry Regiment, *Operational Report,* dtd 31 October 1966, OACSFOR-OT-RD 660507; USARV, *MACOV (Mechanized and Armor Combat Operations in Vietnam) Study,* dtd 28 March 1967.

Section 7

The principal source used was Headquarters, 196th Infantry

Brigade, *Operational Report*, dtd 8 March 1967, OACSFOR-OT-RD 660511.

Section 8

The principal source used was 9th Infantry Division, *Operational Report*, dtd 8 June 1967.

Chapter 6. Section 1

Principal sources used were Defense Department, *United States–Vietnam Relations, 1945–1967* (Washington: Government Printing Office, 1971), Volume 5; Gen. William C. Westmoreland, *A Soldier Reports* (New York: Doubleday, 1976); BDM Corporation, *A Study of Strategic Lessons Learned in Vietnam* (McLean, Virginia: BDM, 1980), Volume VI; Col. Harry G. Summers, Jr., *On Strategy: A Critical Analysis of the Vietnam War* (Novato, California: Presidio Press, 1982); Gen. Dave R. Palmer, *Summons of the Trumpet* (Novato, California: Presidio Press, 1978); MACV, *Command History, 1966; Original Papers, Vietnam Order of Battle Project*.

Section 2

Principal sources used were 1st Infantry Division, *Fundamentals of Infantry Tactics*, dtd 1 February 1968, OACSFOR-OT-RD 682001; DA Operations Report 1-67, *Observations of a Platoon Leader*, dtd 30 January 1967; DA Operations Report 4-67, *Observations of a Battalion Commander*, dtd 7 June 1967; DA Operations Report 6-67, *Observations of a Brigade Commander*, dtd 27 December 1967; USARV Battlefield Reports, *A Summary of Lessons Learned*, Volume III, May 1967.

Section 3

Principal sources used were DA Operations Report 3-68, *Aerial Observation Lessons Learned*, dtd 15 July 1968; DA Operations Report 1-68, *Summary of Lessons Learned*, dtd 1 February 1968; Headquarters, 1st Cavalry Division, *Operational Report for Period Ending 31 October 1966*, p. 51, OACSFOR-OT-RD 660505; *Original Papers, Vietnam Order of Battle Project*.

Section 4

Principal sources used were Ballistic Research Laboratories Memorandum Report 2030, *U.S. Army Casualties Aboard Aircraft in the Republic of Vietnam* (Aberdeen Proving Ground: 1970); Col. R. L. Cody, "U.S. Army Helicopters as Personnel and Material Carriers" and Lt. Col. E. Lail, "Helicopter Evacuation in Vietnam," both contained in *Aeromedical Aspects of Helicopter Operations in the Tactical Situation* presented to Sessions I and II of the Advisory Group for Aerospace Research and Development in Paris, France, May 1967; Col. Spurgeon H. Neel, *An Overall Survey of Helicopter Operations Problems* (Washington: Office of the Surgeon General, 1967); Lt. Gen. John J. Tolson, *Airmobility, 1961–1971, Vietnam Studies (Washington: Department of the Army, 1973)*.

Section 5

Principal sources used were DA Study, *Aviation Requirements for the Combat Structure of the Army*, dtd 6 June 1965; U.S. Congress, Senate, *Hearings before the Preparedness Investigating Subcommittee of the Committee on Armed Services*, 90th Congress, First Session, 1967 (Washington: U.S. Government Printing Office, 1967).

Chapter 7. Section 1

Principal sources used were 1st Infantry Division, *Operations After Action Report: Operation ABILENE*, OACSFOR-OT-RD 66X001; 1st Infantry Division, *Combat Operations After Action Report: Operation BIRMINGHAM*, OACSFOR-OT-RD 66X232; Headquarters, 1st Battalion, 18th Infantry, *After Action Report: Operation LEXINGTON III*, OACSFOR-OT-RD 66X151; 1st Infantry Division, *Operational Report*, dtd 15 August 1966, OACSFOR-OT-RD 660291; 1st Infantry Division, *Combat After Action Report: Operation EL PASO II/III*, dtd 8 December 1966, OACSFOR-OT-RD 66X043; II Field Force, *Operational Report*, dtd 25 April 1967, OACSFOR-OT-RD 670228; Headquarters, 196th Infantry Brigade, *Operational Report for Quarterly Period Ending 31 January 1967*, dtd 7 March 1967, OACSFOR-OT-RD 670221; Headquarters, 173d Airborne Brigade, *Combat Operations After Action Report: Operation ATTLEBORO*, dtd 30 December 1966, OACSFOR-OT-RD 66X009; 25th Infantry Division, *Operational Report: Operation ATTLEBORO*, dtd 28 April 1967, OACSFOR-OT-RD 66X012.

Section 2

Principal sources used were MACV Operations Report 2-66, *The Battle of Annihilation and the Bong Son Campaign*, dtd 1 April 1966; 1st Cavalry Division, *Operational Report*, dtd 5 May

1966, OACSFOR-OT-RD 660119; Headquarters, 3d Brigade Task Force, 25th Infantry Division, *Operational Report*, dtd 1 June 1967, OACSFOR-OT-RD 660514; Headquarters, 1st Brigade, 101st Airborne Division, *Combat Operations After Action Report: Operation HAWTHORNE*, dtd 22 July 1966, OACSFOR-OT-RD 66X102; Headquarters, 101st Airborne Division, *After Action Report: Operation SEWARD*, dtd 6 November 1966, OACSFOR-OT-RD 66X201; Headquarters, 101st Airborne Division, *Operational Report*, dtd 10 March 1967, OACSFOR-OT-RD 660508; 1st Cavalry Division, *Operational Report*, dtd 15 August 1966, OACSFOR-OT-RD 660292; Infantry Field Historical Team Alpha, *Battle for LZ Bird*, supplement to 1st Cavalry Division, *Operational Report for Quarterly Period Ending 30 April 1967*, dtd 27 October 1967, OACSFOR-OT-RD 670473.

Chapter 8. Section 1

Principal sources used were NAVMC Publication 2614, *Professional Knowledge Gained from Operational Experience in Vietnam* (Washington: U.S. Marine Corps, 1967); Jack Shulimson, *U.S. Marines in Vietnam: An Expanding War* (Washington: U.S. Marine Corps, 1982), Part I; Fleet Marine Force Pacific, *U.S. Marine Corps Forces in Vietnam*, Volume I.

Section 2

Principal sources used were 5th Special Forces Group, *Command Operational Report*, dtd 10 May 1966, OACSFOR-OT-RD 660557; Jack Shulimson, *U.S. Marines in Vietnam: An Expanding War* (Washington: U.S. Marine Corps, 1982), Part II; Brig. Gen. Edwin H. Simmons, "Marine Corps Operations in Vietnam, 1965–1966," *Naval Review* (Annapolis: U.S. Naval Institute, 1968).

Section 3

Principal sources used were Jack Shulimson, *U.S. Marines in Vietnam: An Expanding War* (Washington: U.S. Marine Corps, 1982), Part IV; Fleet Marine Force Pacific, *U.S. Marine Corps Forces in Vietnam*, Volume I.

Chapter 9. Section 1

Principal sources used were USARV, *Summary of Lessons Learned*, dtd 18 January 1968; USARV, *Operational Report 1 Feb–30 Apr 67*, OACSFOR-OT-RD 670461; USARV, *Operational Report 1 May–31 Jul 67*, OACSFOR-OT-RD 670600;

USARV, *Operational Report*, dtd 20 November 1967, OACSFOR-OT-RD 674175; USARV, *Operational Report*, dtd 24 April 1968, OACSFOR-OT-RD 681044; Gen. Dave R. Palmer, *Summons of the Trumpet* (Novato, California: Presidio Press, 1978); Col. Harry G. Summers, Jr., *On Strategy: A Critical Analysis of the Vietnam War* (Novato, California: Presidio Press, 1982); MACV, *Command History, 1967*, Volume I; *Original Papers, Vietnam Order of Battle Project*.

Section 2

Principal sources used were Thomas C. Thayer, editor, *A Systems Analysis View of the Vietnam War* (Washington: Southeast Asia Intelligence Division, 1975), Volume 6; Brig. Gen. Edwin H. Simmons, "Marine Corps Operations in Vietnam, 1967," *Naval Review* (Annapolis: U.S. Naval Institute, 1969); I Field Force Vietnam, *Operational Report*, dtd 17 November 1967, OACSFOR-OT-RD 670486; MACV, *Quarterly Command Reports* for 1967.

Section 3

The principal source used was 101st Airborne Division, *Operational Report*, dtd 29 May 1968, OACSFOR-OT-RD 681291.

Chapter 10. Section 1

Principal sources used were 199th Infantry Brigade, *Operational Report, Lessons Learned: 1 August–31 October 1967*, dtd 15 November 1967, OACSFOR-OT-RD 674237; MACVJ3-053 Report, *Hole Huntin'—Techniques to Detect, Neutralize and Destroy Enemy Tunnels*, dtd 20 December 1968; II Field Force Vietnam, *Operational Report*, dtd 5 April 1967, OACSFOR-OT-RD 670228.

Section 2

Principal sources used were II Field Force Vietnam, *Operational Report*, dtd 15 May 1967, OACSFOR-OT-RD 670751; 1st Infantry Division, *After Action Report: Operation JUNCTION CITY*, dtd 8 May 1967, OACSFOR-OT-RD 67X216; 1st Infantry Division, *Operational Report, 1 February–30 April 1967*, OACSFOR-OT-RD 670468; DA Narrative, *Battle of Ap Cu*, OACSFOR-OT-RD 67X074; 11th Armored Cavalry Regiment, *Combat After Action Report: Operation JUNCTION CITY*, dtd 1 November 1967, OACSFOR-OT-RD 67XO59.

Section 3

The principal source used was Headquarters, 3d Battalion, 39th Infantry, *Combat After Action Report*, dtd 16 August 1967, OACSFOR-OT-RD 67X076.

Chapter 11. Section 1

Principal sources used were the 4th Infantry Division, *Combat After Action Report: Operation SAM HOUSTON*, dtd 28 June 1967, OACSFOR-OT-RD 67X030; I Field Force Vietnam, *Operational Report*, dtd 17 November 1967, OACSFOR-OT-RD 670486.

Section 2

Principal sources used were I Field Force Vietnam, *Operational Report*, dtd 26 August 1967, OACSFOR-OT-RD 670622; 4th Infantry Division, *Combat After Action Report: Operation FRANCIS MARION*, dtd 25 November 1967, OACSFOR-OT-RD 67X112.

Section 3

Principal sources used were 4th Infantry Division, *Combat Operations After Action Report for Period Ending 11 October 1967*, OACSFOR-OT-RD 67X117; 4th Infantry Division, *Combat After Action Report: Battle for Dak To*, dtd 3 January 1968, OACSFOR-OT-RD 68X007; USARV, *Seminar on Attack of Fortified Positions in the Jungle*, dtd 31 January 1968, OACSFOR-OT-RD 68X002; I Field Force Vietnam, *Operational Report*, dtd 15 November 1967, OACSFOR-OT-RD 674078; I Field Force Vietnam, *Operational Report*, dtd 15 February 1968, OACSFOR-OT-RD 681098.

Chapter 12. Section 1

Principal sources used were Fleet Marine Force Pacific, *U.S. Marine Corps Forces in Vietnam, March 1965–September 1967*, Volume I; Maj. Gary L. Telfer and Lt. Col. Lane Rogers, *U.S. Marines in Vietnam: The War of Attrition, 1967* (Washington: U.S. Marine Corps), Chapters 1 and 2; 3d Marine Division, *Command Chronology Reports* for February–April 1967.

Section 2

Principal sources used were Maj. Gary L. Telfer and Lt. Col. Lane Rogers, *U.S. Marines in Vietnam: The War of Attrition, 1967* (Washington: U.S. Marine Corps), Chapters 5, 6, and 9; 3d Marine Division, *Command Chronology Report*s for May–December 1967.

Section 3

Principal sources used were Maj. Gary L. Telfer and Lt. Col. Lane Rogers, *U.S. Marine Corps in Vietnam: The War of Attrition, 1967* (Washington: U.S. Marine Corps), Chapters 3 and 7; 1st Marine Division, *Command Chronology Report*s for April–June 1967.

Chapter 13. Section 1

Principal sources used were Headquarters, Task Force Oregon, *Operational Report*, dtd 6 August 1967, OACSFOR-OT-RD 670802; Task Force Oregon, *Operational Report*, dtd 5 November 1967, OACSFOR-OT-RD 670580; Americal Division, *Operational Report*, dtd 26 November 1967, OACSFOR-OT-RD 674289; 3d Brigade Task Force, 25th Infantry Division, *Operational Report for Quarterly Period Ending 30 April 1967*, OACSFOR-OT-RD 670750; 2d Battalion, 35th Infantry, 3d Brigade Task Force, *Combat After Action Report*, dtd 20 August 1967, OACSFOR-OT-RD 67X186; USARV, *Seminar on Attack of Fortified Positions in the Jungle*, dtd 2 January 1968, OACSFOR-OT-RD 68X002; Maj. Gary L. Telfer and Lt. Col. Lane Rogers, *U.S. Marines in Vietnam: The War of Attrition, 1967* (Washington: U.S. Marine Corps), Chapter 4; *Original Papers, Vietnam Order of Battle Project*.

Section 2

Principal sources used were 1st Cavalry Division, *Operational Report*, dtd 8 August 1967, OACSFOR-OT-RD 670226; 1st Cavalry Division, *Operational Report for Period Ending 31 October 1967*, dtd 20 February 1968, OACSFOR-OT-RD 674236; 1st Cavalry Division, *Lessons Learned: Operation PERSHING*, dtd 30 December 1967, OACSFOR-OT-RD 67X199.

Chapter 14. Section 1

Principal sources used were Headquarters, Provisional Corps Vietnam, *Operational Report*, dtd 4 June 1968, OACSFOR-OT-RD 682349; Thomas C. Thayer, editor, *A Systems Analysis View of the Vietnam War* (Washington: Southeast Asia Intelligence Division, 1975), Volume 1; Lt. Gen. Willard Pearson, *The War in the Northern Provinces*, Vietnam Studies (Washington: Department of the Army, 1975); MACV *Quarterly Evaluation Re-*

ports for 1968; USARV, *Operational Report*, dtd 24 April 1968, OACSFOR-OT-RD 681044; USARV, *Operational Report*, dtd 20 May 1968, OACSFOR-OT-RD 682297; USARV, *Operational Report*, dtd 12 August 1968, OACSFOR-OT-RD 683312; USARV, *Operational Report*, dtd 15 November 1968, OACSFOR-OT-RD 684336; USARV, *Operational Report*, dtd 13 February 1969, OACSFOR-OT-RD 691251; MACV, *Command History, 1968*, Volume I; *Original Papers, Vietnam Order of Battle Project*.

Section 2

Principal sources used were Robert W. Coakley et al., *Use of Troops in Civil Disturbances since World War II*, Supplement II (Washington: Histories Division, Department of the Army, 1974); Paul J. Scheips et al., *Army Operational and Intelligence Activities in Civil Disturbances since 1957*, revised edition, OCMH Study 73 (Washington: Department of the Army, 1972); Assistant Secretary of Defense Memorandum, Subject: Special Pay for Duty Subject to Hostile Fire—Korea, dtd 1 April 1968; Headquarters, 3d Brigade, 82d Airborne Division, *Operational Report*, dtd 12 May 1968, OACSFOR-OT-RD 682329.

Section 3

Principal sources used were Thomas C. Thayer, editor, *A Systems Analysis View of the Vietnam War* (Washington: Southeast Asia Intelligence Division, 1975), Volume 6; 1st Logistical Command, *Operational Report*, dtd 14 May 1968, OACSFOR-OT-RD 682276; 1st Logistical Command, *Operational Report*, dtd 14 February 1968, OACSFOR-OT-RD 681160; MACV, *Command History, 1968*, Volume I.

Chapter 15. Section 1

Principal sources used were 97th Military Police Battalion, *Operational Report*, dtd 13 May 1968, OACSFOR-OT-RD 682013; 716th Military Police Battalion, *Operational Report*, dtd 12 February 1968, OACSFOR-OT-RD 681286; 716th Military Police Battalion, *Operational Report*, dtd 8 May 1968, OACSFOR-OT-RD 681286; 18th Military Police Brigade Report, *Lessons Learned During the VC/NVA Tet Offensive*, dtd 15 Feb 1968, OACSFOR-OT-RD 682144; 199th Infantry Brigade, *Long Binh/Saigon Tet Campaign*, dtd 4 June 1968, OACSFOR-OT-RD 68X018; Col. Hoang Ngoc Lung, *The General Offensives of 1968–69*, Indochina Monographs (Washington:

U.S. Army Center of Military History, 1981); II Field Force Vietnam, *Tet Offensive After Action Report, 31 January–18 February 1968*, OACSFOR-OT-RD 68X039.

Section 2

Principal sources used were 9th Infantry Division, *Operational Report*, dtd 21 August 1968, OACSFOR-OT-RD 682266; II Field Force Vietnam, *Operational Report*, dtd 20 May 1968, OACSFOR-OT-RD 682278.

Section 3

Principal sources used were 1st Cavalry Division, *Combat After Action Report: The Battle of Hue, 2–26 February 1968*, dtd 10 March 1968; 1st Cavalry Division, *The Battle of Quang Tri*, OACSFOR-OT-RD 68X050; Fleet Marine Force Pacific, *Operations of U.S. Marine Forces in Vietnam, February 1968*; Col. Hoang Ngoc Lung, *The General Offensives of 1968–69*, Indochina Monographs (Washington: U.S. Army Center of Military History, 1981); MACV I Corps Tactical Zone Senior Advisor, *After Action Report: Tet Offensive*, dtd 14 April 1968.

Section 4

Principal sources used were I Field Force Vietnam, *Operational Report*, dtd 21 August 1968, OACSFOR-OT-RD 682112; 5th Special Forces Group, *Operational Report*, dtd 14 August 1968, OACSFOR-OT-RD 682179; II Field Force Vietnam, *Tet Offensive Combat After Action Report*, dtd 5 August 1968, OACSFOR-OT-RD 68X039; MACV, *Quarterly SEER* (System for Evaluating the Effectiveness of RVNAF) *Reports* for 1968.

Chapter 16. Section 1

Principal sources used were 3d Marine Division, *Command Chronology Reports*, January and February 1968; Capt. Moyers S. Shore II, *The Battle for Khe Sanh* (Washington: U.S. Marine Corps, 1977).

Section 2

The principal source used was 5th Special Forces Group, *Battle of Lang Vei After Action Report*, dtd 12 August 1968, OACSFOR-OT-RD 68X037.

Section 3

Principal sources used were Capt. Moyers S. Shore II, *The Battle for Khe Sanh* (Washington: U.S. Marine Corps, 1977);

Provisional Corps Vietnam, *Operational Report*, dtd 4 June 1968, OACSFOR-OT-RD 682349; 3d Marine Division, *Command Chronology Reports*, February–April 1968; 1st Cavalry Division, *Operational Report*, dtd 13 June 1968, OACSFOR-OT-RD 682337.

Chapter 17. Section 1

Principal sources used were Provisional Corps Vietnam, *Operational Report*, dtd 20 August 1968, OACSFOR-OT-RD 683363; 1st Cavalry Division, *Operational Report*, dtd 13 June 1968, OACSFOR-OT-RD 682337; Lt. Gen. John J. Tolson, *Airmobility*, Vietnam Studies (Washington: Department of the Army, 1973), Chapter 9; 101st Airborne Division, *Operational Report*, dtd 22 November 1968, OACSFOR-OT-UT 684306.

Section 2

Principal sources used were 3d Marine Division, *Command Chronology Reports* for April–December 1968; Fleet Marine Force Pacific, *Operations of Marine Forces, Vietnam*, reports for April–December 1968.

Section 3

Principal sources used were 101st Airborne Division, *Operational Report*, dtd 24 May 1968, OACSFOR-OT-RD 682315; 101st Airborne Division, *Operational Report*, dtd 15 August 1968, OACSFOR-OT-RD 683306; 101st Airborne Division, *Operational Report*, dtd 22 November 1968, OACSFOR-OT-RD 684306; Americal Division, *Operational Report*, dtd 7 May 1968, OACSFOR-OT-RD 682332; Combat Developments Command Trip Report, *Combat Tactics of Americal Division*, dtd 26 July 1968; Lt. Gen. W. R. Peers, *The My Lai Inquiry* (New York: W. W. Norton & Co., 1979); XXIV Corps, *Operational Report*, dtd 15 November 1968, OACSFOR-OT-RD 684253; XXIV Corps, *Operational Report*, dtd 4 March 1969, OACSFOR-OT-RD 691303.

Section 4

Principal sources used were II Field Force Vietnam, *Operational Report*, dtd 14 August 1968, OACSFOR-OT-RD 683289; II Field Force Vietnam, *Operational Report for Period Ending 31 October 1968*, OACSFOR-OT-UT 684252; II Field Force Vietnam, *Operational Report for Period Ending 31 January 1969*,

OACSFOR-OT-UT 691324; Maj. Gen. William B. Fulton, *Riverine Operations*, Vietnam Studies (Washington: Department of the Army, 1973).
Chapter 18. Section 1
Principal sources used were MACV, *Quarterly SEER* (System for Evaluating the Effectiveness of RVNAF) *Reports* for 1969; MACV, *Quarterly Evaluation Reports* for 1969; USARV, *Operational Report for Period Ending 31 January 1969*, OACSFOR-OT-RD 691251; USARV, *Operational Report*, dtd 31 August 1969, OACSFOR-OT-RD 693179; MACV, *Command History, 1969*, Volume I; *Original Papers, Vietnam Order of Battle Project*.
Section 2
Principal sources used were USARV, *Operational Report*, dtd 11 May 1969, OACSFOR-OT-RD 690248; Col. Hoang Ngoc Lung, *The General Offensives of 1968-69*, Indochina Monographs (Washington: U.S. Army Center of Military History, 1981).
Section 3
Principal sources used were ACTIV Project ACG-78F Report, *Vehicle Convoy Operations in the Republic of Vietnam* (Washington: Army Research Office, 29 January 1972); Army Combat Developments Command Trip Report 8-69, *Convoy Security*, dtd 20 January 1969; Army Combat Developments Command Report, *Route and Convoy Security*, dtd 5 December 1967; Combat Developments Command Trip Report 9-69, *Vulcan Employment in a Ground Combat Role*, dtd 20 January 1969.
Section 4
Principal sources used were BDM Corporation, *A Study of Strategic Lessons Learned in Vietnam* (McLean, Virginia: BDM, 1980), Volumes IV and VII; Douglas Kinnard, *The War Managers* (Hanover, New Hampshire: University Press of New England, 1977); William L. Hauser, *America's Army in Crisis* (Baltimore: The Johns Hopkins University Press, 1973); *Original Papers, Vietnam Order of Battle Project*.
Chapter 19. Section 1
Principal sources used were 3d Marine Division, *Command Chronology Reports* for January–February 1969; XXIV Corps, *Operational Report*, dtd 4 June 1969, OACSFOR-OT-UT 692307; XXIV Corps, *Operational Report*, dtd 23 August 1969,

OACSFOR-OT-UT 693291; MACV Combat Experiences 3-69, *Task Force Remagen,* dtd 7 September 1969; Headquarters, 1st Brigade, 5th Infantry Division, *Operational Report,* dtd 30 May 1969, OACSFOR-OT-UT 692327; Headquarters, 1st Brigade, 5th Infantry Division, *Operational Report,* dtd 18 September 1969, OACSFOR-OT-RD 692327; 101st Airborne Division, *Operational Report,* dtd 20 August 1969, OACSFOR-OT-RD 693240; Lt. Gen. John H. Hay, Jr., *Tactical and Material Innovations,* Vietnam Studies (Washington: Department of the Army, 1974), Chapter 5.

Section 2

Principal sources used were Americal Division, *Operational Report,* dtd 19 August 1969, OACSFOR-OT-RD 692339; Americal Division, *Operational Report,* dtd 30 October 1969, OACSFOR-OT-RD 693290; Americal Division, *Operational Report,* dtd 10 November 1969, OACSFOR-OT-RD 694285; XXIV Corps, *Operational Report,* dtd 9 February 1970, OACSFOR-OT-UT 694298.

Chapter 20. Section 1

Principal sources used were 14th Military History Detachment, *Combat After Action Report: Battle of The Angel's Wing,* dtd 25 March 1969, OACSFOR-OT-RD 69X005; 25th Infantry Division, *Operational Report,* dtd 1 May 1969, OACSFOR-OT-RD 692282; 1st Cavalry Division, *Operational Report,* dtd 30 April 1969, OACSFOR-OT-RD 692094; 1st Cavalry Division, *Operational Report,* dtd 15 August 1969, OACSFOR-OT-RD 693030; 25th Infantry Division, *Operational Report,* dtd 18 December 1969, OACSFOR-OT-RD 693230; II Field Force Vietnam, *Operational Report for Period Ending 30 April 1969,* OACSFOR-OT-UT 692303.

Section 2

Principal sources used were 11th Armored Cavalry Regiment, *Combat After Action Report: Operation ATLAS WEDGE,* dtd 10 December 1969, OACSFOR-OT-RD 69X027; II Field Force Vietnam, *Operational Report for Period Ending 31 July 1969,* OACSFOR-OT-UT 693332; 1st Infantry Division, *Operational Report,* dtd 1 December 1969, OACSFOR-OT-UT 694230; 1st Infantry Division, *Operational Report for Period Ending 31*

January 1970, OACSFOR-OT-UT 701235; Headquarters, 2d Infantry Brigade, *Combat After Action Report: Village Seal of Phu Hoa Dong*, dtd 29 September 1969.

Section 3

Principal sources used were 25th Infantry Division, *Combat After Action Interview Report*, dtd 19 November 1969, OACSFOR-OT-UT 701223; I Field Force Vietnam, *Combat After Action Report: Hawk/Hunter, 1st Platoon, B Company, 3d Battalion (Airborne), 503d Infantry*, dtd 15 May 1969, OACSFOR-OT-UT 69X011; 1st Infantry Division Memorandum, Subject: Night Ambush by 3/D/1-2 Inf., 9 Mar 1969, dtd 17 March 1969, as supplemented by 17th Military History Detachment Combat After Action Interviews.

Chapter 21. Section 1

Principal sources used were USARV, *Operational Report*, dtd 23 February 1970, OACSFOR-OT-RD 701046; USARV, *Operational Report for Period Ending 31 July 1970*, OACSFOR-OT-RD 703176; II Field Force Vietnam, *Operational Report*, dtd 14 May 1970, OACSFOR-OT-UT 702010; II Field Force Vietnam, *Operational Report for Period Ending 31 July 1970*, OACSFOR-OT-UT 703037; 4th Infantry Division, *Operational Report*, dtd 20 August 1967, OACSFOR-OT-UT 703083; 25th Infantry Division, *Operational Report for Period Ending 31 July 1970*, OACSFOR-OT-UT 703026; 1st Cavalry Division, *Operational Report*, dtd 14 August 1970, OACSFOR-OT-UT 703016; 11th Armored Cavalry Regiment, *Operational Report*, dtd 23 August 1970, OACSFOR-OT-UT 703255; MACV, *Quarterly SEER Reports* for 1970; Brig. Gen. Tran Dinh Tho, *The Cambodian Incursion*, Indochina Monographs (Washington: U.S. Army Center of Military History, 1979).

Section 2

Principal sources used were USARV, *Operational Report*, dtd 15 May 1970, OACSFOR-OT-RD 702054; XXIV Corps, *Operational Report*, dtd 23 May 1970, OACSFOR-OT-UT 702217; XXIV Corps, *Operational Report*, dtd 12 August 1970, OACSFOR-OT-UT 703010; XXIV Corps, *Operational Report*, dtd 12 November 1970, OACSFOR-OT-UT 704015; Americal Division, *Operational Report*, dtd 10 May 1970, OACSFOR-OT-UT 702210; 101st Airborne Division, *Operational Report*, dtd

17 May 1970, OACSFOR-OT-UT 702186; 101st Airborne Division, *Operational Report*, dtd 15 August 1970, OACSFOR-OT-UT 703152; ACTIV Project ACG-80F Report, *Fire Support Base Defense* (Washington: Army Research Office, March 1972); Maj. Gen. A. E. Milloy, *Senior Officer Debriefing Report*, dtd 10 March 1971, OACSFOR-OT-UT 71B015; Brig. Gen. Edward H. Simmons, "Marine Corps Operations in Vietnam, 1969–1972," *Naval Review* (Annapolis: U.S. Naval Institute, 1973).

Section 3

Principal sources used were Maj. Gen. Verne L. Bowers, Deputy Chief of Staff, Personnel and Administration, Headquarters, USARV, *Final Report*, dtd 10 September 1970, OACSFOR OT-UT 70B038; Maj. Gen. George S. Prugh, *Law at War: Vietnam*, Vietnam Studies (Washington: Department of the Army, 1975); USARV, *Operational Report*, dtd 15 November 1970, OACSFOR-OT-RD 704181; BDM Corporation, *A Study of Strategic Lessons Learned in Vietnam* (McLean, Virginia: BDM, 1980), Volume VII; Gen. William C. Westmoreland, *A Soldier Reports* (New York: Doubleday, 1976); *Original Papers, Vietnam Order of Battle Project*.

Chapter 22. Section 1

Principal sources used were 101st Airborne Division, *Final Report: Airmobile Operations in Support of Operation LAMSON 719*, dtd 24 April 1971, OACSFOR-OT-UT 71X010; XXIV Corps, *Operational Report*, dtd 17 May 1971, OACSFOR-OT-UT 711180; USARV, *Operational Report*, dtd 15 May 1971, DAFD-OTT 711022; Maj. Gen. Nguyen Duy Hinh, *Lam Son 719*, Indochina Monographs (Washington: U.S. Army Center of Military History, 1979).

Section 2

Principal sources used were USARV, *Operational Report for Period Ending 31 October 1971*, DAFD-OTT 712033; ACTIV Project ACG-75F Report, *Rear Area Security and Base Defense* (Washington: Army Research Office, January 1972); Headquarters, 1st Brigade, 5th Infantry Division, *Operational Report*, dtd 19 August 1971, OACSFOR-OT-UT 712182; 23d Infantry Division, *Operational Report*, dtd 1 November 1971, DAFD-OTT 712166; 101st Airborne Division, *Operational Report*, dtd 19 November 1971, DAMO-ODU 712196; Lt. Gen. A. S. Collins,

Jr., *Senior Officer Debriefing Report*, dtd 1 March 1971, OACSFOR-OT-UT 71B013; Maj. Gen. Thomas M. Tarpley, *Senior Officer Debriefing Report*, dtd 13 July 1972, DAFD-OTT 72B005; 97th Military Police Battalion, *Operational Report*, dtd 28 November 1971, DAFD-OTT 712074; *Original Papers, Vietnam Order of Battle Project*.

Section 3

Principal sources used were USARV, *Operational Report for Period Ending 30 April 1972*, DAMO-ODU 721090; 196th Infantry Brigade, *Operational Report for Period Ending 30 April 1972*, HQDA Ltr. 525-73-13; BDM Corporation, *A Study of Strategic Lessons Learned in Vietnam* (McLean, Virginia: BDM, 1980), Volume VII; Col. William E. Le Gro, *Vietnam from Cease-Fire to Capitulation* (Washington: U.S. Army Center of Military History, 1981); Lt. Col. G. H. Turley, "Easter Invasion, 1972," *Marine Corps Gazette* (March 1973); *Original Papers, Vietnam Order of Battle Project*.

Conclusion

United States Army Europe and Seventh Army, *Annual Historical Summary, 1 January to 31 December 1968*, RCS CSHIS-6 (R2); Ltr, USCONARC TO DA DCSOPS, 14 August 1968, *Subject: Major Command Evaluation of Unit Readiness*, RCS CSGPO-265 (R2); Directorate of Operations, J-3, Headquarters, U.S. Strike Command, *Status of Forces;* Headquarters, United States Continental Army Command, *USCONARC/USARSTRIKE Annual Historical Summary, Fiscal Year 1968*, ATOPS-HST 90507; 2d Infantry Division, *Operational Report for Period Ending 31 July 1968*, OACSFOR-OT-RD 683302; 7th Infantry Division, *Operational Report for Period Ending 31 July 1968*, OACSFOR-OT-RD 683365.

General Sources

Barnes, Peter, *Pawns*, New York: Warner Paperbacks, 1971.

Baskir, Lawrence M., and Strauss, William A., *Chance and Circumstance*, New York: Knopf, 1978.

BDM Corporation, *A Study of Strategic Lessons Learned in Vietnam*, Volumes I–VIII and Executive Summary, McLean, Virginia: BDM Corporation, 1980.

Blaufarb, Douglas S., *The Counterinsurgency Era: U.S. Doctrine and Performance, 1950 to the Present*, New York: The Free Press, 1977.

Bonds, Ray, ed., *The Vietnam War: An Illustrated History of the Conflict in Southeast Asia*, New York: Crown Publishers, 1979.

Bouscaren, Anthony T., ed., *All Quiet on the Eastern Front*, New York: Devin-Adair, 1977.

Boyle, Richard, *Flower of the Dragon*, San Francisco: Ramparts Press, 1972.

Cash, Maj. John A., Albright, John N., and Sandstrum, Lt. Col. Allan W., *Seven Firefights in Vietnam*, Washington: Government Printing Office, 1970.

Collins, Gen. James Lawton, Jr., *The Development and Training of the South Vietnamese Army, 1950–1972*, Vietnam Studies, Washington: Department of the Army, 1975.

Cortright, David, *Soldiers in Revolt: The American Military Today*, New York: Anchor Press, 1975.

Department of Defense, *United States–Vietnam Relations, 1945–1967*, Volumes 1–12, Washington: Government Printing Office, 1971.

Dunn, Lt. Gen. Carroll H., *Base Development in South Vietnam, 1965–1970*, Vietnam Studies, Washington: Department of the Army, 1972.

Eckhardt, Maj. Gen. George S., *Command and Control, 1950–1969*, Vietnam Studies, Washington: Department of the Army, 1974.

Ewell, Gen. Julian J., and Hunt, Maj. Gen. Ira A., Jr., *Sharpening the Combat Edge*, Vietnam Studies, Washington: Department of the Army, 1974.

Fails, Lt. Col. William R., *Marines and Helicopters, 1962–1973*, Washington: U.S. Marine Corps, 1978.

Fox, Roger P., *Air Base Defense in the Republic of Vietnam, 1961–1973*, Washington: Office of Air Force History, 1979.

Fulton, Maj. Gen. William B., *Riverine Operations, 1966–1969*, Vietnam Studies, Washington: Department of the Army, 1973.

Gabriel, Richard A. and Savage, Paul L., *Crisis in Command: Mismanagement in the Army*, New York: Hill and Wang, 1978.

Galvin, John R., *Air Assault: The Development of Airmobile Warfare*, New York: Hawthorne Books, 1969.

Garland, Lt. Col. Albert N., "Infantry in Vietnam," Fort

Benning: *Infantry Magazine*, 1967.

Goff, Stanley, and Sanders, Robert, with Smith, Clark, *Brothers: Black Soldiers in the Nam*, Novato, California: Presidio Press, 1982.

Halberstam, David, *The Best and the Brightest*, New York: Random House, 1972.

Hauser, William L., *America's Army in Crisis*, Baltimore: Johns Hopkins University Press, 1973.

Hay, Lt. Gen. John H., Jr., *Tactical and Material Innovations*, Vietnam Studies, Washington, Department of the Army, 1974.

Helmer, John, *Bringing the War Home: The American Soldier in Vietnam and After*, New York: Free Press, 1974.

Heiser, Lt. Gen. Joseph M., Jr., *Logistic Support*, Vietnam Studies, Washington: Department of the Army, 1974.

Heitman, Francis B., *Historical Register and Dictionary of the United States Army*, Volumes 1 and 2, Washington: Government Printing Office, 1903 (reprinted by University of Illinois at Urbana, 1965).

Herr, Michael, *Dispatches*, New York: Avon Books, 1978.

Hinh, Maj. Gen. Nguyen Duy, *Lam Son 719*, Indochina Monographs, Washington: U.S. Army Center of Military History, 1979.

Hoopes, Townsend, *The Limits of Intervention*, New York: David McKay Co., 1969.

Johnson, Haynes and Wilson, George C., *Army in Anguish*, New York: Pocket Books, 1972.

Johnson, Lyndon B., *The Vantage Point: Perspective of the Presidency, 1963–1969*, New York: Popular Library Edition, 1971.

Just, Ward, *Military Men*, New York: Knopf, 1970.

Kalb, Marvin and Abel, Elie, *The Roots of Involvement: The U.S. and Asia, 1784–1971*, New York: W. W. Norton & Co., 1971.

Kelly, Col. Francis J., *U.S. Army Special Forces, 1961–1971*, Vietnam Studies, Washington: Department of the Army, 1973.

Khuyen, Lt. Gen. Dong Van, *The RVNAF*, Indochina Monographs, Washington: U.S. Army Center of Military History, 1979.

Kinnard, Douglas, *The War Managers*, Hanover, New

Hampshire: University Press of New England, 1977.

Kissinger, Henry, *White House Years*, Boston: Little Brown & Co., 1979.

Le Gro, Col. William E., *Vietnam from Cease-Fire to Capitulation*, Washington: U.S. Army Center of Military History, 1981.

Lewy, Guenter, *America in Vietnam*, New York: Oxford Press, 1978.

Loory, Stuart H., *Defeated: Inside America's Military Machine*, New York: Random House, 1973.

Lung, Col. Hoang Ngoc, *Strategy and Tactics*, Indochina Monographs, Washington: U.S. Army Center of Military History, 1980.

—, *The General Offensives of 1968–69: Indochina Monographs*, Washington: U.S. Army Center of Military History, 1981.

Mahon, John K. and Danysh, Romana, *Infantry, Part I— Regular Army: Army Lineage Series*, Washington: Office of the Chief of Military History, U.S. Army, 1972.

Marshall, Brig. Gen. S. L. A., *Ambush*, New York: Cowles Book Co., 1969.

—, *Battles in the Monsoon*, New York: Morrow, 1967.

—, *Bird: The Christmastide Battle*, New York: Cowles Book Co., 1968.

—, *West to Cambodia*, New York: Cowles Book Co., 1968.

Moskos, Charles C., *The American Enlisted Man*, New York: Russell Sage Foundation, 1970.

Oberdorfer, Don, *Tet!*, New York: Doubleday, 1971.

Ott, Maj. Gen. David E., *Field Artillery, 1954–1973*, Vietnam Studies, Washington: Department of the Army, 1975.

Palmer, Brig. Gen. Dave R., *Summons of the Trumpet*, Novato, California: Presidio Press, 1978.

Palmer, Gregory, *The McNamara Strategy and the Vietnam War: Program Budgeting in the Pentagon, 1960–1968*, Westport, Connecticut: Greenwood Press, 1978.

Pearson, Lt. Gen. Willard, *The War in the Northern Provinces, 1966–1968*, Vietnam Studies, Washington: Department of the Army, 1975.

Peers, Lt. Gen. W. R., *The My Lai Inquiry*, New York: W. W. Norton & Co., 1979.

Polner, Murray, *No Victory Parades: The Return of the Vietnam Veteran*, New York: Holt, Rinehart and Winston, 1971.

Prugh, Maj. Gen. George S., *Law at War: Vietnam, 1964–1973*, Vietnam Studies, Washington: Department of the Army, 1975.

Rogers, Lt. Gen. Bernard W., *Cedar Falls–Junction City, A Turning Point*, Vietnam Studies, Washington: Department of the Army, 1974.

Santoli, Al, *Everything We Had*, New York: Random House, 1981.

Schandler, Col. Herbert Y., *The Unmaking of a President: Lyndon Johnson and Vietnam*, Princeton, New Jersey: Princeton University Press, 1977.

Sherrill, Robert, *Military Justice is to Justice as Military Music is to Music*, New York: Harper & Row, 1970.

Shore, Capt. Moyers S. II, *The Battle for Khe Sanh*, Washington: U.S. Marine Corps, 1969.

Shulimson, Jack, *U.S. Marines in Vietnam: An Expanding War, 1966*, Washington: U.S. Marine Corps, 1982.

Shulimson, Jack, and Johnson, Maj. Charles M., *U.S. Marines in Vietnam: The Landing and the Buildup, 1965*, Washington: U.S. Marine Corps, 1978.

Simpson, Col. Charles M. III, *Inside the Green Berets: The First Thirty Years*, Novato, California: Presidio Press, 1983.

Stanton, Shelby L., *Vietnam Order of Battle*, Washington: U.S. News Books, 1981.

Starry, Gen. Donn A., *Mounted Combat in Vietnam*, Vietnam Studies, Washington: Department of the Army, 1978.

Stubbs, Mary L., and Connor, Stanley R., *Armor-Cavalry, Part I—Regular Army and Army Reserve*, Army Lineage Series, Washington: Office of the Chief of Military History, U.S. Army, 1969.

Summers, Col. Harry G., Jr., *On Strategy: A Critical Analysis of the Vietnam War*, Novato, California: Presidio Press, 1982.

Taylor, Gen. Maxwell D., *Swords and Plowshares*, New York: W. W. Norton & Co., 1972.

Tho, Brig. Gen. Tran Dinh, *The Cambodian Incursion*, Indochina Monographs, Washington: U.S. Army Center of Military History, 1979.

Tolson, Lt. Gen. John J., *Airmobility, 1961–1971*, Vietnam Studies, Washington, Department of the Army, 1973.

Truong, Lt. Gen. Ngo Quang, *The Easter Offensive of 1972*, Indochina Monographs, Washington: U.S. Army Center of Military History, 1980.

U.S. Marine Corps Historical Division, *A Chronology of the United States Marine Corps, 1965–1969*, Volume IV, Washington: U.S. Marine Corps, 1971.

U.S. Marine Corps History and Museums Division, *The 1st Marine Division and Its Regiments*, Washington: U.S. Marine Corps, 1981.

U.S. Marine Corps History and Museums Division, *The 3d Marine Division and Its Regiments*, Washington: U.S. Marine Corps, 1983.

U.S. Marine Corps History and Museums Division, *The Marines in Vietnam, 1954–1973: An Anthology and Annotated Bibliography*, Washington: U.S. Marine Corps, 1974.

Vien, Gen. Cao Van, et al., *The U.S. Advisor*, Indochina Monographs, Washington: U.S. Army Center of Military History, 1980.

Vietnam Veterans Against the War, *The Winter Soldier Investigation*, Boston: Beacon Press, 1972.

Walt, Gen. Lewis W., *Strange War, Strange Strategy*, New York: Funk & Wagnalls, 1970.

Weigley, Russell F., *The American Way of War: A History of the United States Military Strategy and Policy*, New York: Macmillan Co., 1973.

Westmoreland, Gen. William C., *A Soldier Reports*, New York: Doubleday, 1976.

Westmoreland, Gen. William C., and Sharpe, Adm. U.S. G., *Report on the War in Vietnam (As of 30 June 1968)*, Washington: Government Printing Office, 1968.

Winter Soldier Archive, *Soldiering in Vietnam: The Short-Timer's Journal*, Berkeley, California: Winter Soldier Archive, 1980.

Whitlow, Capt. Robert H., *U.S. Marines in Vietnam: The Advisory & Combat Assistance Era, 1954–1964*, Washington: U.S. Marine Corps, 1977.